# #Help

# #Help

## Digital Humanitarianism and the Remaking of International Order

FLEUR JOHNS
*Professor, Faculty of Law & Justice, UNSW Sydney*

**OXFORD**
UNIVERSITY PRESS

Oxford University Press is a department of the University of Oxford. It furthers
the University's objective of excellence in research, scholarship, and education
by publishing worldwide. Oxford is a registered trade mark of Oxford University
Press in the UK and certain other countries.

Published in the United States of America by Oxford University Press
198 Madison Avenue, New York, NY 10016, United States of America.

© Fleur Johns 2023

All rights reserved. No part of this publication may be reproduced, stored in
a retrieval system, or transmitted, in any form or by any means, without the
prior permission in writing of Oxford University Press, or as expressly permitted by law,
by license, or under terms agreed with the appropriate reproduction rights organization.
Inquiries concerning reproduction outside the scope of the above should be
sent to the Rights Department, Oxford
University Press, at the address above.

You must not circulate this work in any other form
and you must impose this same condition on any acquirer.

CIP data is on file at the Library of Congress
ISBN 978-0-19-764887-2

DOI: 10.1093/oso/9780197648872.001.0001

1 3 5 7 9 8 6 4 2

Printed by Integrated Books International, United States of America

**Note to Readers**
This publication is designed to provide accurate and authoritative information in regard to the subject
matter covered. It is based upon sources believed to be accurate and reliable and is intended to be
current as of the time it was written. It is sold with the understanding that the publisher is not engaged
in rendering legal, accounting, or other professional services. If legal advice or other expert assistance is
required, the services of a competent professional person should be sought. Also, to confirm that the
information has not been affected or changed by recent developments, traditional legal research
techniques should be used, including checking primary sources where appropriate.

*(Based on the Declaration of Principles jointly adopted by a Committee of the
American Bar Association and a Committee of Publishers and Associations.)*

> You may order this or any other Oxford University Press publication
> by visiting the Oxford University Press website at www.oup.com.

*For Murray and Penelope*

# Contents

1. Interfaces: New Media of Humanitarian Relation  1
2. Maps: Historical Snapshots and Digital Rewriting  29
3. Populations: From Statistics to Data Science  71
4. Emergencies: Waiting and Watching in the Palliative Present  102
5. States: Analog and Digital  134
6. Law and Policy: Infrastructures of Interface  168
7. Uses: Using, Disusing, and Misusing Digital Humanitarian Interfaces  205

*Acknowledgments*  225
*List of Figures*  229
*List of Acronyms and Abbreviations*  231
*Bibliography*  235
*Index*  265

# 1
# Interfaces: New Media of Humanitarian Relation

## Introduction

Mud. Blood. Confusion. This was the scene painted by US journalist and former humanitarian relief worker, Sheri Fink, recalling her experiences working on medical triage of asylum seekers fleeing the 1999 Kosovo War. She was working alongside "overstretched United Nations refugee officials" seeking to register those seeking asylum for purposes of providing them with material assistance and trying to reunite separated families who were papering refugee camp noticeboards with descriptions of missing children. And somewhere in those dying days of the second millennium, in "the cold, muddy no-man's land between Kosovo and Macedonia," a "new way to help" became apparent. As Fink later remembered, she "walked into a tent" one day and "found a Microsoft team photographing refugees and presenting them with computer-generated ID cards." Staff at Microsoft's European headquarters in Paris had reportedly offered their services to the United Nations. And they had begun to insert what in Fink's perception was "the precision of a computer database" into "the chaos of relief work."[1]

There were, of course, many earlier instances of information and communication technologies (ICT) being deployed in humanitarian efforts, from the use of Morse code telegraphy in emergency response in the early twentieth century to the so-called Spacebridge to Armenia of 1989.[2] (The latter was a satellite-mediated, audio, video, and fax link between four US and two Armenian and Russian medical centers, enabling local physicians access to remote support from US-based physicians following the December 1988 Spitak earthquake in Armenia and the June 1989 gas explosion near Ufa in Russia.[3]) Nonetheless, Fink's 2007 reportage recalling her experiences from the end of the 1990s

---

[1] Sheri Fink, "The Science of Doing Good" (2007) 297 *Scientific American* 98. See further UNHCR, "UNHCR and IOM announce technology partnership to set up system to register Kosovo refugees in Albania" (May 11, 1999), <https://www.unhcr.org/en-au/news/press/1999/5/3ae6b81723/unhcr-iom-announce-technology-partnership-set-system-register-kosovo-refugees.html>.

[2] John W. Farnham, "Disaster and Emergency Communications Prior to Computers/Internet: A Review" (2005) 10 *Critical Care* 207.

[3] Bruce A. Houtchens et al., "Telemedicine and International Disaster Response: Medical Consultation to Armenia and Russia via a Telemedicine Spacebridge" (1993) 8 *Prehospital and*

indicated the growing prevalence of a phenomenon that became known, during the first two decades of the third millennium, as *digital humanitarianism*.[4]

This book investigates digital humanitarianism and its ramifications for international law and politics. This introductory chapter begins by laying out the line of argument advanced throughout the book, before proceeding to explain the main object of this inquiry—digital humanitarianism—and the stakes of the transformation of humanitarianism that it signifies. The reconfiguration of possibilities for politico-legal life being effected in digital humanitarian practice is demonstrated and analyzed in this book through the study of interfaces; this chapter explains what this approach entails and how it compares to other common entry or anchorage points for the analysis of contemporary law and politics on the global plane.

## The Argument of the Book

This book's central line of argument is threefold. First, the politico-legal technologies and practices characteristic of humanitarianism are undergoing a process of transformation associated with the advent of digital humanitarianism. This is both an empirical claim and a polemical claim. It is empirical in that it is based on an investigation of humanitarian practice and thinking within international organizations, national governments, nongovernmental organizations, and businesses carried out over several years, as described later in this chapter. It is polemical in that it involves a problematization of the idea that change on the international plane tends to proceed along progressive, programmatic, deliberative pathways of the kind that international lawyers and other humanitarian professionals are forever laying or charting. It posits something nonscientifically akin to an epistemological break.[5] Contemporary international legal and political order, of which humanitarianism is a crucial feature, is already otherwise. Later chapters will elaborate on how humanitarianism—and its subjects, objects,

---

*Disaster Medicine* 57; Charles R. Doarn and Ronald C. Merrell, "Spacebridge to Armenia: A Look Back at Its Impact on Telemedicine in Disaster Response" (2011) 17 *Telemedicine and e-Health* 546.

[4] Philip Yam, J.R. Minkel, and Keren Schultz, "Updates" (2008) 298 *Scientific American* 18; Woodrow Wilson International Center for Scholars, *Improving Disaster Response and Humanitarian Aid in Times of Crisis* (PR Newswire Association, Inc., 2010); Patrick Meier, "New Information Technologies and Their Impact on the Humanitarian Sector" (2011) 93 *International Review of the Red Cross* 1239; Patrick Meier and Rob Munro, "The Unprecedented Role of SMS in Disaster Response: Learning from Haiti" (2010) 30 *The SAIS Review of International Affairs* 91; Patrick Meier, *Digital Humanitarians: How Big Data Is Changing the Face of Humanitarian Response* (Routledge, 2015).

[5] "Epistemological Break," in Ian Buchanan (ed.), *A Dictionary of Critical Theory* (2nd ed., Oxford University Press, 2018).

temporalities, epistemes, and architectures—are being transformed and opened to further transformation. The "advent of digital humanitarianism" indicates, in brief, that those actions and institutions that we call humanitarian are becoming increasingly concerned with trying to represent conditions and dilemmas using binary values (often in combination with nonbinary representative schemes) and translating them into computable decision problems with a view to generating actionable inferences or other triable outputs. More is said on this later in this chapter.

Second, this process of transformation is bringing about slippages, misreads, mismatches, and blind spots as digital humanitarianism goes awry of surrounding governance frameworks, political institutions, and routes and rituals of contestation. As we shall see in later chapters, some international legal claims, relationships, subjectivities, and responsibilities are becoming more or less unrepresentable digitally, even as international law continues to underwrite infrastructures on which digital technology depends. Humanitarianism, in its international legal versions and of other kinds, has always been power-laden—as much enabling as tempering of power—and there has always been much that it failed to capture or notice. Yet the range of things that humanitarianism can say when it purports to speak "to" power using its traditional politico-legal repertoire has narrowed even further as that repertoire has peeled away from the effects of its digital practice. Conventional international legal frameworks (of treaty, contract, and so on) sustain and secure digital humanitarianism, but are also mangled by it.

Third, digital humanitarianism presents openings as well as closures. Digital interfaces allow for a making-common among people and things that is not necessarily continuous—or not seamlessly so—with the status quo defended by or expressed in existing politico-legal architecture on the global plane. For example, those whose digital avatars or outputs are traceable to a common pool of risk attributes or a common class of vulnerabilities have an entitlement or disentitlement in common that only registers, and only gets made actionable, at digital interfaces. In its generation of novel associations, agonies, and aggregates, digital humanitarian practice could occasion new prospects for political and legal claim and use: arguments for redistribution of resources; reconfigurations of relation; and re-allocations of authority. Digital humanitarianism is marked by powerful continuities, among them: reliance on outsourcing; the prevalence of public-private partnerships and other private or hybrid financing of public infrastructure; various manifestations of global hierarchy and inequality; and ongoing struggles against domination and privation. Yet it also manifests discontinuities, among them: new possibilities of affiliation and disaffiliation; new ramifications of old stratifications; and new repositories and intimations of the common or that which is shared or shareable. The digitization of humanitarian practice is in many respects compounding historical concentrations of power, but it has not been entirely foreclosed. With these argumentative destinations in view, one of the key phrases around which they revolve—digital humanitarianism—merits further explanation.

## Digital Humanitarianism

Humanitarianism at its most generic implies concern with human welfare as a primary or preeminent good, and action taken out of such concern rather than primarily for pragmatic or strategic reasons.[6] Yet given the unending contentiousness of what "human welfare" demands, and whose welfare is and is not worth considering, and the difficulty of ranking motives—especially in the case of collective action—its meaning has never been settled and its invocation is frequently contested. Humanitarianism has often been taken to denote "the desire to relieve the suffering of distant strangers" and to do so on the basis of "humanity, impartiality, neutrality," without regard to other political allegiance.[7] However, actions taken in its name have varied widely over time; some have involved violence and destruction.[8] The history of humanitarianism remains fraught and disputed.

Most conventional stories of humanitarianism's history trace the term's modern meaning to the efforts of Geneva businessperson Henry Dunant to publicize and moralize about the suffering of injured soldiers abandoned on an Italian battlefield after an 1859 conflict between French and Austro-Hungarian troops—and the creation of the International Committee of the Red Cross soon thereafter. Stories of this kind focus on successive phases of institution-building bound up with armed conflict: in the mid-late nineteenth century; the interwar period; after World War II; from the end of the Cold War; and in the 1970s, in the aftermath of official decolonization.[9] Now equally widespread, however, are accounts that look well beyond or beside Dunant and trace humanitarianism to political movements, colonial encounters, imperial ambitions, economic developments, literary ideas, and shifts in moral sentiment from the end of the eighteenth century onward.[10] Throughout, it has become apparent

---

[6] "Humanitarianism, n.," in *OED Online* (Oxford University Press, 2021), <https://www.oed.com/view/Entry/272189> (accessed October 10, 2022).

[7] Michael Barnett, "Evolution without Progress? Humanitarianism in a World of Hurt" (2009) 63 *International Organization* 621, 622–623.

[8] Ryerson Christie, "Critical Readings of Humanitarianism," in *The Routledge Companion to Humanitarian Action* (Routledge, 2015).

[9] Michael Barnett, *Empire of Humanity: A History of Humanitarianism* (Cornell University Press, 2011).

[10] Richard Ashby Wilson and Richard D Brown (eds.), *Humanitarianism and Suffering: The Mobilization of Empathy* (Cambridge University Press, 2008); Rob Skinner and Alan

that humanitarianism has been as commensurate with aims of expanding or maintaining power as with those of ameliorating suffering.[11]

Regardless of its disputed provenance and contested content (or perhaps thanks in part to that indeterminacy), by the year 2000, "humanitarian" had come to be one of the most widely used descriptors of international actors, programs, and practices.[12] In recent decades, it has been used to characterize everything from the use of military force, practices of military targeting, and the policing of human movement to the delivery of food, healthcare, and other emergency relief, the maintenance of refugee camps, efforts to promote democracy, and much more. An expanding range of activities that formerly traveled under the rubric of "development" are now advanced under that of "humanitarianism," the distinction between the two having been increasingly elided since the late 1990s. This is in part attributable to scholars' and practitioners' efforts to draw them together under an encompassing human-rights-based agenda.[13]

The addition of the adjective "digital" to this shape-shifting humanitarianism does not fix its meaning. Yet it does highlight recent shifts in practices and politics among humanitarian donors, practitioners and claimants, and the publics periodically enrolled in their efforts. These shifts are all identified with the growing ubiquity of digital technologies in some parts of the world and the resulting augmentation of data-gathering, -storage, -processing, -analysis, and -dissemination capacities. They are connected, also, to the rising inclination of humanitarian actors of many kinds to look to digital technology to address longstanding aspirations, worries, and criticisms of their work.

First, digital humanitarianism implies a change in the composition, credentials, and archetypal settings of the humanitarian workforce. According to a popular champion of the theme, Patrick Meier, "[a]nyone can be a digital humanitarian, absolutely no experience necessary; all you need is a big heart and access to the Internet."[14] In some respects, this suggests humanitarianism is becoming deprofessionalized. Anyone with access to the internet and appropriate moral or sentimental motives merits recognition as a "humanitarian," Meier insists. And anyone with internet access can potentially self-identify as a would-be humanitarian recipient or distributor. In other respects, however, Meier's

---

Lester, "Humanitarianism and Empire: New Research Agendas" (2012) 40 *The Journal of Imperial and Commonwealth History* 729.

[11] See, e.g., Lauren Benton and Lisa Ford, *Rage for Order: The British Empire and the Origins of International Law 1800–1850* (Harvard University Press, 2016).

[12] B.S. Chimni, "Globalization, Humanitarianism and the Erosion of Refugee Protection" (2000) 13 *Journal of Refugee Studies* 243.

[13] E.g., Hugo Slim, "Dissolving the Difference between Humanitarianism and Development: The Mixing of a Rights-Based Solution" (2000) 10 *Development in Practice* 491.

[14] Meier, *Digital Humanitarians*, supra note 4, at 1.

remarks signal a new influx of professionals into the humanitarian field. If "access to the Internet" has become crucial to engage in or benefit from humanitarian work, then those with authority over resources and infrastructure necessary to ensure that access and skills to make it usable—from the electrical grid, telecommunications infrastructure, and undersea cable network to mobile devices, operating systems, search engines, and more—become pivotal in that work.[15] New sites of humanitarian action emerge accordingly. Satellites, ICT control rooms, remote sensing devices, corporate offices of technology companies, and laptops everywhere become sites of humanitarian endeavor, alongside the "clinics for the poor and refugee camps . . . social administration [facilities] . . . and military garrison[s]" traditionally seen as marking the frontlines of humanitarian action.[16]

Second, digital humanitarianism involves a set of epistemological shifts in the way that need and the needy are discerned, represented, and addressed— or imagined being so. The temporal, spatial, and relational presuppositions of humanitarian action—the "moral landscape" of suffering and succor that is constitutive of humanitarianism in Didier Fassin's influential account[17]—are altered when that action gets mediated by digital interfaces. Temporally, greater emphasis is placed upon the imperative of gaining real-time or near-real-time insights and effecting timely response.[18] The humanitarian emergency becomes identified less with the interruption of time than with the dead time of waiting, as Chapter 4 explains. Spatially and relationally, humanitarianism comes to occupy extremes of proximity and distance. On one hand, humanitarianism is envisaged being tailored to, personalized for, and acting in or on bodies with the utmost intimacy; talk of digital humanitarian wearables is indicative of this.[19] On the other hand, prospects for remote management and amelioration of humanitarian crises—humanitarian action from a sometimes immense, digitally mediated distance—become recurrent preoccupations.[20] The formats in which

---

[15] Bhakti Shringarpure, "Africa and the Digital Savior Complex" (2020) 32 *Journal of African Cultural Studies* 178, 181.

[16] Didier Fassin, *Humanitarian Reason: A Moral History of the Present* (University of California Press, 2011) x.

[17] ibid. ix.

[18] Fleur Johns, "The Temporal Rivalries of Human Rights" (2016) 23 *Indiana Journal of Global Legal Studies* 39; V.M. Walden, I. Scott, and J. Lakeman, "Snapshots in Time: Using Real-time Evaluations in Humanitarian Emergencies" (2010) 19 *Disaster Prevention and Management: An International Journal* 283.

[19] Kristin Bergtora Sandvik, "Making Wearables in Aid: Digital Bodies, Data and Gifts" (2019) 1 *Journal of Humanitarian Affairs* 33; Kristin Bergtora Sandvik, "Humanitarian Wearables: Digital Bodies, Experimentation and Ethics," in Daniel Messelken and David Winkler (eds.), *Ethics of Medical Innovation, Experimentation, and Enhancement in Military and Humanitarian Contexts* (Springer International Publishing, 2020).

[20] Mark Duffield, *Post-Humanitarianism: Governing Precarity in the Digital World* (John Wiley & Sons, 2018) 81.

those whose humanitarian conditions are represented and evaluated are also transformed in ways explored throughout this book. Chapter 3 shows, for example, how the population is reconfigured when assembled for management through digital interfaces.

Third, digital humanitarianism is distinguished from other versions of humanitarianism by its reorientation of the goals of humanitarian action: specifically, their rendering informational. To call something humanitarian has, until quite recently, indicated an orientation toward "manage[ment] [of] [human] populations and individuals faced with situations of inequality, contexts of violence, and experiences of suffering" with a view to mitigating or ending their plight.[21] After UN member states' adoption of the Millennium Development Goals in 2000 and the Sustainable Development Goals in 2015, humanitarianism also came to imply—more concertedly than in the past—an orientation toward measurable improvement in social, economic, and environmental conditions.[22] Digital humanitarianism retains these concerns with ameliorating human suffering and optimizing human life as overarching rationales. Yet the goals toward which digital humanitarianism is most immediately targeted are informational. Digital humanitarianism is oriented toward the creation and maintenance of feedback loops designed to transmit signals of scarcity, profusion, need, and capacity among a range of human and nonhuman referents. Digital humanitarian activity aims to make accessible an incessant stream of digital output on or from the world in a format that is readable as "a surface of pure actuality."[23] Moreover, as we shall see in later chapters, digital humanitarianism purports to make that surface actionable or to create a sense of its potential actionability—except, that is, to obstruct its ongoing extraction of and appetite for data.

In these three main ways—in its enrollees, epistemology, and ends—digital humanitarianism changes what humanitarianism presupposes, what it entails, and what it aspires to become. In April 2016, journalist Erin Blakemore reported in the *Smithsonian Magazine* on actions being taken in the aftermath of a magnitude 7.8 earthquake in Ecuador. Since 1970, writers and editors of the *Smithsonian* had sought to "peer into the future via coverage of social progress and of science and technology."[24] That is what Blakemore purported to do—to invite the magazine's relatively affluent, mainly North American readers to

---

[21] Fassin, *supra* note 16, at 5.

[22] Jeffrey D. Sachs, "Goal-Based Development and the SDGs: Implications for Development Finance" (2015) 31 *Oxford Review of Economic Policy* 268.

[23] Antoinette Rouvroy, "The End(s) of Critique: Data Behaviourism versus Due Process," in Mireille Hildebrandt and Katja De Vries (eds.), *Privacy, Due Process and the Computational Turn: The Philosophy of Law Meets the Philosophy of Technology* (Taylor & Francis Group, 2013) 148.

[24] Carey Winfrey, "Noxious Bogs & Amorous Elephants," (*Smithsonian Magazine*, November 2005), <http://archive.is/gdNP1>, quoting founding editor Edward K. Thompson.

envision, and imagine themselves playing a role in, the future of "humanitarian response" in "a digitally connected world":

> In a less connected past, people really were powerless to help unless they donated money to humanitarian response efforts or made their way to stricken areas themselves. But in a digitally connected world, there are other options, some of which are as easy as looking at a few maps. The gesture may be small, but every tag helps—even if you never leave your seat.[25]

This book investigates the politics and preconditions of this "digitally connected" version of humanitarianism on the global plane with an eye, especially, to its international legal ramparts and its political implications. It probes the "powerlessness," the "power[s] to help," the "options" for doing so, and the modes of representing "stricken areas" that are being evoked and mobilized as governments, international organizations, nongovernmental organizations, and communities have recourse to digital technology with humanitarian claims or purposes in view, and how those actors are changed in the process. This book does so in the conviction that there is much at stake in these shifts, as the next section will explain.

## The Stakes of Digital Humanitarianism

Major shifts in the logic and practice of humanitarianism are not just of concern to humanitarian professionals, those in greatest need or those with, in Meier's words "a big heart"; they are matters of significant global investment, both material and ideological. The Global Humanitarian Assistance Report 2021 reported international humanitarian assistance (that is, funding distributed outside public and private donors' national jurisdictions) having grown by, on average, 12 percent a year between 2012 and 2018, before peaking at US$31.3 billion in 2018 and declining to around US$30.8 billion and US$30.9 billion in 2019 and 2020, respectively.[26] With increasing numbers of people unevenly exposed to hazard due to human-induced global warming and rising economic inequality exacerbated by the COVID-19 pandemic, demands for humanitarian aid and subsistence support may be expected to rise.[27] One may expect, also,

---

[25] Erin Blakemore, "Help First Responders in Ecuador Without Leaving Your Desk," (*Smithsonian Magazine* [2016]), <https://www.smithsonianmag.com/smart-news/help-first-responders-ecuador-without-leaving-your-desk-180958822/> (accessed October 10, 2022).
[26] Development Initiatives, "Global Humanitarian Assistance Report 2021" (*Development Initiatives*, June 22, 2021) 32, <https://devinit.org/resources/global-humanitarian-assistance-report-2021/> (accessed October 10, 2022).
[27] IPCC, *Global Warming of 1.5°C* (World Meteorological Organization, 2018); UN Department of Economic and Social Affairs, "World Economic Situation And Prospects" (*UN Department of*

commensurate expansion in the scope of humanitarian activity on the global plane—some of it mediated by digital interfaces.

As importantly, humanitarianism is a field in which legal, social, and political subjectivities and frameworks for action, relation, and imagination have been shaped and reshaped throughout the modern period—and in which they are still being so shaped. Its transformation is, accordingly, a matter in which all those who enact any form of legal or political agency or affiliation on the global plane have a stake. So prevalent has humanitarianism become as a register of global rectitude, authority, and futurism that any major changes in its subjects, objects, and possibilities for perception and action signal very significant shifts in global politics and prospects for and within international law.

## Interfaces: The Approach of the Book

This book tries to grasp these shifts and make them navigable through the study of digital interfaces, their effects, and preconditions. These are, for the most part, analyzed thematically by attention to one of the primary conditions, subjects, or objects that they purport to assemble or operationalize: maps, populations, emergencies, states. Throughout the book, elements of the makeup of these interfaces and the preconditions for their burgeoning in the humanitarian field are examined, including (in Chapter 6 especially) those international legal and policy infrastructures that help to structure, sustain, and reproduce them.

An interface is commonly understood as a surface forming a boundary between distinct spaces or forms of matter and framing encounter or enabling interaction across them.[28] In the context of ICT, the term "interface" encompasses any standardized means of communication between human users and computers, or among computers and other electronic devices. Examples might include graphical user interfaces (GUIs, explained later) or application programming interfaces (APIs, that is computer software performing a particular function and comprising a modular unit designed to facilitate further software development integrating that unit), but a printer cable might equally constitute an interface.[29]

---

*Economic and Social Affairs*, 2021), Monthly Briefing No. 151, <https://www.un.org/development/desa/dpad/publication/world-economic-situation-and-prospects-july-2021-briefing-no-151/> (accessed October 10, 2022).

[28] "Interface, n.," in *OED Online* (Oxford University Press, 2021), <https://www.oed.com/view/Entry/97747> (accessed October 10, 2022).

[29] Daniel Chandler and Rod Munday, "Interface," in *A Dictionary of Media & Communication* (Oxford University Press, 2016); Daniel Chandler and Rod Munday, "Application Programming Interface," in *A Dictionary of Media & Communication* (Oxford University Press, 2016).

The study of interfaces entails the study of certain relational effects generated by combinations of hardware (computers, screens, keyboards, mouses, cables, and so on), software (such as APIs), and human activity—with the range of human activity potentially implicated in that relation being potentially very broad.[30] For purposes of this book, the relational effects in question are those that inform and emerge from the deployment of digital computation. Interface effects involve "local relationships . . . creat[ing] an externalization . . . an edging, or a framing" for mediation or interaction.[31]

ICT interfaces are characteristically engineered to try to make the interactions in question as frictionless as possible. Interfaces tend to layer interactions and operations in ways that do not presuppose knowledge or even awareness of other interface layers. Interfaces provide "simulated visibility" while "obfuscat[ing] the machine" and its buried commands.[32] As Alexander Galloway has remarked in his book on interface effects, "[e]ven source code is a kind of interface . . . into a lower level set of libraries and operation codes."[33] As Galloway has also highlighted in other work, these layers and relationships do not necessarily involve human bodies, needs, or desires: "digital networks are . . . bodyless, and have little connection to the movements of human desire."[34] Nonetheless, digital interfaces are typically engineered, experienced, and navigated as if they were "apparatus[es] for the production of community" among "virtual [human] bodies."[35]

Interfaces establish parameters for and structure practices of use, and occasion iterative encounters among users, infrastructures, and developers of digital computation. They elicit inputs and assemble outputs in ways that create impressions of usable coherence and directive capacity, at least for as long as they are working well.[36] For example, a GUI is an umbrella term for the computational use of pictorial metaphors to create user-friendly alternatives to programming command lines: a computer desktop arranges data to approximate a physical workspace; an icon offers a shorthand way of accessing and running computer programs; a series of file symbols signify and make usable computer storage capacity; a wastepaper basket icon directs users in the deletion and recovery of data; an inverted teardrop-shaped "pin" operationalizes a process of geo-referencing whereby a digital image file becomes associated with a particular spatial location; and so

---

[30] Chandler and Munday, "Interface," *supra* note 29; Branden Hookway, *Interface* (MIT Press, 2014).
[31] Alexander R. Galloway, *The Interface Effect* (Polity, 2012) 36.
[32] Wendy Hui Kyong Chun, "On Software, or the Persistence of Visual Knowledge" 18 Grey Room 26, 40, 43.
[33] Galloway, *supra* note 31, at 9.
[34] Alexander Galloway, *Protocol: How Control Exists after Decentralization* (MIT Press, 2004) 191.
[35] ibid. 191, quoting Allucquère Rosanne Stone.
[36] Galloway, *supra* note 31, at 39.

on.[37] As the media scholar Lev Manovich has written, interfaces such as GUIs specify "ways to represent ('format') and control the [electrical] signal. And this in its turn changes how media functions—its 'properties' [a]re no longer solely contained in the data but [a]re now also dependent on the interface provided by technology manufacturers."[38]

In these and in other ways, interfaces both call forth and condition human agency vis-à-vis digital technology. As Branden Hookway has observed: the "interface produces a supplementation . . . of agency" that is "to say the interface comes into being as it is actively worked through by [a] user," but "[a]t the same time, by imposing itself as a condition necessary for the expression of human agency, the interface comes to define human agency."[39] Each time that this book refers to a digital interface—such as the HOT Tasking Manager (discussed in Chapter 2); MIND (discussed in Chapter 3); HungerMap LIVE (discussed in Chapter 4); poverty mapping employing satellite image data or the Tamwini (My Food Ration) smartphone application developed by the World Food Programme and the Iraqi Ministry of Trade (discussed in Chapter 5)—it is evoking the combination of socio-technical forces and operations that go into creating, maintaining, and using any of these interfaces as points of engagement and relation. Once again, interfaces are effects not things; they are products of the relations that they frame, activated through engagement. Each of the book's later chapter titles (maps, populations, emergencies, states, norms) both denote a mode of defining human agency that gets operationalized at digital interfaces and allude to a suite of interfaces that make each titled phenomenon appear coherent, while obscuring the layered, socio-technical operations that produce and reproduce them.

Analyzing interfaces is not a practice in which studies of humanitarianism typically engage, especially not those written by scholars of international law. How this compares to other, more typical approaches to the subject matter of this book therefore warrants some attention.

## Interfaces and Their Alternatives

To study interfaces is to choose not to study—or to study only obliquely—that with which much international legal scholarship is concerned. Let us consider some alternative apertures through which to analyze the changing international scene, with an eye especially to its legal and political technologies, and how

---

[37] Daniel Chandler and Rod Munday, "Graphical User Interface," in *A Dictionary of Media & Communication* (Oxford University Press, 2016).
[38] Lev Manovich, "Media After Software" (2013) 12 *Journal of Visual Culture* 30, 37.
[39] Hookway, *supra* note 30, at 17.

they compare or relate to interfaces, namely: doctrines; institutions; platforms; algorithms; ideas.

## Interfaces versus Doctrines

Doctrinal study of digital humanitarianism and its ramifications would involve the identification of legal issues thrown up by the shifts in practice with which this book is concerned. It would entail, also, attempting to resolve these, or offering guidance as to how they might by resolved, through synthesis of, and deduction from, broad categories, concepts, and principles of law or policy, or by analogy to apposite cases or comparable issues from other contexts. Formulating that guidance would ordinarily include the taking of some normative position as to a preferable or beneficial way forward on those issues, justified by reference to standards, policies, or values that the audience is presumed to share with the doctrinal researcher or otherwise regard as authoritative, or for which that researcher makes an explicit argument.

As Chapter 6 discusses further, this book focuses a great deal on "how" questions in relation to interfaces: how do these interfaces work; how do they configure the objects and mobilize the subjects with which they are concerned; how do they represent the forms of authority on which they call; how do they affect what humanitarianism is imagined to be or envisaged becoming by those developing or using those interfaces; how do they alter what claims may be made in the humanitarian field; and so on. In contrast, a doctrinal approach to these interfaces would usually only be interested in such questions to the extent that they aided the tackling of a problem framed as a divergence from, gap in, or conflict with applicable law or policy. Doctrinal analysis is characterized broadly by a concern with perfecting the law, both in the abstract and in its application to particular phenomena. In this instance, that would typically entail trying to bring digital humanitarianism into tighter, tidier, more compliant relation to application legal and policy frameworks.

In contrast to such a doctrinal approach, the slippages, misreads, mismatches, blind spots, and reconfigurations to which this book draws attention in connection with digital humanitarian interfaces are not wrongs that could be made right by the proper elaboration of legal doctrine. Rather, the aim of highlighting the structural discrepancies that digital humanitarian interfaces illuminate is to identify points of potential critical leverage within the "new verisimilitude" that they are propagating (a point to which Chapters 6 and 7 will return).[40] This is

---

[40] Roland Barthes, "The Reality Effect," in *The Rustle of Language* (University of California Press, 1969) 148.

why the book's "empirical" descriptions are described earlier as polemical. The purpose of pointing out these discrepancies is not to falsify the interfaces in question, nor to condemn or correct the path of digital humanitarianism. The aim is to render that path somewhat less premade than it might otherwise appear and to show how many fundamental, deeply controversial, high-stakes questions of collective life and politics are still in contention in its unfolding.

## Interfaces versus Institutions

An analysis of digital humanitarianism through a focus on the institutions involved could conceivably take a number of forms. The most literal version would be to focus on the international organizations that are leading the digital humanitarian charge and to ask how their mandates, financing, priorities, workforces, and *modus operandi* are being affected by this aspect of their work. However, institutionally oriented research has more commonly entailed study of a greater variety of "the more enduring features of social life." This has encompassed the study of such recurring organizational complexes as corporations, families, universities, nongovernmental organizations, churches, governments, stock exchanges, courts, and other entities or role-allocating, rule-bound modes of ordering.[41]

A concern with institutions and institutional change is not absent from this book. In Chapters 4, 5, and 6 especially, institutions and institutional change feature prominently. Wherever readers encounter institutions in this book, however, they will not find them fully consummated or well settled in their properties and purposes. As one of our interviewees observed, speaking of the Missing Maps Project (MMP) (discussed in Chapter 2): "It's nothing. It's not an identity entity as such. It's not an organization. It has no bank account. It's nothing. It's really a collaboration between organizations . . . it's not necessarily about the tools or the ways of working within each organization . . . it's really about the data creation."[42] When studied through the interfaces that they make available, promote, or use, institutions are always *in actu*, always in the making, emergent in the present as well as from the past. Moreover, this "making" entails a much greater range of engagement than the processes of habituation, stabilization, and constraint on which institutionalist analyses have tended to dwell.[43]

---

[41] Anthony Giddens, *The Constitution of Society: Outline of the Theory of Structuration* (Polity Press, 1984) 24, 31.

[42] Interview with Participant AG (April 22, 2020).

[43] Philip Mirowski, "The Philosophical Basis of Institutional Economics" (1987) 21 *Journal of Economic Issues* 1001; Douglass C. North, "Institutions" (1991) 5 *The Journal of Economic Perspectives* 97.

When institutions and institutional change are approached through interfaces, it is not possible to tackle questions of design or reform from a distance—in hindsight or in advance—because we can only grasp how institutions condition and are conditioned by social, legal, and economic life in the course of interacting with or through them at their interfaces. The study of interfaces at work does not deny the significance of institutional histories, but it suggests that there are other forces at work in shaping the present than hysteresis. Institutional power and preferences do not bear upon and constrain interface design and operation so much as get made and remade at interfaces, digital interfaces included.

## *Interfaces versus Platforms*

Many recent studies of change in the global digital economy have focused less on institutions than on the power and performance of platforms. Since the mid-1990s, scholars of industrial organization have examined platforms as "architectures" with three main features: "core components with low variability, complementary components with high variability, and interfaces for modularity between core and complementary components."[44] As glossed by cultural studies researchers, these components engender a "set of relations that constantly needs to be performed"—above all, relations that are generative of digital data.[45] They have also given rise to a capitalist platform-based business model premised on "the centrality of a particular way of (re)configuring networked digital communications infrastructures for data-based surplus extraction" and the indispensability of certain commercial intermediaries affording access to markets for that surplus. As the US legal scholar Julie E. Cohen has observed, platforms "represent infrastructure-based strategies for introducing friction into networks" in ways that create opportunities for the marshaling and monetization of digital data.[46]

YouTube, for example, maintains a core functionality enabling users to search YouTube content, upload videos, create channels, and curate playlists. Its core components are comprised of software and protocols that compress and decompress digital video and enable high-quality streaming of media content over the internet delivered via conventional web servers. YouTube also supports a surrounding social media network through its subscription, "community" and

---

[44] Jean-Christophe Plantin et al., "Infrastructure Studies Meet Platform Studies in the Age of Google and Facebook" (2018) 20 *New Media & Society* 293, 296.

[45] Jose van Dijck, *The Culture of Connectivity: A Critical History of Social Media* (Oxford University Press, 2013) 26.

[46] Julie E. Cohen, *Between Truth and Power: The Legal Constructions of Informational Capitalism* (Oxford University Press, 2019) 40.

comment features and standardized "widgets" such as "end screens" (minimized snapshots of other videos that direct viewers of one video to other content). At the same time, YouTube makes available a range of APIs that support developers embedding YouTube functionality into their own websites and applications. These complementary components and interfaces ensure high volumes of digital data flow through the platform which, in turn, fosters relations (commercial and of other kinds) among dispersed constituencies, including, in the case of YouTube: "audiences; amateur, pro-amateur, and professional content creators; media partners; advertisers; new intermediaries like the multi-channel networks (MCNs); and third-party developers."[47] A platform need not take the form of YouTube, however. Many kinds of businesses—from online marketplaces to search engines, payment systems, and developers of computing hardware and software—now operate according to a platform model.

Studying digital humanitarianism through the lens of platform power would highlight the role of platforms like Twitter and Alibaba in the developments recounted in this book. It would also focus on the ways in which international organizations like the United Nations and nongovernmental organizations such as Médecins Sans Frontières are seeking to develop platform capacities by, for example, developing prototypes that enable interface among a range of platforms and elicit ongoing user engagement in data-generative ways. The HOT Tasking Manager and other tools developed as part of the MMP to foster volunteer engagement with the noncommercial platform OpenStreetMap—discussed in Chapter 2—might be thought of in these terms. So, too, could MIND—the disaster response interface developed by UN Global Pulse, discussed in Chapter 3—be understood as an effort to leverage the platform power of the various data providers that it taps (among them Twitter, Wikipedia, OpenStreetMap, and Google) and indirectly support user engagement with those platforms.

The line of inquiry just prefigured is certainly an important vein of the analysis undertaken in this book. Platforms feature throughout it. However, this book's orientation toward interfaces enables it to grapple with factors and agents that would elude it if it were predominantly platform focused. MIND, for instance, cannot be well understood simply as an expression of some generic platform logic or a manifestation of the priorities of dominant platforms. Its development is as much a manifestation of longstanding pressures on international organizations—to be seen to be doing more with less in financial terms—as it is indicative of the kind of business thinking identified with platforms. Moreover, the type of subjectivity MIND is likely to elicit among users is, as discussed in Chapter 3, action-oriented in a way that is characteristic of the humanitarian

---

[47] Jean Burgess and Joshua Green, *YouTube: Online Video and Participatory Culture* (Polity Press, 2018) 19.

field rather than, predominantly, a consumerist posture. Approaching MIND as an interface enables one to discern how the data-extractive friction that platforms seek to generate may be co-produced with relations and dispositions characteristic of humanitarianism, and how each comes to shape the other.

## *Interfaces versus Algorithms*

Scholarly resources available to aid study of the reciprocal shaping ongoing at digital interfaces are prodigious. Social studies of technology and computation have been ongoing for decades; they were well advanced by the 1980s.[48] Since the 1990s, the algorithm—a set of instructions or step-by-step procedures, usually expressed mathematically and/or in computer code, for performing a specified task, typically by predicting output values on the basis of input data— has assumed particular prominence in this field.[49] This has spawned a number of subfields, among them: social and cultural studies of algorithms or "algorithmic culture"; critical algorithm studies; and investigations of algorithmic governance or regulation.[50] As Tarleton Gillespie has observed, these tend to take the algorithm as an entry point for investigating "the insertion of procedure into human knowledge and social experience" entailing functional and ideological "commit[ment] ... to the computational generation of knowledge or decisions."[51] Given this rich scholarly literature, one might expect this book to push aside the interfaces on which it lingers to investigate their algorithmic preconditions and procedures.

There are, however, two main reasons for preferring interfaces over algorithms in this instance. First, algorithms—machine learning algorithms, at least—are products of data. Algorithms do not stand prior to or remain unchanged by data.

---

[48] Wiebe E. Bijker, Thomas E. Hughes, and Trevor Pinch (eds.), *The Social Construction of Technological Systems: New Directions in the Sociology and History of Technology* (MIT Press, 1987); Donald A. MacKenzie and Judy Wajcman, *The Social Shaping of Technology: How the Refrigerator Got Its Hum* (Open University Press, 1985); Steven Shapin and Simon Schaffer, *Leviathan and the Air-Pump: Hobbes, Boyle, and the Experimental Life* (Princeton University Press, 1985); Lucille Alice Suchman, *Plans and Situated Actions: The Problem of Human-Machine Communication* (Cambridge University Press, 1987).

[49] For relatively early examples, see, e.g., N. Katherine Hayles, "Virtual Bodies and Flickering Signifiers" (1993) 66 *October* 69, 74; Stefan Helmreich, "Recombination, Rationality, Reductionism and Romantic Reactions: Culture, Computers, and the Genetic Algorithm" (1998) 28 *Social Studies of Science* 39.

[50] Alexander R. Galloway, *Gaming: Essays on Algorithmic Culture*, vol. 18 (NED-New edition, University of Minnesota Press, 2006); David Moats and Nick Seaver, "'You Social Scientists Love Mind Games': Experimenting in the 'Divide' between Data Science and Critical Algorithm Studies" (2019) 6 *Big Data & Society*. https://doi.org/10.1177/2053951719833404; Karen Yeung, "Algorithmic Regulation: A Critical Interrogation" (2018) 12 *Regulation & Governance* 505.

[51] Tarleton Gillespie, "Algorithm," in Benjamin Peters (ed.), *Digital Keywords: A Vocabulary of Information Society and Culture* (Princeton University Press, 2016).

They are as much outgrowths of data as they are outcomes of system design or the effects of other elements in their "composite" makeup.[52] Digital data flows fuel algorithmic operations and, when redirected or reformatted, sometimes, their failure. Those flows likewise sustain the training and retraining of machine learning algorithms. And it is through interfaces that the data doing this work is elicited and, at least initially, formatted and classified. To study algorithms without attention to how, where, by whom, and in what formats the data on which they depend is sourced, inputted and used is akin to studying the procedures of a criminal trial without considering how it is that particular people come to be investigated and ascribed with the status of an accused, or how that status affects their relations. Moreover, the study of algorithms risks arresting inquiry in such a way as to suggest that decoding, replacing, or optimizing a particular algorithm might "solve" whatever problems a particular computing operation may be said to pose. Although anyone who is active online is unavoidably engaged in the practice of training algorithms, the algorithm can seem like something apart that a critic may approach without complicity: something amenable to being rooted out and "corrected."

Second, many algorithms are proprietary; the Google PageRank algorithm is an example. Commercial developers typically invoke exclusionary legal rights in algorithms. They do so either by patenting a computational invention, programmable procedure, or business method implemented in software (in jurisdictions where this is possible).[53] Alternatively, or in addition, developers frequently characterize these as trade secrets and confidential information the unauthorized disclosure or "misappropriation" of which may give rise to a cause of action in tort law or contract law and/or constitute an offense under criminal law. In this context, the study of algorithms makes the kinds of effects documented in this book seem fully determined, captured, or of definite yet secretive provenance.

Interfaces are the subject of exclusionary, proprietary claims as well.[54] Yet interfaces are, on their surface, shaped by and contingent on intermediation; they are relational, conjunctural, modular, and manifestly customizable. Users—even those of the most skeptical disposition—are always implicated in their operations. Interfaces are, by their nature, hard to engage critically from a safe distance. They are not "a furtive reality that is difficult to grasp, but [rather] a great surface network in which the stimulation of bodies, the intensification of

---

[52] Louise Amoore, *Cloud Ethics: Algorithms and the Attributes of Ourselves and Others* (Duke University Press, 2020).
[53] Regarding the United States, see Ben Klemens, *Math You Can't Use: Patents, Copyright, and Software* (Brookings Institution Press, 2006).
[54] Jonathan Band and Masanobu Katoh, *Interfaces on Trial 2.0* (MIT Press, 2011); Pamela Samuelson, "The Strange Odyssey of Software Interfaces and Intellectual Property Law," in Mario Biagioli, Peter Jaszi, and Martha Woodmansee (eds.), *Making and Unmaking Intellectual Property: Creative Production in Legal and Cultural Perspective* (University of Chicago Press, 2009).

pleasures, the incitement to discourse, the formation of special knowledges, the strengthening of controls and resistances, are linked to one another."[55] For these reasons, interfaces are more generative to think with for this book's purposes than algorithms.

## Interfaces versus Ideas

Talk of "thinking with" may incline some readers toward another comparator to the study of interfaces, namely: the study of ideas, or the work of intellectual history (the two not being interchangeable; intellectual historians of recent decades have cast their concern as the "history of language in use," claiming to have come "a long way from the isolated study of the 'great ideas' of 'great thinkers'").[56] An intellectual history of digital humanitarianism would investigate the language of its practitioners and proponents in use, scrutinizing texts of "varied provenance" including vernacular writings as much as "great texts."[57] The aim, according to one prominent intellectual historian, would be to engage in "a critical process that relates past, present, and future through complex modes of interaction involving both continuities and discontinuities" in pursuit of an interpretative "com[ing] to terms" with recent history.[58]

The study of interfaces does not distinguish itself from intellectual history by dispensing with textual analysis. This book devotes considerable attention to close reading of texts in use, especially if one takes "text" to encompass any readable surface. What distinguishes the investigation of interfaces—or rather, as explained earlier, interface effects—most sharply from intellectual history is the emphasis that the former places on discrete, discontinuous elements that are, in their own right, senseless.

Being concerned with "unravel[ing] the mental worlds of the past" and "mak[ing] sense of it all," intellectual history cannot tell a story built around data fragments that make no sense: satellite image data and mobile phone metadata, for instance.[59] Many of the interfaces described in this book originate not with an idea but with the practical availability of digital data; the ideas and justifications that come to surround them seem to flow from the accessibility and formatting of data, not the other way around (although the process is more commonly

---

[55] Michel Foucault, *The History of Sexuality. Volume I: An Introduction* (Robert Hurley tr., Pantheon Books, 1978) 105–106.
[56] Annabel Brett, "What Is Intellectual History Now?," in David Cannadine (ed.), *What Is History Now?* (Palgrave Macmillan, 2002) 114, 117.
[57] ibid. 118.
[58] Dominick Lacapra, "Rethinking Intellectual History and Reading Texts" (1980) 19 *History and Theory* 245, 273–274.
[59] Brett, *supra* note 56, at 128.

circular). Digital interfaces are certainly social products, but not ones well understood as originating primarily in "mental worlds" and being sustained by such worlds; they are sustained as much by their technical and financial engineering and data-generative use—including entirely "mindless" or unknowing use, such as the production of call detail record data from the making of a phone call. The interface effects with which this book is concerned are outcomes of discretization, such as that which occurs when analog signals are converted into discontinuous binary numbers or data is "hashed" into distinct alphanumerical sequences. Interfaces do not "unravel" these digital signals; rather, they occasion encounters with their outputs wherein some of their further effects and ramifications may be traced. Intellectual history is not fit for the purpose of coming to terms with digital humanitarianism so manifest because intellectual history cannot represent or decode "a generalized infrastructure of discrete breaks."[60]

In all these ways, this book stands awry of much legal and socio-legal scholarship concerned with emergent international order, the global digital economy, or contemporary humanitarian practice. Its stance in relation to these is best captured by recourse to the prefix "infra": this book is a work of infra-legal, infra-disciplinary, and—as explained in Chapter 6—infrastructural inquiry.

## Infra-investigations: Notes on Method

This book is the outcome of years of research, including around 46 interviews or written question-and-answer exchanges with 38 distinct interviewees affiliated with 18 different organizations, governments, or firms conducted since 2015. These were semi-structured interviews with humanitarian professionals, data scientists, policymakers, and others working in international organizations, governments, nongovernmental organizations, or for-profit corporations and engaged, in various capacities, in the work of digital humanitarianism. An initial point of embarkation for these inquiries—although by no means a case study—was Pulse Lab Jakarta (PLJ) about which more is said later. The digital interfaces and other technological initiatives to which these interviews related varied in their technical dimensions. However, humanitarian deployment of blockchain technologies was excluded from the scope of these inquiries because of the distinct issues that those technologies raise (such as the composition and operation of decentralized autonomous organizations).[61]

---

[60] Alexander R. Galloway, "Mathification" (2019) 47 *Diacritics* 96, 98.
[61] Fleur Johns, "Centers and Peripheries in a World of Blockchain: An Introduction to the Symposium" 115 *AJIL Unbound* 404.

PLJ, established in 2012 by the government of Indonesia and the United Nations, is one of several "Labs" of the UN Global Pulse project, others having been established, at different times, in the United States (New York), Uganda (Kampala), and, most recently, Finland.[62] UN Global Pulse is an initiative that was first announced in 2009 by the then-UN Secretary-General, Ban Ki-moon, to "harness[] real-time data and new technologies to protect vulnerable populations."[63] Each of the Labs through which UN Global Pulse works pursues this goal under distinct budgetary and governance arrangements; in Jakarta, PLJ is jointly overseen by the government of Indonesia (through the Ministry of National Development Planning, known as BAPPENAS) and the United Nations (represented by the United Nations' Resident Coordinator in Indonesia). PLJ has secured project funding and in-kind support from a range of international organizations, governments, not-for-profit entities, and private firms, but since 2015, the Australian government has been a major source of its core program funding, having committed such funding through until 2023.[64] Since establishment, PLJ has initiated or participated in a diversity of projects combining data science and qualitative social research, usually in collaboration with public sector and/or private sector partners. Many of these projects have involved the development of prototypes of digital interfaces and/or proof-of-concept research aimed at exploring or demonstrating the potential of nontraditional digital data sources to yield insights of salience for governments, development, and humanitarian professionals.[65] Selected PLJ projects will be the focus of analysis in Chapters 3, 4, and 5, and Chapter 6 will touch on some of its contractual and other arrangements.

Faced with the dizzying range of technologies, products, professionals, organizations, and research programs active in the digital humanitarian domain across a very large number of jurisdictions, research for this book proceeded, initially, by attention to UN Global Pulse, especially PLJ. It then moved out from there to consider other projects, locations, and interfaces, including quite a number unconnected with UN Global Pulse. This is not, therefore, a book about PLJ or UN Global Pulse; it is certainly not an evaluation of their success, impact, or

---

[62] UN Global Pulse, "Where We Work" (*UN Global Pulse*, February 27, 2018), <https://www.unglobalpulse.org/labs/> (accessed October 10, 2022); UN Global Pulse, "UN Global Pulse Annual Report 2020" (UN Global Pulse, 2021), <https://www.unglobalpulse.org/document/un-global-pulse-annual-report-2020/> (accessed October 10, 2022).

[63] UN Global Pulse, "Taking the Global Pulse: Using New Data to Understand Emerging Vulnerability in Real-Time" (UN Global Pulse 2012) <www.unglobalpulse.org/document/taking-the-global-pulse-using-new-data-to-understand-emerging-vulnerability-in-real-time/>.

[64] Australian Government Department of Foreign Affairs and Trade, "Stability in Indonesia" (*Development Partnership in Indonesia*), <https://www.dfat.gov.au/geo/indonesia/development-assistance/stability-in-indonesia> (accessed October 10, 2022).

[65] Fleur Johns, "From Planning to Prototypes: New Ways of Seeing Like a State" (2019) 82 *MLR* 833.

future prospects. The interfaces produced by and the ongoing work of people associated with UN Global Pulse comprise only some among many threads out of which this book weaves its composite picture of the emergent global phenomenon of digital humanitarianism. The research question animating this book has a broader aperture, namely: how are possibilities for politico-legal life on the global plane reconfigured by the influx of digital technology into humanitarian practice and what intimations does this offer of global ordering to come?

To pursue this question through the study of interfaces is an instance of what I have come to describe more broadly (thanks in no small part to the provocations of Gavin Sullivan) as infra-legal or infra-disciplinary research—a research mode implicated also in the study of infrastructure to which I return in Chapter 6. "Infra-legality" was a term that I first used when investigating international organizations' guidelines and manuals concerned with their handling of dead bodies in the aftermath of natural disaster. In these, dead bodies exerted infra-legal authority. They tended to lie at the "edges of conventional international legal sightlines" but exert "imperative force" from those margins insofar as they helped to constitute and configure those "conditions for [international organizations'] action (or inaction) in the aftermath of disaster."[66] My attention to infra-legality has owed something to, but is not coextensive with, Foucault's study of "infra-law."[67] Paraphrasing, Foucault's work suggests the fruitfulness of bracketing the existence or limits of law and asking, instead, what to "make of these different events and practices which are apparently organized around something that is supposed to be [law]?"[68]

An infra-disciplinary approach to research—or the study of infra-legal phenomena and conditions—is characterized by a tendency to look below or aside of that on which most scholars in one's field focus, without any privileging of the "grassroots" or the "bottom-up." In contrast to socio-legal research, infra-legal inquiry does not seek to explain, evaluate, or validate legal phenomena by reference to the social; it does not posit society as "law's designated relational other," determinative input or consummate output.[69] Investigations of infra-legality illuminate, instead, how legality "passes outside itself" and gets transmitted and shaped through a great miscellany of practices and materials.[70]

In relation to any second element to which it is attached, the prefix "infra" suggests "below," "underneath," "beneath," "lower," "inferior," but also "within."

---

[66] Fleur Johns, *Non-Legality in International Law: Unruly Law* (Cambridge University Press, 2013) 187.
[67] Michel Foucault, *Discipline and Punish* (Alan Sheridan tr., 2nd ed., Vintage, 1995) 222–223.
[68] Michel Foucault, *The Birth of Biopolitics: Lectures at the Collège de France, 1978–79* (Graham Burchell tr., Picador Palgrave Macmillan, 2010) 2–3.
[69] Christopher Tomlins, "How Autonomous Is Law?" (2007) 3 *Annual Review of Law and Social Science* 45, 64.
[70] Foucault, *supra* note 67, at 224.

This encapsulates what an infra-disciplinary or infra-legal approach implies: tunneling at once below and within phenomena under study for an immanent, mutable, heterogenous exteriority. Such an approach focuses on elements that are embedded or ubiquitous within a discipline yet cast as inconsequential, marginal, minor, inoperative, dead, banal, alien, "merely" technical, or beyond understanding within it. In the case of this book, those elements have been digital interfaces—specifically, those being developed and deployed in humanitarian work. As will be apparent from this book's bibliography and acknowledgments, taking this route has required reading into and dialogue with those working in many other scholarly fields.

The goal of such infra-disciplinary burrowing has not been, however, to claim access to some unclaimed treasure within one's "home" discipline nor assert mastery gained from excursions outside it. As Annelise Riles has highlighted, amateur ventures to or beyond the edges of the "proper" domain of legal expertise have long been a matter of routine lawyerly practice. These amount, Riles has suggested, to a recurrent form of experimentalism within legal scholarship.[71] Infra-disciplinary or infra-legal study often involves variants of this amateurism.

For some readers, this might sound like a counterdisciplinary approach to research, that is, one "using cross-disciplinary encounters to learn about one's disciplinary blind spots, hidden assumptions or silences, and to destabilize its certain knowledges and common senses."[72] It is certainly the case that infra-disciplinarity shares features with counterdisciplinarity. Both worry about movement among disciplines offering people escape routes from conflicts in which they would otherwise have to take a stand.[73] By turning to another discipline, legal scholars sometimes claim access to a more authentic or less hierarchical form of knowledge practice, try to claim some purer or higher political ground, or seek out a sense of completion. Likewise, scholars in other disciplines sometimes impress their insights on legal scholarship as a form of corrective. In other instances, legal researchers sometimes belittle their own discipline, and simplify or sanctify other disciplines, for purposes of disciplinary boundary-crossing.[74] Like counterdisciplinarity, an infra-disciplinary approach seeks to resist all these urges and overtures; it refrains from trying to wipe the disciplinary muck off one's boots when wandering outside one's "home" discipline, or upon re-entering it after roving elsewhere.

---

[71] Annelise Riles, "Legal Amateurism," in Christopher Tomlins and Justin Desautels-Stein (eds.), *Searching for Contemporary Legal Thought* (Cambridge University Press, 2017).

[72] T.E. Aalberts, "Interdisciplinarity on the Move: Reading Kratochwil as Counter-Disciplinarity Proper" (2016) 44 *Millennium* 242, 248.

[73] Jan Klabbers, "Counter-Disciplinarity" (2010) 4 *International Political Sociology* 308.

[74] Anne Orford, *International Law and the Politics of History* (Cambridge University Press, 2021).

Yet there are also important differences between infra-disciplinary and counterdisciplinary approaches. Because it is oriented toward the inferior and the seemingly inconsequential, infra-disciplinarity is not concerned with lauding or defending the jurisdiction of law or legal scholarship. An infra-disciplinary approach is not likely to lead where Martti Koskenniemi's counterdisciplinarity took him, in a 2012 article, which was into a final rallying cry for international law as "the last platform on which collective futures may be imagined and constructed without taking the present distribution of wealth and knowledge as a given."[75] Infra-disciplinarity is something upon which one embarks to enliven possibilities latent within a discipline not to redeem it as a whole.

My work on the questions pursued in this book started with some work that I did on financial models—work that was informed by my experience as a practicing corporate lawyer in New York during the 1990s and early 2000s.[76] I became interested in financial models because of their intriguing combination of workaday ubiquity, relative obscurity, and manifest significance in the legal drafting and negotiation of cross-border investment deals and their distributive implications. In international project financing, I observed, financial models were typically built and maintained by investment bankers—usually overworked junior analysts under the supervision of more senior bankers. Reference was often made to a project's financial model during negotiation of a deal's legal documentation. Some contractual provisions were keyed off modeled calculations or outputs; others fed directly into model assumptions. Nonetheless, the model itself was never up for negotiation among the lawyers. It belonged to a different field of practice even though it helped to shape what was considered possible, and which arguments could be entertained, in the legal domain.

I became interested in the oblique force that financial models exert—how a model may operate as a kind of talisman for a project, and anchor key contractual terms, but can never be tackled directly by legal argument or inquiry. I came to understand financial models, in the terms outlined earlier, as infra-legal artifacts or interfaces—and recognized them to be already the focus of a rich literature in their own right, much of it informed by science and technology studies.[77] My interest in models continued into later work—in collaboration with geographers— on controversies over dam development in the Mekong River Basin.[78] In that

---

[75] Martti Koskenniemi, "Law, Teleology and International Relations: An Essay in Counterdisciplinarity" (2012) 26 *International Relations* 3, 26; cf. Aalberts, *supra* note 72 (Aalberts suggests that Koskenniemi's is "in fact a counter-IR-disciplinarity" not counterdisciplinarity "proper").

[76] Fleur Johns, "Performing Party Autonomy" (2008) 71 *Law and Contemporary Problems* 243; Fleur Johns, "Financing as Governance" (2011) 31 *OJLS* 391; Johns, *supra* note 66, at 109–152.

[77] See, e.g., Donald MacKenzie, *An Engine, Not a Camera: How Financial Models Shape Markets* (MIT Press, 2006).

[78] Ben Boer et al., *The Mekong: A Socio-Legal Approach to River Basin Development* (Routledge, 2015).

context, seemingly intractable political conflict often got displaced onto highly technical debates over scientific modeling of things like sediment flows and fish migration. Financial modeling also played a very significant role in Mekong River dam development. In this context, the openness of technical and financial models to endless refinement often served as a proxy for political responsiveness; models' adaptability sometimes made dam-related decision-making that was relatively impervious to public input appear more sympathetic. My interest in models as infra-legal artifacts within international legal practice ultimately led me to this work on digital humanitarianism, for which I laid the first published groundwork in 2013.[79]

The initial link between these different phases and domains of work was a class of algorithms known as Monte Carlo algorithms used in finance since the late 1960s. These are computational algorithms used to simulate the various sources of uncertainty that affect the value of an investment. I encountered these when I was trying to gain a firmer grasp of financial models. They alerted me to further, infra-disciplinary dimensions of those artifacts that I was already approaching in an infra-legal way. That is, while looking at the role of financial models in international legal deals, I found myself looking to their edges—at algorithms embedded within them. And the more that I looked into the work that these algorithms and their data inputs and outputs were doing, in financial and other settings, the more significant seemed the stakes of those operations. I became interested in the iterative interplay between these functions and international legal practices and politics. I wanted to figure out what was getting ruled out, or what was becoming possible, in that kind of interplay and to trace its broader ramifications for international law and politics. That began the line of research that led to the writing of this book.

This is a story about a chain of research questions and how they led from one to another obliquely. What I have done is essentially follow chains of reference and techniques through different fields of contestation to see how legal possibilities get shut down or opened up and how power accrues in and around these techniques along the way. The point has not been to master all of the fields traversed or to pillage them for law's or lawyers' benefit. The point has been to be able to gain enough amateur knowledge to be able to stay with the question in a rigorous way, learning all the while from patient and generous collaborators and interlocutors. By doing so, I have sought to illuminate how what is legally arguable in a particular field gets conditioned by all sorts of things, practices, and actors that lawyers do not typically think it is their business to query or even notice.

My ultimate target throughout all of this has been the politics of my "home" discipline: insofar as I have one, international law. I have taken infra-disciplinary

---

[79] Fleur Johns, "The Deluge" (2013) 1 *London Review of International Law* 9.

routes—here, through the study of digital humanitarian interfaces—in order to be able to make a particular type of intervention in the international legal field. I will return to that field, and how my work relates to work ongoing within it, in Chapter 6. For now, let it suffice to say that I have sought, by these routes, to expand the repertoire of international legal inquiry and practice. I have tried to make relatively closed debates and concentrations of power seem more open and undecided, especially to forces, agents, and technologies sometimes judged either untouchable or powerless within them.[80] My aim in tunneling through other disciplines to investigate the workings of digital humanitarian interfaces has not been securing the purposes of international legal work or evaluating its fulfillment or nonfulfillment of those purposes. Rather, the goal of these digressions has been to loosen international law's grip on its archetypal bearings and to enable work in other directions. I seek, in short, to show how much room for experimentation on alternatives to the status quo is already immanently available.

## Chapter Overview

This book's story of the interfaces and interface effects of digital humanitarianism begins with a focus on maps and mapping in Chapter 2. This chapter begins with a brief overview of the practice of humanitarian mapping, presenting snapshots of that practice from the eighteenth, nineteenth, and twentieth centuries, before tracking it into the twenty-first century with the advent of multidimensional, real-time mapping via digital interfaces for humanitarian purposes. As the chapter discusses, the latter have frequently been conceived as ways of addressing blind spots and shortcomings of conventional maps, not to make mapping more definitive but to make it more responsive, timely, and customizable. The ramifications of humanitarian mapping's digitization are, however, far more ambivalent than such aspirations suggest. Through the juxtaposition and comparison of this series of snapshots, this chapter introduces a dynamic that is crucial to the book as a whole: the dissensus between analog and digital logics animating digital humanitarianism and the differences that this dissensus makes. As Chapter 6 will discuss, in something of a final analysis, this focus on analog-digital tensions and slippages is indebted to structuralist and post-structuralist analyses of international law and policy.

To the question "what differences do these tensions and shifts make to humanitarianism and beyond?", Chapter 3 offers one important part of this book's answer: they transform modes of aggregation and produce proto-polities unlike

---

[80] Richard Joyce, "Anarchist International Law(Yers)? Mapping Power and Responsibility in International Law" (2017) 5 *London Review of International Law* 397.

those that have been predominant to date in international humanitarian work. Chapter 3 argues that humanitarian investment in and deployment of digital interfaces is transforming how people, places, and things are being collectively made to count, or not, in the global sensory economy—and contends that these transformations warrant close attention and collective strategizing. Whereas international humanitarian work has long been concerned with the condition of a population rendered in traditional statistical, demographic terms, digital interfaces are often oriented toward analysis of digital aggregates that have not been purposively, systematically, or randomly sampled. Governments, international organizations, and their many private-sector partners are increasingly captivated by the speculative digital aggregates around which digital interfaces revolve as expressions of the end, the object, and the appropriate field of intervention for governance work. Concern with populations in the statistical, actuarial, or biopolitical sense seems, at times, to kick in only at a lower, later, stage. Populations frequently appear beneath, behind, or embedded within the dazzle of the digital aggregate. Power evoked and oriented by the digital interfaces being developed in the international humanitarian field is less a power to "make live and let die"[81]—although it may ultimately have those effects—than a power to make perceive and let pass. We are only in the earliest stages of developing legal and political vocabularies, rituals, and practices to engage with these developments critically and creatively.

As well as reconfiguring the collective subjects, objects, and modalities of humanitarian governance, Chapter 4 argues that digital interfaces alter the temporalities of humanitarianism through their reshaping of humanitarian emergencies. Watching and waiting in the near term is, above all, the activity that the digital interfaces are shown to encourage, although further action is always anticipated by them as well. Humanitarian emergencies are made to appear cyclical and recurrent by these interfaces—and demanding of continual vigilance. Through the emphasis that they place on continual watchfulness—a task that digital interfaces take on, on behalf of their users—the digital interfaces described in Chapter 4 are shown to foster practices of deferral, expectations of self-reliance, and conditions of "chronic waiting."[82]

States' growing recourse to shifting streams of digital data for purposes of trying to understand the needs, wants, and circumstances of their constituents and affording them humanitarian assistance is giving rise to new ways of seeing and being as a state: these are the focus of Chapter 5, making use of the analog-digital friction introduced earlier. No longer are techniques of simplification,

---

[81] Michel Foucault, *"Society Must Be Defended": Lectures at the Collège de France, 1975–1976* (François Ewald ed., Macmillan, 2003) 247.
[82] Craig Jeffrey, "Waiting" (2008) 26 *Environment and Planning D: Society and Space* 954.

legibility, and planning necessary preconditions to state action. In many instances, an early warning signal assembled from real-time digital data will suffice to prompt states to canvass possibilities for humanitarian action and rule out other registers of political action. Nonstate actors and infrastructures condition and mediate these efforts in politically impactful ways. States of the Global South must especially contend with a litany of data doubles: digital representations of their polities, and social and economic conditions within their territories, assembled by commercial actors and/or other, surveillant states in parallel with, and sometimes in lieu of, national data. This is not in itself new. States of the Global South have long had sovereignty tailored for them by those on a civilizing mission and had to contend with donors' and development practitioners' projection of better versions of their future. Nonetheless, the digital alter egos with which they must contend have proliferated. States are also increasingly engaged in the datafication of feedback loops between people and governments. With these changes in the logics of state governance, practices and preoccupations that digital interfaces tend to elicit from states tug them away from the parameters of statehood presupposed by international law.

Chapter 6 investigates how the digital interfaces depicted throughout the book tend to be produced and reproduced in the way that they do, even as they remain ever open to customization and improvement. It focuses on one dimension of the forces or factors that help to sustain this reproduction: international legal and policy infrastructures. As well as suggesting their heterogeneous provenance and supports, this tracing suggests digital interfaces' openness to reassembly—more thoroughgoing reassembly, that is, than customization or refinement—and multiple possible sites of entry for that purpose. For this and other reasons, Chapter 6 argues that there is value in investigating humanitarian digital interfaces infrastructurally when that is approached not as a tapping of roots, but rather as an extension of structuralist and post-structuralist practices and politics of reading. Chapter 6's revisitation of those practices helps to situate this book in relation to prior work in the international legal field.

Chapter 7 explores the politics of using, disusing, and misusing digital humanitarian interfaces, as a way of exploring what might yet be enlivened or made possible in this medium. The argument of this final chapter is not that all current or intended uses of digital technology for humanitarian purposes are harmful and should be abandoned nor is it an argument for sabotage. Rather, the chapter contends that a wider range of persons and activities than typically attract notice are active in shaping international order through digital media—and that digital humanitarianism may be a setting for communities to enter into contention over the parameters and priorities of international legal and political order. What else might digital interfaces be called to do in international humanitarian work other than mimic reality, demand resilience, or intone the march of progress? What questions might be worth asking, Chapter 7 considers, that have not been asked, or have not been asked widely, in humanitarian work? If, as this book argues, international order is already otherwise than it has been and otherwise than it is commonly thought to be, then what possibilities could emerge from that noncorrespondence? Chapter 7 considers how potentialities may be realized or shut down in the politics of digital humanitarian interfaces' use: that is, the politics of what is considered usable or useful; who qualifies as a user; and what range of uses are enacted or invited by digital interfaces in international humanitarian work. It considers also what possibilities for remaking global order and engaging new constituencies in the process might emerge from the creative, collective "misuse" of digital humanitarian interfaces in the sense of their use in defiance of or beyond prevailing expectations and instructions.

## Conclusion

The shift that Sheri Fink understood as "the precision of a computer database" coming to bear on "the chaos of [humanitarian] relief work" in 1999 emerges into something far more unruly over the coming pages—and is shown to be still emergent.[83] Digital humanitarian interfaces are occasioning new ways of gathering, dividing, distributing, and relating on the global plane. This book shows something of how this is taking place. The digitization of humanitarian knowledge and practice is not a matter of improved operational efficiency, heightened granularity, precision, or inclusion across the board. It is, in this book's rendering, a matter of intensely contested political reordering and legal reconfiguration, very much still underway. Claims of ownership and assertions of entitlement are rife in this domain, and yet digital humanitarianism is still, in many respects, unresolved. The book's final chapter speculates about prospects for digital humanitarianism being collectively made otherwise than it has been to date. Before we get to that point, however, it is vital to survey what digital interfaces have been making of humanitarianism to date: its fields of intervention, figures of authority, and preconditions for action, turning first to digital mapping interfaces.

[83] Fink, *supra* note 1.

# 2
# Maps: Historical Snapshots and Digital Rewriting

## Introduction

Many of the digital interfaces being developed and deployed in the humanitarian field take the form of maps; mapping features prominently amid efforts to digitize humanitarian work. The story of digital humanitarian mapping is, nonetheless, one of both continuity and discontinuity. The digital mapping interfaces described in this chapter continue longstanding recourse to cartography as a technique of governance. Many scholars have shown how significant a role that mapmaking technologies have played in shaping and extending certain modern understandings of social space, economic relations, and political authority.[1] This remains true of digital mapping interfaces.

Continuities notwithstanding, efforts to digitize mapping have often been associated with critiques of modernist governance. The digitization of mapping for governance purposes has frequently been framed as a way of "grasping ... contingent relations as an object of governance and integrating non-linearity into governmental reasoning."[2] The turn to digital interfaces in humanitarian mapping has tended to accompany anxieties about deficits of timeliness and specificity in humanitarian response and the propagation of governance techniques aimed at overcoming these, not through greater comprehensiveness but through greater responsiveness. In some instances, the assemblage of maps via digital interfaces has been identified with enhanced prospects for "giv[ing] voice to those in need, allowing them to project their needs to a global workforce of digital responders."[3]

Rather than focusing on how adequately digital technologies satisfy these hopes or assuage these worries, this chapter uses a focus on mapping interfaces as a way of advancing this book's argument that politico-legal technologies characteristic of humanitarianism on the international plane are undergoing

---

[1] Jordan Branch, *The Cartographic State: Maps, Territory, and the Origins of Sovereignty* (Cambridge University Press, 2014); Thongchai Winichakul, *Siam Mapped: A History of the Geo-Body of a Nation* (University of Hawai'i Press, 1994).
[2] David Chandler, *Ontopolitics in the Anthropocene* (Routledge, 2018) 37.
[3] Amelia Hunt and Doug Specht, "Crowdsourced Mapping in Crisis Zones: Collaboration, Organisation and Impact" (2019) 4 *Journal of International Humanitarian Action* 1, 2.

unresolved transformation. To crystallize these emergent shifts, this chapter introduces a way of reading that is crucial to the book as a whole: it traces analog and digital logics animating digital humanitarianism and highlights some of the displacements and differences that the structural tension between them makes. The chapter begins with a brief overview of the practice of humanitarian mapping, presenting snapshots of that practice from the eighteenth, nineteenth, and twentieth centuries, before tracking it into the twenty-first century with the advent of multidimensional, real-time mapping via digital interfaces for humanitarian purposes. The latter, as we shall see, has been associated with advances in geographic information systems (GIS) and growing recourse to digital platforms and devices to facilitate the crowdsourcing of maps.

Later in this chapter, the practices of digital humanitarianism with which this book is fundamentally concerned will be encapsulated by the Missing Maps Project (MMP) and digital interfaces developed and deployed under that rubric. This is a project borne out of collaboration between the Humanitarian OpenStreetMap Team (HOT)—a US-registered nonprofit—and three other not-for-profit organizations: American Red Cross, British Red Cross, and Médecins Sans Frontières.[4] Launched in 2014, the MMP aims to put "the world's most vulnerable people on the map" by marshaling volunteers to label and validate open-source digital maps of areas that are poorly represented by other maps available online—poor cartographic representation that can make these areas difficult for humanitarian professionals to navigate and assist.[5]

As a preview of what is to come, one of the main interfaces through which the MMP is advanced is the HOT Tasking Manager: a "tool for coordination of volunteers and organization of groups to map on OpenStreetMap."[6] It "divides up a large area of interest into many smaller mapping tasks that individual mappers can 'check out' to complete" by way of collectively assembling a digital map intended for use by humanitarian organizations and other actors in crisis response. Through this interface, groups of users are assigned to teams taking carriage of particular projects and tasks, and team members are granted varying levels of permission to map, validate, and create projects. The code written for each version of HOT Tasking Manager, and any incremental updates, is available via an open-source code repository.[7] Version 4, released in May 2020, was built using React: an open-source, JavaScript programming library for building user interfaces and their components originally created by Facebook, Inc. (now

---

[4] "Missing Maps," <https://www.missingmaps.org/> (accessed October 10, 2022).
[5] Ibid.
[6] Humanitarian OpenStreetMap Team, "HOT Tasking Manager," <https://tasks.hotosm.org> (accessed October 10, 2022).
[7] Mikel Maron, "HOT's Tasking Manager 4: How We Built It" (*Mapbox.com*, May 15, 2020), <https://blog.mapbox.com/hots-tasking-manager-4-how-we-built-it-53ebaa3cafd0> (accessed October 10, 2022)>.

Meta, Inc.), the public company based in Menlo Park, California. Version 4's development also made use of the open-source JavaScript programming library Mapbox GL-JS, created by the private company Mapbox, based in San Francisco, California.[8] That development was funded by Microsoft Philanthropies through their AI for Humanitarian Action program.[9] Microsoft Philanthropies is a not-for-profit entity created by Microsoft, Inc. (a public corporation headquartered in Redmond, Washington) in 2015.[10] The following two screenshots (Figures 2.1 and 2.2) show how different iterations of the interface have appeared to volunteers surveying projects with which they might get involved or engaged in mapping tasks. We will return to this interface toward the chapter's end.

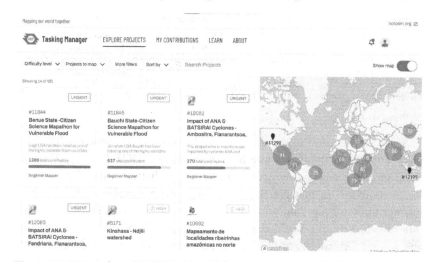

**Figure 2.1** Screenshot of HOT Tasking Manager showing available projects.
© 2022 OpenStreetMap contributors. The Tasking Manager is free and open-source software developed by the Humanitarian OpenStreetMap Team. Reproduced with permission from the Humanitarian OpenStreetMap Team and under an Open Data Commons Open Database License (ODbL) v1.0 from "Explore Projects—HOT Tasking Manager," <https://tasks.hotosm.org> (accessed October 10, 2022). Full terms available at <https://opendatacommons.org/licenses/odbl/1-0>.

---

[8] Prateek Rawat and Archana N. Mahajan, "ReactJS: A Modern Web Development Framework" (2020) 5 *International Journal of Innovative Science and Research Technology* 698; Meg Miller, "Geospatial Data and Software Reviews: Mapbox.Js" (2020) 165 *Association of Canadian Map Libraries and Archives Bulletin.*
[9] Maron, *supra* note 7.
[10] Brad Smith, "Microsoft Deepens Longstanding Commitment to Philanthropy with Expanded Vision, New Organization" (*The Official Microsoft Blog*, December 15, 2015), <https://blogs.microsoft.com/blog/2015/12/15/microsoft-deepens-longstanding-commitment-to-philanthropy-with-expanded-vision-new-organization/ (accessed October 10, 2022)>.

**Figure 2.2** Screenshot of HOT Tasking Manager showing task status.
© 2022 OpenStreetMap contributors. The Tasking Manager is free and open-source software developed by the Humanitarian OpenStreetMap Team. Reproduced with permission from the Humanitarian OpenStreetMap Team and under an Open Data Commons Open Database License (ODbL) v1.0 from "#12081: Impact of Ana & Batsirai Cyclones—Ambositra, Fianarantsoa, Madagascar," <https://tasks.hotosm.org/projects/12081> (accessed October 10, 2022). Full terms available at https://opendatacommons.org/licenses/odbl/1-0 (accessed October 10, 2022).

A key argument of this chapter is that the routing of humanitarian mapping work through digital interfaces such as the HOT Tasking Manager tends to create slippages, misreads, and overruns between digital and analog logics combined in that practice (as those terms are explained later). These incongruities are not failures, because digital humanitarian maps do not aspire to represent the world definitively or comprehensively. Temporariness and adaptability are key to the kind of governance that they seek to effect, as Chapter 3 will further explain. Nevertheless, these structural tensions in the logic of digital humanitarian mapping do create risks of strife that are difficult to address under existing vocabularies of accountability and rubrics of dispute resolution. At the same time, these mismatches create opportunities for countermapping, to which we will turn at the chapter's end—that is, for mapping that, as compared to predominant mapping practices, tries to "increase the power of people living in a mapped area to control representations of themselves and their claims to resources" or otherwise tries "to overcome predominant power hierarchies."[11]

---

[11] Nancy Lee Peluso, "Whose Woods Are These? Counter-Mapping Forest Territories in Kalimantan, Indonesia" (1995) 27 *Antipode* 383, 387; Leila M. Harris and Helen D. Hazen, "Power of Maps: (Counter) Mapping for Conservation" (2005) 4 *ACME: An International Journal for Critical Geographies* 99, 116.

## Analog and Digital

The HOT Tasking Manager is one illustration of an interface in which analog and digital logics are combined in such a way that the digital tends to predominate, as will be shown later. This distinction warrants explanation in general terms before different interfaces are examined in detail. Of course, in the day-to-day work of international humanitarianism, analog and digital logics are frequently entangled and hard to prize apart. Accordingly, it is important to stress that this is a schematic distinction drawn with a particular goal in mind—a goal comparable to that of structuralist analysis (to which Chapter 6 returns), as explained by Roland Barthes:

> The goal of all structuralist activity... is to reconstruct an "object" in such a way as to manifest thereby the rules of functioning (the "functions") of this object. Structure is therefore actually a *simulacrum* of the object, but a directed, *interested* simulacrum, since the imitated object makes something appear which remained invisible, or if one prefers, unintelligible in the natural object.[12]

In this book, the "object" is digital humanitarianism. It is reconstructed here— and shown to be riddled with analog-digital slippages—not because this is how it should or could appear "naturally" in the wild (so to speak), but with an interest or objective in mind. Reading humanitarian interfaces for digital-analog differences is one way in which this book seeks to show that the international order that humanitarian work seeks to maintain and optimize is already noncoincident with itself. This is a reading activity that is interested in generating a sense that alternatives to the status quo may reside not only in some progressive "after" or "next," or some counterfactual past of international order, but are also emergent in its heterogeneous and unstable present. By focusing on digital-analog misfitting, this chapter directs attention away from whether digital or analog practices of humanitarian mapping represent reality "better" or more "accurately." Regardless of their fidelity or infidelity to "the real," the proliferation of digital interfaces in the humanitarian field is propagating a "new verisimilitude" that differs from that in which predominantly analog interfaces tend to trade.[13] This book aims to cast this distance (as between one verisimilitude and another) not as something for law and politics to bridge and resolve, but rather as terrain to be tilled collectively and creatively.

---

[12] Roland Barthes, "The Structuralist Activity," in Richard Howard (tr.), *Critical Essays* (Northwestern University Press, 1972) 214–215 (emphasis in original).

[13] Roland Barthes, "The Reality Effect," in *The Rustle of Language* (University of California Press, 1969) 148.

Return to the basics of the distinction: to describe certain mapping initiatives and interfaces as predominantly analog is to characterize them as concerned with continuous qualities along a scale. Analog logic and technology are concerned, that is, with similarity, comparability, contiguity, sequence, and similarity. Analog differences are differences of degree, not those of opposition or either/or distinction.[14] Analog technologies "map[] continuums precisely whereas the digital computer can only be precise about boundaries."[15] Examples include a ruler, a mercury thermometer, and an accelerator pedal. All of these operate on the basis of continuously variable quantities: spatial positioning, temperature, and valve aperture. Also, units of analog analysis are divisible into smaller units without any necessary loss of significance. Centimeters may be divided into millimeters that may be divided into micrometers that may be divided into nanometers, and so on. In contrast, digital analysis cannot employ units of analysis below the level of the discrete unit on which it depends. Traditional cartographic delineation of governmental or administrative units exemplifies analog mapping technology because the areas in question tend to be nested with comparable units of greater and lesser scale, together comprising the international.

In contrast, digital logic works with discrete units in binary relation: one and zero, on and off, something or nothing. Digital logic is discontinuous and presupposes gaps between elements—gaps that, in digital circuitry, must be spanned by wires, gates, and latches. According to digital logic, no value can be ascribed to any intermediate state between one and zero—an embedded prohibition or agreement that comprises part of the juridical infrastructure of digital technology. As Julian Bigelow pointed out at the famous Macy Conferences of 1946–1953, this "involves a forbidden ground in between and an agreement never to assign any value whatsoever to that forbidden ground, with a few caveats on the side."[16] Accordingly, at any particular point in time or space (for example, in any one pixel of a digital image), a digital signal might leap from one value to another without regard to the state that preceded it, but no interim state or span may be represented.

Digital significations identify and delimit elements in ways that are opposable to all other elements at a particular point in time. The digital is oriented toward either/or events as distinct from an analog concern with both-and processes and more-or-less similarities. Whereas analog communication tends to employ icons that claim some enduring resemblance to the signified (the thing represented),

---

[14] Anthony Wilden, "Analogue and Digital Communication: On the Relationship between Negation, Signification, and the Emergence of the Discrete Element" (1972) 6 *Semiotica*; Anthony Wilden, *System and Structure: Essays in Communication and Exchange* (2nd ed., Tavistock, 1980).

[15] Wilden, *System and Structure, supra* note 16, at 162.

[16] Bernhard Siegert, "Coding as Cultural Technique: On the Emergence of the Digital from Writing AC" 70 *Grey Room* 8, 9, quoting Julian Bigelow in Claus Pias (ed.), *Cybernetics-Kybernetik: The Macy Conferences 1946–1953*, vol. 1 (Diaphanes Verlag, 2003), 187.

digital communication employs symbols (digits) that maintain no inherent connection between signifier and signified; in digital settings any such connection must be learned or ascribed (as and when required). The digital thus presupposes "breaks in referentiality"; its "epistemological power" is not conditional upon maintaining any lasting relation or continuity between the symbolic and the real (in contrast to analog logic according to which degrees of likeness or representational accuracy are often presented on a continuum).[17]

Not all contemporary computing or communication is digital. Analog computing (employing the continuously variable aspects of physical phenomena, such as electrical or mechanical quantities, to model a problem) has enjoyed something of a resurgence of late and quantum information theory has grown in prominence and promise over recent years. Also, digital computing does not expunge all analog logic; the comparability of computers to human minds has been a continuous point of reference in the development of digital computing, for example.[18] Nevertheless, digital logic looms large wherever information and computing technologies are deployed. Blockchain technology (which does not feature in the interfaces discussed in this book but is growing in prominence in digital humanitarian work) exhibits digital logic because of the denotative quality of the cryptographic hashing on which it depends and its reliance on distributed ledger reproducibility, neither of which accommodates more-or-less similarities.[19]

Thanks to the growing prevalence of digital technology in humanitarian work, the difference between analog and digital is making a difference in and to humanitarian mapping, or so the rest of this chapter endeavors to show. Moreover, this difference can prove tactically useful to those who would resist the force of prevailing analog frameworks, as the final part of this chapter and some later chapters will illustrate.

## Humanitarian Mapping

To say something about humanitarian mapping, we must first say something about mapping in general, about which an inordinate amount has been written. It has been speculated that "maps were made before language marks were devised to represent objects and ideas or the sounds of human speech" and have been made more or less continuously ever since.[20] It is fair to say that one cannot

[17] Ibid., 18.
[18] Alan M. Turing, "Computing Machinery and Intelligence" (1950) 59 *Mind* 433.
[19] Fleur Johns, "Centers and Peripheries in a World of Blockchain: An Introduction to the Symposium" (2021) 115 *AJIL Unbound* 404.
[20] Arthur H. Robinson, *Early Thematic Mapping in the History of Cartography* (University of Chicago Press, 1982) 2.

safely generalize about the characteristics of maps, or the purposes that they have served for different peoples, in different places and times.

Undeterred by this immeasurable archive, the twentieth-century American geographer Arthur H. Robinson suggested that maps have tended to serve "three general functions," namely: the recording of geographical features; the provision of guidance to travelers and navigators; and the expression of abstract, hypothetical, or religious concepts.[21] Clearly, these functional categories are nonexhaustive and need not be mutually exclusive. Maps produced and circulated to flesh out the "geo-body" of a nation or an empire, for instance, have typically served all three such functions, as well as others.[22] Robinson's tripartite classification of maps' functions downplays the politically constitutive work done with maps, as well as maps' significance for sustaining property rights and other forms of entitlement and authority. As Brian Harley famously contended, maps are "at least as much an image of the social order as they are a measurement of the phenomenal world of objects."[23] Robinson's account likewise omits maps' polemical and epistemological dimensions—the sense in which a map is at once "an instrument of depiction—of objects, events, places—and an instrument of persuasion [and pedagogy]—about these, its makers and itself."[24] Nikolas Rajkovic is among those who have highlighted how significant modern cartography has been to the "geometrization of planetary legal boundaries" and to the cultivation (among international lawyers and others) of disciplinary reflexes that impede "scrutiny of new and non-geometric matrices of . . . political and economic authority."[25]

As well as playing a role in these constitutive and disciplinary operations, humanitarian mapping falls into the category of what Robinson called "thematic map[ping]": a cartographic practice of "showing the geographical occurrence and variation of a [particular] phenomenon, or at most a very few."[26] Humanitarian mapping has traded especially in the mapping of human pain, claim, and deprivation. And as discussed in Chapter 1, the scope of what gets called "humanitarian" has expanded greatly over the past half-century. Commensurately, the phenomena that practices of humanitarian mapping seek to illuminate vary widely.

---

[21] Ibid., 3.
[22] Winichakul, *supra* note 1.
[23] J.B. Harley, "Deconstructing the Map" (1989) 26 *Cartographica* 1, 7; see also Denis Cosgrove, *Geography and Vision: Seeing, Imagining and Representing the World* (IB Taurus, 2008).
[24] Dennis Wood and John Fels, "Designs on Signs/Myth and Meaning in Maps" (1986) 23 *Cartographica* 54.
[25] Nikolas M. Rajkovic, "The Visual Conquest of International Law: Brute Boundaries, the Map, and the Legacy of Cartogenesis" (2018) 31 *LJIL* 267, 269–270.
[26] Robinson, *supra* note 20, at 16.

What makes a map—or a mapping practice—humanitarian hinges not so much on its substantive or phenomenal concerns as its persuasive and functional ones, or when and how it is brought to bear. Mapping meets the descriptor "humanitarian" when it entails making or modifying maps to try to "promote human welfare" and advocate "action on this basis rather than for pragmatic or strategic reasons."[27] This does not, of course, preclude humanitarian mapping from doing other work as well. Such "other work" includes humanitarian maps' role in the making and defending of nations, empires, and property regimes.

If a map becomes humanitarian based on the purposes to which it is put, then the question arises whether any map may be a humanitarian map. In principle, the answer is yes—at least according to one of our informants immersed in the practice: "It's the end use and the purpose that makes [a map] humanitarian."[28] Those "humanitarian" end uses could be conventional (expressing a desire to alleviate human suffering, as discussed in Chapter 1) or they may be oppositional (articulating an experience of dispossession and privation, as in the examples discussed at this chapter's end).

Deployment of maps for such purposes might, however, not be enough to render a mapping practice humanitarian. Some organizations dedicated to humanitarian mapping subscribe to principles concerning the process of *making* maps whereby that process should also promote human welfare, not just the use of the map that results from it. Some humanitarian mapping tends to overlap, in this respect, with "social mapping." According to this process-oriented approach to mapping, the map is considered "not only an independent source of information, [but] also [a way of] stimulat[ing] discussion, . . . encouraging the participants to engage in dialogue . . . and aiding the problematization of various aspects of life of the population and a settlement."[29] For example, the HOT, mentioned earlier, has adopted a Code of Conduct, in which it affirms "[o]penness, collaboration and participation" as "core aspects of [the organization's] work—from mapping with local communities, remotely and in person, to developing tools, training materials, and processes."[30]

According to the foregoing criteria, there may be some maps that are not amenable to being called humanitarian maps, at least not without controversy, because of the way that they are assembled. Examples of the latter might include maps developed for purposes of resource extraction in ways that explicitly

---

[27] "Humanitarian, n. and Adj.," in *OED Online* (Oxford University Press, March 2020), <https://www.oed.com/view/Entry/89276?redirectedFrom=humanitarian>.
[28] Interview with Participant AD (April 30, 2020).
[29] N.D. Vavilina and I.A. Skalaban, "Social Mapping as a Tool for Public Participation" (2015) 5 *Regional Research of Russia* 66, 67.
[30] Humanitarian OpenStreetMap Team, "HOT Code of Conduct" (*HOT Code of Conduct*), <https://www.hotosm.org/code-of-conduct> (accessed October 10, 2022).

override First Nations' geographic knowledge.[31] At the same time, the process of assembling a digital humanitarian map is often hard to square with commitments to public participation, as will become clear from the discussion below. In general, therefore, digital versions of humanitarian maps tend to lay claim to being humanitarian primarily by virtue of the purposes for which they are intended, not because of the robustness of public engagement in their making or the effects of their use.

## Historical Snapshots of Humanitarian Mapping

To specify what happens when humanitarian mapping is digitized, why digitization matters, and the continuities and discontinuities it manifests, a brief, selective excursion through the history of the practice is apposite. Much has been written of late about the history of humanitarianism.[32] Yet mapping tends to feature only incidentally in those histories; in large part, histories of international humanitarian mapping remain to be written. This chapter does not purport to fill this gap; the approach taken here is episodic and anachronistic, presenting selected "snapshots" depicting humanitarian mapping at different historical junctures, in the eighteenth, nineteenth, and twentieth centuries and at the turn of the twentieth and twenty-first centuries.[33] Each snapshot highlights features that recur amid later initiatives, such as the MMP, and illuminate themes otherwise threaded throughout this book. This counters impressions that digital humanitarian mapping comprises a kind of "neography" that burst onto the international scene in the first decade of the twenty-first century.[34] In past centuries' efforts to craft and disseminate humanitarian maps, we may observe preoccupations that feature prominently among recent efforts to digitize humanitarian insights and practices. These include a concern with the wrangling of data in different formats, emanating from different sources, on different scales, and with assembling these in a way that might make those conditions represented actionable or available for intervention. These were among the difficulties with

---

[31] Dana E. Powell, *Landscapes of Power Politics of Energy in the Navajo Nation* (Duke University Press, 2018).

[32] Matthew Hilton et al., "History and Humanitarianism: A Conversation" (2018) 241 *Past & Present* e1; Agnieszka Sobocinska, "New Histories of Foreign Aid" (2020) 17 *History Australia* 595; Aditi Surie von Czechowski, "Humanitarianism: Histories, Erasures, Repetitions" (2017) 37 *Comparative Studies of South Asia, Africa, & the Middle East* 614.

[33] Cf. Christina Twomey, "Framing Atrocity: Photography and Humanitarianism" (2012) 36 *History of* Photography 255.

[34] Patrick Meier, "A Brief History of Crisis Mapping (Updated)" (*iRevolutions*, March 12, 2009), <https://irevolutions.org/2009/03/12/a-brief-history-of-crisis-mapping/> (accessed October 10, 2022).

which efforts to map disease and other forms of human suffering have long grappled, as our first example will show.

## Eighteenth-Century Disease Mapping

Our first snapshot of humanitarian mapping takes us to late eighteenth-century New York City, not long after the birth of the Republic, when the city was home to about 55,000 people. Specifically, it concerns that city in the year 1797, one of several years between 1791 and 1805 when New York City was "visited" by yellow fever, a visitation causing thousands of deaths.[35] It was "for the purpose of ascertaining [the yellow fever epidemic's] most probable and essential causes" that the New York physician, Valentine Seaman, embarked upon an exercise of what we might now call humanitarian mapping, the results of which were published in 1798.[36] We might call it humanitarian because the concerns most pressing in Seaman's mapmaking were not generic governance concerns such as the distribution of authority and resources (although his maps informed argument on such matters). As a physician, Seaman made and modified maps to try to "promote human welfare" and advocate "action on th[e] basis" of that goal.[37]

At the time, prevailing understandings of the incidence and spread of yellow fever were, Seaman lamented, "often warped by their relators" and tainted by "the superficial scum of newspaper observations, and flying reports."[38] Some believed its spread to be attributable to outsiders and immigrants and looked to cargo ships, in particular, as the source of "an enlivening spark from abroad."[39] Others suspected, as Seaman himself did, that yellow fever was a miasmatic disease that flourished amid "the air of putrid effluvia," such as the gaseous discharge from rotting refuse.[40] It was to test the latter theory, primarily, that Seaman entered numbered dots on copperplate maps depicting the eastern edge of lower Manhattan known as Peck's Slip (now the Seaport District) to plot the residential locations of individuals known to have succumbed to the disease. Also plotted, using circles rather than dots, was a selection of people known to have recovered from illness: some having suffered "severe fevers" and some afflicted by milder fever "of a suspicious nature."[41]

---

[35] Edwin Williams, "Plagues—Account of the Spasmodick Cholera," in *The Treasury of Knowledge, and Library of Reference*, vol. 3 (7th ed., Collins, Keese & Co., 1839) 113.
[36] Valentine Seaman, "An Inquiry into the Cause of the Prevalence of the Yellow Fever in New-York" (1798) I *The Medical Repository* 315, 315.
[37] "Humanitarian, n. and Adj.," *supra* note 27.
[38] Seaman, *supra* note 36.
[39] Tom Koch, "The Art of Medicine: Knowing Its Place: Mapping as Medical Investigation" (2012) 379 *The Lancet; London* 887; Seaman, *supra* note 36, at 328.
[40] Seaman, *supra* note 36, at 316.
[41] Ibid., 318–319.

As was common in cartography prior to the late nineteenth century, Seaman's maps combined textual and symbolic description of a "series of places."[42] Accompanying Seaman's maps was a brief account of the progression of the disease in each person whose death was featured, although Seaman voiced regret that the cases were "too numerous to get an accurate history of them all."[43] Those depicted did not comprise a statistical sample, nor was the map a comprehensive enumeration. They were simply, for the most part, persons whose deaths were attributable to yellow fever in the city in the year 1797 "as far as [Seaman could] learn."[44] Seaman's accompanying narrative also related some sparse details about the last few days or weeks of each person's life (including, in some cases, mention of their occupation or travels) by way of trying to understand when and where they might have contracted and communicated the disease. Also appended were Seaman's observations of the cleanliness and density of occupation of the houses in question, the condition of surrounding streets, and some passing notes about environmental conditions, such as the most common wind direction in certain areas. Some of these environmental factors were represented cartographically. On one map, Seaman used an "S" to symbolize areas of "stagnant filthy water and mud" and an "x" to locate areas of "common convenience to a multitude of people."[45]

In an earlier report, published in 1796, Seaman had assembled a different data composite: combining his personal observations of yellow fever cases with tables of meteorological data taken from observations made by Gardiner Baker at the Exchange Inn in Manhattan.[46] In that context, he happened to mention infestations of mosquitoes in relevant areas, without recognizing these insects as vectors of the disease.[47] Instead, he concluded, in his 1798 publication (in which his maps appeared), that cases of yellow fever were caused by the "junction" of "certain matters emitted from a human body" and "effluvia arising from animal and vegetable substances in a state of putrefaction." Seaman also surmised that certain persons may be "predisposed" to contracting the disease and that "the spark that has kindled the putrid vapors" may, in certain instances, have been "originally introduced from other places."[48] Quarantine measures would, however, be insufficient to keep the disease at bay, he advised, unless urban areas were kept "decently cleaned."[49] These anti-contagionist arguments, and the

---

[42] Branch, *supra* note 1, at 48–49.
[43] Seaman, *supra* note 36, at 319.
[44] Ibid., 322.
[45] Ibid., 323–324.
[46] Valentine Seaman, *An Account of the Epidemic Yellow Fever, as It Appeared in the City of New-York in the Year 1795* (Hopkins, Webb & Co., 1796).
[47] Ibid., 3.
[48] Seaman, *supra* note 36, at 331.
[49] Ibid., 332.

impact of Seaman's work more generally, were later overtaken, on either side of the Atlantic, by debates between contagionists and anti-contagionists in the medical profession and their differing attitudes toward international trade and commerce.[50]

For our purposes, there are several features of Seaman's humanitarian maps that are noteworthy in view of their digital successors (and may be discerned in Figure 2.3).

One noteworthy aspect concerns the relationship that Seaman's maps posited between the particular and the general, and the way that they combined quantitative and qualitative data from multiple sources. Unlike humanitarian maps of the nineteenth and twentieth centuries—that employed the "power of large numbers," thanks to later advances in statistics[51]—Seaman's eighteenth-century maps did not demand the "suppression of small occurrences" in favor of representing statistical trends.[52] On the contrary, Seaman's map generalized from very close attention to "small occurrences." What his maps represented was a rather loose but relatively detailed collection of data about particular bodies: each singled out because of the biological fact of death or fever. This Seaman correlated (nonstatistically, based on geographic proximity) with certain environmental data to draw inferences about the "most probable" causes (again, nonstatistically understood) of a more widespread condition of suffering: in this case, disease. Notwithstanding Seaman's aspiration to "avoid attending to hearsay stories," both the disease data and the environmental data that he presented were assembled from personal reportage and recollection: Seaman's own, firsthand observations and, to a greater extent, information gleaned from others with whom he consulted.[53] These he presented telescopically in the form of dots, circles, and alphanumeric symbols. In visualizing human suffering with such pointillism using "found data" from a diversity of sources, Seaman's humanitarian maps exhibited a quality later magnified exponentially in digital humanitarian mapping: namely, the presentation of "precise inaccuracy."[54]

Also noteworthy is the way in which Seaman's maps presented a composite of public and private data assembled at different times, at different scales, and for a

---

[50] Lloyd G. Stevenson, "Putting Disease on the Map: The Early Use of Spot Maps in the Study of Yellow Fever" (1965) 20 *Journal of the History of Medicine and Allied Sciences* 226; Michael Worboys, *Spreading Germs: Disease Theories and Medical Practice in Britain, 1865-1900* (Cambridge University Press, 2000).

[51] Joshua Cole, *The Power of Large Numbers: Population, Politics, and Gender in Nineteenth-Century France* (Cornell University Press, 2000).

[52] Mark Monmonier, *Cartographies of Danger: Mapping Hazards in America* (University of Chicago Press, 1997) 4.

[53] Seaman, *supra* note 36, at 315.

[54] Daniel A. McFarland and H. Richard McFarland, "Big Data and the Danger of Being Precisely Inaccurate" (2015) 2 *Big Data & Society*.

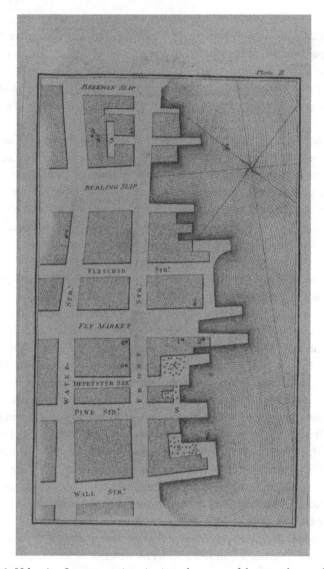

**Figure 2.3** Valentine Seaman, an inquiry into the cause of the prevalence of the yellow fever in New-York (1798), Plate II.

range of purposes, without directing attention toward the difficulty of making them commensurable. Seaman's maps subordinated all these underlying scales to the temporal and spatial scale of the humanitarian condition on which the composite was designed to report. Seaman did so, moreover, disclosing minimal metadata: he "neither acknowledged indebtedness nor claimed originality," but his maps were not his creations *ab initio*.[55] Seaman inscribed his markings upon sections of maps that were, in their entirety, intended to report on a much larger geographic area and on more enduring states than passing epidemics. Seaman created his yellow fever maps by annotating (or having someone annotate) portions of preexisting copperplate maps of the whole of New York City.[56] Despite being expensive to produce, these were commercially published with some regularity during the late eighteenth century for a number of intended audiences: the City of New York was "frequently charted for the benefit of its citizens, its visitors, and its government" and "for a variety of purposes, both private and public."[57] Seaman's markings superimposed private data (namely, his own observations and those of people with whom he consulted) upon hybrid, public-private data: "official" New York City maps commercially published. Seaman did so with a view to eliciting both public and private action on a humanitarian problem: morbidity and mortality attributable to yellow fever. And the resulting composite drew no attention to questions of jurisdiction or authority; to divergent, embedded purposes; or to discrepancies between underlying temporal or spatial scales in the source data. This practice of combining public and private data sources without making clear how (if at all) they may be reconciled, or addressing conflicts or compromises among them, endured as humanitarian mapping was later digitized. Seaman's maps were analog in their concern with the positioning of symbols in context and the extraction of meaning from their relation. Yet they were also proto-digital in the sense of pointing at something—as one does with a finger (or digit)—and thereby pulling it out from an uninvestigated morass.[58]

## Nineteenth-Century Poverty Mapping

The second historical snapshot of humanitarian mapping transports us to late nineteenth-century London. In the interim, both the idea of "society" as an object of inquiry and governmental concern, and the discipline of statistics, had become established. The idea of society as such—as an aggregate, with characteristics and effects distinct from those of individuals and other entities comprising it, that could be studied and targeted by law and policy—took hold in the mid-nineteenth century thanks to the work of early proponents of sociology: August

---

[55] Stevenson, *supra* note 50, at 237.
[56] Tom Koch, "Mapping the Miasma: Air, Health, and Place in Early Medical Mapping" [2005] *Cartographic Perspectives* 4, 11.
[57] Stevenson, *supra* note 50, at 237–238.
[58] Benjamin Peters, "Digital," in Benjamin Peters (ed.), *Digital Keywords: A Vocabulary of Information Society and Culture* (Princeton University Press, 2016).

Comte, Herbert Spencer, and Émile Durkheim.[59] Likewise, representations of facts about society in statistical terms—and accepted methodologies for generating such representations—were both widespread by the mid-nineteenth century, thanks to the rise of statistical thinking documented in the work of Ian Hacking, Lorraine Daston, Marie-Noëlle Bourguet, Theodore Porter, Stephen Stigler, Mary Morgan, Alain Desrosières, and others.

It was in this context, although at some remove from the academic discipline of sociology, that British shipowner and social reformer, Charles Booth, embarked in 1886 upon a major survey of living and working conditions in London.[60] Booth did so utilizing data on some 900,000 people collected via the London School Board Visitors (who were responsible for verifying children's school attendance following passage of the Elementary Education Act of 1870) as well as from other sources.[61] In 1889, this yielded a volume, *Life and Labour of the People* (part of a 17-volume series published between 1889 and 1903), that featured colored maps representing socioeconomic inequality in the East End of London.[62] These 1889 maps depicted the "general condition of the inhabitants" according to a seven-part, hierarchical color scale of relative wealth (with moral overtones) from the darkly shaded "lowest class" characterized as "vicious, semi-criminal" to the golden-colored "wealthy": a composite of the "upper-middle and upper classes," as may be seen in Figure 2.4.[63]

Like Seaman, Booth sought to move away from "sensational stories" toward objective representation of a subset of human bodies, at certain locations in time and space, noteworthy by reason of their heightened vulnerability or need for assistance. More specifically, Booth's aim was to show "the numerical relation which poverty, misery, and depravity bear to regular earnings and comparative comfort, and to describe the general conditions under which each class lives."[64] It has been suggested that Booth's study, at the time of its completion in 1903, "was probably the largest private research project ever carried out in Britain."[65]

Booth's maps were indicative of the rise of "scientific charity" in Britain, the United States, and elsewhere during the 1880s: a movement that sought to

---

[59] Randall Collins and Michael Makowsky, *The Discovery of Society* (8th ed., McGraw-Hill, 2010).
[60] Christian Topalov, "The City as Terra Incognita: Charles Booth's Poverty Survey and the People of London, 1886–1891" (1993) 8 *Planning Perspectives* 395.
[61] Sascha Auerbach, "'The Law Has No Feeling for Poor Folks Like Us!': Everyday Responses to Legal Compulsion in England's Working-Class Communities, 1871–1904" (2012) 45 *Journal of Social History* 686; Topalov, *supra* note 60.
[62] Charles Booth, *Labour and Life of the People*, vol. 1 (rev ed., Macmillan, 1902).
[63] "Charles Booth's London: Poverty Maps and Police Notebooks" (*LSE*, 2016), <https://booth.lse.ac.uk/> (accessed October 10, 2022).
[64] Charles Booth, "Condition and Occupations of the People of East London and Hackney, 1887" (1888) 51 *Journal of the Royal Statistical Society* 276, 277–278.
[65] Ben Gidley, *The Proletarian Other: Charles Booth and the Politics of Representation* (Centre for Urban and Community Research, Goldsmiths College, 2000) 2.

MAPS: HISTORICAL SNAPSHOTS AND DIGITAL REWRITING 45

**Figure 2.4** Section from "Maps Descriptive of London Poverty," Charles Booth, *Inquiry into Life and Labour in London* (1886–1903), digitally represented by London School of Economics and Political Science under a Public Domain Mark.

confront poverty and "improve" and differentiate among the working classes using data-driven measures. A progenitor of contemporary social work, scientific charity sought to ensure that "the everyday activities of living, the hygienic care of household members, the previously trivial features of interactions between adults and children, were ... anatomized by experts, judged in terms of their social costs and consequences and subject to regimes of education or reform."[66] According to scientific charity advocates, no longer should aid to the disadvantaged be guided by "a warm heart and an open hand"; there was "need of knowledge and wisdom and of the organization of the facts."[67] It was important, too, to take account of the complexity of the conditions addressed and the multiple causal factors at play.[68] One technique developed to try to decode this complexity was the social survey, of which Booth's work was one of the earliest examples.[69]

There is much more that could be said, and has been written, about Booth's project and the political and intellectual setting in which it was advanced. For our purposes here, however, there are several aspects of his approach to humanitarian mapping that are noteworthy with regard to the later digitization of the enterprise.

First, it is important to take account of the kind of knowledge that Booth's humanitarian maps sought to create. Booth's maps arrayed voluminous data (far more than had previously been available for comparable purposes); indeed, Booth reported himself "embarrassed by its mass."[70] Yet they made no claim to being comprehensive. As Thomas Osborne and Nikolas Rose have observed, the practice of mapping expansively, "scientifically," and in great detail, does not necessarily evince aspirations for disciplinary control or rationalization. Rather, Booth's maps' novelty and significance "l[ay] in the[ir] routinising of a new set of transactions between knowledge and space" whereby the "doubt" associated with space—the sense of it always eluding or outstripping perception from any one vantage point—could be alleviated by a form of knowledge that was itself spatial.[71]

Booth's poverty maps made the spaces that they depicted seem actionable. They did so by offering points of entry—and prospective moral intervention—into those disparate, confounding phenomena that the maps rendered concurrent, interdependent, and comparable. One could not, according to Booth's maps, register the darker-shaded spaces of poverty without also taking account of the lighter-colored spaces of relative wealth. Through the technology of the map, both extremes were brought within reach of the viewer. Yet no one space was rendered wholly transparent or tractable by its mapping.

---

[66] Nikolas Rose, "Governing 'Advanced' Liberal Democracies," in Nikolas Rose, Thomas Osborne, and Andrew Barry (eds.), *Foucault and Political Reason* (Taylor & Francis Group, 1996) 49.
[67] H.L. Wayland, "A Scientific Basis of Charity" (1894) 3 *The Charities Review* 263.
[68] This causal analysis often extended to moral judgments differentiating between the deserving and undeserving (identifying "indolence" as a cause of poverty, for instance) and invoked ideas from eugenics (by denoting "ancestry" as a factor). See, e.g., ibid.
[69] Martin Bulmer, Kevin Bales, and Kathryn Kish Sklar, *The Social Survey in Historical Perspective, 1880-1940* (Cambridge University Press, 1991).
[70] Quoted in Topalov, *supra* note 6, at 398.
[71] Thomas Osborne and Nikolas Rose, "Spatial Phenomenotechnics: Making Space with Charles Booth and Patrick Geddes" (2004) 22 *Environment and Planning D: Society and Space* 209, 210.

Second, picking up on the analog sense of concurrence that they created, the temporalities of Booth's poverty maps are worth elucidating with an eye to what becomes of these as humanitarian mapping practices are digitized. On one hand, the temporality of Booth's humanitarian mapping was very protracted. Booth conducted his research across 17 years—nearly half a life, given that life expectancy in London in the 1880s was just over 41 years.[72] Once given map form, however, Booth's insights acquired an immediacy and a currency that belied the variable ages of the data presented. The older, accumulated, potentially outdated elements of the data were compressed, together with fresher insights, into a single time scale. This was the temporality of discernment instigated by the act of viewing or using the map: a temporality that proceeded from the body (especially the eye) of the viewer or user.

This immediacy was, however, a becalmed one, not beholden to the vagaries of the now. It was, in particular, at deliberate remove from the "violent demonstrations" provoked by the economic and social conditions of late-nineteenth-century London and the "bourgeois alarm" that accompanied them.[73] Booth's map time held historical time apart from the turmoil of the present, creating a time-space in between. This was envisaged as an interval of agency, albeit only for those scrutinizing the map, not for those among the mapped or engaged in surrounding political conflicts. For the map reader, it availed her of a "visuali[z]able space [and time] for thought," prioritization, and evaluation toward moral and material improvement.[74] Recalling the West End riots of February 1886, Booth's remarks to the Royal Statistical Society in 1887 were revealing of the kind of becalming interlude that he envisaged his maps bringing about:

> This is a serious state of things, but not visibly fraught with imminent social danger, or leading straight to revolution, [...] we can afford to be calm, and to give attempts at improvement the time and patience which are absolutely needed if we are to do any good at all.[75]

In Seaman's and Booth's efforts of analog (and proto-digital) humanitarian mapping, we may observe several technical and representative practices that will become significant for the later digitization of this work. Seaman's maps demonstrated the combination of quantitative and qualitative data, from public

---

[72] John Landers, *Death and the Metropolis: Studies in the Demographic History of London, 1670–1830* (Cambridge University Press, 1993) 171.

[73] Miles A. Kimball, "London through Rose-Colored Graphics: Visual Rhetoric and Information Graphic Design in Charles Booth's Maps of London Poverty" (2006) 36 *Journal of Technical Writing and Communication* 353, 355.

[74] Osborne and Rose, *supra* note 71, at 215.

[75] Quoted in Topalov, *supra* note 60, at 400.

and private sources, and the generalization from a mass of "small occurrences," that would recur, in different forms, in digital mapping dashboards. Booth's poverty maps articulated the goal of amassing and organizing large volumes of data in order to render complex social and economic conditions actionable and to carve out an imaginary space and time for intervention with a view to their measurable improvement, without entering into revolutionary affray. Like Booth's poverty maps, later digital initiatives of humanitarian mapping would sometimes be envisaged as routes for sidestepping political conflict, suspending protest, wrangling chaos into actionable formats, or smoothing over disagreement.

## Twentieth-Century Flood Mapping

The third snapshot from the history of humanitarian mapping takes us away from relatively affluent metropoles and into the last quarter of the twentieth century to focus on flood mapping during and in the immediate aftermath of the 1988 floods in Bangladesh. Bangladesh is, in large part, a riparian nation. The floodplains of three international rivers (the Brahmaputra, the Ganges, and the Meghna) and some 250 smaller perennial rivers account for around 80 percent of its area.[76] Flooding is recurrent during the monsoon season. Even so, the floods that Bangladesh experienced between July and September of 1988 were widely considered the nation's most catastrophic of the twentieth century. Estimates of the total area inundated ranged from 57 percent to more than 70 percent of the territory of Bangladesh.[77] An estimated 30 million people were adversely affected through loss of life, loss of crops, destruction of infrastructure, damage to property, and in other ways.[78]

For purposes of relating the prehistory of digital humanitarian mapping, efforts made to map the 1988 floods and share information about the floods in cartographic form are telling for three main reasons. They evidence a transitional phase of humanitarian mapping during which analog and digital data were newly combined, and the possibilities and difficulties of their combination incipiently explored. They also manifest a transition of another, related kind: namely, the convergence of development and disaster relief thinking and programming toward the end of the Cold War, with mapping cast as crucial to both. Furthermore,

---

[76] James K. Boyce, "Birth of a Megaproject: Political Economy of Flood Control in Bangladesh" (1990) 14 *Environmental Management* 419, 419.

[77] Harun Rasid and M.A.H. Pramanik, "Areal Extent of the 1988 Flood in Bangladesh: How Much Did the Satellite Imagery Show?" (1993) 8 *Natural Hazards* 189; Bimal Kanti Paul, "Flood Research in Bangladesh in Retrospect and Prospect: A Review" (1997) 28 *Geoforum* 121; Rashed Chowdhury, "An Assessment of Flood Forecasting in Bangladesh: The Experience of the 1998 Flood" (2000) 22 *Natural Hazards* 139.

[78] Chowdhury, *supra* note 77, at 139.

efforts to map the 1988 floods in Bangladesh highlight the range of interests and investments that projects of humanitarian mapping tend to elicit, and some of the ways in which humanitarian maps have been materialized and contested.

Up until the 1980s, flood mapping and measurement in Bangladesh were almost entirely dependent on ground observation and human estimation.[79] The mapping of the 1988 floods, however, reflected several key institutional and technological changes during the preceding decades. From the mid-1960s onward, and especially after Bangladesh attained independence in 1971, Bangladesh saw significant inflows of foreign aid.[80] In connection with this, there was a notable expansion of flood control and drainage infrastructure in Bangladesh, entailing the construction of embankments, drainage channels, sluices, and regulators.[81] Alongside this, the newly independent country sought to construct an informational infrastructure for flood prediction and monitoring. In 1972, for instance, a Flood Forecasting and Warning Center (FFWC) was established under the administrative control of the Bangladesh Water Development Board (BWDB).[82] Initially, the FFWC carried out forecasting on the basis of gauge-to-gauge coaxial correlation diagrams (statistical graphs) and Muskingum-Cunge methods (physical-numerical principles used to calculate flood routing) using data recorded from some 11 flood monitoring stations around the country.[83] It was only after the 1988 floods, in 1992, that the FFWC would implement computer modeling for flood forecasting, installing MIKE11—hydrodynamic simulation software developed by the Danish Hydraulic Institute.[84]

Eight years after the FFWC's establishment, in 1980, Bangladesh created the Bangladesh Space Research and Remote Sensing Organization, or SPARRSO, with a mandate to bring the benefits of space technology and research to Bangladesh, through collaboration with NASA (the US National Aeronautics Space Administration), JAXA (the Japanese Aerospace Exploration Agency), and the European Space Agency. By expanding on ground station construction

---

[79] Harun Rasid and M.A.H. Pramanik, "Visual Interpretation of Satellite Imagery for Monitoring Floods in Bangladesh" (1990) 14 *Environmental Management* 815, 815.

[80] Bimal Kanti Paul, "Relief Assistance to 1998 Flood Victims: A Comparison of the Performance of the Government and NGOs" (2003) 169 *The Geographical Journal* 75, 77; Syedur Rahman, "Bangladesh in 1988: Precarious Institution Building Amid Crisis Management" (1989) 29 *Asian Survey* 216, 221.

[81] Rezaur Rahman and Mashfiqus Salehin, "Flood Risks and Reduction Approaches in Bangladesh," in Rajib Shaw, Fuad Mallick, and Aminul Islam (eds.), *Disaster Risk Reduction Approaches in Bangladesh* (Springer Japan, 2013) 76.

[82] Bangladesh Water Development Board, "Flood Forecasting & Warning in Bangladesh" (N.D.), Project Brief, <https://www.bwdb.gov.bd/archive/pdf/190.pdf> (accessed October 10, 2022); Paul, *supra* note 80, at 77.

[83] Md. Sazzad Hossain, "Flood Forecasting and Warning in Bangladesh" (2018) 67 *WMO Bulletin*, <https://public.wmo.int/en/resources/bulletin/flood-forecasting-and-warning-bangladesh> (accessed October 10, 2022).

[84] Bangladesh Water Development Board, "Annual Flood Report" (*Bangladesh Water Development Board*, 2016), Annual Report 12 <http://www.ffwc.gov.bd/images/annual16.pdf>.

efforts undertaken from 1968 onward, SPARRSO availed Bangladesh of direct access to real-time data and imagery from US and Japanese meteorological satellites intended for use in weather forecasting and agro-climatic environmental monitoring. The 1988 floods were monitored in part using advanced very high-resolution radiometer (AVHRR) data (that is, measurements of radiant energy to detect cloud cover and surface water) received by SPARRSO from meteorological satellites operated by the United States' National Oceanographic and Atmospheric Administration.[85]

As noted earlier, however, the 1988 floods marked a time of transition in the types of information used for flood mapping. Satellite data flowed into a decidedly human mélange of data from which insights on the flood were extracted. The extent of flooding in different parts of the country was monitored by a Flood Monitoring Cell established within the Bangladesh President's Secretariat. The staff of this cell was informed by BWDB field engineers and civil servants reporting from district and subdistrict headquarters in inundated areas.[86] The BWDB also sought to use satellite imagery to advise the Flood Monitoring Cell: specifically, interpretations of AVHRR data received from SPARRSO. Yet the interpretation of that data too was largely non-automated. Although that AVHRR data was initially displayed using a digital software package provided by NASA, hard copy versions were generated for interpretation within SPARRSO— copies on which were superimposed Bangladesh's jurisdictional boundaries from the CIA's World Data Base 2 reference system. SPARRSO technical staff analyzed these print outs by reference to a range of other, mostly analog data sources. These included: physiographic and contour maps of Bangladesh; river system maps produced by SPARRSO using aerial photographs and LANDSAT positive transparencies; and maps of Bangladesh's 1954 and 1955 floods. The latter had been prepared by a US consulting firm, IECO, in 1964 after they were commissioned by the East Pakistan Water and Power Development Authority (prior to Bangladeshi independence) to develop a master plan for flood control, with funding from USAID (the United States Agency for International Development). Regard was also had to reports on flood situations from local newspapers.[87] This analysis was carried out daily during the period of inundation, except for eight days in early September 1988 when either a lack of electric power or inundation of the SPARRSO campus prevented the receipt of image data.[88]

---

[85] Rasid and Pramanik, *supra* note 79, at 815.
[86] Rasid and Pramanik, *supra* note 77.
[87] JICA, "The Study for Rural Development Focusing on Flood Proofing in the People's Republic of Bangladesh Final Report" (Japan International Cooperation Agency, 2002), Annex 5, A-9, <https://openjicareport.jica.go.jp/617/617/617_101_11702909.html> (accessed October 10, 2022).
[88] Rasid and Pramanik, *supra* note 79, at 816–817.

Multisource, human interpretation of this kind was, at the time, seen as less costly than fully automated analysis (to the extent that the latter might have been possible) because the latter would have required "specialized computer facilities, relatively expensive computer-compatible tapes, and trained [hu]manpower."[89] In addition, satellite imagery was of limited use because of the unavailability of cloud-free images for the period of the flood's peak.[90] The combination of these various data sources did seem to yield some effective flood forecasting capacity: one observer from the World Meteorological Organization concluded that the FFWC's forecasting for the major river systems proved to be "fairly accurate" throughout the 1988 floods.[91] Nonetheless, these forecasts did not reach all relevant areas' inhabitants. Rahman reports that there was "apparently no effective early-warning system in operation before the 1988 flood." Of 70 inundated villages surveyed, 63 reported receiving no warning of imminent flood, while the remaining 7 were warned by local officials, radio reports, or "local knowledgeable persons."[92]

For all its patchiness, mapping played a central role in the knowledge complex that Bangladesh mobilized to address flood risk and to aid those threatened or harmed by inundation. The official flood map that the BWDB ultimately produced based on the mostly analog interpretive practices described above took the form of a choropleth map of the whole of Bangladesh: a map, somewhat like Booth's poverty maps, that used shading and color to indicate the average value of a particular quantity within a delineated area. This classified flood-affected administrative units (districts and subdistricts or *upazilas*) into one of three categories according to the extent of their inundation over the course of the 1988 floods: in the first category, the area affected was estimated to be over 75 percent; in the second, the area affected was between 25 and 75 percent; and in the third, the area affected was up to 25 percent of the total land area in question.[93] In this way, much as Booth had, the BWDB sought to use maps to open up an actionable space between the recent history of flooding and the present of official review. By 1988, however, this flood mapping space was becoming inundated by data in varying formats emanating from multiple official and unofficial sites.

Apparent in these efforts to map and respond to the 1988 floods was a convergence of development and disaster-related thinking and practice by which digital humanitarianism would later be marked. Initially, disaster relief took priority. During the floods, "[r]esources were diverted to relief-oriented activities at

---

[89] Ibid., 820.
[90] Rasid and Pramanik, *supra* note 77.
[91] Hossain, *supra* note 83.
[92] Atiur Rahman, "Peoples' Perception and Response to Floodings: The Bangladesh Experience" (1996) 4 *Journal of Contingencies and Crisis Management* 198.
[93] Rasid and Pramanik, *supra* note 77.

the cost of most economic and infrastructure-related activities."[94] In the floods' aftermath, however, disaster preparedness—flood preparedness specifically— came to be seen as axiomatic to Bangladesh's prospects for economic development. The controversial five-year (1990–1995) Flood Action Plan launched by the World Bank in 1989, for example, proposed a "comprehensive system of flood control and drainage works" combined with "non-structural measures such as flood forecasting, flood warning, flood preparedness and disaster management": all by way of creating "an environment for sustained economic growth and social improvement" in Bangladesh.[95] At the center of this plan was a series of "crude" maps. These depicted the floodplain; the areas flooded for more than a month during the 1988 floods; areas in which monsoonal rice production was affected by flood; and the suggested locations of embankments.[96] In this context, flood mapping served a developmental narrative in which "economic activity in Bangladesh [was] retarded by the threat of floods" and flood control infrastructure would "provide more room for [industrial and commercial] expansion."[97]

Ultimately, the World Bank's vision in the Flood Action Plan was not realized, due to a combination of civil society opposition and donor reluctance. Rather than constructing a massive, multibillion-dollar run of embankments along the country's major rivers as had been proposed, the Bangladeshi government opted during the ensuing decade for smaller-scale flood-proofing and the strengthening of disaster management capabilities.[98] Nonetheless, the convergence of disaster and development narratives and programming persisted. As Bimal Kanti Paul later observed, from "the early 1990s [onward], a pragmatic combination of 'disaster' and 'development' activities . . . [was] the preferred mode of operation for many NGOs in Bangladesh," many of whom had previously avoided disaster relief work in the belief that it "causes disruption to normal development activities and . . . [engenders] relief dependency."[99] This convergence, noticeable in Bangladesh and elsewhere, would endure as humanitarian mapping became more and more digital.

This convergence notwithstanding, flood mitigation efforts on the Bangladesh floodplain remained conflictual. Conflict was expressed, in part, in contending projects of mapping embedded with different priorities and working with distinct spatial and temporal scales. Flood mapping of the kind advanced in the

[94] Rahman, *supra* note 92, at 204.
[95] World Bank Asia Region Technical Department, "Flood Control in Bangladesh A Plan for Action" (1990), World Bank Technical Paper 119, <http://documents1.worldbank.org/curated/en/521601468743379332/pdf/WTP119-REPLACEMENT-PUBLIC-Flood-Control-in-Bangladesh-a-plan-for-action.pdf> (accessed October 10, 2022).
[96] Boyce, *supra* note 76, at 425.
[97] World Bank Asia Region Technical Department, *supra* note 95, at 4.
[98] Hugh Brammer, "After the Bangladesh Flood Action Plan: Looking to the Future" (2010) 9 *Environmental Hazards* 118, 118–119.
[99] Paul, *supra* note 80, at 77.

aforementioned World Bank report favored large-scale, structural efforts to address flood risk.[100] These efforts were responsive to a range of geopolitical drivers and were overwhelmingly future-oriented, rather than being attentive to past experiences of survival on the floodplain. For example, behind the plan to construct hundreds of kilometers of embankments after the 1988 floods was a French engineering consortium assembled and sent to Bangladesh at the behest of President François Mitterand with the support of General H.M Ershad, President of Bangladesh. Mitterand's wife, Danielle Mitterand, active in human rights campaigns, happened to have been visiting Dhaka at the time of the 1988 floods as President Ershad's guest. With Mitterand's support, an early version of the plan ultimately published by the World Bank was presented at the G7 Summit in Paris in July 1989. Thereafter, Japanese and US skepticism was a significant factor in its demise.[101]

Alongside this type of endeavor, in the wake of the 1988 floods, researchers from an array of disciplines—anthropology, sociology, economics, and geography—set about mapping a wide range of physical, social, and economic phenomena related to floods in Bangladesh, some of which had been "virtually untouched" in studies of Bangladesh prior to the 1980s.[102] Maps literal and figurative were published depicting a variety of environmental and health risks posed by flooding; related distributive processes; human adjustments made in the face of recurrent flooding; peoples' comprehension of flood risk and associated preparedness; effects of different hazard management and flood control strategies; and a broader range of socioeconomic and psycho-social impacts and adaptations beyond damage to and loss of assets or livelihood.[103] Physiographic and hydrodynamic maps previously in circulation were shown to have taken little if any account of local coping strategies and variable levels of preparedness.[104] Growth in the number and variety of nongovernmental organizations (NGOs) active in Bangladesh from the late 1980s to the late 1990s contributed to this rise in flood mapping pluralism.[105] And this burgeoning range of flood studies and maps expressed contending versions of what was valuable and worthy of notice and what should or should not be factored into humanitarian and research work. Apparent among these efforts of mapping was an aspiration for flood data that was more timely, granular, and attentive to local variation than

---

[100] H. Brammer, "Floods in Bangladesh: II. Flood Mitigation and Environmental Aspects" (1990) 156 *The Geographical Journal* 158.
[101] Boyce, *supra* note 76.
[102] Paul, *supra* note 80, at 128.
[103] Ibid.
[104] Brian Cook, "Flood Knowledge and Management in Bangladesh: Increasing Diversity, Complexity and Uncertainty" (2010) 4 *Geography Compass* 750.
[105] Nilufar Matin and Muhammad Taher, "The Changing Emphasis of Disasters in Bangladesh NGOs" (2001) 25 *Disasters* 227.

had been available to date.[106] This aspiration helped to fuel the embrace of digital technologies in flood mapping, in Bangladesh and elsewhere, without bringing an end to contestation over what could and should be mapped.

## End-of-the-Millennium Vulnerability Mapping

The fourth and final snapshot in our selective tour through the history of humanitarian mapping—before we turn to its latest, digital manifestations—is taken from the final few years of the twentieth century and concerns the work of an international organization: the Food and Agriculture Organization (FAO). Its focus is the Food Insecurity and Vulnerability Information and Mapping Systems (FIVIMS) developed under the FAO's auspices in 1997 and 1998.[107]

The goal of creating FIVIMS was to contribute to the reduction of food insecurity and vulnerability globally, the former meaning "undernourish[ment] as a result of the physical unavailability of food, [people's] lack of social or economic access to adequate food, and/or inadequate food utilization." Vulnerability was understood in this context to refer to "the full range of factors that place people at risk of becoming food-insecure."[108] Marshaling information through FIVIMS—especially at the subnational and household levels—would, it was hoped, enable accurate and timely identification of food-insecure and vulnerable groups and provide insight into some of the coping strategies that they were already utilizing, in order to "design and, eventually, evaluate possible policies and interventions."[109]

The plan to create FIVIMS was one of the relatively few "new and specific proposals" that emerged from the five days of multilateral "scoldings and self-flagellation" that was the 1996 World Food Summit, an event arranged under the leadership of the FAO's first African Director-General, Jacques Diouf.[110] Unlike the first such ad hoc international meeting, held in 1974, the 1996 Summit was convened in the face of US reticence as well as ambivalence from other quarters. This was in contrast to the World Food Conference of 1974, which had been called in response to an acute global food crisis, including the Bangladesh famine, and a deteriorating economic situation globally, at the behest (in part)

---

[106] E.g., Rasid and Pramanik, *supra* note, at 820.

[107] Ezzeddine Boutrif, "Establishing a Food Insecurity and Vulnerability Information and Mapping System" (FAO 1998), Appendix to the 17th Session of the Asia Pacific Commission on Agricultural Statistics APCAS/98/7, <http://www.fao.org/3/w5849T/w5849t09.htm> (accessed October 10, 2022).

[108] FAO, *Food Insecurity and Vulnerability Information and Mapping Systems (FIVIMS)* (FAO, 2000) 1, 13.

[109] Ibid., 3.

[110] D. Shaw, *World Food Security: A History Since 1945* (Palgrave Macmillan UK, 2007) 347–354.

of US Secretary of State Henry Kissinger.[111] By 1996, "at the end of a long series of international conferences held over the previous five years," states' appetite for ambitious global plans was dampened.[112] FIVIMS, conceived as an "incremental" and "cost-effective" initiative, was exactly the kind of diminutive change proposal that divided states could get behind.[113]

Mapping, as represented in and by FIVIMS, differed from the efforts of disease, poverty, and flood mapping discussed so far. In FIVIMS, mapping signified but one dimension or task of a dynamic information system. It was to be conducted, moreover, using GIS: computer hardware and software for capturing, storing, analyzing, and displaying spatial data (that is, data related to positions on the Earth's surface). GIS enabled the ingestion, processing, and representation—in a range of formats—of multiple types of data including, potentially, digital data from satellites, aerial drones, or other remote sensing devices; preexisting cartographic and survey data and/or demographic data (in digital or database form); and (potentially) a variety of real-time data, such as mobile phone use or internet search data. The map, therefore, was not a single, visual artifact that could be generated and shared in the way that maps were published, printed, and circulated by Seaman and Booth in the eighteenth and nineteenth centuries and during the 1988 Bangladesh floods. Toward the end of the millennium, mapping became a multinodal, networked activity by which a continuous stream of composite outputs was produced.

Notably, FIVIMS comprised a "framework" for "collaborative networking" and data-sharing both within and among national FIVIMS networks. The latter were to be made up of "all the operating systems of those units that produce or use data and information of relevance to FIVIMS." Each such national FIVIMS network was expected to formulate and work toward a national FIVIMS strategy and work plan, after having first identified and prioritized the "information needs of key food security decision-makers" and conducted an inventory and available data and information. Spanning all of this would be the global FIVIMS. And central to this global architecture was a set of indicators common to all countries that would "permit intercountry analyses and comparisons."[114]

In the Bangladesh flood mapping example, we saw the aim of humanitarian mapping begin to shift away from the creation of a coherent visual scheme that would afford the maps' master-creators room and particular sites for intervention and toward the generation of a stream of geographic data that could be adapted to the vantage points, arguments, and needs of many disparate users. That shift accelerated as mapping became the work of an information system, as in FIVIMS.

[111] Ibid., 121.
[112] Ibid., 353.
[113] FAO, *supra* note 108, at 13–16.
[114] Ibid., 23–25.

FIVIMS was expressly designed to be "demand-driven" and "useful to several groups of people across different sectors of society."[115] Much as the Seaman and Booth maps had combined public and private data from multiple sources, national FIVIMS networks reported sourcing data from governments, international organizations, bilateral aid agencies, and NGOs.[116] In FIVIMS, however, there was greater emphasis on the diversification and effectiveness of mapping outputs and interfaces. Policy documents offering guidance on FIVIMS' implementation argued for "effective product dissemination" adaptive to the "needs, interests and perspectives of the appropriate target users" through media, which could include "radio, posters, town meetings and computer networks."[117]

This understanding of humanitarian mapping, as a practice involving the making of a diversity of products and interfaces that could be actioned by a wide range of users, reflected changed understandings of the role of the state—changes about which Chapter 5 says more. In the mid-late 1990s, the state was still the primary sponsor of geodetic infrastructure, and the main source of geological, meteorological, demographic, land ownership, taxation, and other cartographically relevant data. However, a combination of political and economic factors (including forces favoring privatization and public austerity) was pressuring many states—and the international organizations that they sustained—to try to fund these activities (at least in part) from outside the public fisc.[118] At the same time, the growing ubiquity of GIS systems and handheld devices equipped with Global Positioning System (GPS) technology had vested greater mapping capacity in individuals, communities, and the private sector. From the mid-1990s onward, familiarity with the UNIX operating system was no longer a precondition for using GIS.[119] This lessened demand on states and international organizations for, and diversified the potential sources of, maps amenable to being put to humanitarian purposes.

FIVIMS thus represented an exemplary instance of the first phase of the digitization of humanitarian mapping—a phase characterized by the systematization of the activity and its diffusion across a network of creators, users, and interfaces, albeit still mostly in ways mediated by national governments. In 2011, the FIVIMS work of FAO was integrated into a new joint strategy of the FAO and the World Food Programme on Information Systems for Food and Nutrition

---

[115] Ibid., 15, 17.
[116] P.S. Bindraban et al., *Focus on Food Insecurity and Vulnerability—A Review of the UN System Common Country Assessments and World Bank Poverty Reduction Strategy Papers* (FAO, 2003) 11–12.
[117] FAO, *supra* note 108, at 21–22.
[118] E.g.., David Rhind, "Chapter 1 National Mapping As A Business-Like Enterprise," in Fraser Taylor (ed.), *Policy Issues in Modern Cartography*, vol. 3 (Elsevier, 1998).
[119] Jiří Pánek, "From Mental Maps to GeoParticipation" (2016) 53 *The Cartographic Journal* 300, 302.

Security.[120] This saw emphasis placed on "much greater ownership of [food and nutrition security information] in the individual and community-levels, stressing communication feedback loops to fine tune analysis for different user groups."[121] Humanitarian mapping became a curatorial activity entailing the linking up of different "feedback loops" through which relevant information had to be encouraged, continually, to flow. Implied, too, in this turn toward individual and community-level "ownership" of humanitarian mapping was a growing expectation of self-reliance and self-documentation on the part of individuals and communities in relation to their humanitarian needs—an emergent imperative that we will explore further in Chapter 4.

## The Digitization of Humanitarian Mapping

Much has happened in mapping in the years since the launch of FIVIMS. As will become apparent in later chapters, the digitization of maps and mapping is a recurrent aspect of many actors' growing recourse to digital technology in international humanitarian work. The MMP, introduced earlier, is one example of the digitization of humanitarian mapping in which several of its distinguishing features may be highlighted.[122]

As noted earlier, the MMP mobilizes a combination of remote and local volunteers to help create digital maps of human-inhabited areas that are "unmapped or undermapped," through collaborative analysis and labeling of satellite imagery.[123] Volunteers use a range of different digital applications and interfaces for these purposes: Field Papers (an interface enabling the creation and printing of multipage atlases for manual annotation and the uploading of annotated documents, as shown in Figure 2.5);[124] MapSwipe (an open source mobile application for map labeling);[125] and OpenMapKit (an application allowing users to create mobile phone data collection surveys for field data collection).[126] The

---

[120] FAO Office of Evaluation, *Evaluation of FAO's Role and Work in Nutrition* (FAO, 2011), PC 108/6 29.
[121] Nancy Mock, Nathan Morrow, and Adam Papendieck, "From Complexity to Food Security Decision-Support: Novel Methods of Assessment and Their Role in Enhancing the Timeliness and Relevance of Food and Nutrition Security Information" (2013) 2 *Global Food Security* 41, 43.
[122] Paul Knight, "Missing Maps Project Awarded at the Red Cross Humanitarian Technology Awards—A Year of Blogs—Oct 2020" (*Missing Maps*, October 26, 2020), <https://www.missingmaps.org/blog/2020/10/26/a-year-of-blogs/> (accessed October 10, 2022).
[123] Jane Feinmann, "How MSF Is Mapping the World's Medical Emergency Zones" (2014) 349 *BMJ* g7540.
[124] "About Field Papers" (*Field Papers*), <http://fieldpapers.org/about> (accessed October 10, 2022).
[125] Jess Cahill, "MapSwipe—The Story Continues" (June 25, 2018), <https://www.missingmaps.org/blog/2018/06/25/mapswipe-story/> (accessed October 10, 2022).
[126] "OpenMapKit Website" (*OpenMapKit*), <http://openmapkit.org/> (accessed October 10, 2022).

**Figure 2.5** Image of Field Papers in use.
© 2011, Alexander Kachkaev, "2011-05-10 (0010)," <http://www.flickr.com/photos/kachkaev/5710460686> (accessed October 10, 2022). Also available at <https://wiki.openstreetmap.org/wiki/File:Surveying_with_walking_papers.jpg> (accessed October 10, 2022). Reproduced under a Creative Commons Attribution—ShareAlike 2.0 license; full terms available at https://creativecommons.org/licenses/by-sa/2.0/legalcode (accessed October 10, 2022).

resulting maps are then made available, after validation in accordance with the mapmaking protocols of HOT (an organization mentioned at the start of this chapter), via the free and open platform OpenStreetMap (OSM), with the database structure, organizational practices, and editing software of OSM informing their makeup.[127]

The overall goal of the endeavor is for humanitarian organizations working in and with these "unmapped or undermapped" communities to become better equipped to meet the needs of vulnerable people among them. As Givoni observes, "the project is . . . an exercise in which collaborative crisis mapping is conducted under relatively controlled conditions with a view to building capacities for a collective disaster response to form independently in

---

[127] Georg Glasze and Chris Perkins, "Social and Political Dimensions of the OpenStreetMap Project: Towards a Critical Geographical Research Agenda," in Jamal Jokar Arsanjani et al. (eds.), *OpenStreetMap in GIScience: Experiences, Research, and Applications* (Springer International Publishing, 2015).

the future."[128] Given its commitment to engaging local volunteers in mapping their own communities, alongside remote (external) volunteers, the exercise also serves "to validate HOT's basic commitment to . . . inclusive and egalitarian [mapping] action."[129] One of our informants spoke of this commitment as follows:

> [W]ith the Missing Maps project, what we've been doing is also putting money forward and training and teaching people in local areas to take over responsibility of their own mapping. So little mapping communities have been growing in all these areas and all these places and that puts people on the ground. Now, the best and most effective map is one that's done with local knowledge. We can map from satellite and we can say there's a building there but underneath that roof we don't know whether that is a house, a shop or it's just a roof with no walls which is some of the kind of open cooking kitchens that you find in some of the rural areas of Africa. So we have no idea what's underneath that roof when we draw from satellite imagery. So people on the ground are that important to being able to put local knowledge to the data and the features that we put on the map.[130]

Just as FIVIMS was an expression of concerns about cost-effectiveness within the FAO and among its major state sponsors, and manifest an embrace of incrementalism amid political division, so the MMP has been lauded in part because it has not required "a great deal of funding from MSF [Médecins Sans Frontières]" or its other founding organizations, nor a high level of consensus among participants.[131] Even without these, the MMP and its digital interfaces have helped its sponsoring organizations enlarge and strengthen the volunteer base upon which they draw. They do so by offering volunteers opportunities to get involved "on a more casual basis," without great sacrifice or longstanding commitment "by mapping through the use of their mobile devices while sitting on the sofa for example."[132]

Humanitarian mapping in this casualized, piecework mode—a mode that articulates well with the burgeoning casualization of work and rise of the so-called "gig economy"—entails participation in an information system, as in

---

[128] Michal Givoni, "Between Micro Mappers and Missing Maps: Digital Humanitarianism and the Politics of Material Participation in Disaster Response" (2016) 34 *Environment and Planning D: Society and Space* 1036.
[129] Ibid., 1036.
[130] Interview with Participant AD, *supra* note 28.
[131] Feinmann, *supra* note 123.
[132] Stefan Scholz et al., "Volunteered Geographic Information for Disaster Risk Reduction—The Missing Maps Approach and Its Potential within the Red Cross and Red Crescent Movement" (2018) 10 *Remote Sensing* 1239.

FIVIMS. However, that system has been somewhat de-professionalized in the MMP (or the amateurism of Seaman and Booth has been revived) as nonexperts are afforded novel points of entry to its operational hierarchies and divisions of labor.[133] Some barriers to entry have been lowered. No longer does the exercise demand the commitment of 17 years of anyone's life, as Booth's poverty mapping required of him. Rather, the work of mapping is broken down into assignable microtasks that are meted out to a diversity of concurrent contributors, with varying levels of insight and experience, via the HOT Tasking Manager shown in Figures 2.1 and 2.2.[134] This breakdown and technological dispersal of responsibilities and resulting tapping of new user-supporters are among the factors that have aided the influx into the humanitarian field of new investors of time and material resources, alongside and in combination with states, as discussed in Chapters 1 and 5.

Also significant, among the features that distinguish the MMP from prior humanitarian mapping efforts, is its indication of the growing prominence of "crowds" in the sourcing and analysis (that is, mainly labeling) of digital data from which maps are assembled.[135] Emphasis is regularly placed, amid discussion of the MMP and similar projects, on the quality (in terms of resolution) and quantity of the image data made available by satellite technology and the potential potency of combining this with the latent force of a "crowd."[136] The crowd is unknowable and unplaceable in such accounts because it is made up of a partially remote workforce focused on fragments of a succession of projects. It is an "anonymous workforce" that "bring[s] strangers together to generate new knowledge"—although both the newness and the reliability of the knowledge so generated may be questioned.[137] Even so, an important dimension of both the claim to novelty and the claim to authenticity of the MMP—and hence its claim to authority—is its tapping and mobilization of a "crowd." And crowdsourcing is expressive of the digital logic earlier discussed because it leverages the multinodal, decentralized architecture characteristic of digital technology that

---

[133] João Porto de Albuquerque, Benjamin Herfort, and Melanie Eckle, "The Tasks of the Crowd: A Typology of Tasks in Geographic Information Crowdsourcing and a Case Study in Humanitarian Mapping" (2016) 8 *Remote Sensing* 859; Glasze and Perkins, *supra* note 127; Mordechai (Muki) Haklay, "Neogeography and the Delusion of Democratisation" (2013) 45 *Environment and Planning A: Economy and Space* 55.

[134] Humanitarian OpenStreetMap Team, *supra* note 6.

[135] Daren C. Brabham, *Crowdsourcing* (MIT Press, 2013).

[136] Catherine Turk, "Cartographica Incognita: 'Dijital Jedis,' Satellite Salvation and the Mysteries of the 'Missing Maps'" (2017) 54 *The Cartographic Journal* 14.

[137] Ibid., 21–22; Paul Currion, "'If All You Have Is a Hammer . . .'—How Useful Is Humanitarian Crowdsourcing?" (*Medium*, November 10, 2015), <https://paulcurrion.medium.com/if-all-you-have-is-a-hammer-how-useful-is-humanitarian-crowdsourcing-fed4ef33f8c8> (accessed October 10, 2022).

in turn depends on disparate inputs from any source being translatable into binary code.

Embedded within this celebratory invocation of the digitally mediated "crowd" is a complex and longstanding set of attractions and anxieties that have been explored by scholars such as Elias Canetti and Jodi Dean.[138] These include qualities of egalitarianism often identified with crowds (however ephemerally). They also include recurrent characterizations of the crowd as "a source of new feelings, thoughts, and ideas" deriving from its unruly heterogeneity; that is, the crowd's presumed possession of "the novel consistency of a provisional being."[139] When digital initiatives of humanitarian mapping invoke the power and potential of "crowdsourcing," they mobilize these ambivalent social and political associations. Crowdsourcing so inflected seems to herald possibilities for the transformation of humanitarian practice in a more egalitarian direction, even as crowd members are ordered and ranked in the process.

Nonetheless, the affirmation of the power of "crowdsourcing" that occurs frequently in the practice of digital humanitarian mapping, and the celebration of the participatory opportunities that projects like the MMP create, cannot be "decoupled from the [associated] augmentation of other political capacities to establish security and order in crises."[140] For one thing, crowdsourcing gets filtered through the workforce ordering that digital interfaces effect, as shown by the breakdown of volunteer roles via the HOT Tasking Manager represented in Figure 2.1.[141] Given the hierarchies and divisions of labor embedded in digital interfaces, crowdsourcing may reinforce as much as breakdown hierarchy. The democratization of knowledge-making that digitization is supposed to bring about is invariably bundled with logics of political and economic ordering that tend to compromise those participatory opportunities.

Likewise, beyond the internal operations of the MMP, capacities for surveillant monitoring may be enhanced through crowd-based creation, sourcing, labeling, and sharing of data, even when undertaken for ostensibly benign or beneficial purposes. Consider, for example, the brief "accidental" invasion of Costa Rica in 2010 by Nicaraguan troops who reported to a local newspaper that they mistook the area in question to be Nicaraguan territory because of the area's mislabeling on Google Maps, an incident to which we will return in Chapter 5.[142] In that instance, the deployment of a state's military force was apparently guided by

---

[138] Elias Canetti, *Crowds and Power* (Carol Stewart tr., Farrar, Strauss & Giroux, 1984); Jodi Dean, *Crowds and Party* (Verso Books, 2016).
[139] Jodi Dean, "Enclosing the Subject" (2016) 44 *Political Theory* 363, 363, 378.
[140] Givoni, *supra* note 128, at 1025, 1030.
[141] See also Albuquerque, Herfort, and Eckle, *supra* note 133.
[142] Mark Brown, "Nicaraguan Invasion? Blame Google Maps" (*Wired*, November 8, 2010), <https://www.wired.com/2010/11/google-maps-error-blamed-for-nicaraguan-invasion/> (accessed October 10, 2022).

Google Maps data: data crowdsourced from a range of public and private data providers, including users of Android smartphones on which location services are active and users of the Waze traffic navigation app (developed and owned by Google). One could imagine a similar consequence flowing from freely available online humanitarian maps. Indeed, some digital humanitarian initiatives have seen local participants withdraw because of worries about their security—in Libyan crisis mapping, for instance.[143]

Mapping of crowdsourced data may also enliven prospects for monetization of human-sourced data streams in ways potentially at odds with the interests of the communities engaged in that crowdsourcing. Consider, for example, what happened when a company called Loveland Technologies released an online cadastral map and a free mobile app designed to enable community mapping of property "blight" and tax foreclosure in Detroit, purportedly to help community organizations that were working to rebuild affected communities and support residents to stay in their homes (that is, in pursuit of humanitarian objectives). What reportedly ensued was that the app was widely utilized by external investors to identify opportunities for investment. This facilitated a speculative buy-up of a significant percentage of Detroit residential real estate that pushed secure housing even further out of reach for many.[144]

A third noteworthy feature of the MMP—beyond its reliance on casualization and crowdsourcing—is the anti-formalism that it champions. On one hand, the "positional accuracy" of the kind of satellite data employed in the MMP is strong and improving all the time, when assessed against measures like the US Geological Survey's National Survey's National Map Accuracy Standards.[145] On the other hand, data that is accurate by this measure is known to elide or misrepresent "individual- and community-based memories, affective geographies" and other popular knowledge, all of which could affect the authenticity, plausibility, or actionability of a humanitarian map.[146] Accordingly, the MMP looks to combine the two: supplementing the digital formalism of high-resolution satellite mapping outputs by overlaying these with anti-formal, analog knowledge forms.

The involvement of local volunteers in the MMP is meant to keep a "human in the loop" amid the workings of digital technology—that figure that Louise Amoore shows to be very difficult to call upon in practice "amid the limitless

---

[143] Ryan Burns, "Moments of Closure in the Knowledge Politics of Digital Humanitarianism" (2014) 53 *Geoforum* 51, 51, 58 (discussing controversies over crisis mapping in Libya).

[144] Shilpia Jindia, "Tech Startups to the Rescue? How Technology Can Deepen Inequality in Detroit—And How 'Civic Tech' Could Help End It" (*Medium*, November 23, 2016), <https://medium.com/latterly/tech-startups-to-the-rescue-978ec1f0f68f> (accessed October 10, 2022); Craig M. Dalton and Tim Stallmann, "Counter-Mapping Data Science: Counter-Mapping" (2018) 62 *The Canadian Geographer/Le Géographe Canadien* 93.

[145] Burns, *supra* note 143.

[146] Ibid., 57.

feedback loops and back propagation of the machine learning algorithms," such as those used in satellite image processing.[147] The manual annotation of the MMP's maps drawing upon analog community knowledge (using the Field Papers interface, for example, as shown in Figure 2.5) positions the human volunteer as a visible marker of anti-formalist correctives even as that human mark does not bear directly upon underlying machine learning operations, such as those involved in satellite image processing.

At the same time, these anti-formalist commitments incorporating analog knowledge forms remain a source of concern and conflict for the MMP. Quite apart from the challenges of operationalizing human questioning of automated satellite image processing, the "level of engagement of local communities seems to vary from [MMP] project to project" according to the observations of Carmen Sumadiwiria while studying MMP volunteers in Bangladesh. "One of the barriers to this is that data entered onto the OSM platform by the Missing Maps [P]roject is primarily in English," Sumadiwiria remarked.[148] Sumadiwiria also noted a range of reasons why people asked to provide local knowledge routinely resist doing so, or provide false or inaccurate information, because of their sense of what communities might stand to gain or lose from the mapping initiative, or because of unevenly distributed literacy and other skill levels.[149] Accordingly, the relationship between the relative formality of the digital and its anti-formalist analog correctives never seems to be fully resolved through their combination in the MMP. Their respective limits and incommensurability remain glaring.

In a spirit of anti-formalist renewal, the MMP aspires to reintroduce into humanitarian mapping subjective, human-scale content—the "flying reports" that Seaman sought to overcome—through crowdsourcing especially. Yet it does so in formats that often seem to overstate the robustness, even-handedness, and unquestionability of both the analog and the digital data so assembled. Like Seaman's and Booth's maps discussed earlier, the composite maps generated by the MMP—and the configuration of spaces, objects, and subjects that are assembled through its digital interfaces—draw little or no attention to questions of jurisdiction or authority; to divergent, embedded interests and purposes (and conflicts among them); or to discrepancies between underlying temporal or spatial scales in the source data. Indeed, the digital interfaces of the MMP may downplay the extent to which the digital humanitarian mapping that they occasion not only garbles or fudges the representation of objects and subjects but actually makes these anew—a remaking that later chapters will explore further.

---

[147] Louise Amoore, *Cloud Ethics* (Duke University Press, 2020).

[148] Carmen Sumadiwiria, "Putting Vulnerable Communities on the Map: A Research Report on What Influences Digital Map-Making with Young Volunteers in Bangladesh" (Y Care International, 2015).

[149] Ibid., 23–25.

## Mismatches and Overruns; Closures and Openings

In the casualization, crowdsourcing, and anti-formalism apparent at interfaces such as the MMP, digital humanitarian mapping aspires to be something more than humanitarian mapping was at each of the historical moments earlier surveyed in this chapter. What it fails to overcome, however, is a digital-analog tension already apparent in Bangladesh's efforts to map the 1988 floods. That is the tension between digital knowledge forms, such as digital data from satellites (characterized, both in their assemblage and the kinds of outputs that they yield, by discrete, distinct, bounded elements and relations of discontinuity), and analog knowledge forms, such as data about administrative jurisdictions, community affiliations, or property rights (comprised of differences of magnitude and relations of continuous variation), at work in humanitarian mapping. As humanitarian mapping has been digitized, discrepancies and disjunctions between the two have yielded both the analog misreading of digital actions and the digital overrun of analog frameworks.

One example of the analog misreading of digital actions is the tendency, noted earlier, to interpret the turn to community-driven mapping through crowdsourcing of labeled digital data (in the MMP, for instance) as a dehierarchization of knowledge-power relations. This is an analog assumption because it presumes continuity between the decentralization of data sources and the decentralization of political power—as if the properties of data run through to communities generating that data whereby those communities become more free or more self-empowered by orders of magnitude as they propagate and contribute more—and more diverse—data.

This is an analog misreading because such ongoing, relational effects cannot be presumed or sustained in digital settings. A digital data set does not purport to reflect the conditions of its creation. When digitized and processed automatically, the content of digital data gets subordinated to a binary classification scheme, associated processing parameters, and the imperative of maintaining readily usable interfaces. When people confirm certain features on a map via a digital interface such as those used in the MMP, their identity and the political conditions under which they do so become irrelevant. If the data input meets applicable, quantitative thresholds, it will be incorporated; if not, it will not. Beyond the scope of generic quality control measures, digital data made available to an interface such as the MMP cannot be organized along a spectrum according to its empowering implications; it is either inputted or discarded.

It is misplaced to presume that expanded participation in sourcing data for digital humanitarian mapping interfaces will enhance their political legitimacy for other reasons too. Users do not typically expect digital interfaces to disclose their workings. Predominantly analog knowledge forms routinely relate how and from where they originated or make explicit their sources of authority; this is consistent with analog concerns for continuity. In contrast, digital knowledge forms typically embed sourcing and methodological information relatively deeply into their interfaces to ensure that they appear as frictionless as possible for users. The online interface of the MMP, for instance, refers only vaguely to the involvement of remote and community volunteers.

Moreover, contrary to the previously mentioned expectation, structures of authority operative within digital technology permit the reproduction and extension of hierarchy as much as its disruption.[150] As Alexander Galloway has observed: "It is not the case that networks produce a general waning of organization and control. In fact, it is the opposite: distributed networks produce an entirely new system of organization and control that, while perhaps incompatible with pyramidal systems of power, is nevertheless just as effective at keeping things in line."[151]

The MMP may reflect an aspiration within HOT to enable "mobility between the hierarchical positions they occupy, and a transfer of knowledge from the global north to the global south and back."[152] Nonetheless, analysis of digital data is generally indifferent as to its source or the circumstances of its assemblage, which is one of the reasons why quality assessment of large volumes of volunteered geographic data can be difficult.[153] The effort to invest volunteer labeling of data via digital interfaces with egalitarian implications sets an ill-fitting analog frame around binary digits that symbolize without regard to the conditions of their creation (except for such learned or ascribed links as may be embedded in code).

At the same time, examples of digital overrun of analog social, political, and legal frameworks abound. Digitization of maps and mapping interfaces is potentially antithetical to the making and holding of knowledge in common, and to legal relations that depend on repositories of common knowledge, because of its allowance for customization. A mapping interface that is, as FIVIMS and OSM have been, envisioned as adaptable to a wide range of uses and users has to accommodate conflict among those uses and users. Producers of widely used online maps, such as Google Maps, routinely grapple with how to represent disputed territories. One provisional solution on which they often settle is to customize boundaries and names, resulting in multiple versions of a map being accessible from different geolocations (with geolocations typically attributed

---

[150] Andrew Feenberg, *Questioning Technology* (2nd ed., Taylor & Francis Group, 2012) 76; Haklay, *supra* note 133.

[151] Alexander Galloway, "Protocol" (2006) 23 *Theory, Culture & Society* 317, 317, 318; Alexander Galloway, *Protocol* (MIT Press, 2004).

[152] Givoni, *supra* note 128, at 1025, 1036.

[153] G.M. Foody and others, "Accurate Attribute Mapping from Volunteered Geographic Information: Issues of Volunteer Quantity and Quality" (2015) 52 *The Cartographic Journal* 336.

on the basis of network routing addresses or phones' or other devices' internal GPS).[154] As digital artifacts, these different maps maintain no continuity with one another. Thus, digital customization brings about a surfeit of irreconcilable data, eroding the "common ground" that analog frameworks surrounding the delineation of territorial boundaries and the resolution of territorial disputes (such as traditional "official" maps) strive to maintain. We will return to this tension in Chapter 5.

Digital overrunning of preexisting analog frameworks is also apparent in new capacities to map attachments and movements of itinerant people that do not correspond to traditional jurisdictional attributions or assumptions. Consider, for instance, the possibility of mapping the temporary and circular migratory activity of labor migrants and informal workers inferred from digital mobile phone records.[155] Similar approaches may permit the tracking of short-term movement by tourists or second homeowners.[156] In both settings, digital mapping interfaces bring to the fore the potentially very significant contributions to, or demands on, particular jurisdictions made by itinerant or multi-attached persons who may have no correspondingly significant legal status, rights, or obligations in that jurisdiction.[157] In such instances, digital mapping interfaces could conceivably help inaugurate new claims from or on the jurisdictions in question, from pleas for greater tax contributions by second homeowners to arguments for greater legal protection of informal workers' rights and changes in migration law and policy.[158] And it is precisely the on/off quality and temporal specificity of digital communication that brings these possibilities into view. Nontraditional digital data sources attest to the significance of itinerant persons without regard to their formal legal status or placement on an analog continuum of citizenship rights or tax obligations.

The kinds of digital-analog mismatches just described foster closures as well as openings.[159] Digitization of humanitarian mapping may put more resources—including the digital outputs of volunteer labor marshaled by not-for-profit organizations—in the service of the interests of a dominant few. OSM products,

---

[154] Sterling D. Quinn and Doran A. Tucker, "How Geopolitical Conflict Shapes the Mass-Produced Online Map" (2017) 22 *First Monday*.

[155] Joshua E. Blumenstock, "Inferring Patterns of Internal Migration from Mobile Phone Call Records: Evidence from Rwanda" (2012) 18 *Information Technology for Development* 107.

[156] Erki Saluveer et al., "Methodological Framework for Producing National Tourism Statistics from Mobile Positioning Data" (2020) 81 *Annals of Tourism Research* 102895.

[157] On the need for temporary population statistics and challenges in assembling them, see Elin Charles-Edwards et al., "A Framework for Official Temporary Population Statistics" (2020) 36 *Journal of Official Statistics* 1.

[158] Andreas Back and Roger Marjavaara, "Mapping an Invisible Population: The Uneven Geography of Second-Home Tourism" (2017) 19 *Tourism Geographies* 595; Maribel Casas-Cortés et al., "Clashing Cartographies, Migrating Maps: The Politics of Mobility at the External Borders of E.U.Rope" (2017) 16 *ACME: An International Journal for Critical Geographies* 1.

[159] Burns, *supra* note 143.

including those resulting from the MMP, are readily adaptable to proprietary, profitmaking purposes. For example, Uber, Facebook, Microsoft, Apple, and other major corporate players in the digital economy make growing use of OSM to help refine and support their own products.[160] Discussed earlier were other ways in which digital humanitarian mapping may enhance the very political and economic capacities that it aims to problematize.

Yet these mismatches and overruns also create footholds for possible practices of counter-mapping. That is, they may enliven "effort[s] that fundamentally question[n] the assumptions or biases of cartographic conventions, that challeng[e] predominant power effects of mapping, or that engag[e] in mapping in ways that [potentially] upset power relations" or at least problematize those relations' representation.[161]

One illustration is Hackitectura's mapping of the Strait of Gibraltar.[162] This was one of several initiatives in the "antiAtlas of borders" series created by Hackitectura, a group of architects, artists, activists, and computer specialists active as a cohort between 2002 and 2011.[163] They produced an online map—an interface—depicting a dense profusion of two-way flows of capital, migration, communication, and militarization across the Strait. In connection with the creation and circulation of this map, Hackitectura also organized workshops and short-term "direct actions" against the detention of migrants on either side of the Strait, including "a blockade of a Civil Guard bus with migrant detainees that had just arrived to Tarifa's beach, and a demonstration outside the Foreigner Confinement Centre in Algeciras."[164] In so doing, they sought to create "an alternative understanding of the Spanish-Moroccan border region," as compared to prevailing accounts emphasizing African migrants' abjection before "an abstract geopolitical line."[165]

Hackitectura's counter-mapping initiative made strategic use of exactly the kinds of overruns discussed earlier: leveraging a dizzying profusion of incommensurable digital data to try to overload the "brute geography [of] modern territorialization," cross-hatch the border, and reinscribe the spaces in question, heightening a sense of their density, incoherence, and openness to

---

[160] Jennings Anderson, Dipto Sarkar, and Leysia Palen, "Corporate Editors in the Evolving Landscape of OpenStreetMap" (2019) 8 *ISPRS International Journal of Geo-Information* 232.

[161] Harris and Hazen, *supra* note 11, at 99, 115.

[162] "Hackitectura—Critical Cartography of Gibraltar" (*antiAtlas of borders*, August 14, 2013), <https://www.antiatlas.net/hackitectura-critical-cartography-of-gibraltar-en/> (accessed October 10, 2022).

[163] "Acerca de—hackitectura.net," <https://hackitectura.net/es/acerca-de/> (accessed October 10, 2022).

[164] Jose Perez de Lama, Pablo de Soto, and Sergio Moreno, "Fadaîlat. Through Spaces at Fortress EU's Southwest Border," *Fadaiat: Freedom of Movement, Freedom of Knowledge* (Indymedia, 2006), <http://www.in-no.org/pdfs/furthur2/fadaiat_f2.pdf>.

[165] "Hackitectura—Critical Cartography of Gibraltar," *supra* note 162.

intervention.[166] This surfeit helped to galvanize another multiplicity; the endeavor brought "together migration, labor rights, gender and communication activists, political theorists, hackers, union organizers, architects and artists in a temporary media-lab that could become a permanent public interface between Tarifa [in Spain] and Tangiers [in Morocco]."[167] Their reinscription of the Strait was materialized also in the establishment of a wi-fi link between the project's nodes in Tarifa and Tangiers and various live-streamed events and temporary satellite connections devised "so that movements that hardly know each other [might] begin to work together."[168] Subsequent reflections suggested that "not all objectives . . . [were] met" and some met only "modestly," but the work has remained "a relevant point of reference" for later protests and activism.[169]

A second illustration is the work of Alianza Ceibo, Digital Democracy, and the Waorani people of Pastaza in Ecuador, where the output of a digitally mediated community mapping initiative was tendered as evidence in successful court action launched by the Waorani against the Ecuadorian state. The Waorani objected to the failure of the Ecuadorian state properly to consult them before proceeding to commercialize rights to extract oil resources in the territory of Waorani communities, arguing that this was contrary to the Ecuadorian Constitution and international treaty and customary law.[170] In the Tribunal of Pastaza, which found a violation of Waorani rights and their entitlement to (primarily procedural) reparation (a ruling later affirmed by the Provincial Court of Pastaza and the Constitutional Court of Ecuador), specific mention was made of the Waorani's mapping efforts and the "fundamental" and "special" relationships to territory evidenced thereby.[171] This referenced a three-year process in which 20 Waorani communities used Mapeo, a free, open-source collaborative mapping application developed by the US-based not-for-profit Digital Democracy, to map large tracts of Waorani territory using categories and descriptors in Waotero (the Waorani language) and icons designed by community members.[172] The result was a rich digitized cartographic record of "ancestral knowledge, traditional medicine, sacred and culturally significant sites, symbols, livelihoods and toponymy, as well as non-human beings inhabiting" Waorani territory,

---

[166] Rajkovic, *supra* note 25, at 270.
[167] "Hackitectura—Critical Cartography of Gibraltar," *supra* note 162.
[168] Perez de Lama, de Soto, and Moreno, *supra* note 164.
[169] Hackitectura.net, "Indymedia Straits of Gibraltar," <https://hackitectura.net/en/indymedia-straits-of-gibraltar/> (accessed October 10, 2022).
[170] Margherita Scazza and Oswando Nenquimo, *From Spears to Maps: The Case of Waorani Resistance in Ecuador for the Defence of Their Right to Prior Consultation* (International Institute for Environment and Development (IIED), February 2021).
[171] Ibid., 8.
[172] "Digital Democracy: Waorani Territory Mapping Project" (*Digital Democracy*), <https://www.digital-democracy.org/ourwork/waorani/> (accessed October 10, 2022).

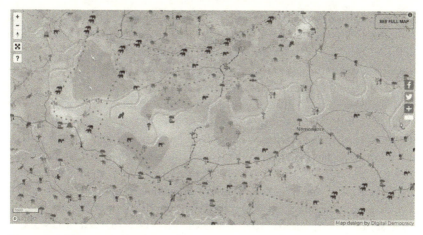

**Figure 2.6** Map created by the community of Nemompare using the Mapeo app in 2015. Cultural and intellectual property of the Waorani of Pastaza, represented by the Alianza Ceibo y Organización Waorani de Pastaza. Source: "Waorani Map— Mapping Ancestral Lands" (Amazon Frontlines), <https://www.amazonfrontlines.org/maps/waorani/> (accessed October 10, 2022). Reproduced with permission from Oswando Gahue Nenquimo Pauchi.

designed to aid defense of their right to consultation prior to any commercial exploitation of that territory.[173] An example is shown in Figure 2.6.

As in that of Hackitectura, the work of the Waorani, Alianza Ceibo, and Digital Democracy leveraged the denotative discontinuity of digital technology to try to fracture the wholeness of territory and interrupt the conventional spectrum and apparent indefatigability of property rights—in this instance, by evoking a deluge of human-nonhuman connections and signifiers. In this context, it was the indifference of digital signals to preexisting states as well as digital technology's accommodation of discrete, multiuser inputs that the Waorani and their allies were able to leverage against more encompassing, analog depictions of presence and absence. Digital mapping enabled the switching on of multiple affiliations to substantiate claims that could be made recognizable under applicable laws.

These collaborative counter-mapping efforts have their limitations and, in the latter case especially, have been matters of community conflict and some skepticism.[174] Counter-mapping tactics of these kinds cannot alone alter law, make resources move, or shift power in significant ways; coalition-building and other political work is essential for that. Moreover, digital counter-mapping exhibits

---

[173] Scazza and Nenquimo, *supra* note 170, at 9.
[174] Ibid., 10–11.

its own exclusions and dependencies.[175] Digital inputs feed into socio-technical complexes with in-built priorities and preconditions. In circumstances like those of the Waorani peoples, for instance, digital maps "remain conditioned by the [need] to meet both State expectations of legibility and [by] the Indigenous pursuit of recognition" under applicable international and national law.[176]

Nonetheless, these efforts of counter-mapping do indicate possibilities for leveraging, for tactical, critical effect, the digital-analog mismatches that the digitization of humanitarian mapping has brought to light. Both organizations' initiatives have gained purchase from the tension between, on one hand, a digital data trail evidencing a dense, discontinuous set of entanglements and attachments and, on the other, the analog technology of a territorial, political, or proprietary boundary presumed continuous. Both organizations have done so, moreover, without recourse to the kind of casualized piecework or crowdsourcing on which the MMP depends, offering an important reminder that not all efforts of digital humanitarian mapping are equivalent. The epistemological conflicts and rival ontologies at the heart of these organizations' ongoing work will be the focus of further attention in coming chapters that explore what digital interfaces make of populations, emergencies, and states in international humanitarian practice.

[175] Thomas J. McGurk and Sébastien Caquard, "To What Extent Can Online Mapping Be Decolonial? A Journey throughout Indigenous Cartography in Canada" (2020) 64 *The Canadian Geographer/Le Géographe Canadien* 49.
[176] Alberto Preci, "Fixing the Territory, a Turning Point: The Paradoxes of the Wichí Maps of the Argentine Chaco" (2020) 64 *The Canadian Geographer/Le Géographe Canadien* 20, 30.

# 3
# Populations: From Statistics to Data Science

## Introduction

Prior chapters have explored how institutions and programs dedicated to humanitarianism are incorporating the production, maintenance, promotion, and use of digital interfaces into their work and engaging a range of new collaborators and investors in the process. Chapter 2 highlighted the tensions and slippages that emerge when humanitarian mapping combines analog and digital logics in ways that prioritize the latter. This chapter focuses on what digital interfaces make of the polities around which humanitarian work is oriented, or how people, places, and things are rallied and associated when their aggregation takes on digital formats. Digital interfaces, this chapter argues, are reconstituting collectives in the international humanitarian field and playing a significant role in such collectives' qualification and effectuation as agents and objects of governance. This chapter focuses especially on digital interfaces' sublimation of populations into digital aggregates.

One 2019 pilot project encapsulates the kinds of collective sublimation with which this chapter is concerned. At that time, Pulse Lab Jakarta (PLJ)—an institution briefly introduced in Chapter 1—developed a prototype website or interface to try to explore possible ways of supplementing existing analog ways of tracking human displacement after disaster, the latter represented especially by the International Organization for Migration's Displacement Tracking Matrix (DTM).[1] This entailed assembling and visualizing location data from approximately 600,000 mobile phones with subscriptions registered to people residing in the districts of Palu, Sigi, and Donggala on the island of Sulawesi in Indonesia: those districts most affected by a massive earthquake that hit that island on September 28, 2018. Subscribers' mobile positioning data from a period immediately before the earthquake (September 1 to September 27, 2018) was compared with data from a period immediately after it (October 1, 2018 to

---

[1] On the changing role of the IOM of which the DTM is indicative, see Megan Bradley, "The International Organization for Migration (IOM): Gaining Power in the Forced Migration Regime" (2017) 33 *Refuge: Canada's Journal on Refugees* 97.

January 31, 2019).[2] The inflow and outflow movements to and from the island that were illuminated by this data were represented on the PLJ interface by red and yellow dots continually in motion.

As noted earlier, this interface was aimed at improving upon traditional analog methods of tracking displacement, foremost among them the DTM. The DTM is a set of procedures, devised in 2004 and since refined, to track and monitor displacement and population mobility in order to inform "decision-makers and responders" during crises and to contribute to better understanding of population flows more generally. For baseline assessment and flow monitoring, it relies on analog technologies of population measurement: individual and household registration, interviews, and surveys, as well as direct observation and focus group discussions. These are carried out by in-country DTM teams, in collaboration with local and national governments.[3]

PLJ sought to overlay the DTM with a prototypical digital rendering of the population: one that could be assembled without the expense, delay, and difficulty of conducting surveys, and which promised, perhaps, greater accuracy or coverage by virtue of its replacement of human reporters and observers with automated ones. In both the DTM and the PLJ prototype, human bodies are represented by proxies: in the first, by quantitative and qualitative data derived from human-to-human interaction specifically carried out for that purpose; in the second, by radio signals and global positioning data emitted from mobile phones, detected and gathered for purposes of maintaining a commercial mobile phone service and then repurposed (after pseudonymization) to a new end. Yet their respective modes of aggregation are quite different—differences that implicate the analog-digital distinctions introduced in Chapter 2.

Taking as its starting point the shift in methods of assembling and analyzing populations indicated by comparison of the DTM to the PLJ's prototypical supplement, this chapter addresses the following questions. How is the terrain of prospective humanitarian governance reconfigured in this shift? What, exactly, is made prospectively governable in each setting? More specifically: If the population is the "end of government" in the first setting (a phrase explained later),[4] then is it still the end of government or international humanitarian governance,

---

[2] Pulse Lab Jakarta, "Understanding Population Movement After the 2018 Central Sulawesi Natural Disasters" (*Medium*, December 17, 2019), <https://medium.com/pulse-lab-jakarta/understanding-population-movement-after-the-2018-central-sulawesi-natural-disasters-70ab95b7741b> (accessed October 10, 2022).

[3] International Organization for Migration, "Methodological Framework Used in Displacement Tracking Matrix Operations for Quantifying Displacement and Mobility" (*International Organization for Migration*, 2017), <https://displacement.iom.int/content/methodological-framework-used-displacement-tracking-matrix-operations-quantifying> (accessed October 10, 2022).

[4] Michel Foucault, *Security, Territory, Population: Lectures at the Collège de France 1977–78* (Palgrave Macmillan, 2009) 105.

in the same way, in the second? And if not, then how and to whom might that change be significant?

In addressing these questions, the chapter begins with a brief discussion of the significance of the population in and for international humanitarian governance. This will focus on Michel Foucault's influential account of shifts, historical and enduring, in how the task of "government" came to be understood and conducted (in which context "government" encompasses a plurality of ways of managing "an economy, at the level of the state as a whole ... [through] supervision and control over its inhabitants, wealth, and the conduct of all and each").[5] In short, Foucault documented how the task of government became one of managing and maintaining the life of a population. Or as Hannah Arendt wrote, in her explication of that which Foucault later elaborated as "biopolitics": "[T]he fact of mutual dependence for the sake of life and nothing else assume[d] public significance and ... activities connected with sheer survival [we]re permitted to appear in public."[6]

Even as "the fact of mutual dependence for the sake of life" remains axiomatic within the international humanitarian field, this chapter seeks to understand how this "mutual dependence" is recast at digital interfaces. The aim is not to evaluate whether digital interfaces deliver what they promise to the intended beneficiaries of humanitarian work (greater accuracy than analog alternatives, for instance). Rather, the aim is to understand how digital interfaces transform archetypes of humanitarian perception, action, and governance. Later chapters—Chapter 7 especially—explore what might be made of this transformation when approached not with a view to its correction but rather on its own, politically generative terms.

The chapter continues with an overview of some of the steps typically taken in the assemblage and measurement of populations for modern humanitarian governance. It contrasts these with recent efforts to represent, manage, and optimize human populations digitally, taking some of the work of UN Global Pulse, and collaborative endeavors in which it has been involved, as illustrative of these. (You will recall, from Chapter 1, that UN Global Pulse labs has worked with an array of public and private collaborators.)

To preview the argument of this chapter, the statistical artifact of the population is undergoing something of a declension or a demotion in formal standing in humanitarian practice (comparable to that which Foucault described the family undergoing at an earlier historical moment)[7] whereby it is becoming an interior dimension of the social formation that humanitarian work addresses.

---

[5] Ibid., 94–95.
[6] Hannah Arendt, *The Human Condition* (University of Chicago Press, 1998) 46.
[7] Foucault, *supra* note 4, at 105.

Governmental attention on the part of some states, nongovernmental organizations, and international organizations is increasingly preoccupied with eliciting and addressing something else, in the first instance, through digital humanitarian interfaces. That "something else" is a succession of digital aggregates—many of them only prototypically formed—that overlay the population as an object of inquiry and concern. Biopolitical governance of populations continues in earnest. Nonetheless, when conducted through digital interfaces, it often gets routed through senso-politics in a distinct register; the chapter explains later what makes that senso-politics distinct from biopolitics in the context of international organizations' humanitarian work. The concluding section of this chapter reflects on what may be at stake in such a shift, or why and to whom it might matter, including how it might bear on the practices and artifacts with which other chapters are concerned.

## The Population in Modern Governance

In statistical work, a population is a "(real or hypothetical) totality of objects or individuals under consideration, of which the statistical attributes may be estimated by the study of a sample or samples drawn from it."[8] The population is marked by variation. Regularities appear at the level of a population that do not necessarily hold true for any one member or subset within it. So generalized, the term has, since the late nineteenth century, referred to a wide array of observable things, including plants, animals, and star clusters. Nonetheless, demographic understandings of population have, over this period, largely "coloni[z]ed the terrain of the term."[9] As Susan Greenhalgh has observed, "counting or estimating the 'vital' attributes of [mainly human] populations such as fertility and mortality, and then manipulating the numbers so as to chart their variations and distributions, are seen as the fundamental activities of the science of population."[10]

This predominance of the demographic is commensurate with at least one version of biopolitics put forward by Michel Foucault, of which there were a number of iterations across his body of work.[11] Biopolitics names the tendency for

---

[8] Nancy Krieger, "Who and What Is a 'Population'? Historical Debates, Current Controversies, and Implications for Understanding 'Population Health' and Rectifying Health Inequities" (2012) 90 *The Milbank Quarterly* 634, 639.

[9] Stephen Legg, "Foucault's Population Geographies: Classifications, Biopolitics and Governmental Spaces" (2005) 11 *Population, Space and Place* 137, 137.

[10] Susan Greenhalgh, "Globalization and Population Governance in China," in Aihwa Ong and Stephen J. Collier (eds.), *Global Assemblages: Technology, Politics, and Ethics as Anthropological Problems* (John Wiley & Sons, Ltd., 2008) 357.

[11] Thomas Lemke, Monica J. Casper, and Lisa Jean Moore, *Biopolitics: An Advanced Introduction* (NYU Press, 2011).

"concrete processes of life in a population" to serve as both the target of and the rationale for "security"—security being a "technology" that Foucault suggested became a governmental preoccupation from the late modern period onward.[12] "Security" in this setting suggests not so much insulation from threat as "a sort of homeostasis" to be achieved by "maximizing ... positive elements ... and minimizing what is risky and inconvenient" to life, including by addressing what and how things should, or should not, circulate.[13] Management of a "population" to this end entails working through an "open series [that] can ... be controlled by an estimate of probabilities."[14] This might sound rather benign, but as many have pointed out, the biopolitical "power of regularization" involved in "making live and letting die" across a population is not necessarily any less intense than the sovereign power of the gallows or the disciplinary power of the prison.[15] They simply operate in different registers (registers that often overlap in practice), by reference to different objects, and elicit different forms of subjectivity and engagement from the governed. Foucault's is not a story of the progressive amelioration of governmental techniques, any more than this chapter is a story of that kind. The point of elucidating the specificity of these overlapping governmental registers is not that some are categorically worse than others, but rather that "everything is dangerous."[16] Moreover, different registers of governance are dangerous in quite distinct ways, and the dangers of each must be navigated on its own terms.

This chapter takes Foucault's account of biopolitical governmentality, with the population as its end, as something of a foil. It does so not to try to rarefy or refute that account or sanctify its author, but rather to work from its limits; that work was, after all, never put forward as transhistorical. It is important to do so because of the intuitive appeal of Foucauldian biopolitics to many trying to understand how power is operating in the global digital economy. Important recent work analyzing legal and political developments in "information capitalism" has identified those developments with the intensification of biopolitics.[17] This chapter proceeds from a worry that this diagnosis may elide aspects of the forms of rule and relation that are proliferating amid this intensification, especially in the realm of digital humanitarianism. As noted already, there remains ample evidence for the biopolitical character of contemporary humanitarian

---

[12] Michel Foucault, *"Society Must Be Defended": Lectures at the Collège de France, 1975-1976* (François Ewald ed., Macmillan, 2003) 249.
[13] Foucault, *supra* note 12, 249; Foucault, *supra* note 4, at 19, 64.
[14] Foucault, *supra* note 4, at 20.
[15] Foucault, *supra* note 12, at 247.
[16] Michel Foucault, "On the Genealogy of Ethics: An Overview of Work in Progress," in Paul Rabinow (ed.), *The Foucault Reader* (Pantheon, 1984) 343.
[17] See, e.g., Julie Cohen, *Between Truth and Power: The Legal Constructions of Informational Capitalism* (Oxford University Press, 2019).

governance.[18] Nonetheless, governance in this mode is increasingly alloyed with other techniques or modulations of power that merit elucidation in their own right. Power evoked and oriented by the digital aggregates with which this chapter is concerned is less a power to "make live and let die"—although it may ultimately have those effects—than a power to make perceive and let pass.

A focus on populations and how they are governed does not, however, result only from engagement with Foucault's work. Such a focus is virtually unavoidable in any study of humanitarian thinking, doctrine, and practice or of the work of international organizations bearing a humanitarian mandate. Populations have been axiomatic to the field of humanitarianism since at least the mid-nineteenth century.[19] As Barnett has observed: "Humanitarianism aspires to save lives. Not just any lives, but the lives of the world's most vulnerable and neglected populations."[20]

In this context, it is telling that several substantial books dedicated to explaining the distinct properties and prescriptions of the humanitarian field do not index the term "population," even though that term appears repeatedly throughout their pages.[21] It is simply taken for granted that the population is one of the primary units with which work in the humanitarian field routinely deals. This is the case even though the goals of humanitarianism are most commonly pitched at both larger and smaller scales, by appeal to "a concept of universal 'humanity' enshrined in the individual human body."[22] Humanitarianism may not aim to "produc[e] an integrated and disciplined national population."[23] Its target populations may only be "perceived and united ... during moments of crisis," as Miriam Ticktin has noted.[24] Yet international humanitarian work is nonetheless oriented toward "biosociological processes characteristic of human masses"—that is, toward populations.[25] The United Nations, for instance, is extensively engaged in documenting those "biosociological processes," including

---

[18] Volha Piotukh, *Biopolitics, Governmentality and Humanitarianism: "Caring" for the Population in Afghanistan and Belarus* (Routledge, 2015).
[19] Michael Barnett, *Empire of Humanity: A History of Humanitarianism* (Cornell University Press, 2011) 1.
[20] Michael N. Barnett, "Humanitarian Governance" (2013) 16 *Annual Review of Political Science* 379, 380.
[21] David Mosse (ed.), *Adventures in Aidland: The Anthropology of Professionals in International Development* (Berghain Books, 2013); Barnett, *supra* note 19; Peter Macalister-Smith, *International Humanitarian Assistance: Disaster Relief Actions in International Law and Organization* (Springer, 1985); Daniel Maxwell and Kirsten Heidi Gelsdorf, *Understanding the Humanitarian World* (Routledge, 2019).
[22] Miriam Ticktin, "From the Human to the Planetary" (2019) 6 *Medicine Anthropology Theory* 133, 139.
[23] Ibid., 141.
[24] Ibid., 140.
[25] Foucault, *supra* note 12, at 250.

by encouraging, supporting, and informing governments' maintenance of "population data system[s]."[26]

When data is assembled for national governments and international organizations to use for governance—including for humanitarian governance—in a format that purports to represent a population, two things happen. First, to state the obvious, representation takes place by proxy. The attributes of interest are not typically studied by comprehensive enumeration of all members of a population, but rather by studying a sample of that population, although the sample will sometimes be very large (as in the taking of a census on a given day). Population thinking almost always requires drawing inferences beyond the reach of the available data, by generalizing from one or more samples. Second, the relation between the sample and the population becomes a live matter of concern. It becomes important to think through what can and cannot be inferred from a particular sample and how we might understand that sample probabilistically in relation to all other possible samples that could be drawn from the population in question. Hence the issue of bias in the sample, and prospects for its detection and correction, come to the fore. Any exercise of assembling or recording a population for governance will typically entail passage through these three post-study-design phases: sampling (including data collection and summary data description); evaluation (calculating and comparing values in the sample in order to try to understand its statistical significance with reference to the population); and inference (drawing inferences about the parameters of a population on the basis of one or more samples).

## The Population in Digital Humanitarianism

The practice of making a population along these lines gets transmuted when it is carried out using immense volumes of largely unstructured digital data that have not, for the most part, been purposively, systematically or randomly sampled. Consider, for example, the various forms of data that stream into one of UN Global Pulse's prototypical interfaces, designed to aid those charged with relief management and planning in the immediate aftermath of natural disaster, and those seeking assistance in that aftermath: MIND (which stands for "Managing Information in Natural Disaster").[27]

---

[26] United Nations Statistics Division, "Draft Handbook on Civil Registration, Vital Statistics and Identity Management Systems: Communication for Development" (April 2019), <https://unstats.un.org/unsd/demographic-social/meetings/2019/newyork-egm-crvsims/docs/draft_handbook.pdf (accessed October 10, 2022)>.

[27] Pulse Lab Jakarta, "Managing Relevant Information in the Aftermath of Natural Disasters: Launching PLJ's Latest Data Analytics Platform" (*Medium*, June 1, 2019), <https://medium.com/pulse-lab-jakarta/managing-relevant-information-in-the-aftermath-of-natural-disasters-launching-pljs-latest-data-de3b4cbae07b> (accessed October 10, 2022).

MIND is an online interface that assembles a number of different "nontraditional" sources of data regarding the human impact of selected natural disaster events and makes these available for a limited period after each such event.[28] It presents information from social media (Twitter); conventional media sources (from "a credible news API"[29] spanning some 50 English-language news websites[30]); crowdsourced references (Wikipedia, OpenStreetMap); and Google search trends that in each case satisfies certain prespecified parameters (as to its geographic and temporal metadata and, in the case of media reports, its textual content). It depicts this information in a dynamic, online map format, using open-source mapping and route-planning applications. According to PLJ, where it was developed, the interface is "designed to complement existing disaster response tools" in order to "aid logistics planning and information management following natural disasters" by "publicly providing stakeholders with timely insights on affected areas, [and] the needs of communities."[31] The events featured are those that are the subject of disaster alerts from the Global Disaster Alert and Coordination System (GDACS): an automated early warning system created in 2004 by the United Nations and the European Commission.[32]

In MIND, as in the example with which this chapter opened, populations made vulnerable by natural disaster are represented by recourse to new forms of proxy. These include data streams assembled for commercial purposes by commercial operators: in the case of MIND, unstructured data amassed, processed, and formatted by Google and Twitter. These data are not "samples" at all in a classical, statistical sense, as discussed further later. The proxies for population well-being that are featured in MIND have not been assembled for the purpose of statistical analysis. Indeed, the primary purpose of the interface is to showcase "nontraditional" data sources that may be of use in the immediate aftermath of natural disaster.[33] This entails deferral of authority to upstream data collectors and dependence on aggregators beyond humanitarian intermediaries' or users' purview. As one of our interviewees remarked: "[T]hese are data sources whose prominence we don't fully understand, right. And I think with all of this, the principle of caveat emptor [that is, buyer beware] applies."[34] Another one of the data scientists with whom we spoke remarked as follows:

---

[28] Interview with Participant D (September 5, 2019).
[29] Pulse Lab Jakarta, *supra* note 27.
[30] Interview with Participant D, *supra* note 28.
[31] Pulse Lab Jakarta, *supra* note 27.
[32] Emergency Relief Coordination Centre, OCHA-Geneva, "GDACS—Global Disaster Alerting and Coordination System," <https://www.gdacs.org/About/overview.aspx> (accessed October 10, 2022).
[33] Interview with Participant D, *supra* note 28.
[34] Interview with Participants AC and D (February 18, 2020).

[A]ll the data [has] its inherent biases and the way it's been collected... because it isn't collected to necessarily meet the aim of your project. It's collected for a different aim. We don't necessarily, as data practitioners, understand that aim straight away. You have to ... follow up, extract that, create partnerships, and still we might not understand it.[35]

These nontraditional proxies are comprised of data with two qualities. First, the data is available more or less in real time. Second, it may arguably be useful to address issues that typically get raised in the aftermath of natural disaster. In other words, the status of these proxies is opportunistic. The potential of the digital data in question to aid governance is only established retrospectively, after the conditions of the data's gathering and processing have been established otherwise, for very different purposes. The difficulties that this approach to data-gathering poses for conventional statistical analysis have been well documented.[36]

To be clear, the aim of MIND is not to encourage humanitarian professionals to dispense with traditional statistical measurement of populations, but rather to supplement that with analysis of digital data that is more timely, can be assembled less expensively, or that yields information that may not otherwise be available in the days and weeks following a natural disaster. MIND does not invite disregard for official data channels. (Humanitarian professionals working in emergency settings have, after all, always tended to call on a range of data sources, often varying in reliability.[37]) Yet MIND does direct particular attention toward digital data sources that deal in available data proxies rather than statistical samples. One of our informants described (with reference to a different project) how analysis of digital administrative data supplements, and differs from, conventional statistical sampling as follows:

We're using [automatic identification system] data on ships, like ships have a black box just like flights have, and it contains a lot of information, and what we're using it for or what we are planning to use it for, is our statistics on harbor activities because so far, or today it's based on information from [our] two biggest harbors... and then estimations of the activities in all the other harbors. And with those new data we can now get exact data from every harbor because we can follow every ship in and out of the harbor. Not only can we get that so we get a full sample, or not even a sample, we get full coverage of the activities in

---

[35] Interview with Participant AE (April 20, 2020).
[36] Denisa Florescu et al., "Will 'Big Data' Transform Official Statistics?," *Q2014: European Conference on Quality in Official Statistics* (2014); Pedro Galeano and Daniel Peña, "Data Science, Big Data and Statistics" (2019) 28 *TEST* 289.
[37] Maxwell and Gelsdorf, *supra* note 21, at 133.

harbors, but we could also if we want to do that we can do it, instead of doing on a yearly basis we could do it more often, if we wanted to do that.[38]

Because of this "full coverage," the degree to which such digital proxies may be representative of the whole population is of diminished concern in a decision-support digital interface like MIND. The question of "fit" in the relationship between sample and population tends to recede. Certainly, work ongoing in the field of computational statistics is concerned with how to carry out statistically sound, reproducible population thinking and prediction when working with high volumes of unstructured digital data.[39] One of our interviewees involved in the Missing Maps Project (discussed in Chapter 2) mentioned that those involved in that project are experimenting with "micro-censusing": surveying small areas comprehensively and then trying to extrapolate from that in statistically robust ways.[40] Nonetheless, at this stage, data scientists, including those working at UN Global Pulse, tend to be quite up front about the fact that the representativeness of unstructured digital data and its coverage of the population are "difficult to assess."[41] As one of our interviewees remarked: "So far people have been very occupied with getting a structure out of the data and trying to make something that makes sense out of that. . . . But the thing is that they [have] not validate[d] if the sample they ha[ve] [i]s a skewed one."[42]

Often digital signals are being mined for attention-directing guidance—to highlight where further investigation may be warranted—rather than to generate a new population-wide data set. As one of our informants explained: "[W]hat we are trying to see is . . . will it be possible to complement [traditional quantitative] information with a different kind of information . . . saying . . . : 'Hey, probably you have to look into other kind of possibilities.'"[43]

How and where attention may move in response to such digital prompts becomes contingent upon a range of things, including the composition of the digital data in question. As noted earlier, the forms of digital data most readily available in large volumes are, in many instances, unstructured, commercial data. Commercial platforms like Google and Twitter are primarily concerned with the profiling, classification, and ranking of individuals for the delivery of tailored advertising and other saleable services.[44] Mobile phone providers are

---

[38] Interview with Participant R (December 4, 2018).
[39] Bradley Efron and Trevor Hastie, *Computer Age Statistical Inference* (Cambridge University Press, 2016); Peter Bühlmann and Sara van de Geer, "Statistics for Big Data: A Perspective" (2018) 136 *Statistics & Probability Letters* 37.
[40] Interview with Participant AG (April 22, 2020).
[41] Florescu et al., *supra* note 36, at 3.
[42] Interview with Participant R, *supra* note 38.
[43] Interview with Participant AC and D, *supra* note 34.
[44] Marion Fourcade and Kieran Healy, "Seeing like a Market" (2017) 15 *Socio-Economic Review* 9.

likewise concerned with categorizing customers "into segments that have a consistent demographic, psychographic or usage pattern" for business purposes.[45] It is difficult to adapt the data-gathering infrastructure of organizations so oriented to the purposes of representing populations as a whole and determining relative levels of vulnerability within them. Where one is trying to use data derived from mobile phone use for humanitarian purposes, for instance (as UN Global Pulse has done in a number of collaborative projects[46]), the coverage of that data will typically be circumscribed by factors like the relevant company's (profit-driven) distribution of mobile phone towers, its customer relations management software, its data storage capacity, and so on. Also, it may be difficult to discern whose mobile phone–recorded behavior is being represented at any given time, especially where devices are shared or where one person maintains multiple subscriptions (both of which are common practices in the Global South).[47]

These limiting factors, as well as other constraints on using mobile phone data to generate population proxies, have been highlighted repeatedly by those exploring the potential of such data to supplement traditional data sources in the governance of health and well-being, disaster response, urban planning, and socioeconomic policymaking.[48] One of our informants emphasized this in the following story:

> [J]ust to mention an example that's in the world of official statistics ... the Dutch did a sentiment index based on information from Facebook and Twitter and based on linguistics and using specific words would indicate a specific kind of sentiment either positive or negative and they tried to validate that and say ... people in the Netherlands seems to be more happy in June because they were going on vacation in July and they were also more happy in December because Christmas is the nice time. And then [it] happened a number of years ago, I think it was 6 or 8 years ago, that the Netherlands lost the World Cup Final in South Africa. Not only did they lose but they lost in a very disgraceful way and that took place in June and it was reflected in actually that sentiment ... [and] they used the kind of information they could get from Facebook and Twitter but if the sample was only young people or elderly people or middle aged people

---

[45] Fadly Hamka et al., "Mobile Customer Segmentation Based on Smartphone Measurement" (2014) 31 *Telematics and Informatics* 220, 220.

[46] Pulse Lab New York, "Using Call Detail Records to Understand Refugee Integration in Turkey" (*United Nations Global Pulse*, 2018), <https://www.unglobalpulse.org/projects/using-call-detail-records-understand-refugee-integration-turkey> (accessed October 10, 2022).

[47] E.g., Robert Foster and Heather A Horst (eds.), *The Moral Economy of Mobile Phones: Pacific Island Perspectives* (ANU Press, 2018).

[48] UN Global Working Group on Big Data for Official Statistics, "Handbook on the Use of Mobile Phone Data for Official Statistics" (2019), <https://unstats.un.org/bigdata/task-teams/mobile-phone/MPD%20Handbook%2020191004.pdf> (accessed October 10, 2022).

or men instead of women or whatever, because of the structure of the kind of data we don't know that.[49]

These kinds of problems of signaling and statistical bias could perhaps be surmounted to some degree, such that unstructured digital data from diverse, unconventional sources might yet "become a useful and reliable data source for the field of official statistics" aimed at recording or representing population characteristics, or informing disaster relief.[50] A number of scholars have called for greater convergence between the fields of statistics and machine learning to this end.[51] Yet there are, nonetheless, *other* indications of the demotion of the population in international humanitarian governance in favor of digital aggregates. One such indication relates to the diminished significance of the idea of the population as a "natural" phenomenon.

Foucault's account of the population governance characteristic of modern biopolitics suggested that the population must be made or understood as "natural" for this purpose. This has a very specific meaning; to say that biopolitical governance is oriented toward the "naturalness" of populations does not imply that populations are taken to be unadulterated or simply *there*. It suggests, rather, that governance of a population entails acting upon "a series of interactions, circular effects, and effects of diffusion [that] tak[e] place between each individual and all the others." This presumes that "there is a spontaneous bond between the individual and the others which is not constituted and willed by the state."[52] These bonds form the basis for the "spontaneous production of the collective interest by desire" within a population—desire that governmentality is concerned to cultivate, manage, and guide.[53] It is in this sense that the population is invested, for governance purposes, with a "naturalness ... [a] thickness, with internal mechanisms of regulation." Population governance in Foucault's account entails the state and other governmental actors taking responsibility for these "internal mechanisms" through a range of different "practices and types of intervention." Those interventions aim to "get [those internal mechanisms] to work, or to work with them" so that "they do not veer off course."[54] The population is invested with "naturalness," Foucault explained, in the sense that it "depends on a series of variables" that are not necessarily responsive to "voluntarist and direct

---

[49] Interview with Participant R, *supra* note 38.
[50] Piet J.H. Daas et al., "Big Data as a Source for Official Statistics" (2015) 31 *Journal of Official Statistics* 249.
[51] Leo Breiman, "Statistical Modeling: The Two Cultures (with Comments and a Rejoinder by the Author)" (2001) 16 *Statistical Science* 199; Galeano and Peña, *supra* note 36.
[52] Foucault, *supra* note 4, at 352.
[53] Ibid., 75.
[54] Ibid., 352–353.

action" on the part of a sovereign, but must instead be approached using "enlightened... techniques of transformation."[55]

Humanitarian activities after natural disaster have perhaps never been typified by exacting statistical analysis of target populations' "internal mechanisms." They are necessarily improvisational and often uncoordinated and underresourced.[56] Nonetheless, humanitarian work has long been oriented toward the pursuit of population-level biosocial goals—"sav[ing] lives, alleviat[ing] suffering and maintain[ing] human dignity"—by working with and through affected communities.[57] Even in the chaos and confusion of an emergency setting, humanitarian governance is meant to entail deployment of "enlightened techniques of transformation" within a vulnerable population. A set of global principles on "good humanitarian donorship" adopted in 2003 and updated in 2018 emphasize, for example, the importance of "[p]rovid[ing] humanitarian assistance in ways that are supportive of recovery and long-term development."[58]

When data streams are marshaled at digital interfaces for humanitarian action, however, this sense of the population having an "interior" of relations that governance must try to engage, nurture, direct, and strengthen over the long term gets thinned out. The task of governance framed by digital interfaces is not oriented toward "get[ting] [a population's internal mechanisms] to work, or to work[ing] with them," because those internal mechanisms or bonds "between each individual and all the others" are often not represented in digital data structures designed for segmentation and tailoring (in the case of mobile phone, social media, or search data) or for remote comprehensiveness (when it comes to satellite data).

Governance tools like the MIND interface—that combine multiple forms of digital data—effect a denaturing or denaturalization of the aggregate that is to be governed. No longer does the task of managing "human masses" entail a grappling with their "thickness."[59] Instead, the totality only becomes visible at the intersection of often quite narrow—albeit very voluminous—slipstreams of data (the now ubiquitous "deep dive"). The "bonds" among different data sources, data layers, and data objects are ephemeral and, on the whole, barely articulated. Digital aggregates are not more artificial than populations as targets for governance, but they are assembled differently. Digital aggregates'

---

[55] Ibid., 70–71.
[56] Maxwell and Gelsdorf, *supra* note 21, at 121–141.
[57] Good Humanitarian Donorship (GHD) Initiative, "Principles and Good Practice of Humanitarian Donorship" (2018), <https://www.ghdinitiative.org/ghd/gns/principles-good-practice-of-ghd/principles-good-practice-ghd.html> (accessed October 10, 2022).
[58] Johan Schaar, "The Birth of the Good Humanitarian Donorship Initiative," in *The Humanitarian Response Index 2007* (Palgrave Macmillan, 2008); Good Humanitarian Donorship (GHD) Initiative, *supra* note 57.
[59] Foucault, *supra* note 12, at 250.

representation adheres more to logics of individuation, segmentation, modularity, and multiscalar layering than those of "natural[]" integration.

One of our data scientist informants with experience working in the humanitarian field described the thin, denatured quality of digital data assembled for humanitarian purposes as follows:

> I guess it's almost like a new religion, like the data. There is truth inherently in the data, that the data has the ability to fix the problem, a particular problem. And I would say that they're [that is, humanitarian professionals are] not necessarily like this on a personal level, but they might be like this on a project thinking level, that they are focused on one question, or one problem, and don't necessarily look at the huge, interconnected thinking behind a problem. And if they do, it's definitely not on paper, and if it is on paper, it's definitely very vague, and you use very creative donor language. You know, like disaster risk reduction, resilience, management. A lot of these things don't actually mean anything when you get onto the ground and you're doing a particular project . . . they probably do understand the complexities, but they think that the data can solve that, and they're very—I guess you'd say driven and I wouldn't say like arrogant, but [they proceed] as if all this information has the ability to fix everything and has the right to be used, or can improve things.[60]

Recall that the MIND interface combines earth observation data with text and image data sourced from social media platforms, wikis, and traditional media sources. Whatever the "bonds" that one might discern among these data objects and scales, they do not appear either "spontaneous" or "thick" or, in the preceding interviewee's words, "interconnected." Rather, they are assembled around the artifact of "natural disaster" (which PLJ intends to encompass "cyclones, earthquakes, tsunamis, floods, volcanic eruptions and wildfires").[61] Moreover, the category "natural disaster" is itself a digital "data derivative."[62] Recall that the MIND interface is triggered by automated disaster alerts issued by GDACS. GDACS is, in turn, "fed" by a range of mostly automated data streams from seismological organizations, meteorological organizations, and composite data sources of other kinds.[63] GDACS' alerts also provide the geographic coordinates used to filter the various other digital data sources assembled in MIND.[64]

---

[60] Interview with Participant AE, *supra* note 35.
[61] Pulse Lab Jakarta, *supra* note 27.
[62] Louise Amoore, "Data Derivatives: On the Emergence of a Security Risk Calculus for Our Times" (2011) 28 *Theory, Culture & Society* 24.
[63] Emergency Relief Coordination Centre, OCHA-Geneva, *supra* note 32.
[64] Pulse Lab Jakarta, *supra* note 27.

This cumulative data aggregate and others like it—and the terrain of prospective governmental intervention that they call up—are not just creations of data. They are also comprised of a series of contracts and treaty mandates, including those agreements under which data access and sharing have been secured; we will discuss these aspects of digital interfaces' infrastructure in Chapter 6.[65] They are also held together by a series of undisclosed estimations, calibrations, and adjustments: those manipulations necessary to integrate data assembled at very different scales and for very different purposes.[66] (Gross divergences in scale pose an acknowledged problem in the use of satellite image data for poverty mapping, for instance.[67])

Cumulative data aggregates like those presented at the MIND interface do, nonetheless, depict some biosocial relations and invite governmental attention to these: relations among social media users geotagged to a particular area; people vulnerable to the adverse geophysical effects of a disaster captured in sensor data; and those seeking information via Google from computers or devices located within the directly affected area. Yet these relations only become apparent incidentally, at the user interface. At this point, they have the status of a passing given, rather than appearing as objects of inquiry or particular interest. As Luciano Floridi has observed, it is characteristic of contemporary digital technology that the composition of interfaces and the phenomena that they feature is "functionally invisible."[68]

Moreover, insofar as digital interfaces like MIND do represent relations among their constituent elements, these are not relations marked by that which Bruce Curtis has argued is a key feature of "population": namely, its "dependen[ce], in the first instance, on the establishment of practical equivalences among subjects, objects or events."[69] The population, in Foucault's account, is a "set of elements in which we can note constants and regularities even in accidents" and which are thereby "immersed within the general regime of living beings."[70] The MIND interface is concerned, still, with regularities in the form of data patterns, correlations, and predictive possibilities, but this no longer implies placement in a series extending "from biological rootedness through the species up to the surface."[71]

[65] Fleur Johns and Caroline Compton, "Data Jurisdictions and Rival Regimes of Algorithmic Regulation" (2020) 16 *Regulation & Governance* 63; Cohen, *supra* note 17.
[66] Sean Kandel et al., "Research Directions in Data Wrangling: Visualizations and Transformations for Usable and Credible Data" (2011) 10 *Information Visualization* 271.
[67] Hossein Hassani et al., "Big Data and Energy Poverty Alleviation" (2019) 3 *Big Data and Cognitive Computing* 50, 59.
[68] Luciano Floridi, *The Fourth Revolution: How the Infosphere Is Reshaping Human Reality* (Oxford University Press, 2014) 38.
[69] Bruce Curtis, "Foucault on Governmentality and Population: The Impossible Discovery" (2002) 27 *The Canadian Journal of Sociology* 505, 508.
[70] Foucault, *supra* note 4, at 74–75.
[71] Ibid., 75.

The operating goal of the MIND interface is precisely to constitute governmental terrain—or a field of potential humanitarian action—out of *non*equivalence, or to extricate actionable data points from out of "the general regime of living beings." Its immediate concern is not the commensuration or tending of bodies, but the detection of physical properties or changes—traceable to humans, nonhumans, or combinations of the two—and the generation of corresponding outputs by which human and nonhuman attention may be directed. Its operation is senso-political: to make perceive and let pass, as previously noted.

In order to provide urgent humanitarian relief, a user of the MIND interface is invited to disassemble aggregate data on disasters into singular social media postings—records of dividuated perception.[72] She is invited to experience continuously shifting dissimilarity within the data, even while addressing the aggregate. And these variegated data strains don't necessarily correspond to bodies or biological entities; they are, as geographer Louise Amoore has written, lines of sight.[73] They are slipstreams in data, configured at the confluence of filtering parameters. Whether the experiences that they intimate are real or imagined is not of any great consequence to those to whom the MIND interface is addressed, at least not in the first instance. The constitution of a field of potential governmental action, or the narrowing or redirection of the aperture of governmental attention: these no longer require much by way of bio-social data. An instrumentally engineered digital conflux of seemingly actionable discrete data points will suffice, it seems, to flesh out a field of potential action and direct humanitarian attention across it (at least for purposes of an initial "Hey, . . . you have to look..."[74]).

Consider, for example, the way that users are invited to navigate the MIND interface. Each user may navigate an experience of the disaster event in question through a front layer of their choice. They may choose to foreground social media accounts (sourced from geotagged postings on Twitter). They might front-end logistical and geographical information, such as road type (sourced from OpenStreetMap, a free, editable world map with geospatial data labeled by registered users who number in the millions worldwide as discussed in Chapter 2, and from OpenRouteService, an open-source route planner developed by Heidelberg University). They might seek basic demographic and transport infrastructure information (sourced from Wikipedia). They might start with extracts from news reports regarding the impact of the disaster in question (sourced through automated text analysis of news reports). Or they could begin with internet search trends from those within the impacted area (sourced

---

[72] Gilles Deleuze, "Postscript on the Societies of Control" (1992) 59 *October* 3.
[73] Louise Amoore, "Lines of Sight: On the Visualization of Unknown Futures" (2009) 13 *Citizenship Studies* 17.
[74] Interview with Participant AC and D, *supra* note 34.

from Google Trends). Alternatively, they might work through their own "custom layer" to visualize their own data set against this disaster setting.

UN Global Pulse has showcased the operation of MIND in a website featuring a succession of images showing a magnitude 7.5 earthquake that impacted the island of Sulawesi in Indonesia in late September 2018 visualized through each of the six layers of the MIND interface.[75] Each has presumably been designed to elicit concern and support action corresponding to UN Global Pulse's broad mission of "sav[ing] lives and better[ing] livelihoods."[76] Each takes the primary lens of, respectively, the Twitter layer, the Wikipedia layer, the traditional news layer, the Google Trends layer, and the customized layer.

What becomes discernible in these different versions of the MIND interface? More specifically, what becomes of the population within these? Historian Alison Bashford has characterized twentieth-century political engagement with population problems—spanning concern with reproduction, mortality, migration, food, agriculture, soil, and more—as "experiments in globality, the imaginative activity through which the 'daily work of human beings' was linked to the idea of a global polity."[77] In successive versions of the MIND interface, however, the imaginative work encouraged is of quite a different order.

When viewed through the Twitter layer, the MIND interface sifts a life-threatening event into a loose arrangement of pinpricks corresponding to social media postings, with each dot open to individual scrutiny for those so inclined. Through the highly conditioned, preformatted medium of social media, this layer introduces would-be beneficiaries to unspecified would-be helpers, joined by the prospect of claim and response. Viewing a natural disaster through the Wikipedia layer, the user is invited to imagine herself as intervener, motivated by these claims or otherwise to try to gather rough-and-ready information about the event and possibly to travel to the area most affected, mindful of the many obstacles in her way. When MIND is instead configured to foreground the traditional news layer or the Google Trends layer, the interface pulls back from the locus of disaster, representing it only by a single map point. Instead, these layers of MIND cast the natural disaster event as part of a dynamic series of newsworthy items and searchable topics.

Through these different iterations of the interface, the problem on which the MIND interface invites users to dwell is constantly shifting. It is no longer that of safeguarding a population linked to "the long, modern trajectory of an

---

[75] UN Global Pulse, "MIND: Managing Information in Natural Disasters" (*UN Global Pulse*, N.D.), <https://www.unglobalpulse.org/microsite/mind/> (accessed October 10, 2022).

[76] UN Global Pulse, "UN Global Pulse Annual Report 2018" (2018) 7, <https://www.unglobalpulse.org/sites/default/files/UNGP_Annual2018_web_FINAL.pdf>.

[77] Alison Bashford, *Global Population: History, Geopolitics, and Life on Earth* (Columbia University Press, 2014) 17.

aspirational one world."[78] Rather, the world of MIND is a world parsed according to the passing interests of the time-poor and the information-overloaded. As one of our interviewees from elsewhere in the digital humanitarian sector (not someone who worked on the MIND interface) explained: "[W]e are trying to get the entire sector to speed up and data helps create that urgency."[79]

Users may be alerted, momentarily, to the faint clamor of the imperiled and the impoverished (those disproportionately affected by natural disasters[80]) via social media reportage made available at the MIND interface. But they are invited to curate the representation of need as they see fit. One of the data scientists that we interviewed observed that policymakers or officials presented with new digital tools tend to "focus on ... the visual[s] and not so much [on] the contents."[81] This recalls Lillie Chouliaraki's description of humanitarian organizations' adoption of a "technologize[d] and particularize[d]" style of communication "that 'cleanses' public communication of sentimentalist argument and introduces individual judgement [at the point of encounter] as our primary resource for engaging with suffering as a cause"—a style she dubs "post-humanitarian."[82]

It becomes hard, in this setting, either for claimants to advance or users to assess claims of need in relation to one another, or to consider what they might mean to and for others. As one of the interviewees whom we quoted above noted, it becomes hard to "look at the huge, interconnected ... problem" when working through the MIND interface or other interfaces like it.[83] Claims presented through Twitter may tend toward individualism because there is no way of reflexively assessing their relation to others' comparable or concurrent needs, nor of grasping the limits of the resources that may be available to address them (an aspect of the experience of "context collapse" associated with Twitter use).[84] The only *relative* indicator presented in the MIND interface is the degree to which an assertion of need made via a Twitter posting corresponds to a pattern in Google Trends or in text-mined news reports. That, however, may encourage even less reflexivity about relative merit or urgency since it may reinforce the sense that the most "high-arousal" claims across all three settings (Twitter, Google search, and the news media) warrant greatest attention.[85]

---

[78] Ibid.
[79] Interview with Participant AK (July 16, 2021).
[80] Chester Hartman and Gregory Squires (eds.), *There Is No Such Thing as a Natural Disaster: Race, Class, and Hurricane Katrina* (Routledge, 2006).
[81] Interview with Participant D (July 27, 2018).
[82] Lilie Chouliaraki, "Post-Humanitarianism: Humanitarian Communication beyond a Politics of Pity" (2010) 13 *International Journal of Cultural Studies* 107, 121.
[83] Interview with Participant AE, *supra* note 35.
[84] Alice E. Marwick and danah boyd, "I Tweet Honestly, I Tweet Passionately: Twitter Users, Context Collapse, and the Imagined Audience" (2011) 13 *New Media & Society* 114.
[85] Jonah Berger and Katherine L. Milkman, "What Makes Online Content Viral?" (2012) 49 *Journal of Marketing Research* 192.

Likewise, the structure of the MIND interface seems inhospitable to nontransactional appeals. Structural concerns that do not translate into a request for some specific good or service, or do not raise a problem that seems readily fixable, may be ill-suited to this setting. This is in part because the claimant appealing for help via a Twitter post must do so without having any clear sense of the identity, capacities, powers, or situation of the addressees.[86] It is in part because conduct rather than meaning is what registers, for the most part, in the digital medium (the fact of the making of a Google search including certain terms, for example, rather than the intent and purpose of that search, or condition of the person making it).[87] And it is in part because the format of Twitter is implicitly transactional: one gets accustomed to posting in exchange for likes or retweets and to expect a fairly rapid call-response interaction.[88]

Indeed, each screen of the MIND interface presumes a slightly different end and employs a slightly different value scale and affective or imaginative register. The Twitter layer, as noted earlier, seems to prioritize the cogency of individual pleas and the pathos of individual plight. The Wikipedia layer values data that is actionable or pragmatically useful for purposes of humanitarian intervention and movement in space from point A to point B. The traditional news and the Google Trends layers seem to value intensity of collective concern, albeit a "collective" assembled and a "concern" expressed via Google or the news media (and, for the time being in this prototype, only the English-language news media).

One cannot say exactly what the humanitarian professionals whom the MIND interface is designed to support might make use of the tool, and its overlapping registers of value, if and when it eventually gets refined for, or adapted by, particular users. (Prototype developers in this domain tend to be aware of the limits of "doing [things] globally." As one informant highlighted: "It is useless in some countries... and then you have different languages... [so] the ideal scenario for the next phase... if you can get the funding, [is] to then do a customized version for a particular user and partly use this money to also properly opensource the core functionality.")[89] In its current form, however, it does not encourage users to be concerned, in the first instance, with addressing or managing a population. This does not represent a loss necessarily, but it does signify an important shift in governmental modes of collective address, the stakes of which are discussed later.

The elements and events that were of concern in Foucault's account of modern population governance were not, moreover, just *any* elements and events. They

---

[86] Eden Litt and Eszter Hargittai, "The Imagined Audience on Social Network Sites" (2016) 2 *Social Media + Society*.
[87] Evelyn Ruppert, "Population Objects: Interpassive Subjects" (2011) 45 *Sociology* 218.
[88] Gina Masullo Chen, "Tweet This: A Uses and Gratifications Perspective on How Active Twitter Use Gratifies a Need to Connect with Others" (2011) 27 *Computers in Human Behavior* 755.
[89] Interview with Participant AC and D, *supra* note 34.

were elements and events characteristic of biological life. The population to be governed was, in Foucault's words, "a global mass that is affected by overall characteristics specific to life . . . like birth, death, production, illness and so on."[90] The kind of governmentality evoked by the MIND interface seems, however, less concerned with evaluating or optimizing biological life. The MIND interface might take as its overarching rationale the preservation of human life and the reduction of morbidity, but its *effective* focus seems more foreshortened.

UN Global Pulse has publicly talked about its work as a matter of producing devices for "social listening," a term also embraced by other UN agencies.[91] But to what exactly is it listening? The MIND interface does not seem aimed at recording and representing a biosocial corpus. Rather, it seeks to elicit and project some holographic digital aggregate that can stand in for that corpus in a scanter, more fleeting mode: an unbonded aggregate that is all process—or process upon process—rather than expressive of any universalized or particularized vital substance. The governmental preoccupations called up by an interface like MIND are not so much biopolitical as senso-political, at least in the first instance. The immediate concern of such technologies is less that of representing bodies and distributing them on a spectrum of health to death than the goal of producing, voicing, and amplifying a summative interlocutor, in real time. That interlocutor does not, moreover, take the form of a polity so much as a temporary, synthetic configuration of concern (a Google trend, for instance), always time-limited and likely to pass, in the near future, into some other aggregation of interest.

Admittedly, there is thread bareness and "ad hocery" in every representation of people, places, and things in the aftermath of a natural disaster, even representations of a traditional, analog kind. As noted earlier, humanitarian professionals working in the aftermath of natural disaster have often had to cobble data together opportunistically.[92] So the kind of shift described here—from population to digital aggregate—may be even more pronounced in other kinds of digital humanitarian projects, beyond disaster relief.

Digital data uses of many, more run-of-the-mill kinds are also being championed (cautiously) by the UN Global Working Group on Big Data for Official Statistics and by UN Global Pulse. PLJ has, for example, explored the prospect of "nowcasting" food price information in Indonesia by analyzing Twitter postings using a set of keywords related to basic commodities.[93] This was

---

[90] Foucault, *supra* note 4, at 377–378.
[91] UN Global Pulse, *Haze Gazer Demo* (May 8, 2018), <https://www.youtube.com/watch?v=YVZV9fpoxTQ>; Soenke Ziesche, "Innovative Big Data Approaches for Capturing and Analyzing Data to Monitor and Achieve the SDGs" (*UN ESCAP*, 2017) 77, <https://www.unescap.org/publications/innovative-big-data-approaches-capturing-and-analyzing-data-monitor-and-achieve-sdgs>.
[92] Maxwell and Gelsdorf, *supra* note 21, at 133–134.
[93] Jaewoo Kim, Meeyoung Cha, and Jong Gun Lee, "Nowcasting Commodity Prices Using Social Media" (2017) 3 *PeerJ Computer Science* e126.

with a view to understanding price dynamics in near-real time, to supplement official consumer price data. PLJ has also investigated the potential of mobile phone data to yield proxy indicators for the socioeconomic condition of a household, working with the National Statistics Office in Vanuatu in the South Pacific. They have established correlations between aspects of mobile phone data and education level, household expenditure, and household income.[94] The hope is that this might help Vanuatu develop a cost-effective alternative or complement to the traditional population survey, to understand how people are faring across the 85 islands of its archipelago. Elsewhere, efforts are being made to use mobile phone data to better understand patterns of human movement across different timescales (labor movement, tourism, etc.), including shifts between daytime and nighttime population.[95]

Regardless of the particular digital humanitarian interface on which one focuses, however, the kind of governmental terrain called up by these interfaces seems close to what Foucault described as a form of highly conditioned "counter-conduct" advanced "in correlation with" the modern system of governmentality—namely, "the idea that at a given moment the nation itself, in its totality, must be able to possess exactly at each of its points as in its mass, the truth of what it is, what it wants, and what it must do."[96] Recall that the MIND interface depends in part on the unpaid labor of countless people, posting and labeling data on social media, Wikipedia, and OpenStreetMap about natural disaster locales and effects, as well as all sorts of other things, generating a continuous stream of labeled data. This evokes an idea on which Foucault elaborated as follows: "This is the idea of a nation entitled to its own knowledge, or the idea of a society transparent to itself and possessor of its own truth, even if it is an element of the population ... which formulates this truth."[97] Such a self-knowing aggregate has been a recurrent feature of revolutionary expectations that "society itself" might "prevail over the state" and over other forms of sovereign power.[98] The self-knowing digital aggregate called up by digital humanitarian interfaces seems reminiscent of this aspiration, but in a politically disassembled form.

Could it be *this*—a digital aggregate (not a nation, necessarily) understood to be "entitled to its own [digital] knowledge"—that is in the process of surmounting the "natural" population as the end of government? In other words, does the task of governing by reference to, say, an anonymized stream of call detail records

---

[94] Zakiya Pramestri et al., "Estimating the Indicators on Education and Household Characteristics and Expenditure from Mobile Phone Data in Vanuatu," *Poster Session 2* (*NetMob*, 2017), <https://www.netmob.org/www17/assets/img/bookofabstract_poster_2017.pdf#page=82>.

[95] Pierre Deville et al., "Dynamic Population Mapping Using Mobile Phone Data" (2014) 111 *Proceedings of the National Academy of Sciences* 15888.

[96] Foucault, *supra* note 4, at 355–357.

[97] Ibid., 357.

[98] Ibid., 356.

corresponding to many millions of mobile phone calls or social media posts corresponding to many millions of accounts, assembled at a digital interface, become something other than a task of population management? Is it, rather, a task of extracting, formulating, producing, and then acting in "a given moment" on some sensory input that an aggregate may be represented digitally as having *in and of itself*, however mediated, selective, and compromised its assemblage?

Just to be clear, the foregoing claim is not that digital representations of environmental, social, and economic conditions of the kind that the MIND interface puts forward *are* in fact spontaneously generated in the aggregate as an expression of some kind of authentic, collective self-knowledge. Rather this is the way that the terrain or object of governance gets reconstituted in the move away from a statistically or actuarially assembled population to a digital aggregate. The objects of senso-political governance produced at digital interfaces are *speculative* in three senses of "speculate."[99] They are assembled through close—even rapt—*observation*, in this instance of available digital traces. They are *conjectural*, in that their pertinence is based on inference and anticipation, in this instance, anticipation of remedial action. And they look to dynamic interactions in the hope of being able to *realize some immediate gain* in knowledge and capacity. In all these ways, the idea of a digital aggregate "entitled to its own [digital] knowledge" is a speculative projection of the work and object of senso-political governance shaped by digital interfaces—one appearing ever more frequently in contemporary international humanitarian practice. This is related to, but entails much more then, the practice of treating development indicators—such as those generated under the rubric of the Sustainable Development Goals (SDGs)—as "ends, in and of themselves" because the digital aggregates toward which interfaces like MIND orient users are constantly in the process of being collectively made.[100]

Governments, international organizations, and their many private sector partners seem increasingly captivated by such speculative digital aggregates as expressions of the end, the object, and the appropriate field of intervention for humanitarian governance. Concern with "populations" in the statistical, actuarial, and biopolitical sense seem, at times, to kick in only at a lower, later stage of governance, beneath or after the dazzle of the digital aggregate. In contrast to the parallel, and in many ways complementary, findings of Engin Isin and Evelyn Ruppert, these speculative digital aggregates do not herald a "new form

---

[99] "Speculate, v.," in *OED Online* (Oxford University Press, 2020), <https://www.oed.com/view/Entry/186112> (accessed October 10, 2022).

[100] Sally Engle Merry, Kevin E. Davis, and Benedict Kingsbury, *The Quiet Power of Indicators: Measuring Governance, Corruption, and Rule of Law* (Cambridge University Press, 2015) 106.

of power... nestled in existing forms."[101] Rather, the proliferation of these digital aggregates indicates a shift in the "how" not the "what" of power: a change in that which relations of power are oriented toward producing not in what they aim to capture.[102] And it is a shift in which there are quite profound political stakes (as there are in many "merely technical" endeavors[103])—stakes to which we will now turn.

## The Stakes of Digital Aggregation in the Humanitarian Field

To this point, this chapter has considered four ways in which humanitarian digital interfaces tend to move attention away from preoccupations with optimizing a population—preoccupations famously characteristic of biopolitical governmentality in Foucault's account and also typical of humanitarianism. First, digital aggregates overlay the population as a matter of humanitarian concern at digital interfaces such as MIND. Second, this loosens surrounding concerns with "fit" or representativeness in sample-population relations. Third, digitization effects a thinning out or denaturalization of the notion of a population in favor of unbonded digital aggregates registrable in real time. Fourth, governmental attention gets redirected away from the probabilistic rendering of the characteristics of a bio-social mass toward speculative, senso-political representations of data-about-data-about-data, often attributed with capacities for automatic self-disclosure.

This story of digitization could be read in a number of familiar ways. Perhaps it might be construed as criticizing the inauthenticity or technocracy of the data-gathering practices in question. If only (so the familiar response goes) there were more consultation with intended beneficiaries in prototype development, then things would be much better. This is not a new idea to UN Global Pulse. Ethics guidance that they have produced or publicly committed to highlights the value of "consultation with groups concerned" and "tak[ing] into consideration the context of data use, including social, geographic, political and religious factors."[104] Furthermore, a number of PLJ projects have employed qualitative,

---

[101] Engin Isin and Evelyn Ruppert, "The Birth of Sensory Power: How a Pandemic Made It Visible?" (2020) 7 *Big Data & Society* 1, 8.

[102] Michel Foucault, Geoff Bennington, and Bernard-Henri Lévy, "The History of Sexuality: Interview" (1980) 4 *Oxford Literary Review* 3, 9 ("Above all, relations of power are productive").

[103] Cf. Duncan Kennedy, "The Political Stakes in 'Merely Technical' Issues of Contract Law" (2001) 1 *European Review of Private Law* 7.

[104] UN Global Pulse and International Association of Privacy Professionals (IAPP), "Building Ethics into Privacy Frameworks for Big Data and AI" (2018) 10, <https://iapp.org/media/pdf/resource_center/BUILDING-ETHICS-INTO-PRIVACY-FRAMEWORKS-FOR-BIG-DATA-AND-AI-UN-Global-Pulse-IAPP.pdf> (accessed October 10, 2022)>; UN Development Group, "Data Privacy, Ethics and Protection: Guidance Note on Big Data for Achievement of the 2030 Agenda" (2017) 5,

ethnographic research techniques to garner insights from prospective users to inform their design work.[105] There is also a strong commitment to using open-source software across the humanitarian sector, including in PLJ. The views of one of our interviewees seemed indicative of those of many when one said: "We should always be doing things so that the general community... can critique our work and run with it in their own context, and hopefully give it back."[106]

Even if want of consultation were the main concern of this chapter (which it is not), it would be difficult to determine a corresponding corrective. In many instances—when one is dealing with data sources via immense volumes of Twitter postings, Google searches, or pseudonymized mobile phone data—it may be difficult to determine exactly who should be consulted regarding this data's humanitarian use and how. As we quoted one of our interviewees earlier, "the principle of caveat emptor applies."[107] And even where public consultation is feasible, it may be politically ambivalent. Questions of authenticity and representativeness in this setting are almost always contested and contestable (as they are in the other digital settings mentioned earlier). As has been shown elsewhere, the effects of public consultation may be as disabling as they are enabling of any reframing of the object of consultation.[108] Senso-politics informed by stakeholder engagement is not necessarily more salutary or progressive than senso-politics without a participatory plug-in.

Alternatively, the foregoing analysis may be construed as lamenting the despoiling of humanitarianism by commercial imperatives. This is not the intended message; humanitarian initiatives and institutions have never been pure of nonpublic, for-profit investments. Humanitarian data infrastructure in the public sector is often riddled with private debts literal and figurative. Even where that infrastructure is well-resourced and well-maintained, it may be compromised or locked up in any number of ways. For example, one of our interviewees described a "nightmare scenario" in which "there's a third party implementor [of public health ICT funded by humanitarian philanthropy] that controls the most important data source that is needed to eradicate polio in [a

<https://unsdg.un.org/resources/data-privacy-ethics-and-protection-guidance-note-big-data-achievement-2030-agenda> (accessed October 10, 2022).

[105] Giulio Quaggiotto, "Tech4Labs Issue 6: Inverting the Logic of Government through User Insights" (*nesta*, June 2015), <https://www.nesta.org.uk/blog/tech4labs-issue-6-inverting-the-logic-of-government-through-user-insights/> (accessed October 10, 2022); Pulse Lab Jakarta, "After Dark: Encouraging Safe Transit for Women Travelling at Night" (2019), <https://www.dropbox.com/s/i42igsae3l67ngu/After%20Dark.pdf?dl=0> (accessed October 10, 2022).
[106] Interview with Participant AE, *supra* note 35.
[107] Interview with Participant AC and D, *supra* note 34.
[108] Shalmali Guttal and Bruce Shoemaker, "Manipulating Consent: The World Bank and Public Consultation in the Nam Theun 2 Hydroelectric Project" (2004) 10 *Watershed* 18; Ben Boer et al., *The Mekong: A Socio-Legal Approach to River Basin Development* (Routledge, 2015) 137–164.

particular] country. We have been trying for three years to get access to that data. The government has been trying for three years to get access to that data. We still do not have access; they still do not have access."[109]

More broadly, evidence abounds of the longstanding entanglement of humanitarianism with its supposed antonym: self-interest. Consider, for instance, historians Lauren Benton and Lisa Ford's examination of the "British-led effort to curb slave trading" in the first half of the nineteenth century, in which "the goal of protecting the rights of the enslaved paled in comparison to the drive [of British imperial powers] to control private jurisdictions and regulate colonial regimes" and thereby "craft a British global empire of law."[110] Likewise, Jessica Whyte's exacting work has shown how well twentieth-century humanitarianism served those seeking to counter Third World challenges to neoliberal economic doctrine.[111]

If the aim of this chapter is not to put forward normative critiques of the work of UN Global Pulse or others along the foregoing lines, then the question arises: Why should it matter if one understands new digital interfaces as operating biopolitically or as generative of senso-political modalities of power? This chapter's concern is not with the durability or generalizability of Foucault's late twentieth-century work, as noted earlier. Rather, what this chapter aims to put forward is a preliminary diagram of some emergent lines of juridico-political relation active within humanitarianism today.

This chapter traces something of what humanitarian governance becomes when the population has, to some degree, faded into the background at digital interfaces. The wager of this chapter is that this shifting of priorities and techniques produces significant discrepancies between prevailing expectations, demands, analyses, and critiques and the kinds of phenomena with which they are now confronted. The remainder of the chapter sets out some of the ways in which existing analytical, political, and legal repertoires may fall short of the practices to which this chapter has drawn attention, and why these shortfalls matter.

Rather than calling forth a population, the kinds of digital aggregates evoked senso-politically by a tool like UN Global Pulse's MIND mimic, to some extent, "the idea of a society transparent to itself"—an idea that has, as noted earlier, sometimes had revolutionary inflections (and may still be politically generative, arguably informing the work of Forensic Architecture, for instance[112]). Those

---

[109] Interview with Participant AK, *supra* note 79.

[110] Lauren Benton and Lisa Ford, *Rage for Order: The British Empire and the Origins of International Law 1800–1850* (Harvard University Press, 2016) 191.

[111] Jessica Whyte, *The Morals of the Market: Human Rights and the Rise of Neoliberalism* (Verso Books, 2019) 232.

[112] Eyal Weizman, *Forensic Architecture: Violence at the Threshold of Detectability* (MIT Press, 2017).

who develop digital humanitarian interfaces often claim to be tapping or enabling more authentic or more democratically dispersed forms of knowledge-making than governmental statistics have traditionally allowed. One of our interviewees observed, for example, that "[t]he truths that are . . . identified . . . through big data cannot be controlled by government."[113] In the contexts under analysis in this book, however, the political intimations of that idea seem attenuated by decidedly nonrevolutionary impulses and ideologies, namely: commercialism (making money); pragmatism (making do); and protection (making tolerable).[114] What becomes of digital aggregates so assembled will be contingent on a range of factors, including how well-equipped people are by prevailing repertoires of politico-legal critique to engage in their contestation.

One recurring claim of this book is that the composition of those digital aggregates into which human and nonhuman proxies are ever-increasingly assembled, wittingly and unwittingly, is a first-order question being worked out in a struggle of conflicting ideas and investments. This is not a struggle well described as wholly beholden to one meta-principle or meta-descriptor or another, whether the term be biopolitics, neoliberalism, or something else.[115]

Digital humanitarianism names terrain on which battles over resources, authority, and polity-formation are being waged. Deals are being struck surrounding data access. Debates are ongoing about the terms on which that access is granted—whether, for example, a mobile phone company should enjoy some sort of quid pro quo for sharing data with governments for humanitarian purposes and, if so, what that might be.[116] Such debates tend to see digital interfaces (and surrounding proprietary and regulatory arrangements) assessed according to a standard of "usefulness" rather than by reference to other considerations, such as their fairness, justness, or their distributive and politically constitutive effects.

The practice of scrutinizing digital interfaces for their usefulness (to which Chapter 7 will return) may be leveraged by companies like Digicel, the mobile phone company that for a time enjoyed market share above 50 percent in 22 national markets across the Caribbean and South Pacific.[117] Companies such as this may emphasize their digital infrastructure's social value or usefulness as part

---

[113] Interview with Participant AH (October 26, 2020).

[114] There is much more to be said about all of these. On the racialization, spatialization, and politics of "protection" for instance, see Kevin Grove, "Disaster Biopolitics and the Crisis Economy," in Jennifer L Lawrence and Sarah Marie Wiebe (eds.), *Biopolitical Disaster* (Routledge, 2018).

[115] To be fair, many who use these terms do not confer upon them the status of meta-principle or meta-descriptor. See, e.g., Peck's vivid account of the collective crafting of neoliberalism: Jamie Peck, *Constructions of Neoliberal Reason* (Oxford University Press, 2010).

[116] Interview with Participant AA (December 17, 2019).

[117] The JMMB Group, "Investor Update: Digicel Group Limited" (April 2019), <https://www.jmmb.com/sites/default/files/Jamaica/Attachments/Research/2019/JMMB_Digicel_InvestorUpdate_APRIL_2019.pdf> (accessed October 10, 2022).

of an argument for self-regulation, casting themselves (with mixed success) as "site[s] of depoliticized innovation."[118]

Debates about what might serve as usable data for humanitarian purposes also fuel contention over *governmental* authority and jurisdiction.[119] With regard to PLJ's work, for instance, disputes over data access and use have at times divided the Indonesian Telecommunication Regulatory Authority (operating under the rubric of the Ministry of Communication and Information Technology) and the Ministry of National Development Planning in Indonesia—ministries with very different histories, orientations, and priorities.[120]

Digital communications infrastructure has also become the target of protest in a range of political debates from Afghanistan to Bougainville and Hong Kong to Wales.[121] We will return to the politics of digital interfaces' use, disuse, and misuse in Chapter 7.

This matters even for those not using digital humanitarian interfaces. While interfaces like MIND are not currently pivotal in decision-making over public resource distribution (a September 2021 report suggested that MIND was not in use[122]), they do indicate a redirection of humanitarian budgets away from other things and toward ICT development. National governments and international and nongovernmental organizations "are using ICT in new and expanded ways" in their humanitarian efforts, as we have seen in prior chapters.[123] Practices and interfaces of the kind discussed in this chapter also reflect growth in ICT-related spending (on devices, phone service, and internet access) among beneficiaries of humanitarian assistance and growth in digitally mediated delivery of humanitarian assistance.[124] The work of UN Global Pulse, and the prototype interfaces

---

[118] Julie E. Cohen, "Law for the Platform Economy" (2017) 51 *UC Davis Law Review* 133, 161.

[119] Interview with Participant R, *supra* note 38. See generally Marion Fourcade and Jeffrey Gordon, "Learning Like a State: Statecraft in the Digital Age" (2020) 1 *Journal of Law and Political Economy* 78.

[120] See generally Susan Eick, "A History of Indonesian Telecommunication Reform 1999–2006" (40th Annual Hawaii International Conference on System Sciences, January 2007); Vedi Hadiz, *The Politics of Economic Development in Indonesia: Contending Perspectives* (Routledge, 2005).

[121] Reuters, "Gunmen Destroy Mobile Phone Tower in Afghan South" ( *Reuters*, March 2, 2008), <https://www.reuters.com/article/us-afghan-violence-idUSISL20878120080302> (accessed October 10, 2022); Patrick Makis and Matthew Vari, "Loloho Digicel Tower Equipment Torched" (*Post Courier*, Papua New Guinea, February 14, 2019), <https://postcourier.com.pg/loloho-digicel-tower-equipment-torched/> (accessed October 10, 2022); Ellen Ioanes, "Hong Kong Protesters Destroyed 'Smart' Lampposts Because They Fear China Is Spying on Them" (*Business Insider*, August 26, 2019), <https://www.businessinsider.com/hong-kong-protesters-smart-lampposts-are-spying-on-them-2019-8> (accessed October 10, 2022); Fiona Leake, "Suspect in Custody Following Arson Attack on 5G Mast" (*5Gradar*, March 10, 2019), <https://www.5gradar.com/news/suspect-in-custody-following-arson-attack-on-5g-mast> (accessed October 10, 2022).

[122] Aleks Berditchevskaia et al., "Collective Crisis Intelligence for Frontline Humanitarian Response" (*NESTA*, 2021) 88, <https://www.nesta.org.uk/report/collective-crisis-intelligence-frontline-humanitarian-response/>.

[123] Mark Haselkorn and Rebecca Walton, "The Role of Information and Communication in the Context of Humanitarian Service" (2009) 52 *IEEE Transactions on Professional Communication* 325.

[124] Allen L. Hammond et al., "The Next 4 Billion: Market Size and Business Strategy at the Base of the Pyramid" (*The World Bank*, 2007) 39127, at 43–51, <http://documents.worldbank.org/cura

that it has developed, suggest ways in which donor and donee attention and imagination are being captured and directed digitally and the kinds of polities or could-be-polities assembled and mobilized in the process.[125] They are indicative, in other words, of emergent senso-political arrangements. We know that how we classify people for governmental purposes changes how those so classified are thought and talked about and organize themselves.[126] Yet we have not yet fully grasped how people's digital aggregation will play out in this regard. Decision-support prototypes like the MIND interface are, accordingly, charged with juridico-political import regardless of how limited their *operational* impact may be upon current international humanitarian practice. They may not be central to mundane decision-making in humanitarian work, but they are indicative of the directions in which many in the humanitarian field are being encouraged, trained, and funded to move. As one of our informants recounted:

> There are a lot of developing countries that are active in the [UN Global] [W]orking [G]roup [on Big Data for Official Statistics] more and more. More and more African countries. We [that is, members of the Working Group] are going to have the next conference . . . in Rwanda. So they are very interested. When we had the training sessions during the conference that we had in Bogotá, Colombia there was a lot of participants from developing countries. But there is a long way before they have the capacity to actually use tools that we are providing for them.[127]

A second major theme of this book, after the first-order question highlighted earlier, is the importance of remaking and transmuting prevailing repertoires of politico-legal critique in the face of the burgeoning digitization of governance. There is a long tradition of thinking of humanitarian disasters as constitutive socially, legally, and politically.[128] However, prevailing debates about the politics of humanitarian disasters have not tended to feature digital interfaces

ted/en/779321468175731439/The-next-4-billion-market-size-and-business-strategy-at-the-base-of-the-pyramid> (accessed October 10, 2022); European Parliament, Directorate-General for Parliamentary Research Services, and Capgemini Consulting, *Technological Innovation for Humanitarian Aid and Assistance* (2019) 30, <http://publications.europa.eu/publication/manifestation_identifier/PUB_QA01119236ENN> (accessed October 10, 2022).

[125] Fleur Johns, "Data, Detection, and the Redistribution of the Sensible in International Law" (2017) 111 *AJIL* 57.

[126] Jennifer Elrick and Luisa Farah Schwartzman, "From Statistical Category to Social Category: Organized Politics and Official Categorizations of 'Persons with a Migration Background' in Germany" (2015) 38 *Ethnic and Racial Studies* 1539.

[127] Interview with Participant R, *supra* note 38.

[128] Fleur Johns, "Guantánamo Bay and the Annihilation of the Exception" (2005) 16 *EJIL* 613; Nasser Hussain, *The Jurisprudence of Emergency: Colonialism and the Rule of Law* (University of Michigan Press, 2019).

like MIND. Scholars and practitioners alike are not accustomed to thinking of commercial geotagging as a socially or politically constitutive practice in its own right (although there is literature on social place-making associated with geotagging).[129] Similarly, there is no political vernacular in circulation with which to understand peoples' posting of geotagged tweets or conducting of Google searches as practices potentially demarcating sites of "vulnerability" and prospective humanitarian intervention. Nor have relations of polity to territory—in legal doctrine or in political idiom—typically been framed in terms of endlessly fluctuating, time-sensitive placement, such as those depicted when one tracks shifts in nighttime and daytime population using mobile phone data.[130] Precisely what kinds of sociality digital aggregates may be understood to be constituting and their amenability to political mobilization—this is a matter of ongoing study.[131]

This chapter has argued that these interfaces operate more senso-politically than biopolitically. Still, it remains the case that humanitarian digital interfaces' development and use are overwhelmingly justified in terms of the biological and economic optimization of human lives. Techno-solutionists everywhere talk of saving, freeing, and improving people.[132] This is definitely the case in the humanitarian field. UN Global Pulse has argued, as noted earlier, that "big data and new technologies can, and should, be used to save lives and better livelihoods."[133] The standard rejoinder to this justification then becomes to point out forms of human immiseration to which digitization has contributed—Virginia Eubanks' powerfully drawn "digital poorhouse," for example[134]—whereupon commitments to optimization are expected to be redoubled. Elsewhere, reformism in this setting has tended to fixate on getting digital proxies to better match their human referents, in less biased, racialized, underinclusive, or overinclusive ways.

But what if the well-being of human populations were becoming more or less incidental to the practice and senso-politics of digital governance, even in that most humanist of domains: that of international humanitarianism? What if the kinds of work in which people and things are being enrolled by

---

[129] E.g., Lee Humphreys and Tony Liao, "Mobile Geotagging: Reexamining Our Interactions with Urban Space" (2011) 16 *Journal of Computer-Mediated Communication* 407.

[130] Guilherme Augusto Zagatti et al., "A Trip to Work: Estimation of Origin and Destination of Commuting Patterns in the Main Metropolitan Regions of Haiti Using CDR" (2018) 3 *Development Engineering* 133; Fleur Johns, "Data Territories: Changing Architectures of Association in International Law," in Martin Kuijer and Wouter Werner (eds.), *Netherlands Yearbook of International Law 2016: The Changing Nature of Territoriality in International Law* (TMC Asser Press, 2017).

[131] E.g., Marion Fourcade and Daniel Kluttz, "A Maussian Bargain: Accumulation by Gift in the Digital Economy" (2020) 7 *Big Data & Society*.

[132] Eugeny Morozov, *To Save Everything, Click Here: The Folly of Technological Solutionism* (PublicAffairs, 2013).

[133] UN Global Pulse, *supra* note 76, at 7.

[134] Virginia Eubanks, *Automating Inequality* (St. Martin's Press, 2018).

digital humanitarian interfaces like MIND were *not* oriented toward faithfully representing and optimizing human lives in the aggregate, but rather creating, investing, and trading in and acting on aggregates of an entirely different sort—namely, digital aggregates understood to be taking effect "on their own terms"?

Senso-political digital interfaces such as MIND tend to maintain a structural imperviousness to critique premised on the demand that those interfaces more closely, fairly, or attentively mirror the human world. First, specialists in this domain have an endless series of technical fixes to answer criticisms of this kind, many of which entail demand for more data and more expansive deployment of digital technology—that is, a doubling down on that which is being queried.[135] Second, there is much work carried out in the sphere of the senso-political for which this mimicry of the real is more or less beside the point: that is, work managing, maintaining, and curating the interplay of data upon data, for instance. Recall how the MIND interface gets operationalized in any one instance: it is triggered by an automated GDACS alert.

To entertain this idea—that an inbuilt structural indifference to archetypal humanist demands and critiques is being engineered into the interfaces of digital humanitarianism—is not necessarily dystopian. It is far from clear that humanist aggregates are, in all instances, superior to digital ones. (Samera Esmeir, in her book *Juridical Humanity*, is among those who have shown how effectively violence has been enabled and justified in the name of humanism and humanity.[136]) Nor is this chapter describing a process of dehumanization; humans remain very much in the frame and all over the surrounding rhetoric. As one of our interviewees working on the development and deployment of digital interfaces for humanitarian purposes explained: "[W]e don't cut human expertise, we don't cut domain expertise, we don't cut human intuition out of the picture; it's actually a blend of both algorithmic power and human intelligence."[137] Nonetheless, the concrete practices and interfaces through which digitization is advancing in the international humanitarian field are transforming how people, places, and things are being made to count, or not, in the global sensory economy of humanitarianism today—and these shifts warrant close attention.

It is in amassing, processing, and visualizing digital data that what counts as worthy of attention is increasingly being determined, not necessarily by addressing peoples' lives as such. And this is not taking place primarily through practices of tending to bodies in the aggregate, although of course those practices continue. Digital data *qua* data or data on data: these are increasingly the objects with which international humanitarian governance is preoccupied. The

---

[135] See, e.g., Pedro Domingos, *The Master Algorithm* (Basic Books, 2017) 261–289.
[136] Samera Esmeir, *Juridical Humanity: A Colonial History* (Stanford University Press, 2012).
[137] Interview with Participant AK, *supra* note 79.

senso-political mezzanines described in this chapter—of which interfaces like MIND are emblematic—*are*, in large part, where sociality and conflict are manifest in the sphere of digital humanitarianism. Broadly speaking, what counts in this senso-political domain of contending digital aggregates is what shows up, or is made to show up, in the data, not what is valuable, worthy, sustainable, normal, natural, necessary, just, or authentic in any broader sense. Reproduction of the real is not the concern that animates this domain so much as making new things stand in for the real. And a critical repertoire closely attuned to these "new things"—that is still only just beginning to take shape. The coming chapter will probe what this might imply for the repertoires of claim-making, sense-making, strategizing, and struggle surrounding humanitarian emergencies.

# 4
# Emergencies: Waiting and Watching in the Palliative Present

## Introduction

In the humanitarian field and elsewhere on the international plane, law and politics throughout the modern period have been conducted, in significant part, in a register of emergency. That is to say, law and politics have often mobilized and been impelled by certain "state[s] of things unexpectedly arising, and urgently demanding immediate action" and associated perceptions of phenomena "issuing from concealment" or rising from below the surface.[1] These are historically contingent surfacings; an emergency is a formation that "has in a particular historical moment been given the important function of addressing some kind of . . . urgent situation."[2] Emergencies may be slow-onset and protracted as discussed later in this chapter. Yet, by their nature, emergencies tend to speak in the present and try to provoke action in the present. They typically address the now, the very recent past, and the near future, and they do so in the imperative tense. Emergencies have manifest in this way at all scales, from the village to the globe, yet practices and imaginaries of international lawyers and other international humanitarian professionals have, perhaps especially, "littered [the international legal plane] with ruptive instances."[3] Recurrently, emergencies have offered prospects for international law's extension and renewal as well as rationales for its regularizing force.[4]

Much of the rich repertoire of powers and liabilities, claim-making and sense-making, right-assertion and struggle built around emergencies is at work in and around the digital interfaces with which this chapter is concerned: interfaces that represent and invite action on humanitarian emergencies. Yet at the same time, the fact of these interfaces being digital brings about certain shifts in

---

[1] "Emergency, n.," in *OED Online* (Oxford University Press, 2021), <https://www.oed.com/view/Entry/61130> (accessed October 10, 2022).
[2] Alain Pottage, "The Materiality of What?" (2012) 39 *Journal of Law and Society* 167, 181, quoting Michel Foucault, "Le jeu de Michel Foucault," in *Dits et Ecrits*, vol. 3 (1994) 299.
[3] Fleur Johns, Richard Joyce, and Sundhya Pahuja, *Events: The Force of International Law* (Taylor & Francis Group, 2010) 1.
[4] Ibid., 1–3.

how emergencies are configured and readied for response. Digital humanitarian interfaces' customizability does not prevent them from having profound structuring and restructuring effects; in fact, it helps to ensure such effects. We have already encountered some of these shifts in prior chapters: changes in how emergencies are mapped and how affected populations are assembled and made governable. This chapter probes these shifts further, exploring resulting transformations in the presuppositions and predicates of humanitarian emergency: by whom an emergency is considered actionable; in what form or format; and within what time frame. Before considering the answers that digital humanitarian interfaces yield to these questions, some remarks on the recent historical framing of international humanitarian emergencies are in order. Later, this chapter will examine the "who," the "what," and the "when" of humanitarian emergencies represented at digital interfaces by reference to two examples: VAMPIRE and HungerMap LIVE. As we will see later, humanitarian emergencies' mediation by digital interfaces either makes them everyone's and no one's problem or renders them actionable by and for a relatively narrow range of people; it turns them from sites of potential unrest into tractable problems of data deficiency; and it renders humanitarian emergencies incessant—something with which those in the present must endlessly try to cope for the benefit of some idealized future beneficiaries.

## International Humanitarian Emergencies

Work in the international humanitarian field trades in understandings of emergency that are closely related to those circulating in the intersecting fields of public law, public health, policing, and emergency management. In all these domains, adoption of the language of emergency is a matter of switching things on and off: switching on certain powers, responsibilities, funding flows, and strategic options; switching off certain preoccupations and procedures identified with routine, nonemergency conditions. Yet precisely which switches move, when, how, and for whom differs among the previously referenced fields. As Wagner-Pacifici has observed, any given emergency event is "intrinsically restless."[5] The parameters of what counts as an emergency are subject to political contestation among those who lay claim to emergency authority, those who seek emergency assistance, and those who are asked to make sacrifices for or otherwise support an emergency's handling.[6]

---

[5] Robin Wagner-Pacifici, "Theorizing the Restlessness of Events" (2010) 115 *American Journal of Sociology* 1351.

[6] Jennifer C. Rubenstein, "Emergency Claims and Democratic Action" (2015) 32 *Social Philosophy and Policy* 101.

A public law emergency may trigger powers and constraints enshrined in national constitutions regarding governmental actors and military personnel and engender debate in those terms. A public health emergency may prompt medical professionals with certain types of expertise to step forward, casting other experts and priorities into the background, alongside the adoption of other health-oriented measures. A local emergency might call forth emergency services personnel and cue community recourse to emergency management plans. Yet those humanitarian emergencies that, by reason of their scale or the surpassing nature of the human needs that they provoke, register *internationally* have especially pervasive effects. Among these, they create rationales for international organizations' continued existence and occasion those organizations assuming responsibilities that might, in other instances, be assumed by other actors or discharged otherwise or not at all. Those responsibilities of international organizations typically entail orchestrating "a large influx of resources aimed at saving lives [and] the creation of temporary and often parallel coordination structures, and a response [often] dominated by food aid."[7] This also involves international organizations trying to tap new sources or enhanced levels of financial support and international legal authority as they respond to requests for assistance that frequently outstrip available resources.

Given this jurisdiction-making aspect of humanitarian emergencies on the international plane, it is unsurprising that international organizations have devoted considerable effort to trying to define the kinds of humanitarian emergencies with which they are concerned. The United Nations' Office for the Coordination of Humanitarian Affairs (OCHA) has, for example, been at pains to distinguish between "slow-onset" and "rapid-onset" humanitarian emergencies, bringing both within its purview. A slow-onset emergency, according to OCHA, "emerges gradually over time, often based on a confluence of different events" including "recurring or cyclical hazard events." A rapid-onset emergency encompasses "catastrophic, sudden-onset events like tropical storms, earthquakes and tsunamis." Both bring about intensifications of vulnerability and "acute humanitarian need."[8] Similarly, the Food and Agriculture Organization (FAO) lists 11 types of emergency with which it is concerned (from "nuclear release and radioactivity" to "transboundary plant pests and diseases"). Among these is a "complex emergency" that is a "major humanitarian crisis that is often the result of a

---

[7] OCHA Policy Development and Studies Branch, "OCHA and Slow-Onset Emergencies" (UN Office for the Coordination of Humanitarian Affairs, April 2011), OCHA Occasional Policy Briefing Series No. 6, 4.
[8] Ibid., 3–4.

combination of political instability, conflict and violence, social inequities and underlying poverty."[9]

Elsewhere within the network of the United Nations and affiliated agencies—specifically, within the UN Disaster Relief Organization (UNDRO) (incorporated into the UN Department of Humanitarian Affairs in 1992, which was itself reorganized to become OCHA in 1998)—it has been acknowledged that "emergencies are a fundamental part of normal life. They are consequences of the ways societies structure themselves, economically and socially; the ways that societies and states interact; and the ways that relationships between the decision makers are sustained."[10] Humanitarian emergencies are indeed "normal" in that their recurrence is structurally presupposed when governmental rationales are fundamentally linked to questions of scarcity and when, as in capitalist settings, scarcity is a precondition for maximizing return on investment.[11] They are also widely and regularly anticipated; the increasing prevalence and intensification of natural disasters has, for example, been both documented and forecast as a matter of climate science for decades.[12]

Humanitarian emergencies may be "normal" (in the sense of their regular recurrence having become economically and ecologically preconditioned), but as scholars and activists have emphasized for decades, they are not "natural" even when precipitated by geophysical, hydrological, meteorological, or climatological occurrences. They result from human decision-making: from the interaction of such hazards and preexisting social, economic, and political conditions and priorities.[13] Those who are most adversely affected by so-called natural disasters tend to be living under economic and political conditions that predispose them to those effects, or render them more exposed than others.[14] Emphasizing the "naturalness" of disaster has been a recurrent way of directing governmental and

---

[9] FAO, "Complex Emergencies: FAO in Emergencies," <https://web.archive.org/web/20220119011912/https://www.fao.org/emergencies/emergency-types/complex-emergencies/en/> (accessed October 10, 2022).

[10] Mark Anderson and Michael Gerber, "Introduction to Humanitarian Emergencies," in David Townes (ed.), *Health in Humanitarian Emergencies: Principles and Practice for Public Health and Healthcare Practitioners* (Cambridge University Press, 2018) 1, quoting UNDRO, *An Overview of Disaster Management* (2nd ed., 1992).

[11] Michel Foucault, *Security, Territory, Population: Lectures at the Collège de France, 1977–78* (Graham Burchell ed., Arnold I. Davidson tr., Palgrave Macmillan UK, 2007) 341–347.

[12] Deborah R. Coen, "The Advent of Climate Science," in *Oxford Research Encyclopedia of Climate Science* (Oxford University Press, 2020); World Meteorological Organization (WMO), "Weather-Related Disasters Increase over Past 50 Years, Causing More Damage but Fewer Deaths" (August 31, 2021), <https://public.wmo.int/en/media/press-release/weather-related-disasters-increase-over-past-50-years-causing-more-damage-fewer> (accessed October 10, 2022).

[13] Ilan Kelman, *Disaster by Choice: How Our Actions Turn Natural Hazards into Catastrophes* (Oxford University Press, 2020).

[14] Terry Cannon, "Vulnerability Analysis and the Explanation of 'Natural' Disasters," in Ann Varley (ed.), *Disasters, Development and Environment* (John Wiley & Sons, Ltd., 1994); Chester W. Hartman and Gregory D. Squires, *There Is No Such Thing as a Natural Disaster: Race, Class, and Hurricane Katrina* (Routledge, 2006).

public attention away from the economically conditioned and racialized distribution of both suffering and concern.[15]

The authoritative classifications of some experiences of collective death and pain as humanitarian emergencies is what makes them actionable as such; this is where digital humanitarian interfaces come in. Some may endure extreme deprivation, suffering, and death without their plight being designated a humanitarian emergency.[16] The power to classify and attract attention to emergencies is unevenly distributed and digital humanitarian interfaces are becoming increasingly important vectors in that attention economy.[17] This all presupposes, of course, nonreliance on divine explanations for humanitarian emergencies following the efforts of Enlightenment thinkers to explain the world in "natural terms alone."[18] Emergencies likely take on other valences in theocracies or among other congregations of intense religiosity.

Much depends, then, on whether and how any devastating event is escalated to the level of an international humanitarian emergency. When emergencies are encountered via digital interfaces developed or adopted by international organizations, the range of actions that may be taken or encouraged differ from those promoted by traditional frameworks (such as specialist expert or nongovernmental organization (NGO) reports). This chapter focuses on three dimensions of the shifts associated with humanitarian emergencies' representation via digital interfaces: for *whom* is the emergency made salient and actionable; *how* is the emergency defined; and *when*, or at what pace and according to what timescale, is the emergency experienced.

## Emergency for Whom?

From an international vantage point, primary responsibility for emergency response is typically understood to reside with nation-states insofar as their territories or nationals are affected (albeit being subject to variable allocation of responsibility within them). This is both a widely held political assumption and an expression of the international law on state jurisdiction. Building on this, states have often sought to expand their jurisdiction, or justify its

---

[15] Eric Klinenberg, "Denaturalizing Disaster: A Social Autopsy of the 1995 Chicago Heat Wave" (1999) 28 *Theory and Society* 239.

[16] Aurora Fredriksen, "Crisis in 'a Normal Bad Year': Spaces of Humanitarian Emergency, the Integrated Food Security Phase Classification Scale and the Somali Famine of 2011" (2016) 48 *Environment and Planning A: Economy and Space* 40, 42.

[17] Fleur Johns, "Data, Detection, and the Redistribution of the Sensible in International Law" (2017) 111 *AJIL* 57.

[18] Susan Neiman, *Evil in Modern Thought: An Alternative History of Philosophy* (Princeton University Press, 2015) 246.

extraterritorial exercise, by reference to humanitarian claims and ideals; historian James Heartfield has called this "humanitarian imperialism."[19] There has also been a centuries-long tradition of states delegating their responsibility for emergency management in whole or in part to corporations, NGOs, and multilateral forces.[20] In recent decades, emergency services have been among those public services funded through public-private partnerships (PPPs) in many jurisdictions.[21]

Digital humanitarianism continues this trajectory of state delegation to, and private sector involvement in, emergency response, development assistance, and humanitarian aid. Yet, as prior chapters have already shown, the development and deployment of digital humanitarian interfaces has established new frontiers and interlocutors in this field. Digital humanitarian interfaces tend to demand data that can attest, in near-real time, to the activities of large numbers of people or the conditions of large swathes of territory. To date, nowhere has a more expansive or effective infrastructure been built for the extraction, storage, and analysis of such data than that created and controlled by commercial digital platforms and device manufacturers.[22] Accordingly, those commercial actors have come to seem indispensable to contemporary efforts to confront international humanitarian emergencies. Because of their vast data hordes and financial might, problems of international humanitarian emergency have become problems that the world's largest digital technology companies are seen as having unique capacity—and responsibility—to address.[23] One of our interviewees encapsulated this view, when recounting how they moved from working in an international organization to working in Silicon Valley in pursuit of humanitarian goals:

> The UN's formula for everything—climate change, COVID-19, food security—is that we need more money and more political will to solve the problem. That's the basic formula for everything. But I could see after a while that there was

---

[19] Heartfield James, *Humanitarian Imperialism in Australia, New Zealand, Fiji, Canada, South Africa, and the Congo, 1837–1909* (Columbia University Press, 2011).

[20] See, e.g., Sanjay Sharma, *Famine, Philanthropy and the Colonial State: North India in the Early Nineteenth Century* (Oxford University Press, 2001); Davide Rodogno, *Against Massacre: Humanitarian Interventions in the Ottoman Empire, 1815–1914* (Princeton University Press, 2012).

[21] For illustrative accounts of its recent history in the United States and South Africa, see, e.g., Ami J. Abou-bakr, "The Emergence of Disaster-Oriented PPPs," in *Managing Disasters through Public-Private Partnerships* (Georgetown University Press, 2013) 15–42; Faranak Miraftab, "Public-Private Partnerships: The Trojan Horse of Neoliberal Development?" (2004) 24 *Journal of Planning Education and Research* 89.

[22] Shoshana Zuboff, *The Age of Surveillance Capitalism: The Fight for a Human Future at the New Frontier of Power* (Profile Books, 2019).

[23] See, e.g., ITU, "Turning Digital Technology Innovation into Climate Action" (International Telecommunication Union, 2019).

a missing pillar of technology innovation and all the money in the world and all the political will in the world wasn't automatically going to produce the innovations that were required to achieve the Sustainable Development Goals. And so that's how I ended up in Silicon Valley.[24]

According to some of their proponents, digital humanitarian interfaces also promise to enroll and mobilize a much broader, more geographically dispersed range of constituencies in addressing humanitarian emergencies than have historically been involved. They ostensibly "democratize" humanitarian emergency response and advocacy[25] and give "voice" to the "voiceless"—although claims of this kind have met with some astute critical scrutiny.[26] As noted in Chapter 2, some scholarly literature has focused on the "crowdsourced" aspects of digital humanitarian work, sometimes cast as a mechanism of "philanthro-capitalist" massification, sometimes as a vehicle for "grassroots" ethico-political projects.[27] Tending toward the latter view, one of our interviewees speculated that public access to digital data might afford disaster-affected communities "a political . . . evidence base for advocacy to mayors and so forth" to try to elicit governmental action to counter those risks. "That's the advocacy end of this," this interviewee continued, "it's how we break this thing wide open."[28] Another interviewee claimed that whereas, in the past, data has been generated by government "and the outputs and the insights [have been] controlled by government and used . . . to justify policy," digital interfaces rally "data [that] cannot be controlled by government" so "it creates this huge nervousness."[29]

Those invited into these openings must do so in accordance with certain expectations, however. Above all, digital humanitarian interfaces foster an expectation of resilience. The prospect of "breaking" humanitarian advocacy and emergency response "wide open" through digital interfaces making data broadly available and usable does not just entail an imagined transfer of capacity or projected amplification of demotic voice (as yet largely unfulfilled). It also involves a conferral of responsibility: an expectation—an imperative, even—that all individuals and communities enhance their self-reliance and continually seek out and realize

---

[24] Interview with Participant AK (July 16, 2021).
[25] Patrick Meier, *Digital Humanitarians: How Big Data Is Changing the Face of Humanitarianism* (Routledge, 2015) 193.
[26] Mirca Madianou, Liezel Longboan, and Jonathan Corpus Ong, "Finding a Voice Through Humanitarian Technologies? Communication Technologies and Participation in Disaster Recovery" (2015) 9 *International Journal of Communication* 19.
[27] Ryan Burns, "New Frontiers of Philanthro-Capitalism: Digital Technologies and Humanitarianism" (2019) 51 *Antipode* 1101; Anne-Meike Fechter and Anke Schwittay, "Citizen Aid: Grassroots Interventions in Development and Humanitarianism" (2019) 40 *Third World Quarterly* 1769.
[28] Interview with Participant N (April 11, 2018).
[29] Interview with Participant AH (October 26, 2020).

positive opportunities to make "life in capitalist ruins" with or without state support.[30] One might say that the very openness and responsiveness of digital humanitarian interfaces tend to make resilience seem mandatory: encouraging people everywhere, but especially those most vulnerable, to engage continually in "the mapping of internal system relations" in order to understand how to deal with "emergent social, economic and environmental conditions."[31] Read in this register, the "wide open" becomes less open; it closes around ever-proliferating versions of the world as it is. The task of living becomes one of accepting and coping with ceaseless change in the here and now, not envisioning or organizing for a future. "[T]he only thing certain is the 'necessity' of contingency itself."[32]

To the question "for whom is the emergency actionable?," those working on and with digital humanitarian interfaces tend to answer, in effect, *everyone*. Everyone with access to digital data, much of it commercially accumulated and controlled, is invited to see themselves as incipiently capable of acting on humanitarian emergencies, provided that their capability is cast primarily in informational terms and shepherded by intermediaries in control of the marshaling of relevant information. Readers may recall the remarks of Patrick Meier, from Chapter 1, that "[a]nyone can be a digital humanitarian, absolutely no experience necessary; all you need is a big heart and access to the Internet."[33]

When one scratches below the surface, however, the *everyone* that digital humanitarian interfaces are imagined empowering all too often becomes, in effect, *no one*.[34] The very profusion of data, the diversity of data sources that digital interfaces marshal, and the associated dispersal of humanitarian responsibilities seem to yield any number of reasons why redistributive or preventative action beyond information-gathering should be deferred. There is never enough data on hand. There is always, it seems, the prospect of more or improved data on the horizon, some configuration of which might make humanitarian action better informed, better targeted, better received. In their forever-incomplete formulation, digital humanitarian interfaces seem to offer as many reasons not to act as they forge potential new pathways for action.

---

[30] Anna Lowenhaupt Tsing, *The Mushroom at the End of the World: On the Possibility of Life in Capitalist Ruins* (Princeton University Press, 2015).
[31] David Chandler, *Ontopolitics in the Anthropocene: An Introduction to Mapping, Sensing and Hacking* (Routledge, 2018) 48–50; see also Suzan Ilcan and Kim Rygiel, "'Resiliency Humanitarianism': Responsibilizing Refugees through Humanitarian Emergency Governance in the Camp" (2015) 9 *International Political Sociology* 333; Mark Duffield, "The Resilience of the Ruins: Towards a Critique of Digital Humanitarianism" (2016) 4 *Resilience* 147; Mark Duffield, *Post-Humanitarianism: Governing Precarity in the Digital World* (Polity, 2018).
[32] Chandler, *supra* note 31, at 202.
[33] Meier, *supra* note 25, at 1.
[34] Will Douglas Heaven, "Hundreds of AI Tools Have Been Built to Catch Covid. None of Them Helped" [2021] *MIT Technology Review*, <https://www.technologyreview.com/2021/07/30/1030329/machine-learning-ai-failed-covid-hospital-diagnosis-pandemic/> (accessed October 10, 2022).

We will return to the question of who is invited to use digital humanitarian interfaces in Chapter 7. Before then, let us consider what form international humanitarian emergencies tend to take when called up on digital interfaces.

## Interfacing Digitally with Humanitarian Emergencies

To be made amenable to solution by humanitarian professionals, emergencies must be made into problems. Often, that entails rendering them as a series of logistical and technical problems.[35] The configuration of those problems shapes the response. In the Philippines, for example, the characterization of 2013's Typhoon Haiyan as a "climate emergency" led to a recovery plan that prioritized climate adaptive relocation away from the nation's shores.[36] In contrast, when the City of Chicago decided to understand their 1995 heat wave as an isolated problem of extreme heat, and not poverty or climate change, they delimited the bounds of their response accordingly.[37]

At the same time, the availability of certain tools out of which emergency response may be crafted often shapes how emergencies are understood.[38] Those flush with digital data and analytics capacity tend to recast humanitarian emergencies as problems to which those data and capacities will deliver answers. In other words, it is sometimes the readiness to hand of particular tools or apparent solutions that drives emergencies' problematization.[39] In particular, enhanced computational capacity and the ability to access high volumes of digital data can seem like proto-solutions to all kinds of social, economic, and political difficulties, provided that those difficulties are framed as computable problems or dilemmas arising from a paucity of data.[40] Digital humanitarianism often works in this way: it is possible to develop digital interfaces relatively quickly and at low cost, so this encourages the framing of any given humanitarian emergency as a problem, at least in part, of informational shortfall or outdated data—a problem, that is, to which digital humanitarianism seems like a solution.

Haze Gazer, a precursor to the MIND interface discussed in Chapter 3 and again in this chapter, is illustrative of this dynamic. Haze Gazer was developed

---

[35] Tania Murray Li, *The Will to Improve: Governmentality, Development, and the Practice of Politics* (Duke University Press, 2007) 7.

[36] Caroline Compton, "The Unheeded Present and the Impossible Future: Temporalities of Relocation after Typhoon Haiyan" (2018) 50 *Critical Asian Studies* 136.

[37] Klinenberg *supra* note 15.

[38] Kate Crawford and Megan Finn, "The Limits of Crisis Data: Analytical and Ethical Challenges of Using Social and Mobile Data to Understand Disasters" (2015) 80 *GeoJournal* 491.

[39] Graham Harman, "Technology, Objects and Things in Heidegger" (2010) 34 *Cambridge Journal of Economics* 17.

[40] Eugeny Morozov, *To Save Everything, Click Here: The Folly of Technological Solutionism* (PublicAffairs, 2013).

by Pulse Lab Jakarta (PLJ) in 2015 to help the Indonesian government understand and respond to haze-related emergencies, recognized both nationally and internationally as a matter of grave concern. This followed the occurrence of unusually severe haze conditions, attributable to deliberate burning of peat and forests, the effects of which was exacerbated by El Niño–related weather, in parts of Southeast Asia in 2015. These caused death, destruction of flora and fauna, widespread health problems, school closures, work disruptions, transport interruptions, and related distress.[41]

Framed as a tool for responding to emergencies of this kind, the Haze Gazer interface enables users to track fire hotspots identifiable by satellite and monitor air quality standards and relative health risk using the Air Quality Index China: "the world's largest aggregator of real-time air quality data."[42] It also incorporates geolocated tweets featuring particular keywords suggestive of haze, after PLJ established a correlation between the number of Twitter posts about haze and the severity of haze events.[43] The interface can also accommodate YouTube videos, using the YouTube application programming interface to identify videos tagged with relevant terms, although PLJ found relatively little relevant video material available.[44] The interface initially included data from the Indonesian government's public complaint system, LAPOR!, but later iterations have not done so.[45] The combination of these thermal, air quality, and social media data is overlaid on OpenStreetMap maps, discussed in Chapter 2. Figure 4.1 depicts the data sources of the Haze Gazer interface.

Analyses of recurrent haze problems in Southeast Asia have often been attentive to the social, economic, and political factors that contribute to them. For instance, one group of scholars has argued categorically that "the underlying causes of fires are social-politic problems" and observed, in 2017, that the "Indonesian government has been attempting to address the problem of forest and land fires for 18 years without great success."[46] In explaining its development of Haze Gazer, PLJ acknowledged these causes, but moved quickly to a more tractable framing of the problem posed by haze-related devastation: that governmental responses had "not previously [been] based on a timely and accurate reading of layered weather data."[47] This recast the problem to fit the solution

---

[41] Pulse Lab Jakarta, "Stories of Change: Haze Gazer & VAMPIRE" (2018), <https://pulselabjakarta.org/ourwork>.
[42] Robert A. Rohde and Richard A. Muller, "Air Pollution in China: Mapping of Concentrations and Sources" (2015) 10 *PLOS ONE*, at e0135749; Interview with Participant B (July 23, 2018).
[43] Mark Kibanov et al., "Mining Social Media to Inform Peatland Fire and Haze Disaster Management" (2017) 7 *Social Network Analysis and Mining* 30.
[44] Ibid.; Pulse Lab Jakarta, *supra* note 41.
[45] Interview with Participant B, *supra* note 42.
[46] Herry Purnomo et al., "Fire Economy and Actor Network of Forest and Land Fires in Indonesia" (2017) 78 *Forest Policy and Economics* 21.
[47] Pulse Lab Jakarta, *supra* note 41.

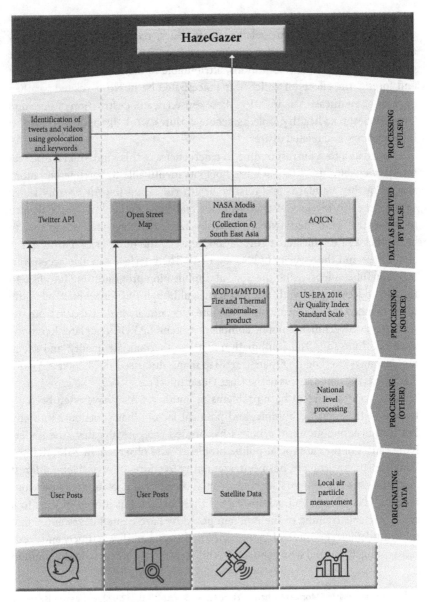

**Figure 4.1** Haze Gazer data sources.

© 2022 Wiley. Reproduced under contributors' license from Fleur Johns and Caroline Compton, "Data Jurisdictions and Rival Regimes of Algorithmic Regulation" (2022) 16 Regulation & Governance 63.

that a digital interface presented. The emergency became not so much an environmental, political, or economic one (bound up with climate change, deforestation, economic dependence on the mining and palm oil industries, and so on) as an informational one: the founding of governmental responses on patchy or dated data, or the inability of government to hear public "voices" of the kind made available by social media. The "operational impact" of the digital interface could then be evaluated not by its amelioration of haze-related suffering or prevention of haze events, but rather by its incorporation of new forms of digital data into government decision-making infrastructures. The "change" that PLJ later celebrated having helped bring about was that "the Executive Office of the President of the Republic of Indonesia (KSP) adopted [Haze Gazer and another of its interfaces] as key building blocks in developing the architecture for its Early Warning System (EWS), which is now a centerpiece of the President's Situation Room."[48]

Haze is, by its nature, a peril that is difficult to make actionable as an emergency insofar as it is all-encompassing and disorienting, with both its causes and effects often only apparent over the long term.[49] Remaking haze according to the parameters and protocols of a digital interface made it seem more immediately actionable than it might otherwise have appeared; it helped to craft a humanitarian emergency event. Visualized on the Haze Gazer interface, haze became traceable to discrete "hot spots." Meanwhile, social media postings directed attention toward those suffering adverse health effects, depicting them as would-be claimants of emergency assistance, their visibility on the interface seeming to imply that they were being seen and heard by someone with power to respond. Not depicted, however, were any connections (of ownership or investment, for instance) among haze "hot spots." Nor did the interface represent anyone carrying out legal or illegal logging or draining peatland to make way for palm oil and rubber plantations or for mining, nor investing in those industries or otherwise deriving financial benefit from them, despite these being widely recognized as among the most significant causes of haze.[50]

By refashioning Indonesia's haze emergency as a problem of information and voice, Haze Gazer effectively marginalized a range of possible policy responses to prevent haze's recurrence, including some (such as debt relief to alleviate government reliance on timber or palm oil royalties or the devolution of forest ownership and/or management responsibilities to local institutions offered incentives for conservation) that have been shown to be effective in reducing deforestation

---

[48] Ibid.
[49] A.L. Hinwood and C.M. Rodriguez, "Potential Health Impacts Associated with Peat Smoke" (2005) 88 *Journal of the Royal Society of Western Australia* 133.
[50] Purnomo et al., *supra* note 46.

(and hence lessening haze from land-clearing fires).[51] In the very process of making Indonesia's haze problem an emergency actionable as an information vacuum that digital data might fill, this digital interface evacuated the space of possible action surrounding that emergency of many strategic options that might otherwise have been available to address it.

## Emergencies' Emergence and the Rhythms of Digital Interface

As is apparent from the Haze Gazer example, digital interfaces representing humanitarian emergencies do not just reshape and reprioritize those emergencies' constituencies, causes and effects. Digital interfaces also modulate the temporality of emergency, that is: the time frame within which it is perceived; the pace and intervals at which action is invited in and on that emergency; and its relation to past, present, and future times.

Emergencies are often encountered, analyzed, and reproduced according to a certain temporal "canon" characteristic of international humanitarian work. Employing this idea of a "canon," Catherine Brun has observed that "[h]umanitarian action primarily aims for temporary solutions that tend to make people stuck in a humanitarian system for years."[52] As Brun highlights, work on humanitarian emergencies aims at the immediate future but tends to make that near-term elastic, potentially even unending. This is an elasticity identifiable with the phenomenology of "chronic waiting" and surviving, both frequently cast as debased modes of persistence (including by Brun herself).[53] In the first instance, then, international humanitarian emergencies have often inhabited a temporary yet malleable time-space traced around the event horizon of their initial occurrence or, in the case of slow-onset emergencies, their coming to international humanitarian practitioners' attention.

Beyond this temporary and expandable survival-space close to the now, international humanitarian work on emergencies also tends to be futurist in a far more vaulting posture. One version of this is the "reproductive futurity" analyzed by queer theorist Lee Edelman, a futurity that takes as its emblematic figure of political possibility "the Child" in need of protection (an idealized figure, as distinct from any actual, locatable children). Humanitarian emergencies become vehicles

---

[51] Alexander Pfaff et al., "Policy Impacts on Deforestation: Lessons Learned from Past Experiences to Inform New Initiatives" (Nicholas Institute, Duke University, June 2010).

[52] Cathrine Brun, "There Is No Future in Humanitarianism: Emergency, Temporality and Protracted Displacement" (2016) 27 *History and Anthropology* 393.

[53] Didier Fassin, *Life: A Critical User's Manual* (Polity, 2018), 81–83; cf. Craig Jeffrey, "Waiting" (2008) 26 *Environment and Planning D: Society and Space* 954.

for reproductive futurism insofar as political measures taken under the rubric of an emergency are often aimed, at least in part, at making the future more secure for subsequent generations in vague, generalized terms and eliciting forbearance from people in the present on that basis. As Edelman has written: "[A]s the repository of variously sentimentalized cultural identifications, the Child has come to embody for [many] the telos of the social order and come to be seen as the one for whom that order is held in perpetual trust ... always at the cost of limiting the rights [and possibilities that] 'real' citizens are allowed."[54] Approached in this temporal register, the emergency must always be pillaged for its offerings to the unborn or just-born people of tomorrow: lessons learned, promises extracted, and so on. In this idealized embodiment, the emergency is invested with a telos. Yet, in the deference that this demands of those living through humanitarian emergency, that telos is "reinscribed in the present."[55] Those consigned to the temporality of survival are still invited by international humanitarian endeavors to dream of modernist progress, but those dreams belong to the Child and to Humanity. They do not, for the most part, open possibilities for political renegotiation or the building of radically different pathways from the here and now. *Pace* Brun, there is a future in humanitarian emergency, but it is, all too often, an overdetermined, occupied future, already staked out and claimed "in the name of [H]umanity"—a future from which those in the present are disconnected and disengaged.[56]

The digitally rendered emergency tends to present a compressed version of this temporality and telos. As to the first, digital humanitarian interfaces often assume the burden of waiting while their users are released from that task, or at least encouraged to experience some sense of release, whether in the capacity of would-be donor, prospective intervenor, or data-contributing claimant. "I will wait for you," the digital interface seems to say to its users as it processes incoming streams of data. Perceived through a digital humanitarian interface, the emergency is forever emergent. Each of those interfaces discussed in prior chapters, and later in this one, depends on some digital trigger or switch before it makes available its analysis of any given humanitarian emergency. The MIND interface discussed in Chapter 3 awaits input from the Global Disaster Alert Coordinating System disaster alert application programming interface, for example. Once so prompted, the digital interface in turn prompts its users. Countries on the HungerMap LIVE interface, discussed later, change color when automated analysis of relevant data inputs suggests (or yields a "prediction" of) food scarcity. Duly alerted, users are invited to envision themselves in a posture

---

[54] Lee Edelman, *No Future: Queer Theory and the Death Drive* (Duke University Press, 2004) 10–11.
[55] Chandler, *supra* note 31, at 214, quoting Timothy Morton, *Hyperobjects: Philosophy and Ecology after the End of the World* (University of Minnesota Press, 2013) 95.
[56] Edelman, *supra* note 54, at 153.

of acting, no longer waiting, albeit acting on a problem that has been formatted already as an informational problem, as discussed earlier.

As to the second (the telos of futurism), digital humanitarian interfaces emphasize tinkering with emergencies' existing components and employing digital technology to make something out of those incrementally and iteratively. That is how digital interfaces tend to invite futures to be constructed. What gets foregrounded in the process are those proximate futures that may be teased out of the present. Any larger, more remote or vastly different future is cast beyond reach. As discussed earlier, the future beyond the near term is already spoken for in digital renditions: by the idealized figure of the Child, or Humanity. What is accessible to those living through humanitarian emergencies is a nearer-term future belonging to whomever has their hands on the levers of the now. And engagement with a digital interface invites users to experience themselves as holding those levers and well situated to leverage the emergency. One of our interviewees articulated this sense of real-time readiness as follows:

> [T]he basis of our approach [to humanitarian interface development] is incrementality; that you only build the increments that you know aren't being built and you try to optimize all of the things which can ... interact with that increment, and that *you never build ahead*.[57]

In these ways, digital interfaces remake emergencies, temporally speaking. When represented via digital interfaces, the experience of waiting often associated with humanitarian emergencies (whether rapid-onset or slow-onset) is displaced onto the interface and remade as a matter of awaiting the most up-to-date information or a prompt of "early warning." Meanwhile, the futurism characteristic of humanitarianism gets foreshortened. As much as digital interfaces promise progress for the benefit of later generations, they orient their current users toward managing and tinkering with what they already know and have to ensure their own resilience.[58]

## Awaiting Emergencies with VAMPIRE and HungerMap LIVE

Digital interfaces' remaking of international humanitarian emergencies' protagonists, substance, and temporalities is further demonstrated by two

---

[57] Interview with Participant L (August 2015) (emphasis added).
[58] Caroline Compton, "The Temporality of Disaster: Data, the Emergency, and Climate Change" (2020) 1 *Anthropocenes—Human, Inhuman, Posthuman* 14.

interfaces designed to address food insecurity and hunger: VAMPIRE and HungerMap LIVE. Readers will recall, from Chapter 2, the interagency efforts led by the FAO, at the end of the twentieth century, to marshal a combination of analog and digital data and technologies to reduce food insecurity through the Food Insecurity and Vulnerability Information and Mapping Systems (FIVIMS). As was noted in that chapter, food insecurity was characterized for these purposes as "undernourish[ment] as a result of the physical unavailability of food, [people's] lack of social or economic access to adequate food, and/or inadequate food utilization," while vulnerability was understood to refer to "the full range of factors that place people at risk of becoming food-insecure."[59] While supported by the FAO, FIVIMS was expressly designed to be "demand-driven" and "useful to several groups of people across different sectors of society," as noted in Chapter 2.[60] Within FIVIMS, the role of government nonetheless remained central; governments were envisaged entering into "partnership with all actors of civil society, as appropriate" to develop and maintain relevant systems addressing and mapping food insecurity.[61] In contrast, digital humanitarian interfaces to address food insecurity—of which VAMPIRE and HungerMap LIVE are indicative—tend to place "greater ownership . . . in the individual and community-levels."[62]

## *VAMPIRE*

VAMPIRE (an acronym for Vulnerability Analysis Monitoring Platform for Impact of Regional Events) is an integrated map-based visualization tool designed to track the impact of drought, crop failure, and associated price volatility on the food security of vulnerable populations. It was developed between 2014 and 2016 through a partnership between PLJ, the government of Indonesia, and the World Food Programme (WFP) (with support, during pilot studies, from the Korea Advanced Institute of Science and Technology and the FAO). It was designed to aid government decision makers in allocating resources to avert hunger-related humanitarian emergencies and in better understanding the impact of climate anomalies on those living below or close to the poverty

---

[59] FAO, "Food Insecurity and Vulnerability Information and Mapping Systems (FIVIMS)" (FAO, 2000) 1, 13.

[60] FAO Committee on World Food Security, "Guidelines for National Food Insecurity and Vulnerability Information and Mapping Systems (FIVIMS): Background and Principles" (FAO, 5 June 1998), 24th Session, <https://www.fao.org/3/w8500e/w8500e.htm> (accessed October 10, 2022).

[61] Ibid.

[62] Nancy Mock, Nathan Morrow, and Adam Papendieck, "From Complexity to Food Security Decision-Support: Novel Methods of Assessment and Their Role in Enhancing the Timeliness and Relevance of Food and Nutrition Security Information" (2013) 2 *Global Food Security* 41.

line.[63] By 2018, versions of VAMPIRE had reportedly been installed into the situation room of the Indonesian President's Office and adopted by the Ministry of Disaster Management in Sri Lanka, while the PLJ indicated that it was "in the process of open sourcing the tool to enable uptake elsewhere."[64] Work on the latter, however, was apparently overtaken by the PLJ turning its attention to the development of MIND, discussed in Chapter 3.[65]

Factors motivating the development of the initial Indonesian module included Indonesian government concern about food security during the 2014–2015 El Niño cycle, informed by recollections of drought, food commodity price spikes, and resulting public rioting and antigovernment protest from an earlier El Niño season, in 1997–1998.[66] In 1998, a confluence of severe drought and the Asian financial crisis caused extreme food price volatility and devastating food shortages.[67] This in turn precipitated violent public demonstrations against the regime of General Mohammed Suharto, hastening its downfall.[68]

Built with this history of hunger-related protest in view, VAMPIRE overlays socioeconomic data on drought data. The first is derived from the Indonesian National Socio-Economic Household Survey, conducted by Central Bureau of Statistics twice yearly, and a one-off WFP survey designed to test assumptions in a sample of districts identified as vulnerable. The second encompasses measures of vegetation health and rainfall anomalies derived from satellite image data made available at no cost by NASA and the US Geological Survey. This combination of data is overlaid on a digital map focused on selected countries (initially, Indonesia and Sri Lanka).[69] In its initial, prototype version, this map could be viewed through three layers: a baseline data layer, featuring traditional national survey data on poverty levels and household food security sourced from the Indonesian government and the WFP; a climate data layer, visualizing rainfall anomalies and vegetation health indices drawing on data from NOAA in the United States; and an impact layer, visualizing the results of algorithmic analysis

---

[63] Pulse Lab Jakarta, *supra* note 41.
[64] Pulse Lab Jakarta, "Fusing Datasets to Track the Impact of Disasters in Indonesia and Beyond ... VAMPIRE Is on It!" (*Medium*, January 30, 2018), <https://medium.com/pulse-lab-jakarta/fusing-datasets-to-track-the-impact-of-disasters-in-indonesia-and-beyond-vampire-is-on-it-ed13fe8e6ff6>.
[65] Interview with Participant AC and D (February 18, 2020).
[66] Pulse Lab Jakarta, *supra* note 41 at 5.
[67] FAO, "Drought and Financial Crisis Leave Indonesia Facing Record Food Deficit" (April 24, 1998), <https://web.archive.org/web/20001025060236/https://www.fao.org/NEWS/GLOBAL/GW9810-e.htm> (accessed October 10, 2022).
[68] Bumba Mukherjee and Ore Koren, "Food Riots, Urbanization, and Mass Killing Campaigns: Indonesia and Malaysia," in Bumba Mukherjee and Ore Koren (eds.), *The Politics of Mass Killing in Autocratic Regimes* (Springer International Publishing, 2019).
[69] Hal Hill, "What's Happened to Poverty and Inequality in Indonesia over Half a Century?" (2021) 38 *Asian Development Review* 68; Pulse Lab Jakarta, *supra* note 41.

of a combination of the two other layers to identify "priority areas where people may require assistance."[70]

VAMPIRE was initially going to incorporate food price data too, but attempts to do so were abandoned because of difficulties accessing relevant government data and challenges of crowdsourcing reliable food price information from social media (the latter overly skewed toward urban areas).[71] Later, PLJ and WFP staff speculated publicly about the potential of VAMPIRE to incorporate mobile phone data to provide information on the movement of affected communities and to introduce a text message alert function to notify affected populations.[72] Since being incorporated into the Indonesian government's early warning software, VAMPIRE has reportedly retained its "actual look" while becoming "enriched with substantially more data on food prices."[73]

As to the question of who this digital interface identifies as protagonists of relevant humanitarian emergencies, the users for which VAMPIRE was designed were clearly national government officials. Nonetheless, the story of VAMPIRE's creation underscores the propensity for digital interfaces' development to occasion and promote public-private co-investment. A relevant factor in VAMPIRE's development was the availability of both public funding and private data. The WFP in Indonesia was supported in this work by German government funding via the WFP regional office in Bangkok, to engage in drought monitoring and preparedness efforts. And the fact of PLJ having access to Twitter data (thanks to UN Global Pulse's standing agreement with that company) was influential upon VAMPIRE's design.[74]

As well as showcasing PPP in government delivery of emergency services, VAMPIRE also exemplifies digital interfaces' tendency to demand resilience of affected households and communities in the face of humanitarian emergency, as discussed earlier. PLJ's public speculation that VAMPIRE might be developed further to incorporate text messaging to "notify affected populations" underscores the interface's promotion of community self-reliance.[75] This orientation toward making affected people more responsible for their own survival was also apparent in the early efforts to incorporate food price data gleaned from social media into the interface. In 2014, PLJ experimented with using Twitter data to predict price variations for certain favored commodities in Indonesia: beef,

---

[70] Pulse Lab Jakarta, *supra* note 41
[71] Ibid., at 7, 26.
[72] Anthea Webb and Derval Usher, "A New Tool for Assisting Vulnerable Populations During Droughts" (*Medium*, February 28, 2017), <https://medium.com/pulse-lab-jakarta/a-new-tool-for-assisting-vulnerable-populations-during-droughts-a54e5022cb9e> (accessed October 10, 2022).
[73] Pulse Lab Jakarta, *supra* note 41, at 20.
[74] Pulse Lab Jakarta, *supra* note 41, at 5, 9.
[75] Webb and Usher, *supra* note 72.

chicken, onion, and chili.[76] PLJ later incorporated a practice of paying people to visit local markets and upload images depicted market prices for specified commodities. While the practice was short-lived, one interviewee familiar with the project described this payment as a mechanism for "empowering the citizen to go in and capture this data by themselves, so creating data where it was not."[77] However briefly the pay-for-data practice endured in this context, the importance of "empowerment" through data creation is a recurring motif in digital humanitarian work, particularly in relation to digital interfaces that deal with rapid-onset emergencies.

As to the substance of the humanitarian emergency that VAMPIRE represents, the problem of food insecurity was at least initially framed at this interface as a product of the dynamic conjunction of climactic and market factors. Once the idea of incorporating market price data was abandoned during its development, however, VAMPIRE came to depict food insecurity as an ever-present phenomenon (albeit in different degrees). The design of this interface suggested that the onset of some level of food insecurity could be expected at all times, seemingly without regard to changes in political decision-making or economic policy settings.

For all the ubiquity of food insecurity at this interface, however, what is made actionable by VAMPIRE is not *any* instance or public complaint of hunger or malnutrition, but rather a very particular conception of vulnerability to food insecurity. VAMPIRE equates vulnerability worthy of users' attention to the incidence of "small-scale farmers . . . living below or close to the poverty line and without irrigation."[78] When such persons are located in areas affected by rainfall anomalies, VAMPIRE encourages users to look again. VAMPIRE thus singles out a particular subset of the many "poor and vulnerable" people living in rural Indonesia: namely, small-scale farmers without irrigation.[79] In so doing, VAMPIRE narrows users' aperture of attention to only a fraction of those demonstrably vulnerable to food shortages and food price increases. This is notwithstanding evidence of far more prevalent hunger: according to the Asian Development Bank's data for the 2017–2019 period, 9 percent of Indonesians were undernourished, and in the WFP's August 2021 reporting, 28 percent of Indonesian children under 5 years of age exhibited the effects of chronic

---

[76] UN Global Pulse, "Project Brief: Nowcasting Food Prices in Indonesia Using Social Media Signals" (*UN Global Pulse*, January 2014), <https://www.unglobalpulse.org/document/nowcasting-food-prices-in-indonesia-using-social-media-signals/> (accessed October 10, 2022).
[77] Interview with Participant A (August 21, 2015).
[78] Ibid 8.
[79] Laura Ralston and Sailesh Tiwari, "No One Left behind: Rural Poverty in Indonesia" (*World Bank May*, 2020) 18, <https://openknowledge.worldbank.org/bitstream/handle/10986/34163/No-One-Left-Behind-Rural-Poverty-in-Indonesia.pdf> (accessed October 10, 2022).

malnutrition in 2020.[80] Faced with the many critical problems of food insecurity and undernourishment confronted by Indonesians, VAMPIRE makes a relatively narrow, discrete selection of these problems tractable, beginning with the translation of their plight into a problem of data deficiency. Moreover, possible connections between those specific areas highlighted for users' attention elude the digital interface entirely.

Moreover, the fact that avoidance of the kind of public discontent evident in 1998 was cited by VAMPIRE's creators as a motivating factor in its development conveyed an impression of hunger as most problematic when translated into "voice" or public protest.[81] Visualized instead as an information problem that the interface itself might address, VAMPIRE made food insecurity seem already well in hand.

VAMPIRE also reinforces the dependence of digital interfaces' design upon the apparent readiness-to-hand of certain data and resources—that is, the contingency of the way that they ultimately come to configure humanitarian emergencies. According to one public account, VAMPIRE's creation was attributable to the gathering in Jakarta of professionals with relevant expertise, interests, and technologies: several key officials within the WFP arrived in Jakarta in 2014 "looking for an opportunity to work with PLJ"; a Geographic and Information System (GIS) analyst came on board who was "looking for an organization at which [they] could evaluate and improve GIS processes"; and PLJ's Chief Data Scientist "had been experimenting with Twitter data analysis" and "saw this as a logical extension of that work."[82] As to their readiness-to-hand, one PLJ publication quoted a WFP source saying that "[a] concept—for what would become VAMPIRE—became clearer, and it also became clear that producing it wasn't going to be that difficult."[83]

VAMPIRE likewise accords with the tendency, identified earlier, for digital interfaces to take on the task of waiting, representing emergencies as forever emergent, and demanding constant vigilance. No longer need users seek out information on emergency conditions in the first instance; VAMPIRE takes on the task of watchfulness and early warning. Indeed, VAMPIRE has reportedly "been swallowed up by the [Indonesian] government's Early Warning System."[84]

This digital vigilance brings users closer to occupying a "real time" proximate to emergency—albeit perhaps not as close as initially hoped. Despite the stated

---

[80] Asian Development Bank, "Poverty: Indonesia" (*Asian Development Bank*, May 14, 2021), <https://www.adb.org/countries/indonesia/poverty> (accessed October 10, 2022); World Food Programme, "WFP Indonesia Country Brief" (2021), <https://www.wfp.org/countries/indonesia> (accessed October 10, 2022).
[81] Pulse Lab Jakarta, *supra* note 41, at 5, 12, 23.
[82] Pulse Lab Jakarta, *supra* note 41, at 5, 9.
[83] Ibid., 7.
[84] Ibid., 19.

aspiration of the WFP that VAMPIRE might promote "more real-time analysis" than could be garnered from the National Food Security and Vulnerability Atlas (developed by the WFP and Indonesia's Food Security Agency in 2015), the temporal window of the VAMPIRE never came very close to real time during the pilot phase.[85]

Nonetheless, VAMPIRE does seemingly help government users draw closer to the now. At the time of VAMPIRE's initial development, food shortage reporting in Indonesia was manual and infrequent, with scarcity figures only updated once a year.[86] As of December 2018, Indonesia's national food security assessment, which incorporated VAMPIRE data, was updated every few weeks—at least 26 times a year. This signaled a dramatic increase in the timeliness of food security information available to decision makers in the Indonesian government.[87]

As in other digital interfaces representing humanitarian emergencies, this proximity to an ever-charged present tends to make the future harder to imagine. VAMPIRE does look forward, but only over a very short horizon, attentive to the challenges of forecasting. For the WFP, for example, VAMPIRE has reportedly become "the go-to source on looking forward as to what food security is going to be doing . . . which is particularly helpful when we know that the weather is less predictable than it used to be."[88] VAMPIRE "look[s] forward" but only far enough to recognize that conditions are far "less predictable than [they] used to be." Beyond that, it fosters only the vaguest and most generalized aspirations for some digitally empowered future. When digital humanitarian interfaces such as VAMPIRE fill users' screens with pointillist perils in the present, it potentially becomes harder for those users to draw links between those points and envision how relations among them could potentially be redrawn.

## *HungerMap LIVE*

Humanitarian emergencies are being remade at another digital interface designed to assist those charged with distributing food aid or advocating for its distribution: HungerMap LIVE. In 2018, to try to address omissions and obstacles in its efforts to monitor food security around the globe, the WFP entered into a "partnership" with the Alibaba Foundation. The Alibaba Foundation is a private charitable organization, based in Hangzhou, China, established and funded by the Alibaba Group, a multinational retail, e-commerce, technology, and investment company listed on the New York and Hong Kong

---

[85] Ibid., 7.
[86] Interview with Participants A and B (November 27, 2018).
[87] "Internal Presentation by A and B" (December 4, 2018).
[88] Pulse Lab Jakarta, *supra* note 41, at 22.

stock exchanges. The stated aim of that WFP-Alibaba partnership was to support efforts to achieve Sustainable Development Goal (SDG) 2—the ending of hunger, achievement of food security, improvement of nutrition, and promotion of sustainable agriculture—by tapping the "support and expertise of the Alibaba Group" to "help WFP become even more efficient and effective in its work."[89] HungerMap LIVE is one of the outputs of this partnership. In September 2019, WFP Executive Director David Beasley and Eric Jing of the Alibaba Group announced the creation of a new monitoring system called HungerMap LIVE, saying: "HungerMap LIVE monitors food security in more than 90 countries and issues predictions for places where data is limited."[90] Initially using data from 63 countries over 14 years, the WFP trained machine learning models to generate projections of food insecurity (with "projections" not implying forecasts but rather estimates of current or very recent food insecurity in areas from which insufficient data is available that are instead derived from data drawn from other areas).[91]

HungerMap LIVE presents users with a composite of data relating to food security, weather, population size, conflict, hazards, nutrition information, and macro-economic data. Its main feature is a map on which the prevalence of insufficient food intake at the first administrative level (that is, the highest-level subnational administrative unit in a given nation-state) is visualized through a color scheme of greens, yellows, and reds, and population density is indicated through brightness. When a user places a cursor above a particular administrative unit within any nation-state depicted, two "scores" appear, one indicating the prevalence of people with "insufficient" food consumption (FCS) and one signaling the prevalence of people with a "crisis" or "above crisis" rating on the reduced coping strategy index (rCSI). The stated aim of doing so is to help users—"WFP staff, key decision makers and the broader humanitarian community"—to assess, monitor, and predict the magnitude and severity of hunger in near-real time.[92]

The two scores on which users of this digital interface are invited to focus, in relation to any given subnational administrative unit, are calculated using one of two methods. For one subset of nation-states depicted, they are calculated from actual data gathered by using digital technology to replicate traditional

---

[89] World Food Programme, "News Release: WFP and Alibaba Enter Strategic Partnership to Support UN Sustainable Development Goal of a World with Zero Hunger" (November 5, 2018), <https://www.wfp.org/news/wfp-and-alibaba-enter-strategic-partnership-support-un-sustainable-development-goa>.

[90] MVAMBLOG, "Introducing HungerMap LIVE," (*MVAM: THE BLOG*, October 22, 2019), <https://mvam.org/2019/10/22/introducing-hunger-map-live/>.

[91] Anna Gustilo Ong, "WFP Launches HungerMap Live" (*WFP Stories*, January 20, 2020), <https://www.wfp.org/stories/wfp-launches-hungermap-live> (accessed October 10, 2022).

[92] World Food Programme, "HungerMap LIVE," <https://hungermap.wfp.org/>.

survey methods. The WFP randomly dials phones in selected countries and uses computer-assisted telephone interviewing (CATI) to collect data on demographic variables, food consumption, coping strategies used, and access to food, market, and health services. Data is collected on a rolling basis; it is processed and updated on HungerMap LIVE daily. For another subset of nation-states, in which ongoing data collection of this kind is not conducted, the FCS and rCSI are outputs of a machine learning process. The WFP used the Extreme Gradient Boosting algorithm—an "ensemble of regression trees"—to develop models that generate estimates of the prevalence of food insecurity (FCS or rCSI) for any given administrative unit after training on survey-based calculations of FCS and rCSI from over 70 nation-states. The inputs for these models include the last available measure of FCS and rCSI for that area, as well as data on population density, rainfall, vegetation status, conflict, market prices (such as the WFP's own alert for price spikes (ALPS) indicator), macroeconomic indicators, and undernourishment, drawn from a range of governmental sources, international organizations' reporting, and commercial sources (including the New York–based, commercial macroeconomic data provider, Trading Economics).[93]

As to the question around whom this digital interface is oriented, the answer is, primarily, the WFP itself and the "governments, UN agencies, local/international NGOs, regional bodies and academic institutions" with which it works.[94] It is these figures whose prospective agency and immediate needs loom largest in the world of HungerMap LIVE. Although the interface is ostensibly addressed to the broader humanitarian community and is available for anyone to access online, the constituency at which HungerMap LIVE is primarily aimed is comprised of professionals already concerned with hunger and wanting to know where and when to direct or intensify their efforts.

In contrast to some discussed elsewhere in this book, this digital interface does not presume that everyone and anyone can remedy the plight of those whose unsated hunger it represents. What it does presume is that everyone and anyone can watch and wait as governments and international organizations act on that plight (or do not) with the support of a publicly available website. The WFP's capacity to raise funds from individual giving has been hampered by low levels of historic funding from such sources and poor "brand awareness"; the extent to which it should be investing to try to raise greater private income remains a matter of dispute within the organization.[95] The orientation of HungerMap LIVE

---

[93] Ibid.
[94] World Food Programme, "Vulnerability Analysis and Mapping: Food Security Analysis at the World Food Programme" (November 2018), <https://docs.wfp.org/api/documents/WFP-0000040024/download/>.
[95] WFP Office of Evaluation and Avenir Analytics, "Strategic Evaluation of Funding WFP's Work" (*World Food Programme*, 2020), Evaluation Report OEV/2019/018 34, <https://docs.wfp.org/api/documents/WFP-0000116029/download/> (accessed October 10, 2022).

toward governmental and intergovernmental officers has been designed accordingly, but the availability of this tool online nonetheless gestures toward larger audiences of would-be supporters.

To convey a sense of why HungerMap LIVE is addressed primarily to the WFP and its government collaborators and only secondarily to the public, some background is called for. The WFP was created in 1961, initially as a three-year experiment, under the joint auspices of the United Nations and the FAO, for the distribution of food to promote economic and social development.[96] Its remit later expanded to include meeting refugee and other emergency and protracted relief food needs and promoting world food security.[97] Hunger mapping was not, however, originally part of its mandate. As the WFP sought to service an expanding range of constituencies while operating on comparatively limited resources, it became invested in collecting and presenting information about food security in cartographic form to try to predict famines and rationalize and target the distribution of emergency relief. To this end, the WFP established a cartography unit called Vulnerability Analysis and Mapping (VAM) in 1994 to provide technical services to decision makers in WFP's central office in Rome and regional and national offices.[98] Since then, VAM (together with its subsequent offshoots, mVAM and the Hunger Monitoring Unit) have aided in the assemblage and analysis of information for the design, implementation, and evaluation of all the WFP's country programs.[99] The WFP currently employs around 200 analysts across 80 countries who are supported by VAM to try to ensure the "most efficient use of humanitarian resources by allocating funding according to needs."[100]

VAM has supported WFP country officials' production of historical data sets on socioeconomic variables, food aid deliveries, agricultural land use, rainfall, soil moisture content, market and price movements, and basic infrastructure and logistical data, as well as providing WFP country offices with GIS software for mapping available data. The data that VAM assembles comes from a range of sources. For example, VAM uses satellite data obtained from publicly available government sources and educational institutions. To meet its data needs,

---

[96] See "World Food Programme," UNGA Res. 1714 (XVI) (December 19, 1961) UN Doc. A/RES/1714(XX).
[97] See World Food Programme, *General Regulations and General Rules* (January 2014), <https://docs.wfp.org/api/documents/eef12dfcbda04bddb7012f9c5002f356/download/> (accessed October 10, 2022).
[98] D. Shaw, *The World's Largest Humanitarian Agency—The Transformation of the UN World Food Programme and of Food Aid* (Palgrave Macmillan Limited, 2011).
[99] P. Recalde, "An Overview of Vulnerability Analysis and Mapping (VAM)" (*United Nations*, 2000), <https://web.archive.org/web/20061122074817/https://www.un.org/Depts/Cartographic/ungis/meeting/march00/documentation/wfp_recalde2.pdf> (accessed October 10, 2022).
[100] World Food Programme, *supra* note 94.

however, the WFP has sometimes initiated primary data collection of its own, as is apparent in the HungerMap LIVE interface's use of CATI data.[101]

Since 2013, the WFP has included mobile phone surveys among its data collection techniques. That is, it initiated practices of calling or texting people who may be affected by hunger to track the food security situation in various countries, adding the results to its VAM services. Mobile phone surveys allowed the WFP to obtain up-to-date information more quickly and cheaply from conflict-affected and hard-to-reach areas than alternative survey methods.[102] Nevertheless, challenges to the WFP's food security monitoring efforts persisted, in part because certain areas and people may not reliably be accessed through mobile phones. Such peoples' food security and vulnerabilities to hunger have continued to comprise blank spots in the WFP's hunger mapping work: areas of "no data" or data restricted to "high administrative level[s]," on which the organization has been fixated for some time.[103]

In its apparent filling of these blanks, HungerMap LIVE is among those measures that help generate a sense of progress in and around the WFP: a sense of the organization "mapping [its] way" toward realization of SDG 2, the goal of achieving "zero hunger."[104] To those who fund the organization, and work in and with it, HungerMap LIVE offers confirmation that the WFP is "at the forefront of innovation in the humanitarian world."[105]

For all the surrounding talk of "daily snapshots" and "pinpoint locations," it is the would-be distributors of food aid with whom the WFP works, not its ultimate beneficiaries, who are the main protagonists of the emergency world that the HungerMap LIVE digital interface evokes, their actions made observable by the internet-using public. Those who are experiencing hunger are apparent only as embedded drivers of color change on this interface from cool tones to a more alarming orange or red. The primary emphasis of the digital interface is on those who may be alerted and moved to action by this color change, not those whose suffering is implied by it.

As to the other constitutive elements of the humanitarian emergencies that HungerMap LIVE visualizes, it "presents [these] as a continuing series of problems, challenges and impulsions . . . requir[ing] constant attentiveness and activity": elements that, as Nate Tkacz has observed, are characteristic of digital interfaces configured as dashboards.[106] In this era of dashboard fever, many

---

[101] Recalde, *supra* note 99.
[102] Jean-Martin Bauer, "Mobile Phone Surveys Can Help World Food Programme Reach Hungry People" *The Guardian* (March 10, 2016).
[103] MVAMBLOG, "Mapping Our Way towards Zero Hunger" (*MVAM: THE BLOG*, July 20, 2018), <https://mvam.org/2018/07/20/mapping-our-way-towards-zero-hunger-2/>.
[104] Ibid.
[105] MVAMBLOG, *supra* note 90.
[106] Nate Tkacz, "Connection Perfected: What the Dashboard Reveals" (Digital Methods Initiative Winter School, Amsterdam, January 16, 2015).

digital interfaces take this form. In HungerMap LIVE's case, a sense of emergency in constant flux is reinforced by the ever-changing, country-specific newsfeed that appears in the lower corner of the screen after one selects a particular nation-state from those listed on the drop-down menu. So represented, the humanitarian emergency appears heterogenous, overdetermined, and ubiquitous; it is less the striking exception than the information-saturated norm.

At the same time, HungerMap LIVE still seeks to represent humanitarian emergencies as actionable in a tempered, targeted way. Its design as a dashboard is key to this representation of actionability. The dashboard, Tkacz has reminded us, was originally a physical barrier designed to keep a horse-drawn carriage driver clean of mud thrown up by a horse's heels. It remained primarily protective in early automobile designs. Only later, in the early twentieth century, did "this plank of protective wood [become] slowly garnished with a range of technical instruments—gauges, meters, indicators and warning signals," all aimed at moderating the drivers' attention and informing their reflexes or minute-by-minute decision-making. Because "the information that it conveys is entirely based on the [presumed] needs and perceptual capacities of the driver," or in this instance, the would-be provider of emergency relief, a dashboard "tell us more about the act of driving [or, for our purposes, allocating humanitarian resources] than the operation of the engine" or the plight of those in its path.[107]

Now digitized, dashboards such as HungerMap LIVE still shield their users from the "mud": both the mud of humanitarian emergency itself and the messy, inexact, politically charged process of generating data in, on, and from humanitarian emergency with a view to controversial resource allocation. Notwithstanding the window that HungerMap LIVE's explanatory glossary and methodology section open onto the challenges and choices underpinning it, HungerMap LIVE remains a relatively clean, frictionless, user-friendly interface. Dashboards like HungerMap LIVE do not block encounters with or perceptions of emergency (as original dashboards did the muddy horses' heels striking the street) so much as filter and optimize these inputs to teach those using the dashboard where, when, and how to act, all without suggesting what the full range of possible actions might be. The effects of any such action then become apparent insofar as they change the configuration of the dashboard. This creates a continuous feedback loop: "[T]he purpose of [the] system [becomes] what it does" and what it shows.[108] HungerMap LIVE does not prevent its users from taking action outside its bounds or in ways that might not register as success on its color scale, but it does make the routes that it lays out—routes leading to more gap-filling data-gathering—seem the most readily available to take.

[107] Ibid.
[108] Stafford Beer, "What Is Cybernetics?" (2002) 31 *Kybernetes* 209, 217.

So framed, the humanitarian emergency becomes cybernetic: concerned with realizing systemic steerage possibilities through recursive communication leveraging intrinsic mechanisms of control.[109] Yet the kind of humanitarian action HungerMap LIVE invites is less that of the cybernetic manager of Stafford Beer's twentieth-century imagination: planning adaptively, junking aberrant inputs, effecting low-level responses to try to ensure overall systemic viability.[110] Instead, the user of HungerMap LIVE is invited to engage in something closer to "making do with what we have."[111] Moreover, any call to action that the interface issues is notably stripped of sentiment. Beyond the sense of urgency that HungerMap LIVE's color scheme engenders and the starkness of many of the figures presented, no effort is made to elicit judgments of the "deservingness" of those experiencing hunger, to evoke pathos, or to engender experiences of "intimacy at a distance" on which calls to action in humanitarian emergencies have so often depended.[112] These are among the ways in which HungerMap LIVE encourages users to experience humanitarian emergencies anew—and modifies the forces at work in the international humanitarian field.

As with VAMPIRE, the temporality of HungerMap LIVE is a relentlessly perilous present. The continuously updating interface combines disparate temporalities without drawing attention to their divergence. Data on different geographical areas is updated at different intervals. Phone survey data is collected on a rolling basis and "spread evenly over a past 28/30 calendar days or over a three-month period," and daily updates are generated on that basis with "a slight time lag of 2–4 days to ensure data quality."[113] Meanwhile, machine learning inputs are reported at different intervals, some weekly, some quarterly, some annually. Nonetheless, HungerMap LIVE does not distinguish between these different time scales. Their edges are smoothed, and their junctions made seamless; they are all made to speak to the "near-real time" on which the interface places emphasis. Unlike many humanitarian communications in the past, HungerMap LIVE does not depict the hungry on "a journey or trajectory" toward improvement over the longer term.[114] Nor is this interface attuned to tracking how a slow-onset humanitarian emergency "emerges gradually over time."[115]

---

[109] Norbert Wiener, "Cybernetics" (1948) 179 *Scientific American* 14; Beer, *supra* note 108.

[110] Stafford Beer, "Cybernetics—A Systems Approach to Management" (1972) 1 *Personnel Review* 28; Stafford Beer, *Brain of the Firm: The Managerial Cybernetics of Organization* (2nd ed., J. Wiley, 1981).

[111] Chandler, *supra* note 31, at 157.

[112] Irene Bruna Seu, "'The Deserving': Moral Reasoning and Ideological Dilemmas in Public Responses to Humanitarian Communications" (2016) 55 *British Journal of Social Psychology* 739; Shani Orgad and Bruna Irene Seu, "'Intimacy at a Distance' in Humanitarian Communication" (2014) 36 *Media, Culture & Society* 916.

[113] World Food Programme, *supra* note 92.

[114] Seu, "'The Deserving,'" *supra* note 112, at 744.

[115] OCHA Policy Development and Studies Branch, *supra* note 7, at 3–4.

The present—and the challenge of making that present more "data rich" or "spectacular"—take precedence when humanitarian emergencies are so visualized.[116]

## Conclusion

Returning to the question with which this chapter began—how humanitarian emergencies are transformed when encountered via digital interfaces—it is clear that not everything about emergencies so digitized is shiny and new. Digital interfaces designed to inform and guide action on humanitarian emergencies, such as Haze Gazer, VAMPIRE, and HungerMap LIVE, mobilize and depend on emergency logics long prevalent in law, politics, and economic policy on the international plane. They are also informed by the preoccupations of, and conflicts within, the organizations underwriting their development: UN Global Pulse, PLJ, the Indonesian government, the WFP, as well as their commercial "partners," Twitter and Alibaba.

Nonetheless, there are recurrent patterns apparent in emergency-making via digital interfaces. They tend to make humanitarian emergencies everyone's and no one's business: potentially detectible by a much broader constituency via the internet, yet actionable only in relatively narrow, predefined ways. In the case of Haze Gazer, those affected by haze in and around Indonesia are invited to voice and "share" their experiences via Twitter, YouTube, and the like. The fact of these mediated voices registering on Haze Gazer became a sort of immediate proxy for government attention and policy response. Nothing is said on the interface itself about what response might be appropriate, but the interface nonetheless engendered a sense of the public having been heard. VAMPIRE likewise focuses public attention on the novelty of the tools that national government officials have at their disposal including the (yet unrealized) prospect of members of the public receiving text message alerts when at risk of being affected. This serves to gently shepherd public attention away from the kinds of public protests that were provoked by food shortages and price spikes in Indonesia in 1998. HungerMap LIVE casts the public in more of an observer role. In effect, it asks those accessing the public website to watch as the WFP and other humanitarian professionals may be envisaged using the interface to calibrate and target their available resources toward areas of greatest need.

Read together, these digital interfaces tend to make of haze and hunger less matters of mainstream contestation, claim-making, and investment over the long term than matters of experts, officials, and other specialized personnel

---

[116] Árpád Rab, "Social Media and Emergency—New Models and Policies Enhancing Disaster Management" (2015) *X ME.DOK Média-Történet-Kommunikáció* 45.

doggedly working through a carefully graduated, color-coded, up-to-the-minute list of priorities. Digital humanitarian interfaces surely do not foreclose public protest or political organizing; indeed, one could envision their "misuse" for such purposes (as will be discussed in Chapter 7). Yet these interfaces do, on their face, seem to direct users' attention toward other endeavors: data-generation and -gathering, for instance.

As depicted on digital interfaces, humanitarian emergencies are shaped to fit the solution that these interfaces appear to offer, that is, emergencies are remade as computable problems and dilemmas arising from a paucity of data. Viewed through Haze Gazer, the mortality, morbidity, and economic loss attributable to haze become problems of data deficiency: governmental reliance on poor data, or the historic inattention of government to public pleas of the kind made through social media. VAMPIRE translates food insecurity vulnerability analysis into a tractable dilemma amenable to computation, namely, the exposure of "small-scale farmers ... living below or close to the poverty line and without irrigation" to anomalous weather events. HungerMap LIVE represents global hunger cybernetically (as a continuous, communicative feedback loop created with a view to systemic optimization and control) but dispenses entirely with twentieth-century cyberneticians' aspiration to overhaul "faulty systems... [that] have become robust."[117] Despite its data composites implying significant relations between hunger and macroeconomic policy settings, HungerMap LIVE does not suggest that the global system of food distribution is amenable to ambitious policy reform. Rather, it directs policymaking attention toward piecemeal measures that might move selected subnational zones from red to green in near-real time.

The temporalities and rhythms with which humanitarian emergencies are inflected by these digital interfaces are also noteworthy. Humanitarian emergencies are made cyclical and recurrent by these interfaces—and demanding of continual vigilance. No longer, it seems, is the humanitarian emergency that which "suspends" time; instead, the "crisis situation" comes to signify or occupy the "dead time" of waiting—an inversion of the scenario sketched by Pierre Bourdieu.[118] Through the emphasis that they place on continual watchfulness—a task that digital interfaces take on, on behalf of their users—the digital interfaces described in this chapter foster a more generalized sense of "chronic waiting," the proliferation of which has been documented by the geographer Craig Jeffrey and others.[119] Insofar as waiting is often identified with submission (by Bourdieu, among others), these interfaces engender

[117] Beer, "Cybernetics—A Systems Approach to Management," *supra* note 110, at 37.
[118] Pierre Bourdieu, *Pascalian Meditations* (Richard Nice tr., Stanford University Press, 2000).
[119] Jeffrey, *supra* note 53.

dispositions of hyperattentive acceptance, all (ironically) in the name of making the conditions that they represent newly actionable with a view to a brighter future for Humanity. Again, the point is not that digital humanitarian interfaces will cause people to accept suffering uncomplainingly in all cases. Rather, read as interventions in a sensory economy (whereby international organizations' tools and techniques help structure perception and distribute global attention), these interfaces incline users toward acceptance of moderate management over agitation for change.

Admittedly, it would be a stretch to argue that digital interfaces of the kind discussed in this chapter are changing the way that humanitarian emergencies are understood and experienced comprehensively. Their take-up still appears to be quite limited, as noted in Chapter 3. From the vantage point of most mainstream, mundane practice in the international humanitarian field, they might well appear ornamental rather than pivotal. Nonetheless, such digital interfaces are frequently championed as harbingers of things to come, and they continue to attract material and rhetorical investment within international humanitarian organizations; in these ways, as well as others, they loom far larger in humanitarian imaginations than the limited extent of their use might suggest.

To grasp the significance of these transformations on legal and policy debates and practices, consider an improbable counterscenario: the translation of debates over tax law and policy into a comparable format. Some researchers have observed that climactic conditions already have a significant impact on tax revenues.[120] Others have been exploring possibilities for real-time tax revenue forecasting.[121] On this basis, one could perhaps imagine international organizations constructing a digital interface to show vulnerabilities in the public fisc in relation to climate-change-related anomalies in near-real time around the world and to direct international humanitarian professionals' and government officials' attention to addressing its "hot zones."

Such a project is improbable, however, because tax law and policy tend to be cast as a confounding mix of untouchable complexity and political sensitivity, as well as being domains in which the strategic range of action is often understood to be constrained by the prevailing entanglement of public and privatized forms of governance.[122] It would be improbable to envision tax law and policy as incidents of climactic conditions or to contemplate international humanitarian

---

[120] Mihai Mutascu, "Influence of Climate Conditions on Tax Revenues" (2014) 8 *Contemporary Economics* 315.

[121] See, e.g., Yu Zhilou and Ji Hua, "Research of Tax Revenue Intelligent Forecast System" (International Forum on Information Technology and Applications, Kunming, July 16–18, 2010).

[122] John Snape, "Tax Law: Complexity, Politics and Policymaking" (2015) 24 *Social & Legal Studies* 155.

professionals deploying in a tax-related humanitarian emergency, because tax law and policy are so intensely, controversially political in most accounts—typically perceived as the outcome of highly charged, ongoing negotiation. The WFP does speak to tax law and policy obliquely—in its support for national safety nets, for instance.[123] Yet the prospect of the WFP creating and sharing publicly a digital interface designed to facilitate targeted action by humanitarian professionals to address shortfalls in tax revenues in near-real time is at the very least unlikely—perhaps even unthinkable. It is certainly unimaginable to envision the WFP doing so in partnership with Alibaba, a close collaborator of the Chinese government.[124]

It is telling, in comparison, that digital interfaces of the kind discussed in this chapter characterize air quality, hunger, and food insecurity as matters amenable to real-time or near-real-time humanitarian response by international humanitarian organizations as well as national government officials—and relatively uncontroversially so. It is a precondition for their being so framed that haze, hunger, and food insecurity be presumptively detached from the kinds of highly charged political negotiations understood to surround issues of tax law and policy and prospects for their reform. The link to weather and climatic conditions—noteworthy in Haze Gazer and VAMPIRE and, to a lesser extent, in HungerMap LIVE—is one means of effecting this detachment. Real-time or near-real-time representation is a second mechanism of severance. What is placed resolutely beyond the purview of these digital interfaces—and those guided by them—is any wholesale evaluation of systems of global food production and distribution, including mechanisms by which food production and distribution are financed, or any critical scrutiny of their public and private law and policy ramparts.

Watching and waiting is, above all, the activity that the digital interfaces discussed in this chapter encourage, although further action is always anticipated by them as well. And watching and waiting are often derided as superfluous—as squandered labor or mere loitering, as Achille Mbembe has observed.[125] Craig Jeffrey has suggested that we need not think of waiting in this way. In his research on youth unemployment in Northern India, Jeffrey observed waiting being carried out as "an active, conscious, materialized practice in which people forge new political strategies, in which time and space often become the

---

[123] World Food Programme, "WFP's Safety Net Policy: The Role of Food Assistance in Social Protection—Update 2012" (June 2012), <https://www.wfp.org/publications/wfps-safety-net-policy-role-food-assistance-social-protection>.
[124] Fu Lai Tony Yu, "Private Enterprise Development in a One-Party Autocratic State: The Case of Alibaba Group in China's E-Commerce" (2018) 54 *Issues & Studies* 1850001.
[125] Achille Mbembe, "Aesthetics of Superfluity" (2004) 16 *Public Culture* 373.

objects of reflection, and in which historical inequalities manifest themselves in new ways."[126] Yet whether the watching and waiting that digital humanitarian interfaces engender might be activated along these lines depends, in part, on what these interfaces are making of states and state authority—a dimension of their effects and intimations to which the next chapter will turn.

[126] Jeffrey, *supra* note 53, at 957.

# 5
# States: Analog and Digital

## Introduction

Digital interfaces have been shown so far to be altering the mapping and timing of humanitarian emergencies and the way that humans and nonhumans are aggregated and called to action for purposes of international humanitarian governance. This chapter examines what the digitization of humanitarian practice discussed in prior chapters might mean for states and for those subject to or dependent on state power—states being the traditional (albeit far from exclusive) agents in the foreground of international legal, social, political, and economic life. This chapter's tale is, in part, a story of the extension and intensification of state capacities: the kinds of effects about which many commentators and scholars of critical algorithm studies are exercised. Yet it is also a story of states' transformation: the reorientation of states' priorities and practices around digital data collection imperatives and cultivation of associated modes of governing. Rather than worrying about digital computation and artificial intelligence having "taken on the roles and register of the state," as Kate Crawford has for example,[1] this chapter explores how states may be taking on the logics of digital interfaces in their humanitarian endeavors, and with what implications.

Before surveying some indicia of states' digitization in the humanitarian field, it is important to clarify, for comparative purposes, the kinds of analog state activity that this chapter calls to mind. Accordingly, we begin by recalling something of what a state has been to students and practitioners of international humanitarianism; that is, how states have carried out activities with a primary stated goal of promoting human welfare internationally. This account cannot purport to be comprehensive or disinterested. As Samuel Moyn has observed, "perhaps the most important point about humanitarianism . . . is that there have been many alternative versions of it" and it has "always turned out to be a specific political project in practice."[2] Nonetheless, this chapter recalls states pursuing humanitarianism along three familiar tracks, with those tracks often intersecting and usually traversed concurrently.

---

[1] Kate Crawford, *Atlas of AI* (Yale University Press, 2021) 186.
[2] Samuel Moyn, *Human Rights and the Uses of History* (Verso Books, 2014) 46.

First, states have engaged independently in international humanitarian endeavors as part of the conduct of their foreign relations, especially in current and former colonial territories. Second, states have combined with other states in regional and intergovernmental collaborations, especially via international organizations, to carry out humanitarian work. Third, states have deputized, enrolled, or partnered with nonstate actors—including faith-based organizations and commercial firms—to discharge humanitarian responsibilities on their behalf internationally.

All three of these humanitarian pathways have been pursued to date predominantly according to analog logic, as explained in Chapter 2 and further later in this chapter. However, states are being rerouted somewhat from these conventional analog tracks as they have growing recourse to digital technology in their humanitarian work (although the latter retains significant analog dimensions). In that rerouting of international humanitarian practice, the logic of statehood itself has also shifted. Later in this chapter, we explore these shifts by attention to each of a state's basic, constituent elements, as classically enumerated for international legal purposes in Article 1 of the 1933 Montevideo Convention on the Rights and Duties of States: population; territory; government; and foreign (inter-state) relations and some exemplary interfaces. First, though, a preliminary question merits attention: What is this "state" with which this chapter is concerned, or how has the modern state been understood, quite apart from its doctrinal parsing in the Montevideo Convention? And how does this chapter's focus on the state sit with the foregrounding of interface effects in this book?

## Being a State

Theorization of the state has waxed and waned for centuries, but Max Weber's conceptualization of the modern state as a specific mode of rulership, forged and maintained in social struggle, has exerted persistent influence in late modern social and legal thought. To Weber, an "institutionally organized political enterprise" only warranted being called a "state" if "and to the extent that, its administrative staff [could] lay claim to a monopoly of legitimate physical force in the execution of its orders." A state was further characterized, in Weber's writing, by that claim of forceful, legitimate rule being leveled over "a definite territory."[3] Moreover, the "particular conditions of [the] modern economy," in Weber's rendition, came to "require" the "legal compulsion of the state."[4] Nonetheless, the domains in which the state might be encountered in this form are myriad. Weber

---

[3] Max Weber, *Economy and Society* (Keith Tribe tr., Harvard University Press, 2019) 135–136.
[4] Ibid., 145.

emphasized that "there is no conceivable purpose that political organisations [such as states] have not at one time or other pursued" and that activities of the modern state range "from provision of food to patronage of art."[5] In this mode, the modern state has also been a template for the international—a way of partitioning and envisioning relations across global time-space.

If one approaches the state via the interfaces generated by and identified with it, as this book advocates doing, a wide range of experiences and effects of statehood come into view. As Didier Fassin has written, any one state is "more than a bureaucracy with rules and procedures"; it is encountered and sustained through relations maintained and work done by "[o]fficers, magistrates, guards, social workers, mental health specialists" and many others, both within and outside state territory.[6] In Clifford Geertz's version, the state is a "rather hurriedly concocted social device designed to give form enough and point to a clatter of crossing desires, contending assumptions, and disparate identities."[7] The state endures and gets reproduced materially and ideationally, as numerous writers have shown, through its control of the supply of money, its "coding" of capital, its marshaling of military, carceral, and legislative force, its educational institutions, its rituals of representation and gathering (such as elections and national holidays), its patronage of the arts, and in a litany of other ways.[8] It also gets reproduced through the operation of countless interfaces through which interaction with the state is invited or simulated. Some recent forms of these interfaces will be examined in this chapter.

## The Humanitarian State, Three Ways

The focus of this chapter is not the modern state in general so much as the humanitarian state, or the state at work in the international humanitarian field. More specifically, this chapter's concern is the kinds of interface effects that are regularly produced by and identified with the state in this domain. To date, the humanitarian state has tended to carry out its work largely according to analog logic, as that was explained in Chapter 2.

---

[5] Ibid., 137.
[6] Didier Fassin (ed.), *At the Heart of the State: The Moral World of Institutions* (Pluto Press, 2015) x.
[7] Clifford Geertz, "What Is a State If It Is Not a Sovereign?" (2004) 45 *Current Anthropology* 577, 583.
[8] Karl Marx, *The German Ideology* (C.J. Arthur ed., International Publishers, 1972); Pierre Bourdieu, *On the State: Lectures at the Collège de France, 1989–1992* (David Fernbach tr., Polity Press, 2014); Katharina Pistor, *The Code of Capital: How the Law Creates Wealth and Inequality* (Princeton University Press, 2019); Dylan Riley, "The New Durkheim: Bourdieu and the State" (2015) 2 *Critical Historical Studies* 261.

We all know that the states of the world are incredibly varied in their properties and powers. Yet we rely on analogy to treat them as legally, politically, and economically comparable and to place them on a single, common plane or, as is often the case, on a developmental continuum. States must be made analogous to one another in order to be made formally equal in law. Thinking through analogy is but one form of analog logic. Not all instances of analog logic entail recourse to analogy, but to draw an analogy is to deploy analog logic, much as a protractor, a ruler, a mercury thermometer, or an accelerator pedal employs analog logic—by marking and comparing relative positions along a continuum.[9]

Statehood is typically "computed," so to speak, by reference to continuous variables and proportions, or by placing and moving units along a spectrum. According to this analog logic, as discussed in Chapter 2, each constituent unit of analysis can, in principle, be divided into ever smaller units without necessarily becoming useless or meaningless. The state may be historically preeminent, but it does not comprise an indivisible unit of analysis or a discrete phenomenon; it is typically divided into provinces, cities, and other administrative units. International law always understands states, and their constituent units, in relation to one another and according to their resemblances and differences of scale and degree. On/off distinctions are not unknown to the international legal order of states. Binary classifications such as legal/nonlegal or national/international are important in the operationalization of statehood and in states' humanitarian work. Mostly, however, government officials, international lawyers, humanitarian professionals, and others talk, think, and work along a continuum stretching from the less to the more when concerned with states' rights and responsibilities on the global plane. Accordingly, international humanitarianism today spans "a continuum from pure aid (e.g., emergency relief) to ... development."[10]

This analog logic may be contrasted with a digital logic increasingly apparent in states' humanitarian practices and investments, recalling the schematic distinction introduced in Chapter 2. Once again, in the day-to-day of states' humanitarian work, analog and digital are frequently concomitant. In lieu of stressing this entanglement, however, this chapter emphasizes the analog-digital cleavages apparent in this work to gain some leverage on what is unresolved—and might possibly be made more negotiable—within it. Digital logic bears increasingly on the humanitarian practices of states on the global plane as those practices get routed, in various ways, through digital interfaces. To grasp how this plays out, it is necessary first to recall some analog archetypes of state humanitarianism.

---

[9] Anthony Wilden, "Analogue and Digital Communication: On Negation, Signification, and Meaning," in *System and Structure: Essays in Communication and Exchange* (Tavistock Publications, 1972).

[10] Tom Arcaro, *Aid Worker Voices* (CreateSpace Independent Publishing Platform, 2016) 17.

State humanitarianism might seem to some like an oxymoron insofar as humanitarianism has often been cast as ameliorative of the excesses of state-based ordering. Pursuit of humanitarian objectives internationally has frequently been justified by reference to the limits of states capacities or wills, and the need to try to overcome those limits, often by appeal to nonstate referents (empires, peoples, individuals, markets, religious orders, humanity). When a state is said to have "failed" to maintain itself as such—or when a state is perceived as not having discharged its Hobbesian responsibility to ensure the security of those who are subject to its sovereign authority—the efforts of other states and international organizations to do things within its territory, with or without the target state's collaboration, are typically called "humanitarian."

At the other end of an analog spectrum of state capacity, relatively successful states have also frequently sought to enlarge their authority by pursuing humanitarian initiatives beyond their territorial borders. As historians Lauren Benton and Lisa Ford have shown, for example, "British officials [of the early nineteenth century] self-consciously described schemes to overhaul judicial administration in newly acquired imperial territories as projects to shore up the property rights and privileges of vulnerable people."[11] Accordingly, the first analog mode in which this chapter depicts states having engaged in humanitarian projects is in the service of maintaining or enlarging their authority, or that of the empires of which they are part.

To characterize humanitarianism as a state-promoting activity is not to depict an "autonomous humanitarian space" having been sullied and distorted by grubby sovereign avarice, as in David Rieff's rendition.[12] Rather, it is to recall a long history of humanitarian powers' and projects' co-production with powers and projects of imperialism and colonialism, as elucidated in a still-expanding body of historical scholarship scrutinizing the sixteenth to nineteenth centuries.[13] It also recalls a widely documented—if still contested—consolidation of state humanitarianism in the late twentieth century, during and after the Cold War, summed up by Jenny Edkins as follows:

---

[11] Lauren Benton and Lisa Ford, *Rage for Order: The British Empire and the Origins of International Law 1800–1850* (Harvard University Press, 2016) 88–89.

[12] David Rieff, *A Bed for the Night: Humanitarianism in Crisis* (Simon & Schuster, 2003).

[13] Peter Stamatov, *The Origins of Global Humanitarianism: Religion, Empires, and Advocacy* (Cambridge University Press, 2013); Amanda B. Moniz, *From Empire to Humanity: The American Revolution and the Origins of Humanitarianism* (Oxford University Press, 2016); Caroline Shaw, *Britannia's Embrace: Modern Humanitarianism and the Imperial Origins of Refugee Relief* (Oxford University Press, 2015); Yannan Li, "Red Cross Society in Imperial China, 1904–1912: A Historical Analysis" (2016) 27 *Voluntas: International Journal of Voluntary and Nonprofit Organizations* 2274; Penelope Edmonds and Anna Johnston, "Empire, Humanitarianism and Violence in the Colonies" (2016) 17 *Journal of Colonialism & Colonial History* <doi:10.1353/cch.2016.0013> (accessed October 10, 2022).

A series of boundary debates—about the relief-development continuum, about the degree of political involvement or "human rights advocacy" that humanitarians should engage in, about questions of "coordination" of humanitarian and military action—marked stages in the movement from relatively independent, poorly resourced and fairly marginal humanitarian groups of the Cold War period to a hugely well-resourced state humanitarianism, where the so-called "non-governmental" sector remains central, but as a subcontractor to state agencies.[14]

In practical terms, this saw humanitarian work become a core part of states' foreign relations programs and budgets—as well as their military operations (the latter a dimension of humanitarianism on which this book does not directly focus). Many states created specialized national bureaucracies dedicated to international aid, emergency relief, and development assistance during the years following the Second World War. These have continued to be key vehicles of state humanitarianism since that time. Some early illustrations are the United Kingdom's passage of the Overseas Resources Development Act establishing the Colonial Development Corporation in 1948, alongside the United States' creation, in the same year, of the Economic Cooperation Agency (to manage the European Recovery Program)—later transformed into the Mutual Security Agency in 1952 and the Agency for International Development in 1961. The year 1961 also saw Japan form an Overseas Economic Cooperation Fund and, in 1962, the Overseas Technical Cooperation Agency, with the former succeeded by the Japanese Bank of International Cooperation in 1999, and the latter incorporated into the Japan International Cooperation Agency in 1974. As historians Kevin O'Sullivan, Matthew Hilton, and Juliano Fori have observed of the various factors underpinning this version of state humanitarianism:

[D]ecades of research into the history of official [state] aid have provided us with a nuanced picture of the dynamics that drive development co-operation, from realist influence-buying to the pursuit of social-democratic principles on the world stage.[15]

The work of historian Thomas Haskell suggests that we must also take into account the "intensification of market discipline, and the penetration of that discipline into spheres of life previously untouched by it" and the effect of these upon

---

[14] Jenny Edkins, "Humanitarianism, Humanity, Human" (2003) 2 *Journal of Human Rights* 253, 254.
[15] Kevin O'Sullivan, Matthew Hilton, and Juliano Fiori, "Humanitarianisms in Context" (2016) 23 *European Review of History: Revue Européenne d'Histoire* 1, 3.

the advance of official state humanitarianism.[16] This has informed states' cost-benefit analysis around humanitarian programs, for instance.

Readers of this book have already encountered states pursuing humanitarianism in this mode—that is, as a core part of their domestic and foreign relations—and spearheading the turn to digital humanitarianism while doing so. Some of the work of Indonesia's National Development Planning Agency, known as BAPPENAS, is exemplary—through its joint venture vehicle Pulse Lab Jakarta (PLJ), for example, introduced in Chapter 1 of this book and examined in other writing.[17]

The second, related mode in which states have typically conducted their humanitarian affairs and been experienced as humanitarian actors, is by assembling themselves into various kinds of regional or transnational arrangements, including by establishing and supporting international and intergovernmental organizations. This occurred during a period of intensive institution-building in the late nineteenth century and again in the aftermath of both the First and Second World Wars. Once again, there is a rich body of historical scholarship on which to draw to understand this organizationally oriented strain of state humanitarianism, including its entanglement with colonialism. Illustrative of states' efforts—in combination with nonstate actors—to expand the reach of their humanitarian operations and aspirations via international organization was the 1863 creation of the Swiss-based International Committee of the Red Cross. This took place at a conference comprised of official state delegates as well as representatives of nongovernmental organizations. This was later complemented (and challenged) by the establishment of the League of Red Crescent Societies in 1919 by the national Red Cross societies of the United States, Great Britain, France, Italy, and Japan.[18] The League of Nations was another key site of and vehicle for state humanitarianism during the interwar period, although it was but one organization among a number that played a role in the "transnational turn" in humanitarianism after World War One.[19] Keith Watenpaugh has noted some of the distinctive features of humanitarianism of this period as follows:

---

[16] Thomas L. Haskell, "Capitalism and the Origins of the Humanitarian Sensibility, Part 1" (1985) 90 *American History Review* 339, 342.

[17] Fleur Johns, "From Planning to Prototypes: New Ways of Seeing Like a State" (2019) 82 *Modern Law Review* 833; Fleur Johns, "State Changes: Prototypical Governance Figured and Prefigured" (2022) 33 *Law & Critique*, <https://doi.org/10.1007/s10978-022-09329-y> (accessed October 10, 2022).

[18] Michael Barnett, *Empire of Humanity: A History of Humanitarianism* (Cornell University Press, 2011) 79–82; Melanie Oppenheimer et al., "Resilient Humanitarianism? Using Assemblage to Re-Evaluate the History of the League of Red Cross Societies" (2021) 43 *The International History Review* 579.

[19] Bruno Cabanes (ed.), "Human Disasters: Humanitarianism and the Transnational Turn in the Wake of World War I," in *The Great War and the Origins of Humanitarianism, 1918–1924* (Cambridge University Press, 2014).

While still possessing elements of its predecessor, modern international humanitarianism, as embodied by the League, was envisioned by its participants and protagonists as a permanent, transnational, institutional, and secular regime for understanding and addressing the root causes of human suffering. It ... was distinct in its reliance on social scientific knowledge-based approaches to the management of humanitarian problems—expanding late-nineteenth-century notions of "scientific philanthropy" on a massive scale.[20]

Some international organizations created during the interwar period remain prominent in humanitarianism today, including in digital humanitarianism—the International Labour Organization, for instance (created in 1919).[21] Some international organizations that were created well prior to that likewise feature amid digital humanitarianism—the International Telecommunication Union (or ITU, created in 1865), for example, about which we will say more later and in Chapter 6. The international organizations that feature most prominently in this book are, nonetheless, those that states established in the waning years or aftermath of World War Two, mostly in and around the United Nations. International humanitarian organizations created at that time included: the UN Relief and Rehabilitation Administration (created in 1943, later absorbed into the United Nations); the Food and Agricultural Organization (created in 1945, in turn it spawned the World Food Programme (WFP) in 1961); the UN Children's Fund (created in 1946); the World Health Organization (created in 1946); and the International Relief Organization (created in 1947, succeeded by the UN High Commissioner for Refugees in 1950). With this mid-twentieth century proliferation of international organizations, state humanitarianism (and for that matter humanitarianism by non-state actors) entered "a new phase of global governance."[22]

States' pursuit of humanitarian goals through international organizations—and those organizations' undertaking of humanitarian initiatives in their own right—have remained prominent, but these have increasingly entailed incorporation of digital technology. The ITU's efforts are indicative. In 2017, the ITU Telecommunication Standardization Sector Focus Group on Machine Learning for Future Networks including 5G inaugurated an AI [Artificial Intelligence] for Good Global Summit, to which Chapter 6 will return. This was conceived as a "meeting of United Nations agencies, AI experts, policymakers and industrialists

---

[20] Keith David Watenpaugh, "The League of Nations' Rescue of Armenian Genocide Survivors and the Making of Modern Humanitarianism, 1920–1927" (2010) 115 *The American Historical Review* 1315, 1319.

[21] See, e.g., International Labour Organization, "EIIP Technical Brief: Using Digital Technologies in Employment-Intensive Works" (International Labour Organization, July 2020).

[22] Barnett, *supra* note 18, at 110–112, 111.

[to] discuss how AI and robotics might be guided to address humanity's most enduring problems, such as poverty, malnutrition and inequality."[23] As one of our interviewees recounted, the ITU staff involved "wanted to . . . create an action oriented conference, where everything around the summit is designed to identify practical applications of AI, to advance the state of Sustainable Development Goals, and also how to scale the solutions."[24] Prototypes and "practical applications" that have emerged from these kinds of settings appear throughout this book.

The third genre of state humanitarianism—inextricably linked to the foregoing modes—has entailed states' enrolment of proxies and partners of various kinds, including faith-based organizations and commercial firms. This is a practice of some longstanding, as illustrated by the range of responsibilities of early modern charter companies. The 1602 Charter of the Dutch East India Company (the VOC), for instance, did not just delegate to that company exclusive rights to conduct trade and commerce in certain areas, including powers to appoint governors and keep armed forces in foreign places. It also charged the company with installing "officers for other essential services so to keep the establishments in good order."[25] Recent decades' research has shown that "the functions of the Company extended to . . . government responsibilities, and even . . . organizing agricultural production," as well as "regulating regimes of slavery, administering the slave trade and enforcing corvée duties" while maintaining and providing for a large casual and contract labor force.[26] It may seem anomalous to characterize a company engaged in the slave trade as a delegate or partner of the humanitarian state. Nonetheless, it remains the case that the VOC was charged with a broad range of international developmental responsibilities, all in the name of enhancing the welfare of white, Dutch people (at the expense of many non-Dutch, non-white peoples' lives). That the VOC's pursuit of these objectives entailed violence, brutality, exploitation, and dispossession has been true too of other humanitarian initiatives.[27] As well as corporations, religious organizations have likewise long been partners in the humanitarian endeavors of states—the entanglement of the Quaker anti-slavery movement of the nineteenth century with British imperial state-making being one illustration.[28]

[23] Declan Butler, "AI Summit Aims to Help World's Poorest" (*Nature*, June 6, 2017), <https://web.archive.org/web/20190430190609/https://www.nature.com/news/ai-summit-aims-to-help-worlds-poorest-1.22112> (accessed October 10, 2022).
[24] Interview with Participant X (October 17, 2019).
[25] Peter Reynders (tr.), "A Translation of the Charter of the Dutch East India Company" (Australasian Hydrographic Society, 2009), <https://rupertgerritsen.tripod.com/pdf/published/VOC_Charter_1602.pdf> (accessed October 10, 2022).
[26] Matthias van Rossum, "Labouring Transformations of Amphibious Monsters: Exploring Early Modern Globalization, Diversity, and Shifting Clusters of Labour Relations in the Context of the Dutch East India Company (1600–1800)" (2019) 64 *International Review of Social History* 19, 22.
[27] Talal Asad, "Reflections on Violence, Law, and Humanitarianism" (2015) 41 *Critical Inquiry* 390.
[28] Stamatov, *supra* note 13.

The corporate and religious entities with which states have partnered in their humanitarian efforts have not always proven amenable to state discipline. Nonstate actors exercise humanitarian authority and advance humanitarian agendas independently, not just as delegates of state power. Religious organizations have typically pitched their humanitarian missions on a larger scale than that of any one state. States' corporate and religious partners have often cut across, defied, or redirected state authority in humanitarian affairs. (Indeed, some nongovernmental humanitarian organizations refuse funding from some governments to maintain their room to maneuver vis-à-vis states; Médecins Sans Frontières is a case in point.) Even so, public-private partnerships (whether named as such or not) have been a recurrent feature of states' engagement in international humanitarian work.

If public-private partnership in the delivery of humanitarian programs has been ongoing for several centuries, its current manifestations—and its connection to the development and deployment of digital interfaces—nonetheless owe much to decisions made at the end of the twentieth century. In the 1990s, state members and leaders of the United Nations, alongside those of other international organizations, began to orient the organization around an imperative of states engaging and defending markets in their humanitarian efforts, marginalizing an approach oriented toward the meeting of "basic needs" that found favor in the 1970s.[29] This was traceable in part to the United Nations experiencing financial crisis and many contributing states undergoing public austerity programs during the 1980s.[30]

In 1997, only four weeks after his appointment as Secretary-General of the United Nations, Kofi Annan spoke at the World Economic Forum Annual Meeting in Davos-Klosters, declaring "market capitalism has no rival. . . . In today's world, the private sector is the dominant engine of growth; the principle creator of value and wealth."[31] The following year he insisted that "the business of the United Nations involves the businesses of the world."[32] By the time Annan invited business leaders to conclude the Global Compact at the 1999 World Economic Forum meeting, he was "pleased to acknowledge that, in the past two years, our relationship has taken great strides. We have shown through cooperative ventures—both at the policy level and on the ground—that the goals of

---

[29] Samuel Moyn, *Not Enough* (Harvard University Press, 2018) 189–192.

[30] Tapio Kanninen, *Leadership and Reform: The Secretary-General and the UN Financial Crisis of the Late 1980s* (Martinus Nijhoff Publishers, 1995).

[31] Quoted in Sandrine Tesner, *The United Nations and Business: A Partnership Recovered* (Macmillan, 2000) xxii.

[32] Ann Zammit, *Development at Risk: Rethinking UN-Business Partnerships* (The South Centre and UNRISD, 2003), 30, quoting United Nations Secretary-General Kofi Annan in a 1998 speech to the World Economic Forum.

the United Nations and those of business can, indeed, be mutually supportive."[33] From Annan, the message to UN member states at the close of the millennium was clear: pursue your humanitarianism through the market or you will be left behind.

In the decades since Kofi Annan's bearing-setting statements, states' humanitarian endeavors have continued to involve a range of private sector and civil society organizations. The lineup of these has, however, been somewhat reconfigured of late. New actors have come onto the scene, as foreshadowed in Chapter 1. In January 2020, for example, Microsoft opened a "representation office to the United Nations" in New York City.[34] Amazon Web Services (AWS) has been partnering with the WFP to address famines.[35] AWS also provides infrastructural support for the work of UN Global Pulse analyzed throughout this book.[36] Google is working with the UN Environment Programme.[37] Twitter entered into its collaboration with UN Global Pulse (outputs of which have been discussed in prior chapters), with the stated goal of advancing attainment of the Sustainable Development Goals (SDGs).[38] "[I]ndustry participation, from Audi ... Siemens ... Microsoft and Intel and [a] who's who [of companies] in the tech industry" has been integral, one informant told us, to the ITU's efforts to foster the development of artificial intelligence to address humanitarian needs.[39] In prior decades, multinational ITC companies such as these would not have been strongly identified with humanitarian action; today they are deeply embedded in states' and international organizations' humanitarian work and frequently perceived to be at the forefront of that work. This is but one indication of shifts in humanitarian practice that affect how states approach the task of governance and how various constituencies call upon state power on the global plane. It is to these shifts that we will now turn.

---

[33] Kofi Annan, "Secretary-General Proposes Global Compact on Human Rights, Labour, Environment, in Address to World Economic Forum in Davos Press Release SG/SM/6881" (*United Nations*, February 1, 1999), <https://www.un.org/press/en/1999/19990201.sgsm6881.html> (accessed October 10, 2022).

[34] "Microsoft Appoints Senior Government Affairs Leaders in Brussels and New York, Establishes New York Office to Work with the United Nations" (*EU Policy Blog*, January 17, 2020), <https://blogs.microsoft.com/eupolicy/2020/01/17/senior-gov-affairs-leaders-appointed-brussels-new-york/> (accessed October 10, 2022).

[35] "Helping to End Future Famines with Machine Learning" (*Amazon Web Services*, November 29, 2018), <https://aws.amazon.com/blogs/publicsector/helping-to-end-future-famines-with-machine-learning/> (accessed October 10, 2022).

[36] Interview with Participant N (April 11, 2018).

[37] "'UN Environment and Google Announce Ground-Breaking Partnership to Protect Our Planet" (*UN Environment Programme*), <https://www.unenvironment.org/news-and-stories/press-release/un-environment-and-google-announce-ground-breaking-partnership> (accessed October 10, 2022).

[38] "Twitter for Good" (*Twitter*), <https://about.twitter.com/en_us/company/twitter-for-good.html> (accessed October 10, 2022).

[39] Interview with Participant X, *supra* note 24.

## Being a Humanitarian State, Digitally

To explain the restructuring of statehood manifest in states' efforts of digital humanitarianism and at digital interfaces expressive of those efforts, this chapter works with a doctrinal archetype of statehood that will be familiar to many readers of this book. For international legal purposes, the state is classically depicted as it is in the first article of the 1933 Montevideo Convention. This treaty's formula is a law textbook staple; the lawful assertion and recognition of statehood upon independence is understood to require satisfaction of four criteria: permanent population, defined territory, government, and the capacity to enter into relations with other states.[40]

As a matter of international legal doctrine, states are not required to demonstrate satisfaction of the Montevideo criteria on an ongoing basis. Any one state's satisfaction of these four criteria is only doctrinally at issue at the point of a would-be state's assertion of independence or effort to secede. Nonetheless, it remains an expectation of legal, political, and economic relations on the global plane that states work to maintain these properties and capacities. This chapter revisits this classical recipe for what constitutes a state, internationally legally speaking, to put forward an argument as to change at the level of humanitarian practice. States are now expected to demonstrate each of these four capacities in the international humanitarian sphere by recourse to digital interfaces. The 1933 Montevideo Convention criteria still pertain as a matter of international legal doctrine to those aspiring to statehood. Nonetheless, each of the ingredients of this standard recipe for statehood is becoming increasingly *separated from itself* as a matter of states' humanitarian practice. The prevailing logic of statehood and state humanitarianism has been, in large part, an analog logic, as discussed earlier. This is now interspersed, in states' daily operations, with a digital logic, as shown in this chapter. The emergence of digital-analog conflict apparent in the mundane work of states discharging humanitarian responsibilities makes many of the inferences that international lawyers and other humanitarian professionals typically draw about states, and how they operate internationally, potentially unreliable. It is also giving rise to new measures of relative worth to which national political communities are now held when vying to establish or maintain their statehood, including their authority as humanitarian actors. States and would-be states are increasingly held to, and must struggle to meet, a standard of datafication in order to maintain their statehood's viability, as explained later.

Given the many ways in which a digital logic is permeating that of statehood, the question now posed for states is not how to "catch up" with the digital and

---

[40] Convention on Rights and Duties of States (adopted by the Seventh International Conference of American States on December 26, 1933, entered into force December 26, 1934) 165 LNTS 19.

try to enmesh it within their mostly analog regulatory nets. Such an approach externalizes forces that are already integral to the workings of statehood. Instead, the questions posed for states by developments in digital humanitarianism are something like the following. What might states and other political communities make of those digital-analog cleavages apparent in their humanitarian work? How might these cleavages be leveraged in ideological and material struggles in which states are implicated? What possibilities for reusing legal and political infrastructures and remaking legal and political relations could these schisms yet open up? Chapter 7 will have more to say on these questions. First, the argument concerning states' digitization will be laid out by reference to the four criteria of the Montevideo Convention.

This chapter returns to the Montevideo Convention of 1933 not just because of its summative doctrinal content but also to recall an earlier instance of struggle over the recoding of international legal order—struggle to which a tactical analogy is drawn here. As Arnulf Becker Lorca has observed in his book *Mestizo International Law*, the Montevideo Convention comprised part of a concerted effort by scholars, governments, and scientific associations during the first few decades of the twentieth century to "modernize the classical legal order inherited from the previous century."[41] This effort was driven in large part, Becker shows, by Latin American states and other industrializing nations of the semi-periphery. To contemporary eyes, the Montevideo Convention's stipulation of the formal requirements of statehood can seem dusty, and relevant only to a relatively small number of sites where peoples are still battling for statehood. However, Becker reminds us that "[s]een from the perspective of the semi-periphery, . . . [c]odification [of statehood] opened a precious opportunity for discussing and changing the basic structure of international law."[42] What the Montevideo Convention delivered in 1933 was a "blow to the standard of civilization"—that is, the requirement that would-be states and decolonizing peoples demonstrate that they are "civilized" enough to attain membership of the international legal community (although that standard has had a long and complex afterlife).[43] It also helped decolonized and decolonizing states to argue for "nonintervention as a consequence of [states'] equality" in international law against the incursions of ex-colonizers or powerful neighbors.[44] As such, it is a helpful reminder that elemental transformations of global order do take place periodically and will do so again. Digital humanitarianism is, in this book's account, a

---

[41] Arnulf Becker Lorca, *Mestizo International Law A Global Intellectual History 1842–1933* (Cambridge University Press, 2015) 305.
[42] Ibid., 305.
[43] On that afterlife, see, e.g., Ntina Tzouvala, *Capitalism as Civilisation: A History of International Law* (Cambridge University Press, 2020).
[44] Becker Lorca, *supra* note 41, at 307, 350.

sphere in which structural displacements and cleavages in global ordering are once again becoming apparent.

Even so, the recodification of international legal and political order underway at digital interfaces and elsewhere in the work of digital humanitarianism is of quite a different kind to that brought about by the Montevideo Convention. As indicated earlier, what is being recodified is not international legal doctrine but rather humanitarian practice and the kinds of infrastructure that such practice instantiates and demands (on which more will be said in Chapter 6). The changes highlighted in this chapter concern the day-to-day work of states maintaining themselves as states in relation to their constituents, international organizations, and other states, especially in their humanitarian endeavors—work to which the Montevideo Convention is not directly relevant. Nonetheless, the openings and instabilities that these changes intimate in international law's predominantly analog architecture go once again to the basic structures and constituent units of internationalism—those partly renegotiated at the time of that Montevideo Convention. And peoples and places in the semi-periphery and the periphery are once again crucial drivers and bearers of this change.

## Assembling a Permanent Population, Digitally

How, then, does digital logic make trouble with longstanding expectations of states having "permanent populations" attributable to and governable by them for humanitarian purposes? According to most international law commentary, the term "permanent population" connotes a relatively stable, organized community of people that a state might call its own, and for whom it assumes responsibility, allowing for diasporic affiliations and migration. In practice, it almost always implies a people counted by a census or through fiscal information-gathering and related determinations of nationality. As discussed in Chapter 3, a population, as distinct from a people or a polity, is a statistical category assembled for purposes of comparison—both internal comparison (between its constituent subcategories) and external comparison (among populations). Whether or not a state can reliably rally a "permanent population" is really only a question for debate at the point of a state's assertion of independence or secession. Even so, international humanitarian affairs are routinely conducted as if every state were—albeit in different ways—answerable to and answering for a more or less permanent population.

The way in which states lay claim to and purport to represent a population is, however, changing in ways detailed in Chapter 3. This is because states—especially states with limited resources—are increasingly looking to digital data to assist them in analyzing their populations' characteristics, preferences and conduct. States' analyses of their populations are increasingly permeated with digital logic and conducted via digital interfaces. And the digital aggregates that states assemble for analysis do not fit neatly into the statistical categories into which states have traditionally apportioned people as "populations." Governmental concern is increasingly directed toward fleeting digital aggregates and the actionable insights that they may yield. Behind this, the statistical characteristics of a biosocial corpus—that is, a permanent population—often seem to have become second-order concerns. The "permanent populations" that states seek to govern are increasingly visualized in ever-shifting real-time or near-real-time data, not in classical demographic terms. This moment-to-moment digital rendition of a state's inhabitants conflicts profoundly with the analog notion of a population bequeathed to international law by several centuries of statistical thinking. This conflict was explored in Chapter 3, so we will not revisit it here.

## Defining and Controlling Territory, Digitally

What, then, of each state's possession of a defined territory as an incident of its statehood and a way of delimiting the primary sphere of its humanitarian responsibilities? If permanent populations are giving ground to impermanent digital projections of the peoples that states aspire to govern as suggested in Chapter 3, are those people still mapped more or less onto a particular patch of the globe for international humanitarian purposes? The answer is both yes and no. Territoriality still performs the bounding, placement functions that it long has in international law. Territory still effects a presumptive distribution of resources, rights, and life prospects across the globe. It still matters, when determining international legal rights and obligations and life chances, in which state's territory a person was born, resides, and does business. Nonetheless, the way that territory is understood and analyzed for humanitarian and other purposes is being fundamentally reconfigured as states, international organizations and nongovernmental organizations turn more and more to the automated analysis of the earth's surface employing massive, distributed, digital data streams and a vast, globally dispersed infrastructure to store and transmit them.[45]

This "turn" can be observed in the Humanitarian OpenStreetMap Team (HOT) Tasking Manager interface discussed in Chapter 2: for instance, in the collaborative mapping project to update and validate maps of the road network in Senegal depicted in Figure 5.1. For this project's purposes, public,

---

[45] Fleur Johns, "Data Territories: Changing Architectures of Association in International Law," in Martin Kuijer and Wouter Werner (eds.), *Netherlands Yearbook of International Law 2016: The Changing Nature of Territoriality in International Law* (TMC Asser Press, 2017).

**Figure 5.1** Screenshot of HOT Tasking Manager: Senegal—Consolidated Mapping Projects.

© 2022 OpenStreetMap contributors. The Tasking Manager is free and open-source software developed by the Humanitarian OpenStreetMap Team. Reproduced with permission from the Humanitarian OpenStreetMap Team and under an Open Data Commons Open Database License (ODbL) v1.0 from "#1085—Senegal—[Consolidated Mapping Projects—Base Roads Check vs Open Data References]," <https://tasks.hotosm.org> (accessed October 10, 2022). Full terms available at <https://opendatacommons.org/licenses/odbl/1-0>.

open data references are employed, such as gROADS (the Global Roads Open Access Data Set, developed under the auspices of the CODATA Global Roads Data Development Task Group of the nongovernmental International Science Council), or digitized Landsat (US) and Russian topographic satellite reference data (used by the WFP).[46] Tellingly, the gROADS data set compiles road network data from multiple sources ranging in age from the 1980s to 2010 depending on the country (although most countries have no confirmed date); as a result, its "spatial accuracy varies."[47] Nonetheless, the representational value of this data derives from its use of a consistent data model and its amenability to updating. So "validated," the territory of Senegal becomes something that can, at least in principle, be assembled and reassembled moment by moment from a variety of sources, not an enduring substrate for governmental jurisdiction—as might have

---

[46] Humanitarian OpenStreetMap Team, "Consolidated Mapping Projects—Base Roads Check vs Open Data References" (*Open Street Map Wiki*), <https://wiki.openstreetmap.org/wiki/Consolidated_mapping_projects_-_base_roads_check_vs_open_data_references> (accessed October 10, 2022).

[47] Center for International Earth Science Information Network—CIESIN—Columbia University and Information Technology Outreach Services—ITOS—University of Georgia, "Global Roads Open Access Data Set, Version 1 (GROADSv1)," <https://sedac.ciesin.columbia.edu/data/set/groads-global-roads-open-access-v1> (accessed October 10, 2022).

appeared in an official state map, for instance. Fragmentation and instability are constitutive of territoriality so rendered, not undermining of it. This recalls an observation, from Chapter 2: that digital interfaces propagate a "new verisimilitude" that differs from that in which predominantly analog interfaces tend to trade.[48]

In these and other ways, territory is being increasingly "digitized" in international humanitarian work. At the same time, the territorial location of digital assets and infrastructure (such as satellite positioning) is of growing significance in international legal affairs; the digital, in other words, is ever more unevenly territorialized. Once again, this brings contemporary practices and manifestations of statehood into tension with the conventional analog architecture of international order. The location of satellites and other data-transmission and -receiving infrastructure, for example, matters enormously in enlivening or disabling states' variable information-gathering capacities. This can, in turn, have implications for human mobility as states make policy based on information so gathered. As Mimi Sheller has observed, with reference to the aftermath of the 2010 earthquake in Haiti, the opening up of territory to digital purview for purposes of disaster response often "reinforce[s] . . . uneven mobility regimes."[49]

Of course, the practice of rendering territory informational for humanitarian and other international legal purposes is not a wholly new phenomenon. The division of a spherical world into evenly spaced meridians using latitude and longitude, for example, is of ancient provenance, although it was not until the eighteenth century that these were reliably measured.[50] Furthermore, it was through a late-nineteenth-century conference and treaty regime that one such meridian became a common, international point of reference for locational and timekeeping purposes.[51] This ensured capacity to measure, survey, and describe parcels of territory with accuracy and created a way of experiencing time-space in common at a global scale—a precondition for the global framing of the humanitarian field. Datafication in this mode has long been vital to the projects and potency of humanitarianism.

The representation of territory in and as digital data has, however, intensified to a very significant degree with the advent of orbital satellites, the satellite-based radio navigation system known as the Global Positioning System and

---

[48] Roland Barthes, "The Reality Effect," in *The Rustle of Language* (University of California Press, 1969) 141.

[49] Mimi Sheller, "The Islanding Effect: Post-Disaster Mobility Systems and Humanitarian Logistics in Haiti" (2013) 20 *Cultural Geographies* 185.

[50] James Evans, *The History and Practice of Ancient Astronomy* (Oxford University Press, 1998); Nel Samana, *Global Positioning: Technologies and Performance* (Wiley, 2008).

[51] W.G. Perrin, "The Prime Meridian" (1927) 13 *The Mariner's Mirror* 109; Rebekah F. Higgitt and Graham Dolan, "Greenwich, Time and the Line" (2010) 34 *Endeavour* 35.

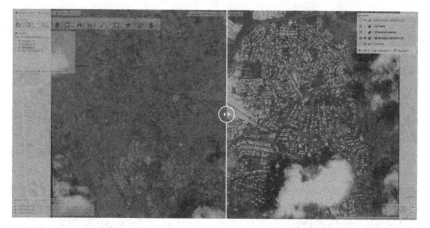

**Figure 5.2** Screenshot of UN Global Pulse showing automated analysis of slum dwellings in Uganda using PulseSatellite.
© 2022 UN Global Pulse. Reproduced with permission from UN Global Pulse, as appeared in "PulseSatellite: Human-AI Interaction for Satellite Analysis," <https://www.unglobalpulse.org/microsite/pulsesatellite/> (accessed October 10, 2022).

technologies of automatic sensing, Google mapping, and the like as discussed in Chapter 2. A profusion of sensor networks and advances in their sophistication have fostered aspirations to seed the planet with continuously operating data-collection and data-generation nodes. Digital interfaces such as PulseSatellite (a collaborative web-based tool developed by UN Global Pulse and UNOSAT (the UN Satellite Center) to extract the most relevant information from satellite imagery for use in humanitarian contexts) seek to give these continuous data streams humanitarian efficacy, as shown in Figure 5.2.[52]

This breaks with analog logics of territory because digital transmission from ubiquitous sensor nodes has, at the level of discrete pixels (in the case of images) or samples (in the case of sound), an all-or-nothing quality—a quality that can be especially appealing for humanitarian organizations operating under conditions of global uncertainty. When digitally sensed, territory can be switched on or off or made potentially actionable or not at a microscale; it becomes reproducibly discontinuous. Digitally encoded images or sounds can be transmitted in near-perfect reproduction up to the point where the noise level (or the amount of unwanted signal interference) occludes a significant number of bits, at which point their transmission will completely fail. No longer does a territory's oversight for

---

[52] Tomaz Logar et al., "PulseSatellite: A Tool Using Human-AI Feedback Loops for Satellite Image Analysis in Humanitarian Contexts" (Proceedings of the AAAI Conference on Artificial Intelligence, New York, 2020).

governance hinge upon some continuously variable (analog) physical quantity, such as positioning relative to known cultural or political landmarks.

In regulating nuclear testing with a view to safeguarding human life, for example, the Comprehensive Nuclear-Test-Ban Treaty Organization (CTBTO) operates a global network of seismic stations, hydroacoustic centers (detecting sound waves in the oceans), listening stations for atmospheric infrasound (low-frequency acoustic waves that can travel long distances), and radionuclide detecting stations.[53] With digital data so collected, the CTBTO seeks to determine when and where a nuclear device of any size is detonated and to evaluate the lawfulness of that detonation under applicable international law. Through such digital infrastructure, events become locatable with great precision without regard to claim or declaration on the part of heads of state. Digital mediation makes it seem almost as though territory might speak for itself.

Territory's digitization is also apparent in states' development work. One of the state officials with whom we spoke emphasized the potential of digital data transmitted by ubiquitous "smart meters" to augment states' statistical capacities with a view to delivering against the SDGs. Our informant began by talking about the usefulness of data sourced with participants' consent from household energy consumption meters, then continued:

[T]here are smart areas in lorries, there are smart meters in harvesters, there are smart meters in other things now, and we think that we can use that either as a new source for existing statistics or a source for new statistics. So that's what we are planning to do.[54]

Territory so "datafied" through the dispersal of "smart . . . things" and thereby made actionable to humanitarian ends still performs bounding, distributive and placement functions for international legal purposes, as noted earlier. Yet it does so in a distinctively digital mode. State territoriality becomes a matter of managing, maintaining, and analyzing a dynamic, information-rich, time-sensitive "planetary skin" comprised of discrete digital bits. The term "planetary skin" here references the work of the Planetary Skin Institute: a nonprofit organization co-founded by Cisco and NASA in 2008-2009 with the goal of building a platform for planetary eco-surveillance.[55] NASA has since made available online an

---

[53] "Monitoring Nuclear Weapons: The Nuke Detectives," *The Economist* (September 3, 2015); Timothy Oleson, "Beyond the Bomb: The World's Nuclear Watchdog Expands Its Science" (*Earth Magazine*, April 7, 2015), <https://www.earthmagazine.org/article/beyond-bomb-worlds-nuclear-watchdog-expands-its-science>.
[54] Interview with Participant R (December 4, 2018).
[55] Jonathan D. Stanley, "Planetary Skin Institute ALERTS: Automated Land Change Evaluation, Reporting and Tracking System" (*Association for Computing Machinery*, 2011), <https://dl.acm.org/doi/10.1145/1999320.1999388> (accessed October 10, 2022).

opensource virtual globe, compatible with multiple operating systems, through its NASA WorldWind initiative.[56] And Hewlett-Packard continues to advance the Central Nervous System for the Earth (CeNSE) project: a highly intelligent network of billions of nanoscale sensors designed, HP Labs say, "to feel, taste, smell, see, and hear what is going on in the world."[57] All of these projects depend on the partitioning, ordering, and naming of cells for unique spatial indexing.

Territory so digitized is less predisposed to or demanding of continual fencing and bounding in the manner conventionally required to sustain states' territorial claims, border enforcement activities, and property rights—although conventional bordering activity continues apace. Analog borders on the global plane are typically presumed to be continuous and unbroken, barring interstate disputes. Analog property rights in international law tend to vary by degrees along a spectrum: from sovereign rights of exclusion and immunity to variable rights of exploration and extraction in different domains. Digitized territory has more of a pixelated quality; it allows for much more granular differentiation between this piece of territory and that. As noted earlier, digital representations of territory suggest that states' international legal authority might be switched on or off in precise locations and at particular times. As one of our informants remarked, when speaking of the work of humanitarian mappers discussed in Chapter 2, "[w]hen HOT [that is, the Humanitarian OpenStreetMap Team] does any mapping at all we don't do boundaries and things like that."[58] Rather, HOT's concern is with assembling meaning from an array of discrete units. In Figure 5.3 we see an instance of poverty being predicted digitally by the Asian Development Bank down to the level of four square kilometer grid-spaces, with the implication that need for or entitlement to state assistance might be meted out accordingly. Meanwhile, for states, the task of patrolling state boundaries is becoming as much about data collection, indexing, distribution, curation, and personalization as it is about explicit marking of boundaries. For these reasons, states worry as much about their access and proximity to digital infrastructure—to the world's satellites and undersea cables, for instance—as they do about maintaining and defending their physical borders.

State territory so digitized fits awkwardly into conventional analog frameworks and institutions on the international plane, including those surrounding the humanitarian field. These offer relatively few means for states to contest digitized boundaries or to raise concerns about transboundary incursions or exclusions

---

[56] Francesco Pirotti et al., "An Open Source Virtual Globe Rendering Engine for 3D Applications: NASA World Wind" (2017) 2 *Open Geospatial Data, Software and Standards* 4.
[57] Hewlett-Packard, "CeNSE, HP Official Site" (2014), <https://web.archive.org/web/20211118013713/https://www.hp.com/us-en/hp-information/environment/cense.html#.YZWug-zP0lI> (accessed October 10, 2022).
[58] Interview with Participant AD (April 30, 2020).

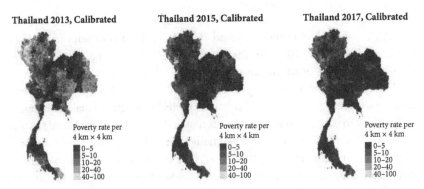

km = kilometer
Note: The images present the calibrated machine learning based estimates of poverty rates for every (approximately) 4km × 4 km grid.
Source: Calculations generated by the study team.

**Figure 5.3** Calibrated machine learning–based estimates of poverty rates for every 4 km × 4 km grid (approximately).
© 2021 Asian Development Bank. Reproduced under Creative Commons Attribution 3.0 IGO license without changes from "Mapping the Spatial Distribution of Poverty Using Satellite Imagery in Thailand" (Asian Development Bank, April 2021) 43, <https://www.adb.org/publications/mapping-poverty-satellite-imagery-thailand> (accessed October 10, 2022). Full terms available at https://creativecommons.org/licenses/by/3.0/igo/legalcode.

of a digital kind. International legal institutions continue to prioritize the resolution of conventional territorial boundary disputes and the analog delimitation of humanitarian fields. Yet unconventional disputes and complex overlaps are arising in the context of territories' digitization. In 2010, for example, just before Costa Rica instituted proceedings in the International Court of Justice (ICJ) against Nicaragua in a border dispute, Nicaraguan military and government officials admitted to an "accidental" invasion of Costa Rican territory (an incident mentioned briefly in Chapter 2). This involved Nicaraguan troops taking down a Costa Rican flag and erecting a Nicaraguan one on Costa Rican territory. The invasion was attributable, the Nicaraguan troop commander said, to an error on Google Maps that misrepresented the location of the border between the two countries by some 2.7 kilometers.[59] This did not come up explicitly in the later ICJ proceedings. Nonetheless, satellite and aerial image data were tendered in support of Costa Rica's claims that Nicaragua had been illegally dredging their territory.

---

[59] Mark Brown, "Nicaraguan Invasion? Blame Google Maps" (*Wired*, November 8, 2010), <https://www.wired.com/2010/11/google-maps-error-blamed-for-nicaraguan-invasion/> (accessed October 10, 2022).

As it happened, the court found this digital evidence (the satellite and aerial image data) "insufficient" because it was unclear; some images were obscured by the tree canopy.[60] In other words, the on/off quality of digital data rendered it useless in this instance. The court went on to chart the land and maritime boundaries between the two countries and to require Nicaragua to remove a military camp from Costa Rican territory. It had nothing at all to say, however, about the way that the two states should manage conflict in these boundaries' digital expression. Nor did the court set any limits on these states maintaining a virtual presence in each other's territory through remote sensing activities. According to the ICJ, state jurisdiction is immune to quantization noise (that is, the distortion that occurs when analog signals are converted into digital signals or vice versa); only the analog version of state authority is readable. Nonetheless, the kind of noise that became apparent at the Nicaraguan–Costa Rican border when that limit became digitally mediated could open prospects, at least in principle, for negotiability of state jurisdiction in humanitarian affairs on which more will be said later.

In so far as international law surrounding statehood, and delimitation of states' humanitarian jurisdiction, *does* speak about territory in informational terms, its conventional guidance may be unreliable when regard is had to expansive digitization of territory and the uneven territorialization of digital data. Early in the Cold War, addressing a dispute between Communist Albania and the United Kingdom in the *Corfu Channel Case*, the ICJ famously stated that "it is every State's obligation not to allow knowingly its territory to be used for acts contrary to the rights of other States."[61] This raised the prospect of states being held legally responsible—and potentially vulnerable to "humanitarian intervention" or other countermeasures—for activities traceable to their territory that unlawfully harm other states. In effect, the ICJ treated state territory as a data repository, presuming that territorial sovereignty and data sovereignty typically travel together. This is an analog framing of states' lawful responsibility because it presupposes and derives meaning from continuous variation in physical phenomena (or rather from a combination of geophysical and geopolitical phenomena). A state's territory is presumed to be charged with information in continuously varying degrees. In some areas, a government may be presumed to see and know all, while in other, more remote areas, less governmental insight and control may be presumed. The digitization of territory has, however, broken these things apart.

---

[60] *Certain Activities Carried Out by Nicaragua in the Border Area (Costa Rica v Nicaragua) and Construction of a Road in Costa Rica Along the San Juan River (Nicaragua v Costa Rica), Judgment* [2015] ICJ Rep. 665, 665, para. 81.
[61] *The Corfu Channel Case (UK v. Albania)* [1949] ICJ Rep. 4.

Capacities for insight or oversight can no longer be presumed to follow from territorial title or proximity to metropolitan centers. Rather, the distribution of such capacities is increasingly uneven. The range of devices emitting and receiving digital data, and the reproducibility and combinability of those data, together with differential access to and control over ICT infrastructure, have seen a small number of digital harvesters acquire data volumes and analytical capacity that far outstrip those of most states—data and capacity that they are typically willing to share only with paying clients. Most of these dominant data harvesters are private, but states like Bahrain, China, Denmark, Israel, Singapore, and the United States are immense data hoarders as well. As a result, some companies and some states have immense repositories of digital data pertinent to much of the world's territory. Meanwhile, many states have less data about people and devices located on their own territories than large commercial digital platforms do.

Even where it is available, though, remotely sensed digital data can obscure as much about a territory as it reveals, in part because of its binary on/off quality. As one of our informants remarked: "[W]e have no idea what's underneath that roof when we draw [a building] from satellite imagery" (as in Figure 5.2, for example).[62] That same informant recalled "the double earthquake in Nepal in 2014," remembering that "Nepal, for about seven days afterwards, was... covered in clouds and none of the satellite imagery companies could get any post-disaster imagery for us."[63] At times, these kinds of data deficits on the part of states may be treated as a mark of those states' "unwillingness and inability" to govern and used to justify even more intrusive surveillance and data-gathering on their territory, thereby entrapping the states concerned in a downward spiral of digital-data-borne domination.[64] Territory's digitization is adding new dimensions to the politics of humanitarian intervention.

Halfway through this chapter's review of the Montevideo Convention's four criteria for statehood, we can already discern some of the many digital-analog conflicts with which relations among states become riddled when statehood gets routed and received via digital interfaces in the humanitarian field. States' permanent populations are increasingly assembled in digital formats for purposes of states trying to understand, serve, and govern them through mainly analog architecture (the latter presupposing comparability and equivalence among populations). State territory is increasingly accessed and controlled in the form of disparate databases and discontinuous data streams to which very uneven access is available and which tend not to track preexisting analog political or administrative boundaries. International legal institutions—such as courts

---

[62] Interview with Participant AD, *supra* note 58.
[63] Ibid.
[64] Ntina Tzouvala, "TWAIL and the 'Unwilling or Unable' Doctrine: Continuities and Ruptures" (2015) 109 *AJIL Unbound* 266.

and tribunals—persist in their efforts to manage a global chessboard of equal sovereign states imagined on a continuum, each with a defined territory and a permanent population for whose humanitarian needs they are primarily responsible. Meanwhile, the edges and interiors of those state territories are being re-expressed in digital formats and in discrete, microscale units of which international law has little grasp. This is taking place under hybrid regimes of public and private law and the de facto jurisdiction that large digital platforms and other major commercial players enjoy—normative infrastructures about which more will be said in Chapter 6. These digital dynamics are in incendiary friction with the predominantly analog structures, principles, and assumptions under which much of states' humanitarian work has been carried out to date.

## Governing Digitally

What does this all make of the governmental capacities that international law and international institutions expect of their member states, in the humanitarian field and otherwise? This is the third of the qualifications that the Montevideo Convention demands of a would-be state: a state should have a government. This has been taken to imply the existence of centralized or federated administrative and legislative organs. *How* those organs routinely govern is undergoing change.

It is important to note, from the outset, that the expectation that states maintain a government has never been incompatible with the delegation of governmental powers and state responsibilities to private or hybrid public-private actors. As noted earlier, practices of states contracting in and out for the discharge of governmental duties and the exercise of governmental powers have long been widespread in international humanitarian work. Even so, the contemporary practice of "government" around the globe has taken on new dimensions. Some of these involve the intermediation of digitality.

Digital technology increasingly mediates states' interactions with their employees, citizens, and residents. Data scientists are now routinely involved in the production of official government statistics; the United Nations has championed this through its Global Working Group on Big Data for Official Statistics. As one of our informants described, the factors that have motivated this work are multiple:

> [T]he [Global Working Group on Big Data for Official Statistics] was set up by the UN in 2014 at a time where there was a lot of worry in official statistical institutions about being obsolete in relation to the data sources and that maybe other like tech companies or others would take over the reporting on actually basic statistics on the economic development, labor market, so on so

forth. Now it turned out that that never happened, there was no need to be super worried about that. And then it evolved into a working group with a focus on how can official statistical institutions use those new data sources either as an input to existing statistics, making maybe the reporting burden from companies and citizens lower, and it's also very much [tackling] an issue in relation to timeliness—could you get data on a more timely basis so that instead of making yearly statistics or quarterly statistics you can make monthly statistics, maybe actually in some cases you could make like day to day statistics if you actually wanted to do that.[65]

By way of one example of the emergent digitization of governmental work in the humanitarian sphere, specialists from the Asian Development Bank's Statistics and Data Innovation Unit have been working with the Philippine Statistics Authority, the National Statistical Office of Thailand, and the World Data Lab to examine the feasibility of poverty mapping using satellite imagery and associated geospatial data.[66] The goal of this work has been to address some of the limitations and costs of traditional poverty estimation techniques. A second aim has been to try to meet the expectation of the 2030 Sustainable Development Agenda that government development indicators will be disaggregated by location, gender, age, and income. To this end, automated analysis of satellite data is being used to infer the intensity of night lights. That intensity has, in turn, been used as a proxy for economic development on the assumption that places that are brighter at night are generally more economically developed—or less poor—than those places that are less well lit. On this basis, machine learning algorithms have been trained on combinations of satellite luminosity data and official government poverty estimates for small areas to try to generate poverty estimates for other areas and scales. Figure 5.3 provides a visual representation of the resulting poverty predictions differentiated at a far smaller scale than previously published official poverty rates which were typically calculated by *tambon* (or subdistrict). One can see from this how poverty gets pixelated and made discontinuous with preexisting governmental jurisdictional limits when rendered digitally, recalling the transformations of territory discussed earlier.

Digital data is mobilized in these ways, and through these kinds of interfaces, in the hope of refining discrete, unit-by-unit reporting against an analog poverty scale (proceeding from more to less poor). The assumption that economic

---

[65] Interview with Participant R, *supra* note 54.
[66] Asian Development Bank, "Mapping the Spatial Distribution of Poverty Using Satellite Imagery in the Philippines" (*Asian Development Bank*, March 2021), <https://www.adb.org/publications/mapping-poverty-satellite-imagery-philippines> (accessed October 10, 2022); Asian Development Bank, "Mapping the Spatial Distribution of Poverty Using Satellite Imagery in Thailand" (*Asian Development Bank*, April 2021), <https://www.adb.org/publications/mapping-poverty-satellite-imagery-thailand> (accessed October 10, 2022).

conditions can be inferred from the intensity of night lights is, however, known to be unsound in some settings, especially in large urban areas and in the very poorest areas. Because of this, satellite luminosity data is considered most promising for states where conventional data sources are worse or nonexistent. In these settings, for all its flaws, remotely accessed digital data may be better than the alternatives. Wherever conventional governmental statistics are considered weakest, the pressure to digitize governmental data-gathering and associated humanitarian resource delivery is greatest. This is but one illustration of the burgeoning digitization of government on the periphery under the rubric of humanitarian goals such as the SDGs.

In the process of having growing recourse to digital data in these and other ways, state governments are being recomposed and reoriented. Many countries' governments now include chief information officer, chief technology officer, and chief innovation officer roles, as well as countless, related subordinate roles, such as the "e-governance champions" that India has sought to embed in its line ministries.[67] In Australia, the InnovationXChange that operated within the Department of Foreign Affairs and Trade (DFAT) between 2015 and 2020 is exemplary of these kinds of changes in emphasis and investment oriented toward humanitarianism's digitization. As one of our informants described it, this initiative's original aim was to "experiment, partner, and learn, and it was very much focused on the aid program. So, it was experimenting with different approaches than DFAT had used previously in the aid program." From 2018 onward, however, "the remit [broadened] beyond just innovation and aid, to innovation in the way DFAT goes about its business broadly, so foreign policy, trade and security."[68] The Organization for Economic Co-operation and Development (OECD) tracks and encourages this kind of digital transformation of the public sector in the OECD Digital Government Index.[69]

Late-twentieth-century enthusiasm for public–private partnerships has thus become newly focused on engaging and mimicking technology leaders from the private sector in the performance of core state functions, including in state humanitarianism. Resulting efforts of digitization have seen ICT companies' products and staff become influential mediators of governmental and intergovernmental operations in the humanitarian sector. Palantir is one notable

---

[67] "United Nations E-Government Survey 2020: Digital Government in the Decade of Action for Sustainable Development" (UN Department of Economic and Social Affairs, 2020).

[68] Interview with Participant V (May 5, 2019); Lisa Cornish, "Under New Management, DFAT Dumps Innovation Role" (*Devex*, February 14, 2020), <https://www.devex.com/news/sponsored/exclusive-under-new-management-dfat-dumps-innovation-role-96559> (accessed October 10, 2022).

[69] OECD, "OECD Digital Government Index (DGI): Results and Key Messages" (2020) Highlights Brochure: OECD Working Papers on Public Governance 3, <https://www.oecd.org/gov/digital-government/digital-government-index-2019-highlights.pdf> (accessed October 10, 2022).

example. In 2019, the WFP announced its entry into a five-year "partnership" with Palantir aimed at helping the WFP better use its data to streamline the delivery of food and cash-based assistance in emergency relief operations around the world. This followed an initial pilot program in Iraq in which Palantir helped reduce WFP's food basket costs by more than 10 percent. It did so by making small changes in these baskets' content, such as swapping out one commodity for something similar or changing procurement sources, all without reducing aggregate nutritional value.[70] Much as automated securities trading arbitrages small, digitally discernible differences in value that only become apparent through the processing of vast volumes of digital data, Palantir introduced a litany of small on/off adjustments into WFP operations to optimize their performance against analog scales (both nutritional and budgetary). And Palantir is just one of the digital players involved in the humanitarian work of the WFP and in government programs supported by the WFP. In Iraq, the Public Distribution System was digitized in collaboration with the WFP with food aid distribution mediated by a dedicated smartphone application—"Tamwini" (My Food Ration)—launched by the WFP and the Iraqi Ministry of Trade.[71]

In its digital version, Iraq's Public Distribution System has also incorporated iris-scanning technology, reportedly supplied by a UK company, IrisGuard; this has been a feature of WFP relief distribution in Jordan as well.[72] Digital iris-scanning to dis-individuate claimants of humanitarian relief entails a very different mode of governmental detection of, and interaction with, applicants for such relief than the taking of names, addresses, and other personal, familial, and communal information by an official.[73] Iris-scanning verifies identification discretely from the automated comparison of iris code (a digital representation of patterns extracted from an image of the iris) to stored banks of the same. It is an on/off process that presumes no relation to others, in contrast to analog, interview-based techniques of identification. In these and other ways, the practice of digitizing governmental and intergovernmental operations in

---

[70] World Food Programme, "Palantir and WFP Partner to Help Transform Global Humanitarian Delivery" (February 5, 2019), <https://www.wfp.org/news/palantir-and-wfp-partner-help-transform-global-humanitarian-delivery>.

[71] World Food Programme, "WFP and the Iraqi Ministry of Trade Launch a Food Ration Smartphone App for 1.6 Million People in Iraq" (June 28, 2021), <https://www.wfp.org/news/wfp-and-iraqi-ministry-trade-launch-food-ration-smartphone-app-16-million-people-iraq> (accessed October 10, 2022).

[72] World Food Programme, "WFP Supports Iraq in Modernising Its Public Distribution System" (January 9, 2019), <https://www.wfp.org/news/wfp-supports-iraq-modernising-its-public-distribution-system> (accessed October 10, 2022); World Food Programme, "WFP Introduces Iris Scan Technology to Provide Food Assistance to Syrian Refugees in Zaatari" (October 6, 2016), <https://www.wfp.org/news/wfp-introduces-innovative-iris-scan-technology-provide-food-assistance-syrian-refu> (accessed October 10, 2022).

[73] Fleur Johns, "Data, Detection, and the Redistribution of the Sensible in International Law" (2017) 111 *American Journal of International Law* 57.

the humanitarian field is making of those something other than they have previously been.

Let me be clear about what Palantir, IrisGuard, and the interfaces that they use exemplify in these contexts: the point is not that these actors are introducing a new corporate, profit-making logic into international legal practices and expectations of government in the humanitarian sphere. Corporate logic and actors have long been influential in states' humanitarian work, as noted earlier. The point is rather that Palantir and other technology companies active in the humanitarian sphere are vectors of digital logic now pervading practices of government in the humanitarian field at both national and international scales. And the embedded micro-transformations effected according to that logic are often in irresolvable tension with the analog assumptions by which international law and humanitarian work have long been marked.

Poverty evaluation or the assessment of food needs, for example, have traditionally entailed focus on variables presumed continuous and cardinal, such as income and consumption. One may be more or less poor or hungry, falling above or below a particular numerical measure (such as a poverty line). The measurement of night lights renders poverty, instead, in discrete, qualitative terms to generate grid-level estimates of poverty headcount (or the proportion of people in each grid section that fall below the national poverty line). The gathering of data from mobile phones for purposes of food aid rationing and distribution likewise attenuates humanitarian need to the scale of individual mobile phone subscribers. In each case, the analog measure of humanitarian need (the poverty line, for example) persists, but digitization translates it into a series of discrete values—that is, the values ascribed to each unit in the relevant poverty estimation grid or in a neural network's gridding of independent variables (the latter involving a grid cell of 100 square meters in the Asian Development Bank's experimental work mentioned earlier[74]).

## Relating to Other States, Digitally

What, then, of states' capacity to enter into relations with other states in their own right, for humanitarian and other purposes, without subordination of their foreign relations decision-making to any other state? This is an essential criterion for statehood according to the Montevideo Convention, and, once again, it is a state capacity presumed in much international humanitarian work. With the changes in government programs described in this chapter, the techniques

---

[74] Asian Development Bank, "Mapping the Spatial Distribution of Poverty Using Satellite Imagery in Thailand," *supra* note 66, at 29.

and logics of state-to-state relation in the humanitarian field are also changing. Governments of the Global South in particular must now figure out not just how to relate to other states but also how to relate to a litany of data doubles that shadow them everywhere.[75] That is, they must accommodate the concurrent digital representation of their polities, and visualizations of social and economic conditions within their territories, that are assembled by commercial and intergovernmental actors in parallel with, and sometimes in lieu of, official national data sets. This is not in itself new: governments of the Global South have long had to contend with donors' visions of their future, and the private compilation of statistics has long been a feature of humanitarian record-keeping and reporting. Nonetheless, the digital alter egos with which these governments must now contend have proliferated and are being invested with growing authority.

IBM's Project Lucy launched in 2014, for example, mobilized a pan-African, evolutionary narrative to support a vast digital data extraction initiative. (The project took its name from the fossilized remains of a human ancestor uncovered in Ethiopia in 1974.) Its goal was both to advance IBM's cognitive computing capacities and to develop commercially viable "solutions" to challenges faced by African states in healthcare, education, water and sanitation, human mobility, and agriculture.[76] Initiatives of this kind, as Deval Desai has observed, have tended to redirect the logic of reform away from reformist policy transplantation or technology transfer from North to South and toward local feedback loops of site-specific reflexivity, optimization, and resilience, often shepherded by commercial data harvesters.[77] For example, in 2020–2021, the Indonesian Ministry of Foreign Affairs teamed up with PLJ and BAPPENAS to "develop a machine learning visualization tool using [natural language processing of manually labeled] declassified documents to analyze digital information received from its global outposts and extract insights to inform diplomatic engagement," seeking to enhance its capacity to conduct informed dialogue with foreign governments and other stakeholders.[78]

The business of accounting for oneself as a state in the world has thus become dependent, in part, on states gathering, analyzing, and serving up digital data.

---

[75] Linnet Taylor and Dennis Broeders, "In the Name of Development: Power, Profit and the Datafication of the Global South" (2015) 64 *Geoforum* 229.

[76] IBM Research, "The Possibilities of Project Lucy" (*IBM Research Blog*, October 13, 2014), <https://www.ibm.com/blogs/research/2014/10/the-possibilities-of-project-lucy/> (accessed October 10, 2022).

[77] Deval Desai, "Reflexive Institutional Reform and the Politics of the Regulatory State of the South" (2021) 16 *Regulation & Governance*, <https://doi.org/10.1111/rego.12336> (accessed October 10, 2022).

[78] Annissa Zahara, Utami Diah Kusumawati, and Dwayne Carruthers, "Adapting to Data-Driven Diplomacy with Machine Learning" (*UN Global Pulse*, February 25, 2021), <https://www.unglobalpulse.org/2021/02/adapting-to-data-driven-diplomacy-with-machine-learning/ (accessed October 10, 2022)>.

Independence in the traditional Montevideo Convention sense still matters immensely of course. Yet state-on-state dependence is just one among several modes of subordination with which political leaders must grapple, alongside the kind of state-on-platform dependence that Project Lucy augurs, for instance. Moreover, the expectation embedded in the Montevideo Convention that a state will, by entry into lawful relations with other states, join them on an unbroken continuum of sovereign statehood seems to miss how much states' capacities are subject to discontinuous classification and ranking in the day-to-day conduct of international affairs, in part according to their data-collection and reporting capabilities. As in the OECD Digital Government Index mentioned earlier, states' relative capacities are being broken down and rated according to an increasingly disparate array of metrics generated by a widening range of public and private actors from their analyses of all kinds of digital data. State decision-making in international humanitarian affairs must take account of an ever-increasing variety of data sources and states' discrete positioning in a growing range of indices.

## The Digital Futures of Statehood

As we have seen, states' insight into their "permanent populations" increasingly requires those populations' recasting as digital aggregates. Territorial control no longer implies a commensurate level of informational control. Government operations are moving into discrete, proprietary digital registers. A state's decision-making independence in foreign affairs is only as effective as its access to digital data to inform and justify that decision-making. Mismatches or elisions between digital presentation and analog "ground truth" are widespread. And all these shifts and tensions are manifest most acutely on the periphery and semi-periphery of global order or in the Global South.

It might appear from discussion to this point that prevailing international legal norms and institutions have barely moved a jot in the face of statehood's digital unmaking, although Chapter 6 will show how extensively they are implicated in these changes. Nonetheless, the international order of states presupposed by humanitarian work *is* being challenged by the emergence of yet another dimension of global inequality: statehoods' uneven digitization. The cumulative effect of these shifts and the difficulties that states face in navigating them amount to a de facto reintroduction of something that recalls the standard of civilization as a criterion for statehood. As noted earlier, the 1933 Montevideo Convention was meant to put an end to that standard. Prior to that treaty, a wide range of international legal agreements and texts endorsed the idea that a state could only be legally recognizable as such if it had a degree of civilization sufficient to enable it to observe the principles of international law. States' lawful authority was ranked against an analog scale running from the most to the least civilized. The Montevideo Convention formally abandoned that requirement (although it has had a lengthy afterlife).[79] Today, however, digital-analog conflicts in international law are such that states are subject to a standard of datafication as both a criterion for statehood and a measure of their statehood's ongoing viability. States are expected to work continually toward ever-greater digital data access, accumulation, productivity, and control to demonstrate capability to conduct themselves internationally, with relative independence, in the humanitarian sphere and more broadly. This demand for datafication has strong echoes of the standard of civilization. Yet it operates according to a distinct, digital logic. States could always be more or less civilized, but Panama can only ever be placed in this place or that place in the OECD Digital Government Index mentioned earlier.

Precisely as would-be states have gained access to some of the conventional markers of statehood anticipated by the Montevideo Convention, the goal posts have been digitized—and have moved accordingly. Analog gains do not necessarily translate into digital ones nor register at digital interfaces. Palestine attained nonmember observer state status at the United Nations in 2012. And the Palestinian Central Bureau of Statistics has been running censuses (with difficulty) for several decades.[80] Yet the vast digital repositories and analytical capacities of the Israeli State render those classical, analog markers of independence (referable to physical installations, comparable institutions, and statistical data sets) somewhat moot. Palestinians must be included in Israel's digital population registry to get electronic identification cards and passports necessary for internal and external movement and engagement.[81] Likewise, the Saami Nordic Convention has been signed and was, at the time of writing, awaiting ratification in Finland, Sweden, and Norway. Yet there is, at this time, no aggregate record of the Saami spanning the extensive digital record-keeping of the Finnish, Swedish, and Norwegian governments, and Saami identity management practices remain intensely contested.[82] In these and many other settings, racialized minorities and colonized peoples often tend to experience a double digital bind: they are overrepresented in some digital data sets (such as those assembled for policing and the marketing of high-risk, high-cost financial products); they are

---

[79] Tzouvala, *supra* note 43.

[80] Ola Awad and Sufian Abu Harb, "Palestinian Census 2017—Harnessing the Modernization Initiative" (2020) 36 *Statistical Journal of the IAOS* 77.

[81] Maciej Cesarz, "The Diversity of Citizenship of Palestinians and Its Impact on their Mobility: Passport and Visa Issues" (2018) 47 *Polish Political Science Yearbook* 284.

[82] Hugh Beach, "Self-Determining the Self: Aspects of Saami Identity Management in Sweden" (2007) 24 *Acta Borealia* 1; Håkon Hermanstrand, "Identification of the South Saami in the Norwegian 1801 Census: Why Is the 1801 Census a Problematic Source?," in Håkon Hermanstrand et al. (eds.), *The Indigenous Identity of the South Saami: Historical and Political Perspectives on a Minority within a Minority* (Springer, 2019); Laura Junka-Aikio, "Can the Sámi Speak Now?" (2016) 30 *Cultural Studies* 205.

underrepresented in data sets enabling of political self-assertion and international engagement. Uneven datafication engenders discontent.

If, as argued in this and prior chapters, digital-analog conflicts are more pervasive and carry potentially higher stakes than ever before in international legal relations, in the humanitarian domain and otherwise, what guidance does international law and policy offer those trying to navigate these conflicts, whether on behalf of, in alliance with, or against the state? The predominant approach is to try to resolve these conflicts into an analog scale—to trump the digital with the analog—which is ironically a sublation of the analog because of its dependence on binary, on/off logic. One illustration is the *Framework for The Ethical Use of Advanced Data Science Methods in the Humanitarian Sector* developed by the International Organization for Migration and the City of The Hague. This Framework emphasizes "safety and security" primarily in the sense of personal data protection and the taking of measures to obstruct unauthorized access. It likewise prioritizes "control" of data by human referents presumed knowable and traceable. On this basis, it foreshadows data subjects potentially restricting or conditioning data processing and enjoying meaningful rights to that data's rectification or erasure should data usage become "unsafe." The Framework envisages, further, that certain individuals might elect to "opt out" or "remove themselves from [a] database."[83] UN Global Pulse's *Risk, Harm and Benefit Assessments Tool* is also exemplary in this regard. The Tool is "built on the principles of proportionate data use" and on "balancing the risks and potential harms to individuals and groups of individuals caused not only by data misuse, but also its non-use."[84] This language of control, proportion and balance evokes the measurable quantities and degrees characteristic of analog logic—a logic cast as corrective of the "risks and potential harms" of digitization.

It will be immediately apparent that this is not a corrective designed to address the kinds of elemental transformations apparent in contemporary articulations of statehood in the humanitarian domain. These instruments address digital technology like a harmful artifact or substance that can be whittled or diluted to a point of acceptability by reference to analog considerations of proportion and balancing and by keeping bad actors and bad data out of the system. They take little account of the awkwardness of the fit between digital and analog logics and its implications for analog standard-setting along these lines. They take little account of the material struggles in which proxy-representation at digital interfaces has become pivotal. Likewise, these instruments take no account of

---

[83] Kate Dodgson et al., "A Framework for the Ethical Use of Advanced Data Science Methods in the Humanitarian Sector" (International Organization for Migration, City of the Hague Data Science Initiative 2020).

[84] UN Global Pulse, "Risks, Harms and Benefits Assessment Tool" (2016), <https://www.unglobalpulse.org/policy/risk-assessment/> (accessed October 10, 2022).

the impossibility for many of stepping back or opting out from being digitally sensed, ranked, and monetized, especially for those on the periphery or semi-periphery of international order whose capacities for claim and livelihood may depend on digital articulation and assessment.

It seems, then, that international legal measures old and new, hard and soft—from the Montevideo Convention to the aforementioned Framework and Tool—are mostly incoherent in the face of the digital provocations highlighted in this chapter. They seek to place the discontinuous on a continuum, to make the discrete comparable, and to synthesize the binary into a single, rational whole. As a result, these measures tend to miss many of their marks, all while affirming a sensibility in which failures are frequently cast as developmental—as if imbalances of power were a consequence of insufficient dedication to innovation. Measures such as the aforementioned Framework and Tool do not equip humanitarian professionals to work with and through digital interfaces. For those working in the humanitarian field to imagine themselves choosing between digital and analog approaches (as the Framework and the Tool demand) is to partake of a nonchoice because it presupposes the binary that it seeks the option of negating and disregards the ubiquity and indispensability of digital infrastructure in many parts of the world.

Revisiting and remaking relations among international order's constituent units and rethinking prevailing approaches to digital technology's "use" in light of the emergent fissures probed in this and prior chapters: this is what the provocations of the digital prompt those working in the humanitarian field to do, or so Chapter 7 will argue. Statehood allows for the parceling of property and the funneling of assets and power, but it is also an infrastructure for collectivizing agency and resources both among those assembled in any one state and between states. At Montevideo in 1933 and at other times and places, international lawyers and others tried to rework prevailing schemes of sensing-in-common; mechanisms of mutualism; ways of marshaling and distributing political energies and material resources. This is what the modernist effort to recodify statehood in 1933 entailed, at least in part: it sought to reorient international effort and aspiration away from civilizing missions and toward radical equality. That radical equality was identified not with sameness or continuity but with the nonpresence of a self-declarable statehood (digital in its self-sufficiency) that could only be made effective in (analog) relation. Accordingly, Article 3 of the Convention affirmed that the "political existence of the state is independent of recognition by the other states" but that a state's exercise of rights will always be conditioned by "the exercise of the rights of other states according to international law."[85]

---

[85] Convention on Rights and Duties of States (adopted by the Seventh International Conference of American States on December 26, 1933, entered into force December 26, 1934) 165 LNTS 19.

STATES: ANALOG AND DIGITAL    167

In 1933, at a moment of global political and economic collapse, people gathered in Uruguay to undertake the improbable task of restating the basic units, preconditions, and objects of their work. Today, before the provocations of the digital, those who work in the international humanitarian field are being called upon to do that again. The next chapter will examine some of the legacy infrastructure with which this work must engage. Whereas this chapter has shown how digital mediation problematizes analog logics of statehood and vice versa, Chapter 6 indicates the extent to which analog law and policy infrastructures supporting digital mediation are themselves plural and unsettled.

# 6
# Law and Policy: Infrastructures of Interface

## Introduction

Contemporary international humanitarianism has been presented in this book through the study of a series of interfaces: the Humanitarian OpenStreetMap Team (HOT) Tasking Manager used in the Missing Maps Project; Haze Gazer; Managing Information in Natural Disaster (MIND); HungerMap LIVE; and so on. In those interfaces' effects, we have discerned evidence of the transformation of international legal and political relations. We have charted the rearticulation of humanitarian problems, the reconfiguration of humanitarian fields of action, and the relocation of humanitarian investment, attention, and authority. Digital interfaces offer us a partial read on these shifts in motion. They also suggest some possible sites of intervention in relation to these shifts. It is the aim of this chapter to heighten these shifts' and sites' tactical navigability. To do so, this chapter investigates some of the infrastructures shaping and sustaining the interfaces depicted throughout this book and being shaped by them in turn: international legal and policy infrastructures, specifically. This investigation gives the digital interfaces discussed throughout this book a history, in that it shows something of how these interfaces have been produced and reproduced in law and policy on the global plane. It also induces a sense of these interfaces' normative incoherence, their openness to reassembly, and their potential value as sites at which to re-enter the international legal and political fray. This chapter moves, then, from interfaces to infrastructures and back again.

To traverse this route, the chapter begins by discussing what may be significant or distinctive about investigating laws and policies as *infrastructural* in relation to the interfaces probed throughout this book: discussion that situates this book in relation to prior work in the international legal field. This explains, too, how one might discern possibilities latent within the transformations explored in this book, unequal accumulations of power notwithstanding. Attention then turns to canvassing briefly what is already well known about the juridical infrastructure of the global digital economy before turning to some of its less widely scrutinized dimensions on which humanitarian digital interfaces especially depend, namely: international treaties, multistakeholder arrangements, international organizations' guidelines, contracts, ethical codes, and finally goals, targets, and other protocols.

A key argument of this chapter is that study of the "reality effect[s]"[1] being generated on the global plane by humanitarian digital interfaces' prevalence may be aided, first, by revisiting what has been learned from the structural and post-structural analysis of international law and policy; and second, by pursuing investigations informed by that lineage, including investigation of the law and policy infrastructures that are shaping and being shaped by humanitarian digital interfaces. Referencing the analog-digital dynamics to which this book has continually returned, this chapter shows how much of what is cast as indicative of the unstoppable advance of the digital is sustained by analog instruments and techniques—and emphasizes that these are marked by dissensus and irresolution. As noted earlier, this reverses the move made in Chapter 5. That chapter highlighted how digital mediation of global relations destabilizes analog architectures of international legal ordering. Digital signs do not, it showed, point to stable analog referents. This chapter shows how analog legal and policy infrastructures supporting digital mediation are themselves piecemeal and unstable. Analog legal and policy infrastructures do not secure digital meanings. The point, in short, is to show that there are many points of entry to the developments described throughout this book and that their course is anything but preordained.

## On Interfaces, Structures, and Infrastructures

To examine international legal infrastructures on which humanitarian digital interfaces depend, and on which those interfaces concurrently exert influence, is to create a structural simulacrum of their heterogeneous makeup. That is what "infra" implies when combined with "structure." As discussed in Chapter 1, the prefix "infra" suggests "below," "underneath," "beneath," "lower," "inferior," but also "within."[2] Accordingly, infrastructure encompasses any structural element that has sunk into, or receded from view within, operative practices, arrangements, and technologies.[3] It implies concern with what is embedded within structure and cast as inferior, inconsequential, marginal, or minor within it, possibly only attracting attention when it breaks down. Bodies, roads,

---

[1] Roland Barthes, "The Reality Effect," in *The Rustle of Language* (University of California Press, 1969) 141.
[2] "Infra-, Prefix," in *OED Online* (Oxford University Press, 2021), <https://www.oed.com/view/Entry/95607> (accessed October 10, 2022).
[3] Susan Leigh Star and Geoffrey C. Bowker, "How to Infrastructure," in *Handbook of New Media: Student Edition* (SAGE Publications, 2006).

computer protocols, trees, undersea cables, and legal instruments can all operate infrastructurally, as can many other phenomena. Infrastructural investigation involves a tunneling into what might otherwise appear as a total, autonomous phenomenon to probe what may be embedded within or presupposed by it—and hence some of the ways in which it is dependent or vulnerable. Infrastructural analyses also show how structures plug into and play with other structures.

How, then, should we understand the *structural* properties of the interfaces that we have examined in prior chapters, for purposes of investigating their infrastructural preconditions? In what sense, for example, are the digital-analog tensions and displacements on which we have remarked throughout this book structural? Addressing these questions demands a brief detour through some of the international legal literature with which this book is in conversation.

This book's investigation of humanitarian interfaces' digital-analog tensions up to this point has been indebted—albeit mostly in an unsung way—to work carried out in the 1980s (and since) in international law.[4] During that decade, scholars of international law David Kennedy and Martti Koskenniemi (alongside people working in other legal fields) drew upon work from the late nineteenth century onward in linguistics, anthropology, semiotics, psychoanalysis, literary theory, political economy, and social theory associated with a movement dubbed structuralism. This is a movement (of sorts) that is "still going on" today, albeit sometimes "under denominations that we cannot immediately recognize," which is why this chapter runs structuralism and post-structuralism together and treats both as ongoing.[5]

Key to this "movement" was the insight that communication and representation—including communication and representation via legal principles and practices—are not transparent to themselves or to those engaged in communicating or representing. The sense-making or authoritative effects of a particular action or statement cannot be deduced from the intention of those making it, nor attributed to some universal rationality or doctrinal scheme, structuralist analyses showed. In studies informed by structuralism, effects of legal signs (say, words or rituals expressing judgment or agreement or artifacts invested with facticity) are outcomes of the iterative conjunction of signifiers (in the texts, gestures, signals, or artifacts in question) and their referents or signifieds (the ideas, objects, and subjects to which those may be understood to refer). The immanent, surface-level manifestations of legal argument and other forms of sense-making exhibit arbitrariness and contradictoriness in that viable arrangements of signifiers may be made to refer to different signifieds and to

[4] Justin Desautels-Stein, "International Legal Structuralism: A Primer" (2016) 8 *International Theory* 201.
[5] Etienne Balibar, "Structuralism: A Destitution of the Subject?" (2003) 14 *Differences* 1, 2.

produce a range of inconsistent effects. At the same time, relations among these elements of signification exhibit grammatical regularity apparent in certain recurrent patterns across their iterative manifestations.

Structuralism and post-structuralism do not presuppose signs' fungibility or flatness; they are not blind to hierarchy. On the contrary, the centrality of the sign in structuralist accounts of sense-making, and post-structuralist elaborations of those, demonstrates the prominence and persistence of hierarchy. That is because the sign's status depends upon its differentiation from that which is not recognizable as primary or pertinent in representational or meaning-making operations. Every sign is a setting-aside of something derided as peripheral to signification; post-structuralist scholarship has shown this at length. Moreover, those elements set aside within grammatical hierarchies are analogous to those neglected or "sunk" elements of structure with which the study of infrastructure is concerned. In the version put forward here, thinking infrastructurally encompasses thinking structurally and post-structurally.

Infrastructural approaches to the study of law carry forward structuralist and post-structuralist insights about the non-intentionality of relations (that is, that individual consciousness, will, choice, and identity, for instance, are outcomes not determinative origins of relations); the radical instability of those relations; and their iterative regularization through hierarchical differentiation. Yet infrastructural approaches take these insights beyond the range of signification and human-to-human relations and carry them into socio-technical complexes: complexes that combine heterogenous, human and nonhuman elements. As Cornelia Vismann demonstrated so effectively (in her study of files, for instance), the post-structural study of grammar can aid investigation of a wide range of techniques, things, and media that continue to make possible "the myth of the subject as legislator, instigator, . . . perpetrator" and maker of meanings.[6] Its effectiveness and range of potential deployment are by no means confined to language or text.

Translated into terms that speak to this book's immediate concerns, international legal scholarship informed by structuralism and post-structuralism teaches us to approach humanitarianism through differential relations. Any particular humanitarian claim or initiative—the development and use of a digital humanitarian interface, for example—cannot be assured of having humanitarian effects, or being received or accepted as humanitarian, by virtue of the designs, intentions, values, or ideas of those advancing it, nor by reference to the supposedly universal properties, needs, or ends of humanity. Nonetheless, differences constitutive of what gets recognized or authorized as humanitarian in any one

---

[6] Cornelia Vismann, "Cultural Techniques and Sovereignty" (2013) 30 *Theory, Culture & Society* 83, 88.

instance (differences experienced, say, between the humane and inhumane, or the altruistic and the self-interested) do exhibit a reproducible syntax. That syntax delimits the range of viable argument as to what humanitarian practice could or should entail, and what humanitarian relations may encompass or not, and what kinds of claims or struggles might be tenable in the humanitarian field at any one place and time (which sometimes takes the form of argument about what is or is not lawful or consistent with policy "best practice").

The syntaxes that structuralist and post-structuralist techniques help us to trace in and through humanitarian interfaces are not metalanguages; the differences comprising them are not universalizable or stable. Nor are they wholly linguistic or semiotic; they include "chain[s] of substitutions activated by the replacement of media and things."[7] Prior chapters discussed, for instance, the replacement of analog by digital logics in international humanitarian work and the syntactical differences that these replacements have put into operation, suggesting that these are integral to the making and remaking of relations on the international legal and political plane. These differences are emergent in practices that are both situated in the field of humanitarianism and constitutive of that field. They encompass intersubjective effects, but they do not always depend on the making of meaning or knowledge. They are often generated by material things and processes at some remove from human meaning-making or knowing. In this sense, recurrence of the differences that delimit the ambit of humanitarian practice has a machinic quality (both literally and figuratively). It does not depend on people perceiving or thinking in terms of those differences. Subjective decision-making and discretion are still rife—indeed unavoidable—throughout structural analyses, but they do not decide the effects that texts produce nor are they necessarily axiomatic to those analyses. As Terry Eagleton memorably said of structuralism: it "is 'anti-humanist,' which means not that its devotees rob children of their sweets but that [structuralist texts] reject the myth that meaning begins and ends in the individual's 'experience.'"[8]

To the question of what sustains the reproduction of this highly contestable grammar across time and space, in the humanitarian field and elsewhere, international legal scholars informed by structuralism and post-structuralism have offered a range of responses. Some have sought to understand this (ironically) through the phenomenological study of consciousness: specifically, legal consciousness (shot through with bad faith) understood in Duncan Kennedy's rendering as "an enormously plastic, loose congeries of ideas, each of which appears from moment to moment to have the force of many army divisions and then no

---

[7] Ibid., 91.
[8] Terry Eagleton, *Literary Theory, An Introduction* (University of Minnesota Press, 2008) 98.

force at all."[9] Others have treated structural relations' reproduction—including in ways constitutive of humanitarianism—as explicable by the study of history.[10] Sometimes this has entailed tracing historical movements of ideas and ideologies (an exercise related to, but also distinguishable from, the phenomenological study of consciousness).[11] Elsewhere, it has involved tracking historical distributions of property, capital, and other forms of legal entitlement.[12] In still other instances, structural change and persistence in the humanitarian field have been cast as outcomes of historical struggle over hierarchy in both its ideal and its material instantiations, sometimes sublimated into conflicts and convergences of style.[13]

In international legal writing informed by structuralism and post-structuralism, what has tended to span these responses (with some exceptions) is a refusal to explain systematicity either as an expression of the necessity of the actual (the historical, the empirical, or the scientific) or as a natural outgrowth of the imaginary (ideas, concepts, ideologies). Instead, the "true subject" to which many of these writings have returned again and again is "the structure itself": "a system of differential relations according to which the symbolic elements determine themselves reciprocally, and a system of singularities corresponding to these relations and tracing the space of the structure."[14] Moreover, this structure is always on the move, just as digital interfaces and their analog and digital properties have been shown to be throughout this book: always "open to new values or variations . . . [and] capable of new distributions, constitutive of another structure."[15]

This tendency of structuralist and post-structuralist analyses to evoke alterity immanent within systematicity—to highlight latent possibilities for a structure to turn up or into something other than itself—explains why structuralism has been characterized as polemical even while it tends to make no explicit arguments for reform.[16] Scholarly work informed by structuralism has always

---

[9] Duncan Kennedy, *A Critique of Adjudication: Fin de Siècle* (Harvard University Press, 1997) 338. See further Susan S. Silbey, "After Legal Consciousness" (2005) 1 *Annual Review of Law and Social Science* 323; Lynette J. Chua and David M. Engel, "Legal Consciousness Reconsidered" (2019) 15 *Annual Review of Law and Social Science* 335.

[10] See, e.g., Samuel Moyn, *The Last Utopia: Human Rights in History* (Harvard University Press, 2010).

[11] See, e.g., Martti Koskenniemi, *The Gentle Civilizer of Nations: The Rise and Fall of International Law, 1870–1960* (Cambridge University Press, 2002); Martti Koskenniemi, "A History of International Law Histories," in *The Oxford Handbook of the History of International Law* (Oxford University Press, 2012).

[12] See, e.g., Thomas L. Haskell, "Capitalism and the Origins of the Humanitarian Sensibility, Part 1" (1985) 90 *The American Historical Review* 339.

[13] See, e.g., David Kennedy, *The Dark Sides of Virtue: Reassessing International Humanitarianism* (Princeton University Press, 2004).

[14] Gilles Deleuze, "How Do We Recognize Structuralism?," in *Desert Islands and Other Texts, 1953–1974* (Semiotexte, 2004) 177–178.

[15] Ibid., 191.

[16] Balibar, *supra* note 5, at 3.

fostered a sense of the unruly and unknown within it, without forging programmatic pathways out of structure.[17] For international legal scholars, investigations of structure have almost always entailed examination of how and where structures come apart or do not operate with consistency, illuminating "deviant approaches" within professional routines.[18] This in turn gives rise to questions about how and where structures could be (or are already) otherwise, even as the conditions under which they are sustained are in many respects formidable and enduring, often violently so. In part due to these provocations, the question of how change does and does not occur in and around structure is a question to which writing in the international legal field has continually returned.[19]

The focus on the opposition of analog to digital and their entanglement in humanitarian digital interfaces throughout this book is quite explicitly indebted to structuralist and post-structuralist analyses of international law and policy; other features of this book's analysis are more indirectly so. As depicted in this book, humanitarian practice is generating and shaped by a field-wide structure of analog-digital relations in which the analog is only recognizable as such when differentiated from digitality and vice versa, and the two are often hard to disentangle. Nonetheless, these analog-digital relations are routinely unsettled in the practice of humanitarianism. In particular, the priority historically afforded the analog in this relation is, in many contemporary settings, being inverted. This is apparent in the serial interactions that digital humanitarianism interfaces occasion. Chapter 3, for example, showed how digital interfaces tend to cast statistically measurable populations into the background of the interactions they elicit, so that digital aggregates otherwise assembled come to the fore.

As in analyses informed by structuralism and post-structuralism, this book has depicted transformations being wrought by the development and use of digital interfaces in humanitarian work—and associated investments of resources and attention—as interventions that appear and "disappear in the production of their ... effects."[20] In other words, these transformations are iterative interface effects, not the inevitable outcome of the piling up of money and mission statements around so-called digital humanitarianism. (The latter would be more in line with accounts of humanitarianism's takeover by philanthro-capitalism.[21]) Transformations in international legal order underway are, at least in part, "reality effects" of humanitarian digital interfaces' development, promotion, and

[17] Fleur Johns, *Non-Legality in International Law: Unruly Law* (Cambridge University Press, 2013).
[18] Martti Koskenniemi, "What Is Critical Research in International Law? Celebrating Structuralism" (2016) 29 *Leiden Journal of International Law* 727, 732.
[19] See, e.g., Ingo Venzke and Kevin Jon Heller (eds.), *Contingency in International Law: On the Possibility of Different Legal Histories* (Oxford University Press, 2021).
[20] Balibar, *supra* note 5, at 6.
[21] *Cf.* Anand Giridharadas, *Winners Take All: The Elite Charade of Changing the World* (Vintage, 2019).

use. That is, these digital interfaces' impacts in the world are not limited by the extent to which they might (or might not) be determining outcomes of decision-making in the humanitarian field. Irrespective of their determinative impacts, they are advancing a "realistic enterprise.. As Roland Barthes said of the role of seemingly dispensable, nonpredictive, fragmentary descriptions of "concrete reality" characteristic of modern realist literature, humanitarian digital interfaces signify "the real" by purporting to collude directly with referent objects "in the name of referential plenitude" (or comprehensive representation). Yet they touch that plenitude lightly.[22] They are, in other words, propagating a "new verisimilitude," to use a phrase borrowed from Barthes that bears repeating.[23]

As producers of reality effects, humanitarian digital interfaces operate more through problems of use than through problems of meaning or intention. The transformations recounted in this book are more use- than idea-driven as Chapter 7 will explore further. In generating reality effects, digital interfaces "act promiscuously," as Wendy Hui Kyong Chun has discussed; they are not faithful to their developers' or users' purposes or intentions. (Chun gives the example of a wireless network's routine reading of all packets—segments into which data is broken for network transmission—that are in its range before deleting those not directly addressed to it.)[24] The questions to which these interface effects direct attention, therefore, are not so much "what do they mean" or "what are they intended to do" questions as "how do they work" and "how can they be used" questions. In this book, we have continually returned to the sorts of "how" questions canvassed in Chapter 1: How are digital humanitarian interfaces working; how is humanitarianism practiced or activated through these interfaces; how are people, places, digits, and things brought into relation in these practices (independent of what their relation might ultimately mean or cause); how is the digitization of humanitarian practice taking and having effect on the international plane in its reconfiguration of these relations; how could the digitization of humanitarian practice potentially have other effects or occasion other relations? Chapter 7 will dwell on questions of possible use.

Promiscuity notwithstanding, the study of infrastructure—including legal and policy infrastructure, as in this chapter—helps elucidate the range of media, investments, and forms of work that go into making digital interfaces usable and making their interface effects recur. The relations into which people, places, digits, and things are brought by humanitarian digital interfaces are

---

[22] Barthes, *supra* note 1, at 148. Cf. Walter Benjamin, "The Task of the Translator," in Marcus Bullock and Michael W. Jennings (eds.), *Walter Benjamin: Selected Writings Volume 1, 1913–1926* (Harvard University Press, 1996).

[23] Barthes, *supra* note 1, at 147.

[24] Wendy Hui Kyong Chun, *Updating to Remain the Same: Habitual New Media* (MIT Press, 2016) 51.

not random; infrastructural investigations show how they come to be patterned. *Pace* some criticisms of structuralist and post-structuralist analyses, they grapple continually with power's uneven distribution and prospects for its unpicking. And one dimension of this uneven, unpickable patterning is legality. Particular understandings of legality and rightfulness are generated as effects of digital interfaces' proliferation and use—proliferation and use that are in turn conditioned by legal and other forms of infrastructure, as this chapter shows. Importantly, however, the infrastructures investigated in this chapter do not lie *behind* the differential relations configured by digital interfaces, explored in prior chapters. Digital interfaces' law and policy infrastructures do not comprise "a furtive reality that is difficult to grasp, but [rather] a great surface network in which the stimulation of bodies, the intensification of pleasures, the incitement to discourse, the formation of special knowledges, the strengthening of controls and resistances, are linked to one another, in accordance with a few major strategies of knowledge and power."[25] Investigations of infrastructure relate to structuralist and post-structural analyses of structure as investigations of infra-law (per Foucault) or infra-legality (per my prior work) relate to most doctrinal, sociological, or normative analyses of law.[26] They illuminate how legality "passes outside itself" and gets transmitted and shaped through a great miscellany of practices and materials.[27]

It is worthwhile making explicit that this approach charts an alternative route to that taken in critical international legal scholarship that has revolved around history and historiography; this book mostly bypasses debates so preoccupied, as Chapter 1 explained when differentiating the study of interfaces from possible alternatives.[28] That is the case even though studies of infrastructure often pillage historical materials, as in Chapter 2's historical "snapshots." This book's focus on currently operating infrastructure mostly sets aside questions about the present's continuity with the passions and projects of particular people in the past. It emphasizes, rather, how dispersed and needy of daily repair are the underpinnings of digitally mediated hierarchy, without disavowing hierarchy's power or persistence. All the interfaces and infrastructures canvassed in this book require routine maintenance, care, and validation; they must continually enroll a labor force in that affirming work, as prior chapters have shown. And they must advance arguments for the continuance and expansion of that work, as this chapter shows. This is the kind of quotidian, repetitive, relational, unattributed,

---

[25] Michel Foucault, *The History of Sexuality. Volume I: An Introduction* (Robert Hurley tr., Pantheon Books, 1978) 105–106.
[26] Michel Foucault, *Discipline and Punish* (Alan Sheridan tr., 2nd ed., Vintage, 1995) 222–223; Fleur Johns, "Death, Disaster and Infra-Legality in International Law," in *Non-Legality in International Law: Unruly Law* (Cambridge University Press, 2013).
[27] Foucault, *supra* note 26, at 224.
[28] Jennifer Pitts, "The Critical History of International Law" (2015) 43 *Political Theory* 541.

ongoing work to which some historical studies are inattentive when trying to grasp the properties and potentialities of international legal ordering. The study of interfaces and their infrastructures facilitates understanding of how particular structural properties get extended, linked, repurposed, reproduced—and how they sometimes do not. It suggests that those repositories and accumulations of power enabled by law are in some ways fragile. Infrastructural studies show, too, how different problematics intersect and combine, and in so doing highlight points of disjunction, failure, and "immanent externality": that is, they evoke a sense of the latent unruliness discussed earlier.[29]

When understood in relation to structuralism and post-structuralism, as proposed here, the study of infrastructure does not revolve especially around the study of physical installations. It encompasses but is not confined to the analysis of large socio-technical systems on which infrastructure studies initially dwelled, decades ago. It does not presuppose infrastructures' spatial or temporal fixity, in contrast to Benedict Kingsbury's and Nahuel Maisley's work, nor envision infrastructure as external to peoples or publics as they seem inclined to do (although it shares many interests and concerns with that work).[30] Rather, the study of infrastructure for which this chapter argues investigates a variety of human and nonhuman forces, relations, practices, and technologies operating in combination—all with the sunk quality and structuring effects highlighted earlier.[31] Study so pursued inverts relations of foreground and background upon which causal explanations for the present and programs for the future commonly rest.[32] It breaks down humanitarian "discourses" and "imaginaries" into heterogeneous elements populating chains of association and substitution on which all sorts of people work, and in which a range of actors are invested, and highlights their brittleness and neediness. It backgrounds the more spectacular transformations around which humanitarianism's history has typically been told, and toward which reformist attention has typically been directed, in order to probe conditions, actions, and technologies both enabling and delimiting of these transformations in their ongoing operation.

The infrastructural focus of this chapter is nonetheless highly selective: it focuses on particular legal and policy infrastructures, and not those most commonly identified with the global digital economy. Such an investigation helps address some questions about how the interface effects discussed throughout this book have been generated, how they tend to recur, and how they relate to

---

[29] Balibar, *supra* note 5, at 5.
[30] Benedict Kingsbury and Nahuel Maisley, "Infrastructures and Laws: Publics and Publicness" (2021) 17 *Annual Review of Law and Social Science* 353.
[31] Star and Bowker, *supra* note 3.
[32] On "infrastuctural inversion," see Geoffrey C. Bowker, *Science on the Run: Information Management and Industrial Geophysics at Schlumberger, 1920–1940* (MIT Press, 1994).

other effects. It does so without requiring resort to stories of universal, common origins and without any claim to methodological objectivity, all while keeping people—indeed, a wide range of actors and interlocutors—in the frame. The next section of this chapter shows that the interfaces examined throughout this book are powered by a diversity of international legal and policy infrastructures. Tracking, strategizing around and leveraging these power sources is key to the prospects for generative use, reuse, disuse, and misuse canvassed in the book's final chapter.

## International Legal Infrastructures of Interfaces

Like other practices in the global digital economy, digital humanitarian initiatives are often characterized as taking place in lawless, ungoverned spaces.[33] Nonetheless, a dense array of international, regional, national, and subnational laws, guidelines, and standards—both "hard" and "soft"[34]—are implicated in developments in the global digital economy and have borne upon the development and deployment of the digital interfaces discussed throughout this book. International laws and policies informing the advance of digital humanitarianism on the global plane are playing a role in the reconfiguration of global order and are in turn being reoriented by digitization.

Legal scholars have elsewhere documented how the design, operation, and take-up of digital interfaces can be traced to specific law and policy shifts at certain places and times. Some have celebrated the shifts in question and called for more.[35] Others have been critical.[36] Important work has highlighted how much enclosure, subordination, and monopolization in the digital economy have been effected or enabled by law—often in the name of openness, freedom, and innovation.[37] To a more limited extent, the reverse has also been demonstrated: that strategic engagement with laws and policies aimed at shoring up existing power

---

[33] Shoshana Zuboff, *The Age of Surveillance Capitalism: The Fight for a Human Future at the New Frontier of Power* (Profile Books, 2019) 231, 252, 281.
[34] Daniel Thürer, "Soft Law," in Rüdiger Wolfrum (ed.), *Max Planck Encyclopedia of Public International Law (Online)* (Oxford University Press 2011), <https://opil.ouplaw.com/home/mpil> (accessed October 10, 2022) ("Social norms... [that] influence the behaviour and decisions of actors participating in international relations... rang[ing] from purely moral or political commitments to strictly legal ones").
[35] Anupam Chander, "How Law Made Silicon Valley" (2013) 63 *Emory Law Journal* 639.
[36] Rebecca Haw Allensworth, "Antitrust's High-Tech Exceptionalism Antitrust and Digital Platforms" (2020) 130 *Yale Law Journal Forum* 588.
[37] Julie E. Cohen, *Between Truth and Power: The Legal Constructions of Informational Capitalism* (Oxford University Press, 2019).

structures in the digital domain sometimes occasions those structures being called into question.[38]

Much of this prior work has, however, focused on national law and policy—especially US law and policy—and their extraterritorial extension via private international law (conflict of laws) doctrine and by other means. Far less attention has been devoted to the roles that international law and international organizations have played in this context. When international law and international organizations have been targets of analysis, emphasis has been placed on international trade and investment law and on institutions of economic governance.[39] Against this trend, a key claim of this book is that international laws and international organizations concerned with humanitarianism are just as noteworthy as vectors of transformation in the global digital economy. To understand how major digital platforms are seeking to extend their business models' reach and serviceable lives and to envision what later iterations of those business models might look like, one cannot neglect those platforms' global humanitarian engagements nor how these are being authorized and shaped by international law and policy. Likewise, one cannot neglect these matters if one wishes to foreshadow how nation states might seek to govern the global digital economy in the future through increasingly chaotic climactic and informational conditions. Attending to international organizations', governments', and other humanitarian agencies' investments in digital technology (investments both material and discursive), and the law and policy frameworks informing and securing those, is key to understanding what might yet become of the global digital and sensory economy.[40] Tracking commercial protagonists, transactions, considerations, and conflicts only gets one so far.

Accordingly, the second part of the chapter examines several key types of international legal and policy infrastructure on which humanitarian digital interfaces both depend and bear, starting with treaties. These merit the descriptor infrastructural for several reasons including their ubiquity, their relative reliability or persistence, and their invisibility in many analyses of digital interfaces' operation and effects.[41]

---

[38] Di Wang and Sida Liu, "Performing Artivism: Feminists, Lawyers, and Online Legal Mobilization in China" (2020) 45 *Law & Social Inquiry* 678.

[39] *See, e.g.*, Cohen, *supra* note 37, at ch. 7.

[40] Fleur Johns, "Data, Detection, and the Redistribution of the Sensible in International Law" (2017) 111 *American Journal of International Law* 57.

[41] Jean-Christophe Plantin at al., "Infrastructure Studies Meet Platform Studies in the Age of Google and Facebook" (2018) 20 *New Media & Society* 293, 294.

## International Treaties

Multilateral and bilateral treaties are classical archetypes of analog ordering, in the terms introduced in Chapter 2, being concerned with connecting entities through their comparable capacities for binding agreement, the latter understood as a force of continuous variation. Nonetheless, such treaties stipulate the powers and establish the mandates of international organizations advancing digital humanitarian initiatives and the conditions under which they are advanced. At the same time, the exercise of treaty powers is also being shaped by the affordances of, and advocates of investment in, digital technology. The Constitution and Convention of the International Telecommunication Union (ITU) 1992 (as amended) is one example.[42] One of our informants described how the composition and powers of the ITU set out in that treaty are informing the organization's digital humanitarian work, and how the ITU is reorienting itself in part around that work. A particular illustration about which they spoke was the ITU's 2017 inauguration and annual co-hosting of the AI for Good Global Summit (mentioned in Chapter 5)—a forum in which digital humanitarian interfaces at various stages of development are showcased:

[O]ne of [the ITU's] core [mandates], and . . . that applies to all UN agencies, is how can we help to advance progress towards the Sustainable Development Goals. And when we created the Summit we really saw the potential of AI [artificial intelligence] to help many of the [Sustainable Development Goals (SDGs)] accelerate or make progress . . .

[O]ne of the things that's unique about ITU, and actually made us well placed to host this Summit, is that we're the only UN agency that has both member states as members and private companies and universities as members. So we have 193 member states and we have about 800 private companies . . . these are telecom operators, software [developers], so basically the whole ICT ecosystem. And then we also have academia, so about 150 top universities as members, and they all participate in our standards making process. So ITU has always had a very strong public/private partnership balance and I think we wouldn't have been able to pull off the Summit if we didn't have that . . . I think that's where we're also set apart of the other UN agencies in that we have a very strong hold in industry. Without that we wouldn't be able to do standards work at all, really.[43]

---

[42] International Telecommunication Union, "Final Acts of the Additional Plenipotentiary Conference: Constitution and Convention of the International Telecommunication Union" (International Telecommunication Union, 1992).
[43] Interview with Participant X (October 17, 2019).

In other instances, the development of digital humanitarian interfaces has proceeded under a different kind of international legal mandate. The UN Development Programme (UNDP), for example, is the main international organization under the rubric of which several labs of UN Global Pulse operate. One of our interviewees observed of Pulse Lab Jakarta (PLJ) that it is "this little flexible dynamic unit," but it "still ha[s] to abide by UNDP regulations" and "to use UNDP templates."[44] The authority that UNDP exercises in this context is derived from a 1965 resolution of the UN General Assembly utilizing powers conferred upon the General Assembly by another multilateral treaty, the UN Charter.[45]

These multilateral agreements are publicly accessible, but many of the bilateral agreements under which digital humanitarian interfaces are being developed and deployed are not. This is for a range of reasons, including the fact of some of these agreements taking informal forms—that of a memorandum of understanding, for instance, commonly seen as a "more flexible, lower-profile alternative" to a formal treaty.[46] For example, the 2012 Memorandum of Understanding between the Government of the Republic of Indonesia (represented by the Minister for National Development Planning) and the United Nations (represented by the UN Resident Coordinator in Indonesia) that provided for the establishment and oversight of PLJ (referenced in Chapter 1) is a bilateral agreement that is not publicly available.[47] A second example—not strictly a treaty, but rather an agreement between the United Nations and a US corporation—is the agreement providing for UN Global Pulse to have access to Twitter data free of charge, including the Twitter "firehose" (an application programming interface that delivers 100 percent of tweets to end users in real time).[48] That agreement is likely treated as commercial-in-confidence from the Twitter side and kept from public purview for that reason.

The behind-the-scenes work done toward and by these multilateral and bilateral agreements underwriting the advance of digital humanitarianism—providing for legal authority, funding, data, and more—highlights some important features of the international legal infrastructure of which they comprise a part. The distribution of background entitlements and shaping of reproducible syntax in the global digital economy is not just occurring in the commercial sphere. It is not wholly concerned with the construction or

---

[44] Interview with Participant A (August 21, 2015).
[45] "United Nations Development Programme" UNGA Res. 2093(XX) (December 20, 1965) UN Doc. A/RES/2093(XX).
[46] Kal Raustiala, "The Architecture of International Cooperation: Transgovernmental Networks and the Future of International Law" (2002) 43 *Virginia Journal of International Law* 1, 30.
[47] "Memorandum of Understanding between the Government of the Republic of Indonesia and the United Nations" (August 15, 2012) (on file with the author).
[48] Interview with Participant A, *supra* note 44.

expansion of private economic power.[49] Also at issue is the reconfiguration and redistribution of *public power* in national and international formats. Multiple forms of capital are at play in this reshaping, not just economic capital.[50] For example, when the ITU marshals its network and directs resources and attention toward goods and services employing artificial intelligence, casting these as essential to help the world progress toward reaching the SDGs, the ITU gathers and distributes social capital. It puts that social capital behind those producing and distributing such goods and services, and it promises more to communities who support their advance.

Major commercial players upon which so many other analyses of the global digital economy typically focus remain important parts of this picture. For example, ITU's AI for Good Summit has featured speakers from multinational information and communication technologies (ICT) firms such as Google, Microsoft, IBM, NEC, and ABB, as well as a range of other telecommunications, manufacturing, ICT services, and financial investment firms. Yet the authority and entitlements that these actors wield are entangled with those of academics, international organizations, nongovernmental organizations, and national governments. As much as the latter often gain validation, "relevance," and funding from collaborating with large corporations, the reverse is also true; major digital platforms and other commercial actors routinely seek legitimacy from the not-for-profit and public sectors, arguably more so in the face of "techlash."[51] The future of the global digital economy is not a one-way street being laid by the likes of Google. Howsoever it shapes up will be, at least in part, an outcome of struggle among a wide variety of public, private, and hybrid actors, including those active in the humanitarian field.

## Multistakeholder Arrangements

In addition to the multilateral and (mostly nonpublic) bilateral agreements under which digital technologies are being deployed in the humanitarian field, policies of multistakeholder engagement are broadly favored in this domain, as they have been in international governance of the Internet generally, albeit with mixed results.[52] The United Nations—a major proponent of these kinds of

---

[49] Cf. Amy Kapczynski, "The Law of Informational Capitalism" (2020) 129 *Yale Law Journal* 1460.
[50] Pierre Bourdieu, "The Forms of Capital," in J.G. Richardson (ed.), *Handbook of Theory and Research for the Sociology of Education* (Greenwood, 1986).
[51] Salome Viljoen, "The Promise and Limits of Lawfulness: Inequality, Law, and the Techlash" (2021) 2 *Journal of Social Computing* 284.
[52] Jeremy Malcolm, *Multi-Stakeholder Governance and the Internet Governance Forum* (Terminus Press, 2008); Kal Raustiala, "Governing the Internet" (2016) 110 *American Journal of International Law* 491; Jeremy Malcolm, "Arresting the Decline of Multi-Stakeholderism in Internet Governance,"

arrangements since the turn of the millennium—has defined multistakeholder partnerships as "voluntary and collaborative relationships between various parties, both State and non-State, in which all participants agree to work together to achieve a common purpose or undertake a specific task and to share risks and responsibilities, resources and benefits."[53] One of our interviewees from an international organization active in digital humanitarianism spoke, tellingly, of multistakeholder arrangements as an essential part of its future:

> [W]e have to move beyond bilateral relationships with countries, bilateral relationships with companies ... bilateral relationships with UN agencies when we're ... soliciting projects and start moving more toward ... boot-strapping and incubating initiatives that have the eventual owners [and users] ... onboard from day one. So these are multistakeholder partnerships.[54]

In research conducted for this book, my collaborators and I often observed or were told about the participation of multiple stakeholders in the development of digital humanitarian interfaces. This took five main forms: government officials' input and collaboration in the development of particular tools;[55] interagency dialogue around their development (for example, consultation among different UN agencies and between UN agencies and nongovernmental organizations);[56] ethnographic and other qualitative research surrounding the development and refinement of such tools (for example, by the Social Systems Team of Pulse Lab Jakarta);[57] digitally facilitated enrolment of communities in data-generation or validation (as in the World Food Programme's computer-assisted mobile phone surveys, for instance: one of the data sources for HungerMap LIVE, discussed in Chapter 4);[58] and other consultation with "domain experts" in the course of particular projects.[59]

---

in *Consumers in the Information Society: Access, Fairness and Representation* (Consumers International, 2012).

[53] UNGA Res. 60/214 (August 10, 2005) UN Doc. A/RES/60/214.
[54] Interview with Participant N (April 11, 2018).
[55] See, e.g., Pulse Lab Jakarta, "Using Big Data Analytics for Improved Public Transport" (Pulse Lab Jakarta, 2017), <https://pulselabjakarta.org/assets/uploadworks/2018-08-02-13-21-05.pdf> (accessed October 10, 2022).
[56] See, e.g., Pulse Lab Kampala, "Using Machine Learning to Analyse Radio Content in Uganda: Opportunities for Sustainable Development and Humanitarian Action" (UN Global Pulse, September 2017), <https://www.unglobalpulse.org/wp-content/uploads/2017/09/Radio-Analysis-Report_Preview.pdf (accessed October 10, 2022).
[57] See, e.g., Iriantoni Almuna et al., "Pulse Stories. After Dark: Encouraging Safe Transit for Women Travelling at Night" (UN Women, Pulse Lab Jakarta, 2019).
[58] Jean-Martin Bauer, "Mobile Phone Surveys Can Help World Food Programme Reach Hungry People" *The Guardian* (March 10, 2016).
[59] See, e.g., UN Global Pulse, "Project Brief: Mapping the Risk-Utility Landscape of Mobile Data for Sustainable Development and Humanitarian Action" (July 2015), <https://www.unglobalpulse.

In these various modes, multistakeholderism continues an anti-formalist drive to engage a diversity of social, economic, and political actors in international law and policy work—a drive apparent since the mid-twentieth century and discussed in Chapter 2 already.[60] Multistakeholderism underwrites digital interfaces' reality effects: their claim to "referential plenitude" in Barthes' terms discussed earlier.[61] Through their operationalization in digital interfaces developed with engagement from a diversity of actors, law and policy are meant to "pass[] outside [them]sel[ves]" and encompass the world.[62]

Nevertheless, the range of stakeholders embraced by these effects is quite limited: the "multi" of multistakeholderism in the humanitarian field remains quite narrow, prospects for crowdsourcing notwithstanding. None of the previously referenced instances of stakeholder engagement entailed, for instance, prospective beneficiaries of humanitarian assistance being cast as direct participants in decision-making surrounding digital interfaces. For all the commitments to multistakeholder consultation and user-centered design that we heard repeated, the range and roles of "stakeholders" or "users" involved never seemed to be up for much negotiation or significant expansion.

Indeed, the prospect of creating greater space for lay or democratic participation in decision-making around the use of digital technology in the humanitarian field seemed to engender some ambivalence among our interviewees. For one thing, end users are not always seen as being sufficiently forward thinking or skilled for this work. Some interviewees with whom we spoke indicated that a lack of relevant qualifications or skills in partner organizations, and sometimes a want of computing power within those organizations, made partnership difficult when developing digital humanitarian interfaces.[63] One interviewee spoke of feeling "frustrated" because "at the end this is what the end user wants: A dumbed down version of everything."[64] Another—one of the interviewees from whom we quoted earlier—worried about end users' short-sightedness and their heterodox desires:

> [W]e try to take a pretty kind of agile approach, you know really stay very close to [intended users] [in a] very, very iterative [way] and we don't do a project for

org/document/mapping-the-risk-utility-landscape-of-mobile-data-for-sustainable-development-and-humanitarian-action/> (accessed October 10, 2022).

[60] Anne Orford, *International Law and the Politics of History* (Cambridge University Press, 2021) 206–217 (discussing various manifestations and influences upon antiformalism in the international legal field).
[61] Barthes, *supra* note 22.
[62] Foucault, *supra* note 26, at 224.
[63] Interview with Participant AI and AJ (November 12, 2020).
[64] Interview with Participant AF (April 28, 2020).

the most part unless we have the user on board from day one.... [But] the challenge is ... that old saw about ... the interview with Henry Ford, he said if I ask people what they wanted they would have sat up and asked for a horse.[65]

We will return to the politics of use and the qualification and disqualification of users in Chapter 7.

In other ways, also, interviewees underscored the difficulty of advancing broadly framed versions of user-centered design or stakeholder engagement in digital interfaces' development, despite the embrace of these ideas across the sector. One obstacle noted was the iterative and often technical nature of the consultations involved. A businessperson with experience working with governments, international organizations, and nongovernmental organizations on such endeavors described their process of working with clients as follows:

> We have a set of integration, standardization and harmonization tools that we use and apply on a case-by-case basis to the customer's systems, to their data, to their use cases. A lot of that is done algorithmically but it gets manually validated in a partnership—a technical partnership—between our staff and their technical experts who actually sit down and look at the results of the algorithm's work and basically a human validates and says, "Yes, this is correct. These two indicators should be matched; they mean the same thing. These two district names should be matched; they mean the same thing." So the grunt work is done by the algorithm, but ... the outputs of that get manually checked.... We have multiple layers of validation.[66]

A further set of factors seen to contribute to the difficulty of expanding the "multi" of multistakeholderism are sector-specific regulations, data localization policies, confidentiality agreements, and pseudo-proprietary contractual arrangements surrounding data retention and usage.

Some of these have impeded multiparty decision-making about digital interfaces' development, arguably for good reasons not canvassed here. Arrangements for the sharing and recombination of publicly held data *should*, after all, be politically challenging to negotiate, given the range of stakes in play. Nonetheless data localization regulations and legacy contractual rights were understood by some interviewees to make it hard for multiple stakeholders to collaborate on digital interface development.

The laws and policies in question were characterized repeatedly as challenges, constraints, barriers, and problems to be overcome in the course of "moving

---

[65] Interview with Participant N, *supra* note 54.
[66] Interview with Participant AK (July 16, 2021).

forward" or maintaining "progress." For example, one of our informants charged with trying to broker data-sharing arrangements within the UN Global Pulse network observed that the "biggest challenge" for organizations engaged in digital humanitarianism "is access to data—access to data and also regulatory compliance." They continued:

> We . . . had an issue with accessing mobile data, . . . social media comes to us through connections agreements that are made at Global Pulse level in New York, so we have access to social media and we have access to the firehose of Twitter, we have tools that the research team use to look into social media; [but] we really want to go beyond that . . . we want to move forward now. And another [type of data] that we want to use is mobile data, call detail records, of telephones—anonymized, confidential de-identified—so what we're interested in looking at is patterns of movement. . . . But we talked with the telecommunications companies maybe—we started talking to them about two years ago and they were really interested and said 'No problem, we can give you data', and something happened . . . and . . . the telecom regulator [in the relevant national jurisdiction], basically said "No, we don't agree to giving you access to this data". . . . We were given [satellite image data] last year and told an hour later [by the geospatial information regulator in the same national jurisdiction] to hand it back straight away.[67]

Why exactly these initial undertakings to share data were overridden was unclear; the interviewee in question alluded vaguely to "the [national] government [having] got involved."[68] Another interviewee suggested, however, that ad hoc decision-making of this kind may be a consequence of unfavorable law and policy settings in the jurisdictions in question:

> [The jurisdiction in question] doesn't have any regulatory basis . . . [for] innovation and data sharing to begin with, even among government institutions. So what they do is they do ad hoc contract[s] or agreement[s] for data sharing and [engage in] negotiation, very ad hoc as well, so that is basically the biggest constraint.

The businessperson from whom we quoted earlier lamented, similarly, that laws and policies in some jurisdictions surrounding cloud hosting often impede data-sharing to enable multistakeholder engagement:

---

[67] Interview with Participant A, *supra* note 44.
[68] Ibid.

Sometimes ... the law allows cloud hosting but then the policy says it can only be hosted on the government's cloud, which is not much better than a server in the basement and that also becomes a barrier.[69]

The same interviewee also highlighted that the prior implementation of particular software (and associated contractual agreements) can effectively tie up public data in particular, private hands, potentially impeding the involvement of other actors:

> I would say the biggest barrier to progress ... is that the implementors who are funded to work in this space create monopolies using the government's data and they take away the control of the data from the country. We see that everywhere that we work ... then what happens is that we can only help government coordinate that emergency response if some third-party implementor decides it's in their interests to follow the government's instructions and share the government's data with us ... many implementors use their technical expertise to basically dominate these countries and make themselves the effective owners of the country's data.[70]

We will return to the role of contractual agreements in conditioning the design and deployment of humanitarian digital interfaces later.

What emerges from this brief sketch of multistakeholder arrangements at work in the development and deployment of digital interfaces is the propensity of norms of openness to underwrite closure. Ostensibly, work on digital interfaces advances inclusive, consultative decision-making. As has transpired in other settings, however, multistakeholderism tends to get whittled away until a relatively narrowly configured "multi" is seen as qualified to get involved. Just as Donders et al. have observed of multistakeholder consultations in a European policymaking context, multistakeholderism may do as much to shore up legacy interests and affirm preexisting positions as open them to question. For all the talk of government being made more open through digital interfaces' recourse to nontraditional data sources and end-user engagement, multistakeholderism surrounding these interfaces turns out to be quite commensurate with "old-style politics of pleasing one stakeholder and then the other."[71] Multistakeholderism

---

[69] Interview with Participant AK, *supra* note 66.
[70] Ibid.
[71] Karen Donders, Hilde Van den Bulck, and Tim Raats, "The Politics of Pleasing: A Critical Analysis of Multistakeholderism in Public Service Media Policies in Flanders" (2019) 41 *Media, Culture & Society* 347, 362.

structures digital interfaces' development and use, but the ensuing relations are often marked as much by closure as openness or negotiability.[72]

## International Organizations' Guidelines

In addition to treaties and multistakeholder arrangements, interfaces such as those that readers have encountered throughout this book are shaped by guidance from international organizations on a range of substantive topics, including disaster mitigation and data protection. To be clear, it is not the case that digital interfaces are direct outputs of this kind of subject-specific guidance; guidelines on disaster relief do not stipulate explicitly that states must employ digital tools. Rather international institutions' guides on disaster relief and data protection tend to soften the ground for such initiatives, encouraging states to be supportive and permissive when asked to share data or otherwise support digital interfaces' development for instance. Everywhere one looks, international institutions are building an embrace of ICT "innovation" into their guidance on humanitarian best practice.

Illustrative of this kind of ground-softening in digital interfaces' favor is that effected by the Guidelines for the Domestic Facilitation and Regulation of International Disaster Relief and Initial Recovery Assistance (IDRL Guidelines) produced by the International Federation of Red Cross and Red Crescent Societies (IFRC). Paragraph 18(2) of the IDRL Guidelines stipulates, for instance, that states affected by disaster "should waive or expedite the granting of any applicable licenses and reduce any other barriers to the use, import or export of telecommunications and information technology equipment by assisting States and assisting humanitarian organizations or on their behalf in disaster relief and initial recovery assistance" and grant "assisting States and eligible assisting humanitarian organizations priority access to bandwidth, frequencies and satellite use for telecommunications and data transfer associated with disaster relief operations." This is indicative of how international soft law instruments facilitate humanitarian organizations gaining access to digital data and ICT infrastructure and incline national governments toward granting that access.[73]

The Sendai Framework for Disaster Risk Reduction 2015–2030 (endorsed by the UN General Assembly pursuant to states agreement at the 2015 Third UN World Conference on Disaster Risk Reduction) is another example.[74] It

[72] Mark Raymond and Laura DeNardis, "Multistakeholderism: Anatomy of an Inchoate Global Institution" (2015) 7 *International Theory* 572, 611.
[73] IFRC, "Guidelines for the Domestic Facilitation and Regulation of International Disaster Relief and Initial Recovery Assistance (IDRL Guidelines)" (2007), <https://disasterlaw.ifrc.org/media/1327> (accessed October 10, 2022).
[74] UNGA Res. 69/283 (June 23, 2015) UN Doc. A/RES/69/283.

has similarly helped to predispose governments and other actors favorably toward the use of digital tools for disaster prediction and response. Section 24(f) of that Framework provides, for instance, that "it is important" for those who have agreed to the Framework to "promote real time access to reliable data, make use of space and in situ information, including geographic information systems (GIS), and use information and communications technology innovations to enhance measurement tools and the collection, analysis and dissemination of data."[75] As well as helping to create favorable conditions for digital interfaces' development, the inclusion of this language in the Framework illustrates how the prospect of ICT "innovation" attracts international institutional attention on the global plane.

The United Nations' and other international organizations' standards on data protection also bear upon (and reflect the influence of) digital humanitarian interfaces' deployment. These standards help to make digitization safe for humanitarian professionals or suggest that it may be so. For example, the UN Principles on Personal Data Protection and Privacy, adopted in 2018, set out a basic framework for the processing of personal data by, or on behalf of, UN organizations in carrying out their mandated activities (personal data being defined for this purpose as information, contained in any form, relating to an identified or identifiable natural person). These establish individual data subjects' consent and their "best interests" as the twin fulcra upon which the "fair[ness] and legitima[cy]" of data processing depend when carried out by UN organizations.[76]

The 2018 UN Principles were not, however, well attuned to the processing of high volumes of aggregate or composite data, including data derived from third parties, as is presupposed by most of the interfaces examined in this book. In such settings, the ideal figure of an individual, consenting data subject may not serve well as a practical touchstone or source of legitimacy. As one of our informants observed:

[The emphasis on informed] consent is taken from the healthcare domain. . . . I can go into a hospital, the surgeon says well the good news is we can treat this, it's a very complex procedure, you don't need to know the details but here are the possible outcomes and the probabilities page. That's informed consent. That's literally all I need. Now here you're being asked to share this data set and make informed consent. Little could you possibly know that five years from now that data will be combined with data that will be produced

---

[75] United Nations Office for Disaster Risk Reduction, "Sendai Framework for Disaster Risk Reduction 2015–2030" (2015).
[76] United Nations, "Principles on Personal Data Protection and Privacy" (2018), <https://unsceb.org/principles-personal-data-protection-and-privacy-listing> (accessed October 10, 2022).

only three years from now by an [app] that doesn't even exist. . . . You're talking about . . . future applications and things that couldn't have even been anticipated so it doesn't [work] . . . just doesn't work, it's broken. . . . How do you verify . . . [that] your consent was informed? In some cases it may be even be theoretically impossible.[77]

The International Committee of the Red Cross (ICRC) Handbook on Data Protection in Humanitarian Action (2020) grapples a little more with the limits of consent-based data governance in humanitarian settings. It specifies that the "vital interests" of individuals (viewed in the aggregate) may serve as the legal basis for the collection of personal data, without the need to obtain data subjects' consent, if "important grounds of public interest" are triggered.[78] This fosters an expectation that there will be circumstances—especially those identified with disaster or emergency—in which international organizations may assert the legitimacy of their digital applications without the imprimatur of consent if they determine that the use of digital data assembled will deliver "vital" collective benefits. The unavailability of an individual subject from which to obtain consent thus prompts a devolution of authority back onto a data-bearing humanitarian actor to be exercised on the basis on their biopolitical assessment of the "vital interests" of a population. As discussed in Chapter 3, however, digital interfaces may make these kinds of assessments harder not easier to make, trading as they often do in nonpopulation digital aggregates.

International soft law instruments such as the guides just discussed thus help to smooth the way for the kind of digital interfaces discussed in this book. They do so in part by dispensing with the need for a consenting subject or offering proxies for that subject. That is the case even though those interfaces are more often characterized as outcomes of private-sector-led innovation than expressions of international organizational investment in the global digital economy. Guidelines of the kind just discussed offer only some rationales for that investment, however. Other justifications are budgetary.

The turn to humanitarian digital interfaces has emerged out of the confluence of international organizations' expansive institutional mandates and national-level austerity politics of various stripes. As was observed by an interagency task force of the United Nations reporting on financing for sustainable development in 2021: "National data collection programs . . . have long been underfunded by national Governments as well as the

---

[77] Interview with Participant N, *supra* note 54.
[78] Christopher Kuner and Massimo Marelli, *Handbook on Data Protection in Humanitarian Action* (2nd ed., ICRC, 2020) 67, <https://www.icrc.org/en/data-protection-humanitarian-action-handbook> (accessed October 10, 2022).

international development community. Funding to statistics and data from external sources has been stagnant since 2014. Yet demand for data has never been higher."[79] Demand for disaggregated data in particular has been driven higher by states signing up to the SDGs and agreeing to report against SDG indicators requiring gender breakdowns and reporting on a range of "vulnerable" groups. One of our interviewees explained international organizations' turn to digital interfaces by noting that they "have less resources [than states] so they need to use [them] wisely ... to identify what they think ... most people need..[80] Digital humanitarian interfaces are routinely called upon to address funding and informational shortfalls in combination.[81]

Yet humanitarian digital interfaces do not just pose answers to informational and budget challenges confronted by states and international organizations; their development is also constrained by them. The most frequently cited reason for national statistics offices not implementing digital applications or using alternative data sources is budget constraints limiting their ability to fund the necessary training of existing staff.[82] The answer to these kinds of dilemmas for many in the humanitarian sector since the late 1990s has been (among other things) partnership: multistakeholder partnership, discussed above, but also public-private partnership (the popularity of which throughout the UN system was noted in Chapter 5). For example, a core objective of the UN Working Group on Big Data for Official Statistics, one informant explained, is to promote "partnership and advocacy.... I am talking about how to make a PPP, public private sector partnership."[83] This is encouraged, also, by SDG 17, one of the targets for which calls for "promot[ion] [of] effective public, public-private and civil society partnerships."[84] Given the prominence of public-private partnership in their inception, the interfaces examined in this book are also artifacts of private law—specifically, contract law.

---

[79] UN Inter-agency Task Force on Financing for Development, "Financing for Sustainable Development Report 2021" (*United Nations*) 187, <https://developmentfinance.un.org/fsdr2021>.

[80] Interview with Participant D (July 27, 2018).

[81] See, e.g., Jennifer L. Cohen and Homi Kharas, "Using Big Data and Artificial Intelligence to Accelerate Global Development" (The Brookings Institution, November 15, 2018), <https://www.brookings.edu/research/using-big-data-and-artificial-intelligence-to-accelerate-global-development/> (accessed October 10, 2022).

[82] UN Statistics Division, "Global Assessment of Institutional Readiness for the Use of Big Data in Official Statistics" (UN Statistics Division, 2020), Background document E/CN.3/2020/24, <https://unstats.un.org/unsd/statcom/51st-session/documents/UN_BigData_report_v6.0-E.html> (accessed October 10, 2022).

[83] Interview with Participant K (November 21, 2018).

[84] United Nations Department of Economic and Social Affairs, "Sustainable Development Goals—Goal 17," <https://www.globalgoals.org/17-partnerships-for-the-goals> (accessed October 10, 2022).

## Contracts

Treaty infrastructures and international guidelines supporting the development and deployment of digital interfaces in the humanitarian field tend to perform landscaping functions in relation to those interfaces. They distribute powers, structure perspectives, and cultivate predispositions on which these interfaces depend. Contractual agreements (to which one or more national law(s) or, in some instances, international law is/are applicable) do this as well, but they also establish more specific blueprints for investment in such interfaces and for their design and operation. They identify explicitly who should (and should not) be regarded as having a stake in these interfaces' use; their respective roles and responsibilities; and the purposes toward which they should be oriented.

Unlike the data localization and other national regulatory requirements alluded to earlier, most contracts and regimes of contract law are perceived by sector participants as enabling legal measures: generative meeting points rather than barriers to be overcome. This betrays the wide-ranging influence of an archetype of contracting as "will-based interpersonal agreement between parties presumed as equals."[85] Contracts surrounding digital interfaces' development, however, routinely belie that archetype. Such contracts "form miniature legal orders in and of themselves" and play a role in the assembly, maintenance, or undermining of other legal orders.[86]

The impetus to constitute such a miniature-yet-nested legal order is often activated by the prospect of digital data becoming available: the offer of data begets contracting to elicit more offers of data. Although interfaces are often characterized as problem-driven, in actuality they are often data-driven: that is, premised opportunistically on some data becoming accessible. Thereafter, contracts operate to structure and condition movements of funding, data, labor, and software rights underpinning digital humanitarian interfaces' development. Humanitarian developers seeking to incorporate data from commercial digital platforms have to reckon, in particular, with their terms of service: a particular variant of standardized contract reproduced and activated globally via digital interfaces (a mechanism sometimes referred to as click-wrap contracting).[87] One of the data scientists working with an international organization with whom we spoke described how they scope out a potential digital humanitarian application, in dialogue with government officials, as follows:

---

[85] Klaas Hendrik Eller, 'Transnational Contract Law," in Peer Zumbansen (ed.), *The Oxford Handbook of Transnational Law* (Oxford University Press, 2021) 514.
[86] Ibid., 516.
[87] Caterina Gardiner, "Principles of Internet Contracting: Illuminating the Shadows'" (2019) 48 *Common Law World Review* 208.

[T]he first step it's basically to identify what can be there, what cannot be there. So, [we discuss] the license [to] all the data itself and agree on what ... data is available. And then through that we're trying to meet in the middle ... I will say that if you want my help these certain things [are what] I need from you. So, for example, the data needs to be provided on a certain level, the details of the data need to come to this different level. And I will try to explain [to] them what I was trying to do and then they will try to explain me what they want. And then we'll try to meet in the middle, that's what I do.[88]

Once this "middle" ground of overlapping institutional objectives and data availability has been preliminarily staked out, contractual texts signal which jurisdictions' authority will be operationalized and inform how these jurisdictions may intersect. For example, the UNDP-originated nondisclosure agreement that academic researchers collaborating with UN Global Pulse must sign invokes the immunity from national law that UN agencies have conferred on them by treaty, stipulating that "[n]othing in or relating to this Agreement shall be deemed a waiver, express or implied, of any of the privileges and immunities of the United Nations, including UNDP and its subsidiary organs."[89]

Among those jurisdictions activated and mediated by contract in connection with digital interfaces' development are national regimes of contract law, as these may be modified in some respects by treaty. These are either brought into relation explicitly (by, say, contractual terms expressly providing for their application to any disputes arising under the contract) or foreshadowed indirectly (by, for example, the inclusion of contractual terms designed to try to circumvent or limit their application). The national law(s) to which the parties agree to submit when contracting to enable the development or use of humanitarian digital interfaces then determine(s) the ambit of their contractual rights and the range of legal remedies to which they could in principle have access in the event of contract breach, and thus delineate(s) the kinds of fault by which they may be concerned in anticipation.[90] For example, the terms of conditions of OpenStreetMap, to which anyone must agree if they wish to contribute data to the Missing Maps Project (discussed in Chapter 2), included, at the time of writing, the following clause (for those resident anywhere in the world except France or Italy):

This Agreement shall be governed by English law without regard to principles of conflict of law. You agree that the United Nations Convention on Contracts

---

[88] Interview with Participant D, *supra* note 80.
[89] "UNDP Mutual Non-Disclosure Agreement" (2018) (on file with the author).
[90] Melvin Aron Eisenberg, "The Role of Fault in Contract Law: Unconscionability, Unexpected Circumstances, Interpretation, Mistake, and Nonperformance" (2009) 107 *Michigan Law Review* 1413.

for the International Sale of Goods (1980) is hereby excluded in its entirety from application to this Agreement. In the event of invalidity of any provision of this Agreement, the parties agree that such invalidity shall not affect the validity of the remaining portions of this Agreement. This is the entire agreement between You and OSMF which supersedes any prior agreement, whether written, oral or other, relating to the subject matter of this agreement.[91]

In practice, however, digital humanitarian interfaces are almost always developed under a cluster of interlocking contracts, rather than a single contract, some addressing funding, some data, some employment or contractor relations, and so on. These will often be subject to different national laws. Far from operating in a lawless space, then, practitioners advancing digital humanitarian initiatives typically grapple with the interaction of a surfeit of laws as well as the conflict of laws principles that govern their interaction. As one developer of digital tools for international and national public sector clients noted:

> It's almost always a case of two bilateral contracts side by side, so we will have something like a framework agreement with the government that sets out the parameters of the relationship, mutual obligations on the parties, mutual intentions to get down to work together, all those things, so there's a broad framework agreement in place with the country, data sharing, data confidentiality, etcetera, etcetera. Then with the funders, it tends to just be a grant agreement, a funding agreement, a contract, something like that. That's generally how it works.[92]

Moreover, these arrangements often have multiple national legal bearings, as the same interviewee went on to explain:

> The agreements that we sign with the countries are always . . . domiciled in that country's jurisdiction. The agreements that we sign with the funders are almost always—the choice of law in that case is wherever the funder tends to be headquartered, so . . . most of the times that's Geneva, for obvious reasons; sometimes it's Washington DC; sometimes it's New York.[93]

National legal domiciles notwithstanding, a recurrent concern of those contracting for the development of digital humanitarian interfaces is the prospect of their being scaled up regionally or globally, or at least adapted for other

---

[91] OpenStreetMap Foundation, "Contributor Terms (Rest of the World)," <https://wiki.osmfoundation.org/wiki/Licence/Contributor_Terms> (accessed October 10, 2022).
[92] Interview with Participant AK, *supra* note 66.
[93] Ibid.

national jurisdictions' purposes. As one interviewee working to advance digital innovation in the UN system observed: "[T]here is experimentation ... but also this idea that we should be able to scale."[94] Recounting a project undertaken with a provincial government, the same interviewee reported: "[I]t was relatively quickly identified that one of the first things to do would be to scale what we did for the [provincial] government to a national thing which ... could probably improve the potential actual utility of this particular thing and make it even more useful."[95] A colleague of that interviewee recalled the process of developing a prototype for the MIND interface (discussed in Chapter 3) that was initially conceived as having a national focus, but soon scaled up:

> [T]he whole idea came up saying let's do [a] regional one. And then through discussions it seems like people were getting excited and said: "How about we do a global one?" And then from the global we could scope down to the regional one. So, when it's finished, I had the global one.[96]

Another interviewee, also working within the UN system, indicated that it may be a prerequisite for humanitarian digital interfaces' development within the United Nations that they address problems at a sufficiently broad scale:

> We'll only take [a donor-proposed project] on if it fits our strategy ... that is to say that ... it has to represent ... an instance of more general problem. In other words, if what we developed can be ... applied across a much larger geography or to solve a broader class of problem ... or ... will necessitate creating some kind of underlying algorithms that will add a lot of value to other things we've already created then we'll take it on. Otherwise, we'll be recommending [to a prospective donor that] they go and find a vendor and do something like that.[97]

These practices of contracting—concluding agreements under different national and international legal regimes; standardized contracting; scaling these contracts' range of operation up or down throughout different iterations of interface design—are all "bequeathing [their] record" to the interfaces discussed throughout this book, just as the digital interfaces in question mediate and condition those contracting practices.[98] Contracts surrounding the development and use of digital interfaces procure a contingent convergence among different

---

[94] Interview with Participant AC (June 11, 2021).
[95] Ibid.
[96] Interview with Participant AC and D (February 18, 2020).
[97] Interview with Participant N, *supra* note 54.
[98] Jacques Derrida, "Des Tours de Babel," in Joseph F. Graham (tr.), *Difference in Translation* (Cornell University Press, 1985) 191.

legal and nonlegal orders: between the background entitlements of the parties and hierarchies embedded in software, for instance.[99] Digital interfaces actualize that convergence by making it usable.

Contracts and digital interfaces work in combination to draw distinct orders provisionally into relation and try to ensure an echo of that relation throughout subsequent translations and iterations of the interface, as it is put into use and, as is often the case, updated, up-scaled, or combined with other interfaces and data sources. This multijurisdictional ordering work "def[ies] a mere efficiency analysis"; it is concerned with much more than reducing transaction costs (*pace* conventional law and economics analyses of transnational contracting).[100] It is as much about crafting spaces and temporalities within which digital interfaces seem viable—indeed essential—tools with which to temper the chaos of the world, as they do in the various ways discussed throughout this book.

In practice, however, contractual relations underwriting and shaping digital interfaces are often deeply embedded in those interfaces—and thus hard for users to scrutinize. Volunteer participants in the Missing Maps Project (discussed in Chapter 2) are unlikely to think of their work as an exercise of rights and discharge of obligations under English contract law, regardless of their acceptance of the choice of law clause quoted earlier. Rather, their work is characterized, on the Missing Maps Project website, as a freewheeling, placeless enterprise: an "open, collaborative project" through which "a global community of mappers" addresses "disasters around the world."[101] Moreover, digital interfaces often integrate submission to (or prospective reliance on) national contract law into banal routines of account sign-up. This is the case in respect of the Missing Maps Project. Those who wish to participate, as a volunteer, in a "mapathon" are invited to take a few "key steps" in order to contribute, the first of which is to create an OpenStreetMap account, a process that includes "agree[ing] [to] the terms and conditions" (including the choice of law clause quoted earlier).[102]

In addition to the embedded practices of contracting for and through humanitarian digital interfaces, these interfaces also rely on an international legal infrastructure that appears much closer to their surface: indeed, one that many interfaces and institutions developing them seek to wear on their proverbial sleeves. That is the infrastructure of ethical codes.

---

[99] On hierarchy within digital networks, see Alexander R. Galloway, "Protocol" (2006) 23 *Theory, Culture & Society* 317.

[100] Eller, *supra* note 85; Fleur Johns, "Performing Party Autonomy" (2008) 71 *Law and Contemporary Problems* 243.

[101] OpenStreetMap Foundation, "Missing Maps," <https://www.missingmaps.org> (accessed October 10, 2022).

[102] See, e.g., Harry West, "Missing Maps Mapathon 2020. UWE Bristol—Department of Geography and Environmental Management" (September 18, 2020), <https://storymaps.arcgis.com/stories/14918b56fedf4e5ab548b9f2431a9ea3> (accessed October 10, 2022).

## Ethical Codes

Alongside the proliferation of humanitarian digital interfaces, recent years have seen an accompanying profusion of ethical policymaking on the international plane designed to regulate conduct in the global digital economy. Many of the policies in question reference one or more resolutions of the UN General Assembly that have sought to regulate intergovernmental and nongovernmental organizations and inform member states' regulation of data governance internationally, such as the Guidelines for the Regulation of Computerized Personnel Data Files adopted in 1990.[103] However, policies concerned with the ethical use of data science in the humanitarian field typically claim authority less on the basis of formal intergovernmental procedures than by highlighting the credentials and range of experts involved in crafting them.

The 2020 *Framework for the Ethical Use of Advanced Data Science Methods in the Humanitarian Sector*, produced by a group calling itself the Humanitarian Data Science and Ethics Group with support from Dutch national and local governments, is one example of such a policy (hereafter, the Ethical Use Framework). It announces itself as the "outcome of a consultative process" conducted by "a multistakeholder group" that "refer[red] extensively to existing academic and humanitarian documents... combine[d] research and interviews with various humanitarian field staff officers," and involved "a thorough review process involving diverse data stakeholders and experts."[104] Another, from 2018, is *The Signal Code: Ethical Obligations for Humanitarian Information Activities*, produced by a program of the Harvard Humanitarian Initiative, with funding from the International Organization for Migration, acknowledges a series of individual contributors affiliated with universities and nongovernmental and international organizations (hereafter the Signal Code Obligations).[105]

Generating normative outputs of this kind has become part of the core business of intergovernmental and nongovernmental organizations promoting digital humanitarianism. One of our interviewees, working within the UN system, highlighted the centrality of policymaking to the task of developing digital interfaces in the humanitarian sector:

[D]ata innovation—part of me will say that it's a buzzword. We leverage it. It's a priming ground... you try to bring across disparate data and tr[y] to find out

---

[103] UNGA Res. 45/95 (December 14, 1990) UN Doc. A/RES/45/95.

[104] Kate Dodgson et al., "A Framework for the Ethical Use of Advanced Data Science Methods in the Humanitarian Sector" (Humanitarian Data Science & Ethics Group, 2020), <https://www.humdseg.org/dseg-ethical-framework> (accessed October 10, 2022).

[105] Stuart R. Campo et al., "The Signal Code: Ethical Obligations for Humanitarian Information Activities" (Harvard Humanitarian Initiative, 2018), 5/2018.

ways in which it can be used for completely different purposes than what it may have been intended when created ... But it's not just about the data. It's also about the kinds of techniques and the related systems or things that you may need, policies around that to enable [us] to use it while also minimizing potential harms.[106]

Common to many of these policymaking activities is an effort to present guidance aimed at humanitarian actors as derived from transcendent norms (principles of more general, often legally binding, application), all while placing those norms beyond contention. At the same time, many such policies disavow their own binding status and affirm the primacy of voluntary self-regulation by humanitarian organizations, even while anticipating those organizations' entry into further, legally binding agreements. As such, these policies seek to carve out and occupy an interim decision-making space, positioned both after and before the binding force of law, but nonetheless freighted with duties and obligations. This is a space in which the humanitarian professional—a human figure poised to assist human populations affected by some acute, unmet need—is positioned as central.[107] That figure's recognition and acceptance of "data responsibility" and skills of "data management" are cast as key to the safety, ethical soundness, and effectiveness of data usage in the humanitarian field.[108] And the exercise of this responsibility is cast as a relational, dialogical endeavor itself mediated digitally, as one of our interviewees involved in ethics policymaking made clear when they remarked:

[A]nother important group of actors that I consult, at least in drafting the policy is of course the whole responsible data community that's out there. There is a huge debate constantly going on online, [so] to get input and feedback on first draft we'll certainly reach out to that community.[109]

Given their insistence on humanitarian actors accepting "data responsibility," the ethical guides promulgated in relation to digital humanitarianism seem to suggest, at first glance, a Weberian ethic of responsibility. However, unlike Max Weber's well-known rendering of that term, the orientation of these ethical

---

[106] Interview with Participant AC (June 16, 2021).
[107] Campo et al., *supra* note 105, at 7.
[108] OCHA Centre for Humanitarian Data, "Data Responsibility Guidelines (Working Draft)" (March 2019); Inter-Agency Standing Committee, "IASC Operational Guidance on Data Responsibility in Humanitarian Action" (February 3, 2021)3 <https://reliefweb.int/report/world/iasc-operational-guidance-data-responsibility-humanitarian-action-february-2021> (accessed October 10, 2022); OCHA Centre for Humanitarian Data, "Guidance Note: Data Responsibility in Public-Private Partnerships" (OCHA, February 2020), <https://centre.humdata.org/guidance-note-data-responsibility-in-public-private-partnerships/> (accessed October 10, 2022).
[109] Interview with Participant G (June 13, 2018).

guides is not toward answering for the foreseeable consequences of whatever actions humanitarian professionals might decide to take or not. Nor is responsibility here a matter of politics as Weber characterized it, in the sense of taking an interest in the distribution, maintenance, or transfer of power and bearing responsibility for the consequences of its exercise.

Instead, "data responsibility" seems more oriented toward what Weber called an ethic of conviction, characteristic of the civil servant rather than the figure of politics. The latter entails executing faithfully on some higher order derived from a preexisting hierarchy of values, exactly as though the action were taken in accordance with the ethical actor's personal conviction. As Weber explained: "With an ethic of conviction, one feels 'responsible' only for ensuring that the flame of pure conviction, for example, the flame of protest against the injustice of the social order, should never be extinguished."[110] Likewise, amid the ethical codes governing "humanitarian information activities," the foremost imperatives seem to be keeping alive "pure conviction" in humanitarian morality as a basis for protesting injustice.[111] These codes are less concerned with transferring power than establishing measures of rectitude, risk management, and self-restraint.

The UN Development Group's 2017 *Guidance Note on Big Data for Achievement of the 2030 Agenda: Data Privacy, Ethics and Protection* (hereafter, the UNDG Guidance Note) is indicative. It anchors its authority to that of "fundamental human right[s]" but insists that it is not, in its own right, a "legal document," "only a minimum basis for self-regulation." In all instances, the UNDG Guidance Note insists, "[d]ata access, analysis or other use must be consistent with the United Nations Charter and in furtherance of the Sustainable Development Goals." Thereafter, among its practical recommendations is a suggestion that "[a]ppropriate governance and accountability mechanisms should be established to monitor compliance with relevant law" and that "[l]egally binding agreements . . . should be established to ensure reliable and secure access to data." Assessments of the potential "impact that data use may have on an individual(s) and/or group(s) of individuals" must be so encompassing as to exceed the reach of human knowledge: they must extend to any "risks, harms and benefits . . . whether known or unknown."[112] All the while, the most important thing, the UNDG Guidance Note suggests, is to try to keep right-bearing humans continually in view. As one of our interviewees explained, the aim of "processes for regulating the . . . access to and use of insights from this data"

---

[110] Max Weber, "Politics as a Vocation," in David Owen and Tracy B. Strong (eds.), Rodney Livingstone (tr.), *The Vocation Lectures: Science as a Vocation; Politics as a Vocation* (Hackett Publishing, 2004).

[111] Didier Fassin, *Humanitarian Reason: A Moral History of the Present* (University of California Press, 2011) 8–9.

[112] United Nations Development Group, "Data Privacy, Ethics and Protection: Guidance Note on Big Data for Achievement of the 2030 Agenda" (2017) 3, 4, 5, 7.

within the UN system is to "place human rights at the cent[er]."[113] As in Weber's rendering of an "ethic of conviction," the "flame of protest against the injustice of the social order, should never be extinguished."[114]

Other instruments likewise tether their authority to general ethical principles by which humanitarian professionals are bound and focus on the evocation of "shared" value within that community. The Signal Code Obligations, for example, make reference to: the Code of Conduct for Employees of the International Committee of the Red Cross (by its terms, "mandatory for all ICRC employees and constitute an integral part of [the ICRC's] employment contract"); and the Humanitarian Charter adopted by Sphere, a nonprofit association based in Geneva that was originally assembled by a group of humanitarian agencies (that Charter being "in part a statement of established legal rights and obligations, in part a statement of shared belief").[115]

Elsewhere, as in the Ethical Use Framework, guidance offered those engaged in digital humanitarianism is situated within, and said to be derived from, "general" AI ethics principles. Within this context, tailored applications and adaptations are required, the Ethical Use Framework insists, because of the specific nature of humanitarian work. In particular, it remains the case that "almost all humanitarian scenarios using technology will still require large amounts of human oversight."[116] The Framework thus maintains an assumption that Louise Amoore observes "is so often assumed in the ethical and moral debates on algorithmic decisions," namely, that "harms inflicted through machine learning are . . . located primarily in the ceding of human control to machines." No attempt is made in these ethical codes to grapple with the prospect that "what it means to be human is significantly transformed in and through" the digitization of humanitarian work, as explored in Amoore's work and in prior chapters of this book.[117]

As much as it manifests concern at the prospect of human actors ceding responsibility to machines, this policymaking activity is nonetheless generative of computation in its own right. It provides a rationale for the development of dedicated software, for instance. Another of our interviewees, working within the UN system to advance digital humanitarianism, indicated just how much ICT infrastructure may need to be marshaled or created in order to give effect to these kinds of ethical guidelines:

---

[113] Interview with Participant N, *supra* note 54.
[114] Weber, *supra* note 110.
[115] ICRC, "Code of Conduct for Employees of the International Committee of the Red Cross" (ICRC 2018); Sphere, "Humanitarian Charter" (1997), <https://spherestandards.org/humanitarian-standards/humanitarian-charter/> (accessed October 10, 2022).
[116] Dodgson et al., *supra* note 104, at 5–9.
[117] Louise Amoore, *Cloud Ethics: Algorithms and the Attributes of Ourselves and Others* (Duke University Press, 2020) 79.

> [F]irst of all we figure out what the absolute minimum amount of information is that will be possible to achieve the outcomes that we're looking for ... we can't ever be in receipt of information more than that. Which means the generation of the data sets has to be done by the data controller. ... Sometimes the data controller ... doesn't have the capacity to do that and we have to actually write the software for them. That will ... export records and cryptographically hash certain values to create anonymous unique IDs and pseudonymous unique IDS. This kind of thing. And then we have to figure out sort of the modality of access. And the modality of access can vary widely ... there are lots of different options.[118]

There are "lots of different options," and yet the emphasis of much ethical codification surrounding digital humanitarianism seems to be on refining the preexisting normative order into ever more elaborate management procedures and technical protocols.

In their preoccupation with the extension of preexisting principles and their orientation toward management—the preparation of Data Responsibility Plans and quality assessment reports, for instance[119]—the ethical guides discussed in this chapter continually defer the moment of politics in the Weberian sense (that is, they defer the exercise, distribution, or transfer of power). Even ensuring the agency of affected populations tends to be cast as a matter of organizational management rather a matter of power being transferred from one locus to another. Promoting beneficiary agency is depicted as a matter of creating "representative participation and feedback mechanisms" and keeping affected populations "sufficiently informed," without regard for the ways in which agency may be redistributed by digital mediation.[120] This leaves many unanswered questions, such as those of the kind that one of our interviewees raised:

> [T]here hasn't been a playbook for this kind of thing ... what does the public need to know? What kind of transparency is appropriate? ... [T]elling them your mobile communications records are being used in [an] anonymized safe way to predict the spread of disease after [an] earthquake is something you can do. That's not what [members of the public] want to know ... What they want to know is whether their village is in the [disease] risk zone and you're not going to tell them that. Because if you do they're going to spread [the disease] all over the country and you can't manage quarantine. So, so that's tricky ... [W]ith the Ebola crisis it's like the opposite problem ... you want to know the risk maps for

---

[118] Interview with Participant N, *supra* note 54.
[119] OCHA Centre for Humanitarian Data, "Data Responsibility Guidelines (Working Draft)," *supra* note 108, at 63; Campo et al., *supra* note 105, at 44.
[120] Campo et al., *supra* note 105, at 26.

the spread of the disease but you don't necessarily want the government of the country to know that after they close the border with their neighboring country that there are a bunch of potentially infected people heading up to the border and it's guarded by scared 18-year-olds but they can't really stop it . . . So all sorts of risks and even group risks and group harms can show up in . . . this kind of data.[121]

Ethical code-making in and around digital humanitarian practice leaves these kinds of thorny political conundrums and conflicts untouched, much as commitments to multistakeholderism in this field fail to grapple with the amplitude of the "multi" to be engaged. Rather, it tends to be presumed, among digital humanitarian actors and proponents, that agency will flow automatically from affected populations being kept "sufficiently informed," as discussed in Chapter 4. As one of our interviewees remarked: "Data is power but sometimes people who collect it [don't] even realize."[122]

## Goals, Targets, and Other Infrastructures of Humanitarian Digital Interface

The foregoing dimensions of digital interfaces' international legal and policy infrastructure—treaties, multistakeholder arrangements, international guidelines, contracts, and ethical codes—are far from the only institutions and norms on which digital interfaces rely and over which they exert some animating influence. Particularly significant, among those not mentioned so far, is the international regime of goals, targets, indicators, and associated measurement and reporting requirements expressed in and surrounding the SDGs: a composite of treaty, resolutions of international organizations, and other international soft-law instruments.[123] As has been apparent throughout this book, the SDGs, and the need to report against SDG targets and indicators, are frequently cited rationales for digital humanitarian interfaces' development and recurrent referents for their design.

The imperative of states and other international actors taking steps to support the development and use of digital technology, in developing countries especially, is embedded in those targets adopted under SDG 9, "Build resilient infrastructure, promote inclusive and sustainable industrialization and foster

---

[121] Interview with Participant N, *supra* note 54.
[122] Interview with Participant I (August 21, 2015).
[123] Sakiko Fukuda-Parr and Desmond McNeill, "Knowledge and Politics in Setting and Measuring the SDGs: Introduction to Special Issue" (2019) 10 *Global Policy* 5.

innovation."[124] ICT development is also referenced in the targets agreed by UN members in relation to health (SDG 3); education (SDG 4); gender equality and women's empowerment (SDG 5); private sector development (SDG 8); and climate change (SDGs 13, 14, and 15).

Digital interfaces also comprise an important medium through which these goals, indicators, and targets are actualized and experienced. As Angelina Fisher has observed, digital interfaces point "towards a different process of indicator construction and dissemination that, in turn, implicates different means by which governance effects are achieved."[125] Sometimes users of digital interfaces are encouraged to feel as though they are working toward SDG attainment simply by interacting with a digital interface. For example, when reporting the World Food Programme's release of HungerMap LIVE (discussed in Chapter 4) to its subscribers, an organization called SDG2 Advocacy Hub (that coordinates global campaigning and advocacy to achieve SDG 2, the goal to "[e]nd hunger, achieve food security and improved nutrition and promote sustainable agriculture") characterized that interface as "a tool for timely action on food insecurity."[126] Regardless of whether any change in outcomes vis-à-vis the SDGs results from their use, digital interfaces train users to treat data availability as a paramount good from which agentive possibilities automatically flow.

More generic international legal infrastructures on which humanitarian digital interfaces depend include a range of protocols, licenses, domains, and standards that are global in their operation and multiple in their national and international points of anchorage, input, and output. Most of the digital interfaces discussed in this book rely, for instance, on free or open-source software licenses. They depend, also, on network protocols and the domain name system. And they are shaped, to varying degrees, by standards issued by the International Organization for Standardization (the ISO) and the International Electrotechnical Commission. Other scholars have traced the roles that such instruments and institutions play in global ordering, their distributive implications, and the forms of contestation that they occasion or foreclose.[127] For purposes of this book, it will suffice to say that humanitarian digital interfaces depend on these international legal infrastructures too. ISO 9001, an international

---

[124] United Nations Department of Economic and Social Affairs, "Sustainable Development Goals—Goal 9," <https://sdgs.un.org/goals/goal9> (accessed October 10, 2022).

[125] Angelina Fisher, "Indicators 2.0: From Ranks and Reports to Dashboards and Databanks" (*Völkerrechtsblog*, November 23, 2021), <https://voelkerrechtsblog.org/indicators-2-0-from-ranks-and-reports-to-dashboards-and-databanks/> (accessed October 10, 2022).

[126] SDG2 Advocacy Hub, "HungerMap LIVE: A Tool for Timely Action on Food Insecurity" (January 22, 2021), <https://sdg2advocacyhub.org/news/hungermap-live-tool-timely-action-food-insecurity> (accessed October 10, 2022).

[127] Alexander R. Galloway, *Protocol: How Control Exists after Decentralization* (MIT Press, 2004); Laura Denardis, *Internet in Everything: Freedom and Security in a World with No Off Switch* (Yale University Press, 2020).

standard for quality management, has been adopted quite widely among larger humanitarian organizations, for instance.[128] Developments in the humanitarian field may yet inform future directions taken in these standard-setting domains.

More could be said about the laws and policies on which humanitarian digital interfaces rely and the interpretation of which those interfaces influence. There is more to this "great surface network in which the stimulation of bodies, the intensification of pleasures, the incitement to discourse, the formation of special knowledges, the strengthening of controls and resistances, are linked to one another" and to the plight and pleas of those in need of humanitarian assistance.[129] The point of this chapter is not, however, to present an exhaustive mapping of all international legal instruments and practices with which humanitarian digital interfaces are in continuous, juris-generative relation. Rather, the point is, as noted at the outset, to suggest the many points of entry that these digital interfaces exhibit and the many forms of investment on which they depend, some of which could be leveraged strategically in yet unforeseen ways. There is, accordingly, nothing unalterable about the priorities embedded in digital interfaces and their infrastructures, even as the heterogeneous powers involved in their reproduction are considerable. There are, as the next chapter will explore, many prospects for rethinking and enlivening a politics of use in this context.

---

[128] Dorothea Hilhorst, "Being Good at Doing Good? Quality and Accountability of Humanitarian NGOs" (2002) 26 *Disasters* 193, 362.
[129] Foucault, *supra* note 25, at 105–106.

# 7
# Uses: Using, Disusing, and Misusing Digital Humanitarian Interfaces

### Introduction

Mud. Blood. Confusion. This book opened with these, but they have not been in abundance throughout its pages. Of course, humanitarianism has always been as much about white four-wheel drive cars and air conditioning as it has been a messy scrabble for survival.[1] Yet mediation by digital interfaces seems to make of humanitarianism an even cleaner, more clinical practice than it might otherwise appear. As we have seen throughout this book, however, that orderliness is always in the making and unmaking. As Orit Halpern has observed, "[h]umanitarianism ... constantly erupt[s] out of the translations between our myriad databanks and interfaces" and the "politics ... of that transformation are still being negotiated." Halpern continued: "This is the nature of politics now, negotiated at the level of attention and nervous networks, structured into our architectures of perception and affect; feedback providing the opening to chance and the danger of repetition without difference."[2] This is what the politics of international legal and political ordering consist of now too: negotiation and struggle amid the "erupt[ions]," "translations," "opening[s]," and "danger[s]" of digital humanitarianism and cognate practices.

This politics is a politics of use. It is in the politics of use, not for the most part in the politics of principle, that the direction of the epistemic shifts to which this book has drawn attention is being set. What gains power in contemporary international legal and political relations is what gets used and who or what is deemed useful and how. According to the doctrine of sources concerning customary law, what gets used may also be what becomes lawful insofar as use amounts to "a general practice accepted as law."[3]

Usefulness is especially salient in the digital humanitarian field. The benchmark of usefulness and measures of use are recurrent points of reference for

---

[1] Lisa Smirl, *Spaces of Aid: How Cars, Compounds and Hotels Shape Humanitarianism* (Zed Books, 2015).
[2] Orit Halpern, *Beautiful Data: A History of Vision and Reason since 1945* (Duke University Press, 2014) 238.
[3] Statute of the Court (1946) UKTS 67 art. 38(1)(b).

humanitarian digital interfaces' design, customization, and deployment, as noted in Chapter 3. Readers may recall, from prior chapters, developers recounting their efforts to develop interfaces that are "useful to several groups of people across different sectors of society" (in Chapters 2 and 4) and to "improve the potential actual utility of [a] particular [interface] and make it even more useful" (in Chapter 6).[4] Interfaces without recordable use or users become junk; they become "dead": "obdurate relic[s] of old decisions, old technologies and old bureaucracies"[5]—relics with which the international humanitarian field is littered. Things that fall out of use and that people regarded as useless—including would-be users without an interface adapted to their use—tend to become superfluous.[6]

There is much to be negotiated, then, in terms of use. Prior chapters have repeatedly suggested that prospects for *doing otherwise* in legal and political relations on the global plane may be opened by the mismatches and tensions between analog and digital in international humanitarian work. This chapter explores how these potentialities may be realized or shut down in the politics of digital interfaces' use: that is, the politics of what is considered usable or useful; who qualifies as a user; what range of uses are enacted or invited; how and why digital interfaces might be generatively disused or misused in international humanitarian work. Use, as Sara Ahmed has discussed at length, can be conservative, even fatal: maintaining well-traveled paths; discouraging deviance; assigning some peoples, places and things to categories of the useless or unused and, on that basis, submitting them to exploitation or appropriation. Yet use and nonuse can also be ways of stopping, resisting, questioning, reinhabiting—in Ahmed's terms, queering—use.[7] This chapter will engage with Ahmed's work, in particular, as it probes what this could entail in the context of the making use (or not) of digital humanitarian interfaces. That is, this chapter explores whether disuse or misuse of digital interfaces could enliven prospects beyond the status quo. That is not to say that status-quo-disrupting use of digital humanitarian interfaces is always, everywhere predictably better than their status-quo-affirming use. Use-effects are challenging to evaluate normatively because usage always changes that which is used which in turn shapes further use, as discussed later. One cannot assess the effects of use from a secure position. Nonetheless, with the global

---

[4] Interview with Participant AC (June 11, 2021); FAO Committee on World Food Security, "Guidelines for National Food Insecurity and Vulnerability Information and Mapping Systems (FIVIMS): Background and Principles" (FAO 24th Session, June 2, 1998) 17, <https://www.fao.org/3/w8500e/w8500e.htm> (accessed October 10, 2022).

[5] Jathan Sadowski, "'Anyway, the Dashboard Is Dead': On Trying to Build Urban Informatics" [2021] *New Media & Society* 1, 7.

[6] On the production of superfluity in international law and politics generally, see Susan Marks, "Law and the Production of Superfluity" (2011) 2 *Transnational Legal Theory* 1.

[7] Sara Ahmed, *What's the Use? On the Uses of Use* (Duke University Press, 2019).

digital economy—of which digital humanitarianism is a dimension—riddled with oppression, domination, exploitation, deprivation, extractivism, and bias, possibilities for challenging the status quo are worth enlivening.[8]

The first part of the chapter considers what kinds of uses and users are encouraged or mandated by humanitarian digital interfaces, even as they are typically customizable. The chapter then turns to *disuse* and prospects for users or could-be users weakening, resisting, or reorienting certain interfaces through withdrawing use or declining to use. Disuse, as we shall see, may be related to a politics of refusal, although it is not reducible to this.[9] Later discussion will focus on associated potential for *misuse*: that is, generatively reshaping digital interfaces through defiance or questioning of their intended or anticipated purposes, or use against or beyond the scope of instructions. Finally, the chapter will draw out the potential of digital interfaces' use to reshape humanitarianism further on the international plane.

In brief, the argument of this chapter is that the range of prospective users, uses, and forms of user input that *count* for purposes of developing, refining, and reconsidering the need for digital humanitarian interfaces should be expanded, given their incipiently transformative effects on the humanitarian episteme. The argument is not that the use of digital humanitarian interfaces should everywhere be resisted and foiled, but neither should their usage be presumed to follow predictable, measurable, beneficial tracks. The stakes of digital humanitarian interfaces' widespread use are far higher than whether or not they serve the informational needs of identified end users. The legal and political questions broached surrounding their development and deployment should be commensurately far-reaching.

## Use

Each of the digital humanitarian interfaces discussed in this book is addressed to users, including prospective, future users (as discussed in Chapter 4). Interfaces' capacity to attract users and usage on a recurrent basis is understood to be essential to their efficacy—and hence the rationales that they offer for further, comparable investment. Given the infinite reproducibility of digital data and ever-expanding mechanisms for its harvesting, those interfaces that attract

---

[8] Ruha Benjamin (ed.), *Captivating Technology: Race, Carceral Technoscience, and Liberatory Imagination in Everyday Life* (Duke University Press, 2019); Julie E. Cohen, *Between Truth and Power: The Legal Constructions of Informational Capitalism* (Oxford University Press, 2019).

[9] Ruha Benjamin, "Informed Refusal: Toward a Justice-Based Bioethics" (2016) 41 *Science, Technology, & Human Values* 967; Maria Kaika, "'Don't Call Me Resilient Again!': The New Urban Agenda as Immunology . . . or . . . What Happens When Communities Refuse to Be Vaccinated with 'Smart Cities' and Indicators" (2017) 29 *Environment and Urbanization* 89.

greatest use tend to prevail and get replicated rather than being used up. Use begets use, as Sara Ahmed has observed; *"[t]he more a path is used, the more a path is used."*[10] What gets used also tends to be valued irrespective of the cumulative effects of that use. Utility (understood broadly, not in strictly utilitarian terms) is treated as a paramount virtue across digital humanitarian endeavors, including in relation to digital interfaces.

Nevertheless, whether a particular humanitarian digital interface has indeed attracted users and usage—and if so, when, where, and of what kinds—is often difficult to document for a combination of technical and privacy-related reasons. As one of our interviewees observed, speaking of the Humanitarian Data Exchange (HDX), an open platform for sharing data across crises and organizations maintained by the UN Office for the Coordination of Humanitarian Affairs' Center for Humanitarian Data: "In terms of [the HDX's] use . . . we don't track individuals so I don't know, I can't tell you exactly. I mean what I can say is of the 6000 data sets we have on the platform I think 60,000, we get 60,000 downloads of the data a month which is a lot of data going out the door."[11] For these reasons, the development and promotion of generic "use cases"—shareable descriptions of situations in which a product or service could potentially be used—is a matter of some preoccupation in this field.[12]

In view of these preoccupations, it could be said that humanitarian digital interfaces are *required* to be useful or to make themselves and the data and other resources that they marshal appear useful. The orientation of the following interviewee toward "user experience" and creating something that is "actually usable" in the humanitarian field is indicative:

> So you've got technology specialists, you know, data scientists, data engineers, who can kind of hack your data, for want of a better word, and try and come up with a solution. Now . . . we combine . . . it with your domain experts and also your ethnographers so that you have this kind of user experience and *something that is actually useable* that can be implemented.[13]

Use is required not just to demonstrate efficacy and justify investment but also as a way of ensuring recognizability to, and integration within, a governable body or "system" in the international humanitarian field. Use often implies "becoming part," while nonuse can signify no longer being "of service to the whole."[14] Unlike a written report, one interviewee explained, a digital interface is

---

[10] Ahmed, *supra* note 7, at 41 (emphasis in original).
[11] Interview with Participant F (June 13, 2018).
[12] See, e.g., Interview with Participant K (October 2, 2015).
[13] Interview with Participant A (August 21, 2015) (emphasis added).
[14] Ahmed, *supra* note 7, at 11.

"an actual tangible"; it "has to fit in your system and it has to be integrated in your system and *someone has to use it*."[15] Digital interfaces' use both demands and demonstrates systemic "fit" on the part of interfaces and their users alike. Our interviewee continued: "So that's kind of a vital component [of our work] . . . capacity development, capacity building, training, transfer of knowledge— . . . how do we internalize these tools."[16]

Digital interfaces must not just attract users, then, but also train those users to "internalize these tools" in their life and work. Users are only users to the extent that they keep on using and doing so in data-generative ways. As Ahmed has written in relation to use: "Not using: not being."[17] This is one of the reasons why humanitarian digital interfaces such as MIND (discussed in Chapter 3) provide for user customization and lay graphic emphasis on the continual updating of data. The former fosters initial "internalization"; the latter, recurrent use. Like commercial digital interfaces, humanitarian versions are built to elicit and retain user attention.[18]

Use of digital interfaces creates value, but their use-value does not derive from their "satisf[action] of human wants," as in Marx's explanation of use-value,[19] so much as their direction of human attention. A digital interface such as HungerMap LIVE—discussed in Chapter 4—does not make itself useful by sating hunger. Instead, its usefulness stems from its translation of hunger into a relatively novel problem of data deficiency and its satisfaction of a desire to resolve that problem—a problem that it has, itself, helped to engender. In this context, satisfaction implies the capturing of attention; hunger implies data hunger. A digital interface made publicly accessible typically demonstrates usefulness by measures such as numbers of visits, average session duration, pages per session, bounce rate (the percentage of website visitors that navigate away from the site after viewing only one page), and so on.

Marx wrote that "[t]o discover the various uses of things is the work of history."[20] Recent history and prevailing practice suggest that, with respect to humanitarian digital interfaces, "use" of an interface implies online engagement with that interface, regardless of such users' ultimate consumption of associated goods or services or such interfaces' broader, systemic effects. Recall the opening scene of Chapter 1, from the 1999 Kosovo War. Humanitarian digital interfaces only came to the fore historically in the dying days of twentieth-century media

---

[15] Interview with Participant A, *supra* note 13 (emphasis added).
[16] Ibid.
[17] Ahmed, *supra* note 7, at 45.
[18] Rebecca Jablonsky, Tero Karppi, and Nick Seaver, "Introduction: Shifting Attention" (2021) 47 *Science, Technology, & Human Values* 235.
[19] Karl Marx, *Capital, Volumes One & Two* (Samuel Moore, Edward Aveling and Ernest Untermann trs., Wordsworth, 2013) 17.
[20] Ibid., 17.

culture; once "sign-value [had] take[n] precedence over use-value," and after the spectacular "aura" surrounding "images of possessable objects" and their prospective uses (characteristic of twentieth-century media and advertising) had been displaced onto "digitized flows of data," in the words of art historian Jonathan Crary.[21] The "discover[y]" of these interfaces' social and political value is historically unfinished business but appraising *sign value* on the basis of recordable, data-generative engagement is often taken to suffice by way of investigation.

Humanitarian digital interfaces are not, however, equally inviting of all users' attention. Those engaging with them must come to recognize themselves, and make themselves recognizable, as *humanitarian* users in order to qualify as such. One of our interviewees spoke of the process of the HDX acquiring registered users, for example, as follows:

> [T]he way it works is you have to be a registered user, once you're registered you can request to create an organization. We get that request. We make sure that you're part of that org, whatever your org email is. We do some research. There[] [are] only three criteria ... one is ... do you have relevant humanitarian data ... [another is] that you're trusted ... do we know you, have we heard of you, are you just some guy who's created ... the name of a group [that] wasn't ... a registered NGO ... So, so yeah mostly it's people we know.[22]

Becoming "trusted" and "know[n]" for purposes of interacting with a humanitarian digital interface like HDX implies showing yourself to be "for" humanitarianism. Users of humanitarian digital interfaces have preassigned roles: data source, official user, intended beneficiary, and so on.

By directing one's attention to or through a humanitarian digital interface, and performing one of these roles, a user is often presumed to concur with its purposes and priorities and to subscribe to a particular way of performing them, even as the interface may be customizable to some degree. This is in accordance with a pragmatic correspondence drawn between the direction of attention, the exercise of individual will, and the crafting of self. William James famously argued: "My experience is what I agree to attend to. Only those items which I notice shape my mind."[23]

As in the HDX example, the user of a humanitarian digital interface is not typically engaged at random: as "just some guy." Without user qualification and

---

[21] Jonathan Crary, "Spectacle, Attention, Counter-Memory" (1989) 50 *October* 97, 99; Jonathan Crary, "Eclipse of the Spectacle," in Brian Wallis (ed.), *Art After Modernism: Rethinking Representation* (New Museum of Contemporary Art with David Godine, 1984) 287.

[22] Interview with Participant F, *supra* note 11.

[23] William James, *The Principles of Psychology, Volumes I and II* (Harvard University Press, 1981) vol. II, 788.

assent—be it presumptive or actual—humanitarian digital interfaces themselves may be suspected of trying, in Marshall McLuhan's terms, to "tak[e] a lease on our eyes and ears and nerves."[24] That would be inconsistent with their claim to be humanitarian: that is, both individual-rights-defending and devoted to collective benefit (as discussed in Chapters 1 and 6). Instead, digital humanitarian interfaces typically lead their users through an implicit or explicit process of user qualification (as in the HDX example described previously), inviting them to certain modes of use and directing them away from others. This is often conducted in the name of affirming and protecting the rights of a preexistent self (e.g., user privacy rights) even as digital interfaces elicit and shape a recordable performance of that user self *in actu*.

As Ahmed has highlighted, the "for" of a particular use—in this context, the "for" of humanitarianism—may come before or after use.[25] Humanitarian digital interfaces may be designed for a particular use, or they may seek to make use of something preexistent (typically, the availability of digital data). As one of our interviewees said, of the work of Pulse Lab Jakarta (PLJ), they are "good at finding new ways to do things or different ways to apply data . . . that can then be picked up and progressed."[26]

Digital humanitarian interfaces' use does not, however, necessarily conform to this humanitarian "for"; use need not correspond to intended function, as Ahmed highlights.[27] This has been underscored in prior chapters; readers may recall the use of Loveland Technology's well-intentioned mapping app by "wealthy and notorious property barons" in Detroit, discussed in Chapter 2.[28] We will return to unintended uses when discussing misuse later. Before then, let us consider some possibilities associated with humanitarian digital interfaces' disuse.

## Disuse

One of the main ways that those addressed by humanitarian digital interfaces are envisaged being able to "speak back" to those interfaces in particular instances is through their disuse. That is a practice of users abandoning an interface or declining to use it at all. In this context, Ahmed's assessment seems, in the first instance, broadly correct: that "the more time something is used, the more power

[24] Marshall Mcluhan, *Understanding Media: The Extensions of Man* (MIT Press, 1994) 15.
[25] Ahmed, *supra* note 7, at 24.
[26] Interview with Participant AH (October 26, 2020).
[27] Ahmed, *supra* note 7, at 24.
[28] Shilpia Jindia, "Tech Startups to the Rescue? How Technology Can Deepen Inequality in Detroit—And How 'Civic Tech' Could Help End It" (*Medium*, November 23, 2016), <https://medium.com/latterly/tech-startups-to-the-rescue-978ec1f0f68f> (accessed October 10, 2022).

it acquires; the less time something is used, the less power it retains." Disuse of digital interfaces can, accordingly, be "weakening and withering."[29] In settings such as #DeleteFacebook campaigns or in discussion of moratoria on facial recognition software, for instance, disuse can seem like a hybrid political response to digital interfaces' ubiquity, combining "voice" (communication of grievances or proposals for change with a view to modifying a relationship) and "exit" (withdrawal from a relationship) according to Albert Hirschman's famous trichotomy.[30] On the other hand, for those in pursuit of use or users, disuse often registers as failure. As one of our interviewees observed, if "you go to HDX and you find really old data that's not maintained or not useful then we're failing."[31]

Given what is at stake in the digitization of humanitarianism (discussed in Chapter 1), the politics of disuse are salient. Throughout this book, humanitarian digital interfaces have been shown to: foreclose protest, casualize humanitarian assistance, misrepresent and sometimes fracture communities (Chapter 2); rally and format collectives in ways that may be problematic and yet relatively impervious to critique (Chapter 3); encourage watchful acceptance, in lieu of radical redistribution, in the face of actual, imminent or projected devastation (Chapter 4); subject polities to a standard of datafication, for purposes of actualizing their statehood, and otherwise change what is involved in being a state (Chapter 5); and be normatively heterogeneous in their underpinnings (Chapter 6). This is clearly not all that humanitarian digital interfaces are or do, have done, or might yet do; digital humanitarian interfaces' use can have positive effects too. Those propagating and championing them are adept at anticipating and documenting positive use cases, so many good use stories about digital humanitarian interfaces—emphasizing their benefits and value—are already in broad circulation. Nonetheless, in view of all their potentially ambivalent, baleful, or divisive effects, it is worthwhile canvassing *disuse* of digital interfaces as a political possibility open to those with stakes in the international transformations now underway in humanitarian practice. There will be times when it may be strategically advisable to refrain from using digital data available for humanitarian ends, or to stop using interfaces and applications designed for humanitarian use.

As a political strategy or indeed a regulatory one (enforced by a moratorium, for instance), disuse can, however, be difficult to execute. Disuse of widely adopted digital interfaces such as Facebook, for example, is not without social cost, especially in those communities for whom Facebook access ensures internet access free of charge (through Facebook's Free Basics initiative, accessible

---

[29] Ahmed, *supra* note 7, at 70.
[30] Albert O. Hirschman, *Exit, Voice, and Loyalty* (Harvard University Press, 1972).
[31] Interview with Participant F, *supra* note 11.

without data charges). For some, this cost may be too high—hence the propensity of calls for disuse to culminate in "hapless boycott[s]" that generate monetizable data in their own right.[32]

Even where people do follow through on abandoning a digital interface, this may not negate the data-generative effects of disuse. As Taina Bucher has observed, "abstaining from using a digital device for one week does not result in disconnection, or less data production, but more digital data points.... To an algorithm, ... absence provides important pieces of information."[33] Use can also be forced on nonusers by arm's-length engagement or evaluative tools such as third-party tagging, ranking, and endorsement.[34]

In the case of humanitarian digital interfaces, disuse may be especially challenging. When the interfaces in question operate aggregatively and passively (drawing data from mobile phone infrastructure, satellites, automatic identification system ship tracking, or other remote sensing devices, for instance) or mediate peoples' access to basic services (such as water and electricity usage or school attendance), disuse of those interfaces may not be feasible. As Nathalie Casemajor and colleagues have observed, many infrastructures of public, private, and hybrid governance are now premised on the "normative superior[ity]" of active, data-generative "participation" in governance. As a consequence, people may be penalized or "pathologized" for failing to use digital interfaces through which that participation is solicited.[35]

Even so, as Casemajor et al. also demonstrate, nonparticipation—or for our purposes, disuse—can be thought of as politically fruitful and variegated, not solely in terms of the vaunted purity of abstinence.[36] Among other implications, this may occasion the revisiting and recoding of actions derided for their uselessness.

One example of humanitarian digital interfaces' disuse too readily coded as uselessness concerns a tsunami early warning system installed in Indonesia: InaTEWS. InaTEWS was developed after the 2004 Indian Ocean earthquake and tsunami with German, Malaysian, and US support. By design, InaTEWS assembles digital data from a broadband seismographic sensor array and GPS network on land, a system of tide gauges and buoys at sea, and CCTV coastal surveillance. Data so assembled, using satellite-based communication,

---

[32] Yuwei Lin, "#DeleteFacebook Is Still Feeding the Beast—But There Are Ways to Overcome Surveillance Capitalism" (*The Conversation*, March 26, 2020), <http://theconversation.com/deletefacebook-is-still-feeding-the-beast-but-there-are-ways-to-overcome-surveillance-capitalism-93874> (accessed October 10, 2022).
[33] Taina Bucher, *If... Then: Algorithmic Power and Politics* (Oxford University Press, 2018) 2.
[34] Marion Fourcade and Fleur Johns, "Loops, Ladders and Links: The Recursivity of Social and Machine Learning" (2020) 49 *Theory and Society* 803, 815.
[35] Nathalie Casemajor et al., "Non-Participation in Digital Media: Toward a Framework of Mediated Political Action" (2015) 37 *Media, Culture & Society* 850, 864.
[36] Ibid.

is processed through SeisComP3 software to feed a decision support system (known, apparently without irony, as TOAST, for Tsunami Observation and Simulation Terminal) whereby incoming, real-time data interacts with a database of historic scenarios and warnings are issued on this basis.[37]

In late September 2018, an earthquake of magnitude 7.5 shook the island of Sulawesi in Indonesia, home to nearly 17.5 million people. Tsunamis followed; multiple large waves struck central Sulawesi, at Palu and Donggala. More than 1,300 people were killed and nearly 60,000 displaced. (Readers may recall PLJ experimenting with mobile phone call detail record data to track these displacements in Chapter 3.) In the aftermath of these events, information circulated about the failure of InaTEWS to issue early warnings and the various practices of breakdown, misrecognition, and disassembly that may have contributed to this failure.

The Indonesian government's meteorology, climatology, and geophysics agency BMKG (Badan Meteorologi, Klimatologi, dan Geofisika) had, it emerged, issued a tsunami warning, predicting relatively small waves, just after the initial earthquake. However, few people received the text message alerts because cell phone and electrical infrastructure had been damaged by the earthquake. In any event, BMKG ended that warning around 30 minutes after it was issued, relying on data from the nearest operating tidal gauge, hundreds of kilometers away, where only a very small wave was detected. None or very few of the 22 buoys then tethered to the ocean floor that were meant to transmit data about wave height turned out to be working. This was reportedly because they had not been maintained, had been damaged by fishers tying their boats to them, or because "vandal[s]" (as some media reports dubbed them) stole their costly sensors or hauled entire units away to sell for scrap. Those few people who did receive an early warning message were reportedly unsure what to do. Footage and complaints circulated on social media.[38]

---

[37] Sven Harig et al., "The Tsunami Scenario Database of the Indonesia Tsunami Early Warning System (InaTEWS): Evolution of the Coverage and the Involved Modeling Approaches" (2020) 177 *Pure and Applied Geophysics* 1379.

[38] Jonatan Lassa, "Reviewing Indonesia's Tsunami Early Warning Strategy: Reflections from Sulawesi Island" (*The Conversation*, October 3, 2018), <http://theconversation.com/reviewing-ind onesias-tsunami-early-warning-strategy-reflections-from-sulawesi-island-104257> (accessed October 10, 2022); Anjali Singhvi, Bedel Saget, and Jasmine C. Lee, "What Went Wrong with Indonesia's Tsunami Early Warning System" (*The New York Times*, October 2, 2018), <https://www. nytimes.com/interactive/2018/10/02/world/asia/indonesia-tsunami-early-warning-system.html> (accessed October 10, 2022); Shotaro Tani and Erwida Maulia, "Indonesia's Tsunami Warning Blamed as Death Toll Reaches 1,200" (*Nikkei Asia*, October 2, 2018), <https://asia.nikkei.com/Econ omy/Indonesia-s-tsunami-warning-blamed-as-death-toll-reaches-1-200> (accessed October 10, 2022); Stephen Wright, "'None of the 22 Buoys Are Functioning': Tsunami Warning System Might Have Saved Lives in Indonesia" (*National Post*, October 1, 2018), <https://nationalpost.com/news/ world/none-of-the-22-buoys-are-functioning-tsunami-warning-system-might-have-saved-lives-in-indonesia> (accessed October 10, 2022).

Prevailing accounts of the failure of InaTEWS described the system as having been rendered "useless" by the aforementioned combination of factors.[39] The implication was that people and state institutions engaging with the system were useless too. In the case of those vandalizing or stealing buoys, for instance, theirs were characterized as "ordinary criminal" actions.[40] At the same time, the Indonesian government was criticized for "never [having] allocated enough money in the state budget to fund . . . necessary maintenance" of the system; the system was "broken" thanks to a "bureaucratic mess."[41] Meanwhile, to many, the system itself was seemingly beyond reproach. It was still characterized publicly as useful: a "well-designed sensor network that could provide critical information."[42] To some, the obvious next step was to place automated sensors on the sea floor, at further remove from the prospect of meddling by useless humans.[43]

The fishers who tied their boats to remote sensors designed to feed a digital warning system and the persons who stole hardware components to sell for scrap *were* making use of the digital interfaces of InaTEWS, but not in ways consistent with its continuous, systemic use; their use made InaTEWS unusable. Like those who looted markets in Palu after the tsunami, they were prioritizing immediate survival over forecast or promised benefits—over productive or reproductive futurity of the kind discussed in Chapter 4. As looters told reporters: "There has been no aid, we need to eat."[44] As such, they were "useless mouths," in Simone de Beauvoir's terms.[45]

In her 1945 play, *The Useless Mouths*, de Beauvoir tells a fictional fourteenth-century story of the town of Vaucelles, facing starvation while besieged by the Duke of Burgundy and awaiting military aid from the King of France. To make its dwindling food supplies last until that help arrives, the Town Council decides

---

[39] See, e.g., Wright, *supra* note 38, quoting Danny Hilman Natawidjaja, a senior earthquake geologist at the Indonesian Institute of Sciences.

[40] Jonatan Lassa, "When Heaven (Hardly) Meets the Earth: Towards Convergency in Tsunami Early Warning Systems" (Indonesian Students' Scientific Meeting Conference Proceedings, Delft, May 1, 2008) 216; Lassa, *supra* note 37.

[41] Arzia Tivany Wargadiredja, "Indonesia's Tsunami Warning System Is Broken" (*VICE*, October 3, 2018), <https://www.vice.com/en/article/yw954g/broken-stripped-and-stolen-indonesias-tsunami-warning-system-is-a-mess> (accessed October 10, 2022).

[42] Tasha Wibawa and Farid M. Ibrahim, "Tsunami Early Detection Buoys Haven't Worked for Six Years: Disaster Agency" (*ABC News*, October 1, 2018), <https://www.abc.net.au/news/2018-10-01/indonesia-tsunami-early-detection-buoys-broken-for-six-years/10324200> (accessed October 10, 2022), quoting Professor Louise Comfort, an expert in disaster management at the University of Pittsburgh.

[43] Doug Bock Clark, "Why the Tsunami in Indonesia Struck Without Warning" (*The New Yorker*, October 4, 2018), <https://www.newyorker.com/news/news-desk/why-the-tsunami-in-indonesia-struck-without-warning> (accessed October 10, 2022).

[44] "Indonesians Loot Markets after Tsunami Creates Shortage of Food, Water" (*NDTV.com*, September 30, 2018), <https://www.ndtv.com/world-news/indonesians-loot-supermarkets-after-tsunami-earthquake-create-shortage-of-food-water-1924504> (accessed October 10, 2022).

[45] Simone de Beauvoir, *"The Useless Mouths" and Other Literary Writings* (University of Illinois Press, 2011).

to "get rid of the useless mouths... the infirm, the old men, the children... [a]nd the women" by driving them into ditches at the edge of town.[46] Meanwhile, the town's male workers occupy themselves building a belfry from which a flag will be hung and bells will sound when the siege is relieved. As Liz Stanley has written of the play, "[w]hat is 'useful' is indicated in the importance of building the belfry, weaving its flag, guarding its walls, deciding on plans for it, keeping order around it."[47] At the same time, economic "dependence equals uselessness and dependence cannot coexist with value."[48] Those oriented toward near-term survival who signal their dependence on others for basic sustenance are judged less useful than those who work on physical infrastructure identified with the promise of future security; on this basis, the former are judged disposable.

Media reports and commentary condemning those who "vandalized" InaTEWS in order to feed themselves conveyed a similar assessment of their relative value as compared to the value of the InaTEWS system and those working on it. The digital interfaces of InaTEWS were meant to enroll Indonesians in an internationally sponsored project of futurity in the realization of which all would have a role. A 2012 public guide to InaTEWS, *Tsunami Early Warning Service Guidebook for InaTEWS*, emphasized that alongside the roles played by various levels and agencies of government, community members bore responsibilities within this socio-technical system. "Communities are responsible for making the necessary preparations to save themselves from earthquake and tsunami risks," it stressed, while "[i]ndividuals and community organisations are [also] responsible for passing on accurate information and guidance to others."[49] "[C]ontinuous cooperation of all stakeholders" was needed, the guide insisted, to ensure the system's "future development and maintenance."[50] That practice would, in turn, move Indonesia closer to a future of "better preparedness" for the tsunamis that would inevitably strike again: that was preparedness to be secured, above all, by continuous use of digital interfaces.[51]

This was how Indonesian coast-dwellers were supposed to make themselves useful: by dedicating their labor to "future development and maintenance" of the digital interfaces and infrastructure of InaTEWS. This would ensure InaTEWS's continued usefulness as a matter of priority. However, some had other uses for InaTEWS—or at least for its "smart" buoys—as noted earlier. Ironically, these actions testified to exactly the do-it-yourself resilience that many digital

---

[46] Ibid., 56.
[47] Liz Stanley, "A Philosopher Manqué?: Simone de Beauvoir, Moral Value and 'The Useless Mouths'" (2001) 8 *European Journal of Women's Studies* 201, 212.
[48] Ibid., 208.
[49] Jaya Murjaya et al., "Tsunami Early Warning Service Guidebook for InaTEWS (2nd Edition)" (BMKG, August 2012) 22.
[50] Ibid., v.
[51] Ibid.

interfaces seek to inculcate in their users, as discussed in Chapter 4. When self-help measures render a digital interface useless for its intended purposes, however, they become unreadable as uses of that interface—and those involved became unrecognizable as users. Their use is not "for" humanitarianism in its digital mode so it is, and they are, devalued. They are, instead, cast to the systemic margins, labeled criminals, vandals.[52] Indonesian officials did not view "ordinary people where the buoys [were] installed as stakeholders," one researcher observed; their actions were not regarded as "serious feedback to the system."[53] Rather, the system's disuse at the hands of such people was cause for lamentation; according to one US-based expert interviewed, it was "a heartbreak"; "a tragedy for science."[54]

Use-for-survival framed as systemic disuse tends to be cast as deviant or devoid of agentive politics—the latter typically equated with "higher" level decisional or deliberative engagement. Even in the literature on the politics of refusal in the digital economy, it is rare for refusal to take the form of simply (although not at all "simply") trying to survive in the now and sabotaging or neglecting digital technology in the process. Refusal of digital technology is typically envisaged as willful, communicative action: a vocal, explicit expression of "tech-abolitionism," for instance.[55]

The vandalism and neglect of the InaTEWS buoys effectively communicated the failure of the InaTEWS project to articulate a political vision that was compelling to the communities meant to be "responsible" for its advancement. It suggested that their political priorities, and the risks and responsibilities foremost for them, lay elsewhere. As Ahmed has noted, "[a] failure to use something properly can be a refusal to use something properly. . . . A refusal . . . to be impressed by the colonizer's words and things."[56] The actions of those people who vandalized or neglected the smart buoys of InaTEWS did not offer reasoned argument to that effect, however. Their disuse was not an effort of persuasion or a plea for inclusion. Those concerned were living a life in which InaTEWS held little relative value, not appealing for InaTEWS to change. They were taking without giving and only later exchanging the scraps they salvaged. As such, they were realizing what Michel Serres has called (without any moralizing implication) "abuse value": a primary form of value, fundamental to life, borne of transversal non-exchange-based relations, before labor or economics.[57] As a

---

[52] Lassa, *supra* note 38.
[53] Lassa, *supra* note 40, at 216.
[54] Wright, *supra* note 38, quoting Professor Louise Comfort, an expert in disaster management at the University of Pittsburgh.
[55] See, e.g., Seeta Peña Gangadharan, "Digital Exclusion: A Politics of Refusal," in Lucy Bernholz, Hélène Landemore, and Rob Reich (eds.), *Digital Technology and Democratic Theory* (University of Chicago Press, 2021).
[56] Ahmed, *supra* note 7, at 207.
[57] Michel Serres, *The Parasite* (Lawrence R. Schehr tr., Johns Hopkins University Press, 1982).

consequence, their actions were not politically legible according to "late-modern political criticism" that, as Achille Mbembe has written, remains wedded to the ideal of "politics [a]s the exercise of reason in the public sphere."[58] Life as survival tends not to be seen as politically originary, Didier Fassin has observed.[59] Disuse of digital interfaces without any profession of larger meaning, message, or purpose tends to be regarded as useless. And uselessness and those identified with it are dispensable with impunity, unless and until the political potency, variability, and vibrancy of disuse gets reclaimed.

## Misuse

The disuse of the InaTEWS system and use-for-survival of some of its components amounted also to a form of *misuse*. That is an improper or unanticipated use or use in defiance of relevant instructions. Those who tied boats to the buoys, or sold them for scrap, or failed to maintain them, all defied official directives for the system's use. They did not interact with its digital interfaces in accordance with the instructions for use offered by the *Tsunami Early Warning Service Guidebook for InaTEWS*. Concerns about the risk of digital interfaces and data potentially being misused in these and other, harmful ways are ever-present in the humanitarian field.[60] Such risks are a recurrent focus of the ethics instruments discussed in Chapter 6.

Yet, as with disuse, it is possible to think of digital interfaces' misuse as part of a rich political vernacular surrounding their deployment in the humanitarian field. Misuse shows how neither their intended purposes nor their past uses exhaust the possibilities of digital humanitarian interfaces' use, nor predetermine the range of potential users that may engage with such interfaces directly or obliquely.[61] This may be problematic, of course, when one thinks of nefarious, devastating misuse to which humanitarian digital interfaces and associated data might be put. Nonetheless, digital interfaces' misuse may also enliven the plurality and potential changeability of use in socially, politically, and legally generative ways. Just as squatters' occupation of buildings without permission (that is, misusing those buildings) entails "trying to fill those . . . spaces in a different

---

[58] Achille Mbembe, "Necropolitics" (2003) 15 *Public Culture* 11, 13.
[59] Didier Fassin, "Ethics of Survival: A Democratic Approach to the Politics of Life" (2010) 1 *Humanity: An International Journal of Human Rights, Humanitarianism, and Development* 81.
[60] See, e.g., Kristy Crabtree and Petronille Geara, "Safety Planning for Technology: Displaced Women and Girls' Interactions with Information and Communication Technology in Lebanon and Harm Reduction Considerations for Humanitarian Settings" (2018) 3 *Journal of International Humanitarian Action* 3; Reza Montasari and Hamid Jahankhani, "The Application of Technology in Combating Human Trafficking," in Hamid Jahankhani, Arshad Jamal, and Shaun Lawson (eds.), *Cybersecurity, Privacy and Freedom Protection in the Connected World* (Springer, 2021).
[61] Ahmed, *supra* note 7, at 24, 44, 85, 199.

way . . . to throw open the question of what space is for," we might think of the actions of Hackitectura, described in Chapter 2, as digital squatting on the border between states, or misuse of borders and bordering, throwing open the question of what and who borders are for.[62]

Making the most of the generativity of misuse could take many forms. When digital interfaces are designed for revenue-generation—as are mainstream social media platforms, for instance—it may be regarded as a productive "misuse" of those interfaces to reroute data derived therefrom through humanitarian digital interfaces such as those described throughout this book. Likewise, it could be regarded as a generative "misuse" of agricultural data generated in the course of commercial farming of private property to collectivize that data via a worker-owned data cooperative, such as the farmer-owned Grower's Information Service Cooperative (GISC). GISC is organized as a national cooperative association under Texas law to help landowners and tenants engaged in agricultural production to collect, store, manage, and leverage agricultural data that they generate, for collective benefit.[63] It is but one example of a data cooperative: an organizational form burgeoning in a range of configurations around the world.[64]

The challenge, however, is to evaluate the repercussions of digital data amassed for private, for-profit purposes being "misused" for collective, not-for-profit purposes or vice versa. Initiatives such as the GISC tend to be entangled with the value and production systems from which they ostensibly depart by reciprocal flows of data. For instance, the design of Twitter's user interface around a presumptive acceptance of market norms (in the transactional relationships it encourages among users, for instance) persists into MIND (discussed in Chapter 3) and Haze Gazer (discussed in Chapter 4) as they incorporate Twitter data, even as they lay claim to nonmarket, humanitarian values and purposes.[65] Traces of prior use persist, also, when data flows from not-for-profit use back to for-profit use, as when GISC maintains "partnerships" with commercial interface developers IBM and Main Street Data. Even as digital humanitarian interfaces' "misuse" of commercial data and infrastructure may disclose possibilities for

---

[62] Ibid., 211.
[63] Grower's Information Services Coop, "Grower's Information Services Coop," <https://www.gisc.coop/> (accessed October 10, 2022); Murray Fulton et al., "Digital Technologies and the Big Data Revolution in the Canadian Agricultural Sector: Opportunities, Challenges, and Alternatives" (*Canadian Centre for the Study of Cooperatives*, August 2021), <https://usaskstudies.coop/documents/big-data-in-canadian-agriculture-report-fultonetal.pdf>.
[64] Trebor Scholz and Nathan Schneider, *Ours to Hack and to Own: The Rise of Platform Cooperativism, A New Vision for the Future of Work and a Fairer Internet* (OR Books, 2016); Morshed Mannan and Simon Pek, "Solidarity in the Sharing Economy: The Role of Platform Cooperatives at the Base of the Pyramid," in Israr Qureshi, Babita Bhatt ,and Dhirendra Mani Shukla (eds.), *Sharing Economy at the Base of the Pyramid* (Springer, 2021).
[65] Fleur Johns and Caroline Compton, "Data Jurisdictions and Rival Regimes of Algorithmic Regulation" (2020) *Regulation & Governance* (forthcoming).

their heterodox use, those possibilities are implicated in prior and overlapping uses that are more orthodox.

Notwithstanding these entanglements, it may still be worthwhile for those with interests at stake in digital humanitarianism (recalling the stakes discussed in Chapter 1) to experiment with strategic misuse of humanitarian digital interfaces beyond the ambit of their intended functions. Misuse can recast the politics of humanitarian digital interfaces. For example, Claudia Aradau and colleagues employed the Droid Destruction Kit (a virtual machine image—a file that behaves like an actual computer—made available on GitHub, that allows anyone to examine data transmitted by Android apps) to "misuse" Refugee.info (a website designed to help refugees to overcome language barriers and access information to assist them safely navigate routes to Europe[66]). This showed that the website was transmitting data indicating the location of refugees in plain text format, without encryption, making an ostensibly protective interface into a site of vulnerability.[67] Experimental misuse of a humanitarian digital interface such as MIND (discussed in Chapter 3) could conceivably set one data source against another to advance a critique of their limits and occlusions. Imagine, for instance, a strategic deluge of tweets from a disaster-affected area being showcased in MIND that spoke to endemic issues of poverty rather than the disaster impacts flagged by Global Disaster Alert and Coordination System and identified as newsworthy by the relevant news application programming interface. Claimants' digital recognition of one another, via MIND (through its Twitter layer, for instance), could also potentially prompt offline, analog organizing among them, as has been attempted by Hackitectura on either side of the Strait of Gibraltar, in ways described in Chapter 2.

Creative misuse of digital humanitarian interfaces might also draw attention to the limits of a focus on usefulness and the perils of interface developers being oriented toward utility maximization for a delimited group of "end users" at the expense of broader implications and stakes (such as the cumulative effect of digital humanitarian interfaces on how emergencies are understood, for example, discussed in Chapter 4). One such limit is the difficulty of distinguishing the *use* of something made from the *making* of that which is used. Distinguishing an interface developer (who typically bears most of those ethical responsibilities discussed in Chapter 6) from an interface user (who is cast in the comparatively passive role of recipient or beneficiary) is not always straightforward when

---

[66] Konstantin Aal, Anne Weibert, and Reem Talhouk, "Refugees & Technology: Determining the Role of HCI Research" (Group '18: 2018 ACM Conference on Supporting Groupwork, Florida, January 7–10, 2018).

[67] Claudia Aradau, Tobias Blanke, and Giles Greenway, "Acts of Digital Parasitism: Hacking, Humanitarian Apps and Platformisation" (2019) 21 *New Media & Society* 2548.

machine learning algorithms are involved. If a digital humanitarian interface making use of machine learning algorithms is "continuously editing, adjusting, removing, and iterating [itself] in relation to a corpus of data" derived from the activity of "users", then "use" cannot be well understood as a taking hold and deploying something preexistent, preloaded with purposes and biases for which someone, somewhere else holds responsibility.[68]

This has implications for how one might try to ensure ethically responsible deployment of digital humanitarian interfaces: something that is often pinned on interface developers presumed to possess panoptical oversight. If the design of an interface partly takes shape through use, one cannot be assured that "good" or "responsible" design of digital interfaces will ensure their safe, beneficial impacts.

A related difficulty is distinguishing between proper use and improper misuse. If every use of a digital interface is, to some extent, a remaking of that interface, then one cannot easily hold on to claims that bad effects of digital interfaces result from their misuse, not from "proper" use. Rather, even the most compliant, well informed of end users will be implicated in digital interfaces' effects, for good and for ill. Digital humanitarian interfaces' use can never be frictionless or responsibility free even when that use is entirely in accordance with instructions.

The same may be said of the use and misuse of law and policy, such as those discussed in Chapter 6. A typical way of making sense of, and assigning responsibility for, harmful or unequal effects of law or policy is to condemn their misuse by particular people. Existing laws and policies are more or less fine (give or take a bit of tinkering), it is often said; it is the people who misuse them that are the problem. But if every misuse is understood as an amplification of potential uses, and those uses are partly constitutive of that which is used, then this route toward exoneration is no longer readily available. Responsibilities for harm and inequality must be much more broadly dispersed and reform need not be confined to tinkering. As Louise Amoore has written, as users of machine learning algorithms, "[w]e do not stand on the bank and respond to the stream, but we are in the stream, immersed in the difficulties and obligations of forming the text" or the interface.[69] Restated for our purposes here: every use of a humanitarian digital interface immerses users in the difficulties and obligations of forming and actuating those interfaces and, indirectly, extending or affirming the laws and policies underwriting them.

---

[68] Louise Amoore, *Cloud Ethics: Algorithms and the Attributes of Ourselves and Others* (Duke University Press, 2020) 97.
[69] Ibid., 101.

## "Sometimes We Get Crazy with Data": What Digital Humanitarianism Could Become

One of our data scientist interviewees remarked: "for people like me, when we see data, sometimes we get crazy with data. So . . . I'm also still on the learning course in terms of how to proportional[ly] put things in place."[70] Humanitarianism is, indeed, going "crazy with data." Humanitarian digital interfaces are proliferating, and this is transmuting the conventional epistemic units of international legal and political ordering: maps; populations; emergencies; states.

Humanitarian digital interfaces, and those who develop and use them, struggle to "put . . . in place" these transmutations, along with all that which is meant to be pushed *out of place* according to prevailing narratives of human progress, development, intergovernmental coordination, and market equilibrium, namely: disasters, famines, and other unanticipated and unintended harms. As Mary Douglas has discussed, for something to be regarded as polluting or dangerous, it must violate some idealized sense of societal order governing the world; it must appear as "matter out of place."[71] Humanitarian digital interfaces take phenomena so experienced and try to switch their binary coding from out of place to placed; from harmful to salutary; to insert the apparent "precision of a computer database" into "the chaos of relief work" (according to Sheri Fink's recollection, from Chapter 1).[72]

As this book has shown, however, these placements are unstable and unfolding. Chapter 1 highlighted how much one might discern of their dynamics, effects, and preconditions from the study of interfaces: framing and communicative surfaces that structure and enable interaction (especially through computation), in contrast to other apertures through which international legal and political order has typically been analyzed. Chapter 2, concerned with humanitarian mapping, introduced a way of reading these interfaces that has been crucial throughout this book: tracing the analog and digital logics structuring them and highlighting some of the differences that the tension and slippage between these makes.

Chapter 3 probed these differences further, showing how the digital mediation of international humanitarian work tends to gather people, places, and things together and make them seem actionable in new configurations: as digital aggregates assembled senso-politically (inferred from digitized sensory input) often overlaying biopolitical populations as targets of governance. Chapter 4 turned from placement to temporality, highlighting how international humanitarian

---

[70] Interview with Participant D (July 27, 2018).
[71] Mary Douglas, *Purity and Danger: An Analysis of the Concepts of Pollution and Taboo* (Routledge, 2002).
[72] Sheri Fink, "The Science of Doing Good" (2007) 297 *Scientific American* 98.

emergencies' mediation by digital interfaces turns them into near-term problems of data deficiency and renders them incessant: something with which those in the present must endlessly try to cope in the name of idealized future beneficiaries. Chapter 5 argued that these shifts have profound implications for states and statehood, especially among the least-resourced states and would-be states of the world. As states take on some of the logics of digital interfaces in their humanitarian endeavors, Chapter 5 contended, they are giving effect to a standard of datafication on the international plane: a standard that rewards states' pursuit of increased data access, accumulation, and control and disadvantages those states least able or inclined to "datify" their governmental affairs.

Chapter 6 canvassed some of the many laws and policies undergirding these transformations and highlighted the extent to which they do not cohere around a single, normative vision or framework of global order. Rather, they disclose multiple points of entry and leverage of which a range of public, private, and hybrid actors are making use. The politics of this "making use" have been the focus of this chapter. We have seen how humanitarian digital interfaces' use empowers or disqualifies users, and how their disuse and misuse may be politically generative, disclosing pluralities of uses and users beyond those that utility-maximization would invite us to consider. Users are implicated in all that those interfaces do and do not do—and what they, and digital humanitarianism, might yet become. Accordingly, any debate about when, where, and how to incorporate digital interfaces into humanitarian work needs to address and consider the full and disparate panoply of user-makers living and working in those interfaces' sphere of senso-political operation.

To some readers, this might not seem useful. Works of international law are meant to offer reform proposals or regulatory solutions. Humanitarianism is meant to be heartwarming and hopeful; all the more so, when, according to Patrick Meier, "[a]nyone can be a digital humanitarian . . . all you need is a big heart and access to the Internet."[73] Redirecting assessment of digital interfaces' potential humanitarian utility to include prospects for their disuse and misuse: this does not sound very helpful or hopeful.

Perhaps this is hopeful, though, if one takes up Hirokazu Miyazaki's unorthodox definition of hope: as a practice of reorienting the "directionality" of knowledge or technique.[74] Annelise Riles has shown how fruitful this may be for researchers of law and politics.[75] Taking this up, one might start by drawing

---

[73] Patrick Meier, *Digital Humanitarians: How Big Data Is Changing the Face of Humanitarian Response* (Routledge, 2015) 1.
[74] Hirokazu Miyazaki, *The Method of Hope: Anthropology, Philosophy, and Fijian Knowledge* (Stanford University Press, 2004) 11.
[75] Annelise Riles, "Is the Law Hopeful?," in Hirokazu Miyazaki and Richard Swedberg (eds.), *The Economy of Hope* (University of Pennsylvania Press, 2017).

from this book a sense of the orthodox directionality of humanitarian digital interfaces. One might note their orientation toward carving out an actionable interval in the present, distanced from political affray, and inviting people—via digital aggregates proxying for people—to wait in this time-space, coping as best they can, anticipating some unspecified yet benevolent future borne of the promise of digitization. One might note, too, the typical orientation of surrounding norms and practices toward ensuring closer correspondence between humanitarian digital interfaces and that which they are supposed to represent: that is, making them more representative or better representative of the world.

Reorientation of these standard directionalities might entail abandonment of a concern with humanitarian digital interfaces' better or more accurate representation of the world in favor of inhabiting these interfaces *as* a world: a complex world of dissensus and divergent perception. This is arguably the kind of intervention made by the "vandal[s]" of the InaTEWS buoys. They refused to heed the accompanying instructions for use (of which they may not even have been aware). Rather than dedicate the present to "making the necessary preparations to save themselves from earthquake and tsunami risks," they prioritized the "need to eat"[76] now over the need to flee a tsunami later.

Instead of the mode of action toward which their attention was directed—that of "passing on accurate information"[77] to help maintain a tsunami early warning system—the so-called vandals of InaTEWS repurposed the physical infrastructure of humanitarian digitization to non-data-generative ends. In so doing, they offered no solutions; their actions do not amount to a reform proposal or a template to be followed. Yet they did "throw open the question" of what and who humanitarian digital interfaces are for, and what kinds of times, spaces, and relations they make and unmake.[78] Their misuse of humanitarian digital interfaces effectively opened a debate about distributive justice. This was a debate that the InaTEWS system's investors did not otherwise seem to be having with the communities they were intent on helping, at least as far as the merits and demerits of that investment were concerned. These are surely questions to be held open whenever thinking and acting internationally, whether issuing or responding to a cry for #help.

---

[76] Murjaya et al., *supra* note 49, at 22; "Indonesians Loot Markets after Tsunami Creates Shortage of Food, Water," *supra* note 44.
[77] Murjaya et al., *supra* note 49, at 22.
[78] Ahmed, *supra* note 7, at 211.

# Acknowledgments

Sole-authored books are invariably collaborative: outputs of a proverbial engine room jammed with people including contributors, collaborators, supporters, provocateurs, doubters, champions, students, friends, family, and interlocutors. The provenance of this book is likewise collective; indeed, it was originally conceived as a co-authored work, to be written with Caroline Compton. For a range of practical and personal reasons, I ended up writing the manuscript alone. Nonetheless, during a stint as postdoctoral research associate on the project from which this book emanates, Caroline carried out a majority of the interviews referenced in this book's pages. Moreover, the framing and approach of the book (the focus on interfaces, for instance) and the analysis in Chapter 4 especially were figured out, in their earliest stages, in dialogue with Caroline. I am grateful for the times that we spent working and traveling together. Also invaluable to this book's development was the series of conversations maintained over several years with Wayne Wobcke, Caroline Compton, and David Nelken, and more recently with Siti Mariyah and Jayson Lamchek, informing and proceeding alongside this book. Maintaining dialogue across disciplines is difficult, time-consuming, and often thankless; Wayne and Siti, working in computer science and computational statistics, respectively, deserve special credit for their patience and generosity throughout. I feel fortunate to have had such thoughtful and unstinting interlocutors.

I am lucky to have been in the good hands of Merel Alstein, Robert Cavooris, Eleanor Hanger, and Lane Berger of Oxford University Press and the terrific team at Newgen KnowledgeWorks throughout the publication process and I thank them for their support, patience, and attention to detail. Erol Gorur and Alice Zhou provided exemplary research assistance in the finalization of the manuscript, for which I am likewise thankful.

The research underpinning this book was supported by the Australian government through the Australian Research Council's Discovery Projects funding scheme (project DP 180100903). It benefited also from a period of study leave granted to me by the University of New South Wales (UNSW) Sydney; I am thankful to the UNSW Faculty of Law & Justice for that support. Work toward this book was also greatly facilitated by the extraordinary generosity and openness of the staff of Pulse Lab Jakarta and the willingness of all anonymous interviewees to make themselves available and share their insights and experiences, for which

I am immensely grateful. David Nelken was a participating investigator in the grant mentioned above and has been a valuable source of inspiration and guidance from afar. The views expressed herein are, however, those of the author and are not necessarily those of the Australian government, the Australian Research Council, or any organization named in the book. Portions of Chapter 5 were reflected in my Annual Kirby Lecture in International Law delivered at the Centre for Public and International Law of the Australian National University (ANU) in June 2021, later published in the *Australian Yearbook of International Law*. Some passages and ideas from Chapter 5 also appear in Fleur Johns, "International Law and Digitalization," in Eyal Benvenisti and Dino Kritsiotis (eds.), *The Cambridge History of International Law Vol XII* (Cambridge University Press forthcoming).

Once one begins to think of engagements crucial to this book's development, the circle of gratitude widens. Andrew Lang, Tom Poole, and David Nelken were each kind enough to read the manuscript in its entirety and to offer gracious, insightful feedback that will inform later work as much as it aided the editing of this text. Gavin Sullivan offered invaluable comments on several chapters, and I have learned much from conversations with Gavin and with Dimitri Van Den Meerssche as part of our ongoing collaboration. Idil Kaner, Serena Natile, David Nelken, James Millington, and Faith Taylor convened a terrific workshop at King's College London, "Mapping Digital Humanitarianism," at which some early ideas for this book were discussed. Versions of individual chapters of this book were presented also to audiences of the Centre for Law and Society Annual Lecture for 2019–2020 at Queen Mary, University of London; the Institute for Advanced Study (IAS) School of Social Science Seminar Series (Princeton); the International Development Seminar of the MIT Department of Urban Studies and Planning; the International Law Workshop of the University of Michigan; the International Law Colloquium of the University of Georgia; the Annual Kirby Lecture in International Law (ANU College of Law); the Lauterpacht Centre Friday Lunchtime Lecture Series (Cambridge University); the UNSW Law & Justice Staff Seminar Series (UNSW Sydney); the Department of Law or North South University (Bangladesh); the Essex Public International Law Lecture Series (Essex University); the Hertie School Centre for Fundamental Rights Colloquium on "Human Rights and the Automated State" (Berlin, Germany); and the UC Berkeley Social Science Matrix panel discussion "Matrix On Point: Humanitarian Technologies" (University of California Berkeley). I am grateful to the following people for inviting me to make those presentations and hosting me in doing so, and to the audiences at these events for engaging thoughtfully and generously with the work in the process: Maksymilian Del Mar, Isobel Roele, Eva Nanopoulos, and Noam Gur; Didier Fassin, Alondra Nelson, and Marion Fourcade; Jason Jackson and Balakrishnan Rajagopal; Monica Hakimi; Harlan Cohen and Christian Turner; Leighton McDonald; Surabhi

Ranganathan; Michael Crawford, Rosalind Dixon, Jonathan Bonnitcha, Brooke Marshall, and Amy Cohen; Rizwanul Islam; Emily Jones and Meagan Wong; Cathryn Costello and Francesca Palmiotto; and, again, Marion Fourcade.

In addition to the research leave mentioned earlier, work toward this book has been supported in many other ways by the Faculty of Law & Justice at UNSW Sydney for which I am grateful. I would like to register my particular appreciation for my colleagues in the Faculty who do so much to make and maintain a liveable, supportive, equitable, vibrant, and stimulating environment, and all the PhD students with whom I have been lucky enough to work.

I am grateful too for the wonderful cohort of scholars with whom I shared the better part of a year in residence as a member of the School of Social Sciences at the IAS in 2019–2020 (where I was especially fortunate to work with Marion Fourcade) and for the opportunity to visit NYU School of Law and the Guarini Institute for Global Legal Studies during that period (with thanks to Angelina Fisher, Benedict Kingsbury, and Thomas Streinz for their work and conversation): these engagements were vital to this book's gestation.

More recently, I have benefited from the virtual hospitality of the University of Gothenburg (as a Visiting Professor in the School of Business, Economics and Law) and have learned a great deal from my involvement in conversations and writing projects led by Gregor Noll and Matilda Arvidsson there, and by Leila Brännström, Markus Gunneflo, and others at Lund University, and from all the members of the Digital Legalities Reading Group. In various, behind-the-scenes ways, big and small, Katherine Biber, Hilary Charlesworth, Richard Joyce, David Kennedy, Karen Knop, Anne Orford, Sundhya Pahuja, Annelise Riles, and Glenda Sluga have been sources of scholarly support and inspiration during the period of this book's development and writing. Early conversations with Charlotte Epstein were stimulating and helpful. Kate Crawford, Didier Fassin, Marion Fourcade, and Martti Koskenniemi were kind enough to read the manuscript and endorse the book, for which I am enormously grateful.

No doubt I have omitted some names unintentionally. All around, I am tremendously lucky to be in ongoing dialogue with terrific colleagues, fellow travelers, and talented graduate students. Meanwhile, Anna Craig cared for our children regularly during the early years of this book's development with grace and wisdom. My ever-loving parents, Penelope Johns and Murray Johns—to whom this book is dedicated—have remained interested and encouraging throughout, as has my brilliant sister, Diana Johns. Thank you, as always, to Pete, Arlo, Claude, and Ilka, who ballast and brighten my world; words cannot record how much.

# List of Figures

Figure 2.1 Screenshot of HOT Tasking Manager showing available projects. © 2022 OpenStreetMap contributors. The Tasking Manager is free and open-source software developed by the Humanitarian OpenStreetMap Team. Reproduced with permission from the Humanitarian OpenStreetMap Team and under an Open Data Commons Open Database License (ODbL) v1.0 from "Explore Projects—HOT Tasking Manager," <https://tasks.hotosm.org> (accessed October 10, 2022). Full terms available at <https://opendatacommons.org/licenses/odbl/1-0>(accessed October 10, 2022).

Figure 2.2 Screenshot of HOT Tasking Manager showing task status. © 2022 OpenStreetMap contributors. The Tasking Manager is free and open-source software developed by the Humanitarian OpenStreetMap Team. Reproduced with permission from the Humanitarian OpenStreetMap Team and under an Open Data Commons Open Database License (ODbL) v1.0 from "#12081: Impact of Ana & Batsirai Cyclones—Ambositra, Fianarantsoa, Madagascar," <https://tasks.hotosm.org/projects/12081> (accessed October 10, 2022). Full terms available at <https://opendatacommons.org/licenses/odbl/1-0>(accessed October 10, 2022).

Figure 2.3 Valentine Seaman, an inquiry into the cause of the prevalence of the yellow fever in New-York (1798), Plate II.

Figure 2.4 Section from "Maps Descriptive of London Poverty," Charles Booth, Inquiry into Life and Labour in London (1886–1903), digitally represented by London School of Economics and Political Science under a Public Domain Mark.

Figure 2.5 Image of Field Papers in use. © 2011, Alexander Kachkaev, "2011-05-10 (0010)," <http://www.flickr.com/photos/kachkaev/5710460686> (accessed October 10, 2022). Also available at <https://wiki.openstreetmap.org/wiki/File:Surveying_with_walking_papers.jpg> (accessed October 10, 2022). Reproduced under a Creative Commons Attribution—ShareAlike 2.0 license; full terms available at <https://creativecommons.org/licenses/by-sa/2.0/legalcode>(accessed October 10, 2022).

230 LIST OF FIGURES

Figure 2.6 Map created by the community of Nemompare using the Mapeo app in 2015. Cultural and intellectual property of the Waorani of Pastaza, represented by the Alianza Ceibo y Organización Waorani de Pastaza. Source: "Waorani Map—Mapping Ancestral Lands" (Amazon Frontlines), <https://www.amazonfrontlines.org/maps/waorani/> (accessed October 10, 2022). Reproduced with permission from Oswando Gahue Nenquimo Pauchi.

Figure 4.1 Haze Gazer data sources. © 2022 Wiley. Reproduced under contributors' license from Fleur Johns and Caroline Compton, "Data Jurisdictions and Rival Regimes of Algorithmic Regulation" (2022) 16 Regulation & Governance 63.

Figure 5.1 Screenshot of HOT Tasking Manager: Senegal—Consolidated Mapping Projects. © 2022 OpenStreetMap contributors. The Tasking Manager is free and open-source software developed by the Humanitarian OpenStreetMap Team. Reproduced with permission from the Humanitarian OpenStreetMap Team and under an Open Data Commons Open Database License (ODbL) v1.0 from "#1085—Senegal—[Consolidated Mapping Projects—Base Roads Check vs Open Data References]," <https://tasks.hotosm.org> (accessed October 10, 2022). Full terms available at <https://opendatacommons.org/licenses/odbl/1-0> (accessed October 10, 2022).

Figure 5.2 Screenshot of UN Global Pulse showing automated analysis of slum dwellings in Uganda using PulseSatellite. © 2022 UN Global Pulse. Reproduced with permission from UN Global Pulse, as appeared in "PulseSatellite: Human-AI Interaction for Satellite Analysis," <https://www.unglobalpulse.org/microsite/pulsesatellite/> (accessed October 10, 2022).

Figure 5.3 Calibrated machine learning-based estimates of poverty rates for every 4 km x 4 km grid (approximately). © 2021 Asian Development Bank. Reproduced under Creative Commons Attribution 3.0 IGO license without changes from "Mapping the Spatial Distribution of Poverty Using Satellite Imagery in Thailand" (Asian Development Bank, April 2021) 43, <https://www.adb.org/publications/mapping-poverty-satellite-imagery-thailand> (accessed October 10, 2022). Full terms available at https://creativecommons.org/licenses/by/3.0/igo/legalcode (accessed October 10, 2022).

# List of Acronyms and Abbreviations

| | |
|---|---|
| AI | Artificial intelligence |
| AIS | Automatic identification system |
| ALPS | Alert for price spikes |
| API | Application programming interface |
| AVHRR | Advanced very high-resolution radiometer |
| AWS | Amazon Web Services |
| BAPPENAS | National Development Planning Agency (Indonesia) |
| BKP | Food Security Agency, Ministry of Agriculture (Indonesia) |
| BMKG | Meteorology, Climatology, and Geophysical Agency (Indonesia) |
| BPS | Central Bureau of Statistics (Indonesia) |
| BRTI | Indonesian Telecommunication Regulatory Authority |
| BWDB | Bangladesh Water Development Board |
| CATI | Computer-assisted telephone interviewing |
| CDR | Call detail record |
| CeNSE | Central Nervous System for the Earth |
| CIA | Central Intelligence Agency (US) |
| CTBTO | Comprehensive Nuclear-Test-Ban Treaty Organization |
| DFAT | Department of Foreign Affairs and Trade (Australia) |
| DTM | Displacement Tracking Matrix |
| EWS | Early warning system |
| FAO | Food and Agriculture Organization |
| FCS | Food consumption score |
| FFWC | Flood Forecasting and Warning Center (Bangladesh) |
| FIVIMS | Food Insecurity and Vulnerability Information and Mapping Systems |
| GDACS | Global Disaster Alert and Coordination System |
| GIS | Geographic information system |
| GISC | Grower Information Services Cooperative |
| GPS | Global Positioning System |
| gROADS | Global Roads Open Access Data Set |
| GUI | Graphical user interface |
| HDX | Humanitarian Data Exchange |
| HOT | Humanitarian OpenStreetMap Team |
| ICJ | International Court of Justice |
| ICRC | International Committee of the Red Cross |
| ICT | Information and communication technology |
| IDRL | International Disaster Response Law |

## LIST OF ACRONYMS AND ABBREVIATIONS

| | |
|---|---|
| IEC | International Electrotechnical Commission |
| IECO | International Engineering Company Inc. (US) |
| IFRC | International Federation of Red Cross and Red Crescent Societies |
| InaTEWS | Indonesia Tsunami Early Warning System |
| IOM | International Organization for Migration |
| ISO | International Organization for Standardization |
| IT | Information technology |
| ITU | International Telecommunication Union |
| JAXA | Japan Aerospace Exploration Agency |
| JBIC | Japanese Bank for International Cooperation |
| JICA | Japan International Cooperation Agency |
| KAIST | Korea Advanced Institute of Science and Technology |
| MCN | Multi-channel network |
| MIND | Managing Information in Natural Disaster |
| MMP | Missing Maps Project |
| MoFA | Ministry of Foreign Affairs (Indonesia) |
| MSF | Médecins Sans Frontières |
| NASA | National Aeronautics and Space Administration (United States) |
| NGO | Nongovernment organization |
| NOAA | National Oceanographic and Atmospheric Administration (United States) |
| OCHA | Office for the Coordination of Humanitarian Affairs (UN) |
| OECD | Organisation for Economic Co-operation and Development |
| OECF | Overseas Economic Cooperation Fund (Japan) |
| OSM | OpenStreetMap |
| OSMF | OpenStreetMap Foundation |
| OTCA | Overseas Technical Cooperation Agency (Japan) |
| PLJ | Pulse Lab Jakarta |
| PPP | Public-private partnership |
| rCSI | Reduced coping strategy index |
| SDGs | Sustainable Development Goals |
| SPARRSO | Space Research and Remote Sensing Organization (Bangladesh) |
| SUSENAS | National Socio-Economic Household Survey (Indonesia) |
| UNDG | United Nations Development Group |
| UNDP | United Nations Development Programme |
| UNDRO | United Nations Disaster Relief Organization |
| UNHCR | United Nations High Commissioner for Refugees |
| UNICEF | United Nations Children's Fund |
| UNIX | Multiuser, multitasking computer operating system derived from a version originally developed by AT&T Corporation |
| UNOSAT | United Nations Satellite Centre |
| USAID | United States Agency for International Development |

| | |
|---|---|
| VAM | Vulnerability Analysis and Mapping |
| VAMPIRE | Vulnerability Analysis Monitoring Platform for Impact of Regional Events |
| VOC | Dutch East India Company |
| WFP | World Food Programme |
| WHO | World Health Organization |
| XGBoost | Extreme Gradient Boosting |

# Bibliography

## Books

Ahmed S, *What's the Use? On the Uses of Use* (Duke University Press 2019).
Amoore L, *Cloud Ethics: Algorithms and the Attributes of Ourselves and Others* (Duke University Press 2020).
Apprich C et al., *Pattern Discrimination* (Meson Press 2018).
Arcaro T, *Aid Worker Voices* (CreateSpace Independent Publishing Platform 2016).
Arendt H, *The Human Condition* (University of Chicago Press 1998).
Band J and Katoh M, *Interfaces on Trial 2.0* (MIT Press 2011).
Bankoff G, Frerks G, and Hilhorst D, *Mapping Vulnerability: Disasters, Development and People* (Routledge 2004).
Barnett M, *Empire of Humanity: A History of Humanitarianism* (Cornell University Press 2011).
Bashford A, *Global Population: History, Geopolitics, and Life on Earth* (Columbia University Press 2014).
Becker Lorca A, *Mestizo International Law: A Global Intellectual History 1842–1933* (Cambridge University Press 2015).
Beer S, *Brain of the Firm: The Managerial Cybernetics of Organization* (2nd ed., J. Wiley 1981).
Benjamin R (ed.), *Captivating Technology: Race, Carceral Technoscience, and Liberatory Imagination in Everyday Life* (Duke University Press 2019).
Benton L and Ford L, *Rage for Order: The British Empire and the Origins of International Law 1800–1850* (Harvard University Press 2016).
Bijker WE, Hughes TE, and Pinch T (eds.), *The Social Construction of Technological Systems: New Directions in the Sociology and History of Technology* (MIT Press 1987).
Boer B et al., *The Mekong: A Socio-Legal Approach to River Basin Development* (Routledge 2015).
Booth C, *Labour and Life of the People, vol. 1* (Rev ed., Macmillan 1902).
Bourdieu P, *On the State: Lectures at the Collège de France, 1989–1992* (David Fernbach tr., Polity Press 2014).
Bourdieu P, *Pascalian Meditations* (Richard Nice tr., Stanford University Press 2000).
Brabham DC, *Crowdsourcing* (MIT Press 2013).
Branch J, *The Cartographic State: Maps, Territory, and the Origins of Sovereignty* (Cambridge University Press 2014).
Buchanan I (ed.), *A Dictionary of Critical Theory* (2nd ed., Oxford University Press 2018).
Bucher T, *If... Then: Algorithmic Power and Politics* (Oxford University Press 2018).
Bulmer M, Bales K, and Sklar KK, *The Social Survey in Historical Perspective, 1880–1940* (Cambridge University Press 1991).
Burgess J and Green J, *YouTube: Online Video and Participatory Culture* (Polity Press 2018).
Canetti E, *Crowds and Power* (Carol Stewart tr., Farrar, Straus & Giroux 1984).

Chandler D and Munday R, *A Dictionary of Media & Communication* (Oxford University Press 2016).
Chandler D, *Ontopolitics in the Anthropocene: An Introduction to Mapping, Sensing and Hacking* (Routledge 2018).
Chun WHK, *Updating to Remain the Same: Habitual New Media* (MIT Press 2016).
Cohen JE, *Between Truth and Power: The Legal Constructions of Informational Capitalism* (Oxford University Press 2019).
Cole J, *The Power of Large Numbers: Population, Politics, and Gender in Nineteenth-Century France* (Cornell University Press 2000).
Collins R and Makowsky M, *The Discovery of Society* (8th ed., McGraw-Hill 2010).
Cosgrove D, *Geography and Vision: Seeing, Imagining and Representing the World* (IB Taurus 2008).
Crawford K, *Atlas of AI* (Yale University Press 2021).
de Beauvoir S, *"The Useless Mouths" and Other Literary Writings* (University of Illinois Press 2011).
Dean J, *Crowds and Party* (Verso Books 2016).
DeNardis L, *Internet in Everything: Freedom and Security in a World with No Off Switch* (Yale University Press 2020).
Domingos P, *The Master Algorithm* (Basic Books 2017).
Douglas M, *Purity and Danger: An Analysis of the Concepts of Pollution and Taboo* (Routledge 2002).
Duffield M, *Post-Humanitarianism: Governing Precarity in the Digital World* (Polity 2018).
Eagleton T, *Literary Theory, An Introduction* (University of Minnesota Press 2008).
Edelman L, *No Future: Queer Theory and the Death Drive* (Duke University Press 2004).
Efron B and Hastie T, *Computer Age Statistical Inference* (Cambridge University Press 2016).
Esmeir S, *Juridical Humanity: A Colonial History* (Stanford University Press 2012).
Eubanks V, *Automating Inequality: How High-Tech Tools Profile, Police, and Punish the Poor* (St. Martin's Press 2018).
Evans J, *The History and Practice of Ancient Astronomy* (Oxford University Press 1998).
Fassin D, *Life: A Critical User's Manual* (Polity 2018).
Fassin D (ed.), *At the Heart of the State: The Moral World of Institutions* (Pluto Press 2015).
Fassin D, *Humanitarian Reason: A Moral History of the Present* (University of California Press 2011).
Feenberg A, *Questioning Technology* (2nd ed., Taylor & Francis Group 2012).
Floridi L, *The Fourth Revolution: How the Infosphere Is Reshaping Human Reality* (Oxford University Press 2014).
Foster R and Horst HA (eds.), *The Moral Economy of Mobile Phones: Pacific Island Perspectives* (ANU Press 2018).
Foucault M, *The Birth of Biopolitics: Lectures at the Collège de France, 1978–79* (Graham Burchell tr., Picador Palgrave Macmillan 2010).
Foucault M, *Security, Territory, Population: Lectures at the Collège de France, 1977–78* (Graham Burchell ed., Arnold I Davidson tr., Palgrave Macmillan UK 2007).
Foucault M, *"Society Must Be Defended": Lectures at the Collège de France, 1975–1976* (François Ewald ed., Macmillan 2003).
Foucault M, *Discipline and Punish* (Alan Sheridan tr., 2nd ed., Vintage 1995).
Foucault M, *The History of Sexuality. Volume I: An Introduction* (Robert Hurley tr., Pantheon Books 1978).

Galloway AR, *The Interface Effect* (Polity 2012).
Galloway AR, *Gaming: Essays on Algorithmic Culture, vol. 18* (NED-New edition, University of Minnesota Press 2006).
Galloway AR, *Protocol: How Control Exists after Decentralization* (MIT Press 2004).
Giddens A, *The Constitution of Society: Outline of the Theory of Structuration* (Polity Press 1984).
Gidley B, *The Proletarian Other: Charles Booth and the Politics of Representation* (Centre for Urban and Community Research, Goldsmiths College 2000).
Giridharadas A, *Winners Take All: The Elite Charade of Changing the World* (Vintage 2019).
Hadiz V, *The Politics of Economic Development in Indonesia: Contending Perspectives* (Routledge 2005).
Halpern O, *Beautiful Data: A History of Vision and Reason since 1945* (Duke University Press 2014).
Hartman C and Squires G (eds.), *There Is No Such Thing as a Natural Disaster: Race, Class, and Hurricane Katrina* (Routledge 2006).
Heartfield James, *Humanitarian Imperialism in Australia, New Zealand, Fiji, Canada, South Africa, and the Congo, 1837–1909* (Columbia University Press 2011).
Hirschman AO, *Exit, Voice, and Loyalty* (Harvard University Press 1972).
Hookway B, *Interface* (MIT Press 2014).
Hussain N, *The Jurisprudence of Emergency: Colonialism and the Rule of Law* (University of Michigan Press 2019).
Jacobsen KL, *The Politics of Humanitarian Technology: Good Intentions, Unintended Consequences and Insecurity* (Routledge 2015).
James W, *The Principles of Psychology, Volumes I and II* (Harvard University Press 1981).
Johns F, *Non-Legality in International Law: Unruly Law* (Cambridge University Press 2013).
Johns F, Joyce R, and Pahuja S, *Events: The Force of International Law* (Taylor & Francis Group 2010).
Kanninen T, *Leadership and Reform: The Secretary-General and the UN Financial Crisis of the Late 1980s* (Martinus Nijhoff Publishers 1995).
Kelman I, *Disaster by Choice: How Our Actions Turn Natural Hazards into Catastrophes* (Oxford University Press 2020).
Kennedy D, *The Dark Sides of Virtue: Reassessing International Humanitarianism* (Princeton University Press 2004).
Kennedy D, *A Critique of Adjudication: Fin de Siècle* (Harvard University Press 1997).
Klemens B, *Math You Can't Use: Patents, Copyright, and Software* (Brookings Institution Press 2006).
Koskenniemi M, *The Gentle Civilizer of Nations: The Rise and Fall of International Law, 1870–1960* (Cambridge University Press 2002).
Kuner C and Marelli M, *Handbook on Data Protection in Humanitarian Action* (2nd ed., ICRC 2020).
Landers J, *Death and the Metropolis: Studies in the Demographic History of London, 1670–1830* (Cambridge University Press 1993).
Lemke T, Casper MJ, and Moore LJ, *Biopolitics: An Advanced Introduction* (NYU Press 2011).
Li TM, *The Will to Improve: Governmentality, Development, and the Practice of Politics* (Duke University Press 2007).

Macalister-Smith P, *International Humanitarian Assistance: Disaster Relief Actions in International Law and Organization* (Springer 1985).
MacKenzie D, *An Engine, Not a Camera: How Financial Models Shape Markets* (MIT Press 2006).
MacKenzie DA and Wajcman J, *The Social Shaping of Technology: How the Refrigerator Got Its Hum* (Open University Press 1985).
Malcolm J, *Multi-Stakeholder Governance and the Internet Governance Forum* (Terminus Press 2008).
Marx K, *Capital, Volumes One & Two* (Samuel Moore, Edward Aveling, and Ernest Untermann trs., Wordsworth 2013).
Marx K, *The German Ideology* (CJ Arthur ed., International Publishers 1972).
Maxwell D and Gelsdorf KH, *Understanding the Humanitarian World* (Routledge 2019).
Mcluhan M, *Understanding Media: The Extensions of Man* (MIT Press 1994).
Meier P, *Digital Humanitarians: How Big Data Is Changing the Face of Humanitarian Response* (Routledge 2015).
Merry SE, Davis KE, and Kingsbury B, *The Quiet Power of Indicators: Measuring Governance, Corruption, and Rule of Law* (Cambridge University Press 2015).
Miyazaki H, *The Method of Hope: Anthropology, Philosophy, and Fijian Knowledge* (Stanford University Press 2004).
Moniz AB, *From Empire to Humanity: The American Revolution and the Origins of Humanitarianism* (Oxford University Press 2016).
Monmonier M, *Cartographies of Danger: Mapping Hazards in America* (University of Chicago Press 1997).
Morozov E, *To Save Everything, Click Here: The Folly of Technological Solutionism* (PublicAffairs 2013).
Mosse D (ed.), *Adventures in Aidland: The Anthropology of Professionals in International Development* (Berghain Books 2013).
Moyn S, *Not Enough: Human Rights in an Unequal World* (Harvard University Press 2018).
Moyn S, *Human Rights and the Uses of History* (Verso Books 2014).
Murjaya J et al., *Tsunami Early Warning Service Guidebook for InaTEWS* (BMKG, 2nd ed., August 2012).
Neiman S, *Evil in Modern Thought: An Alternative History of Philosophy* (Princeton University Press 2015).
Orford A, *International Law and the Politics of History* (Cambridge University Press 2021).
Parisi L, *Contagious Architecture: Computation, Aesthetics, and Space* (MIT Press 2013).
Peck J, *Constructions of Neoliberal Reason* (Oxford University Press 2010).
Piotukh V, *Biopolitics, Governmentality and Humanitarianism: "Caring" for the Population in Afghanistan and Belarus* (Routledge 2015).
Pistor K, *The Code of Capital: How the Law Creates Wealth and Inequality* (Princeton University Press 2019).
Powell DE, *Landscapes of Power: Politics of Energy in the Navajo Nation* (Duke University Press 2018).
Rieff D, *A Bed for the Night: Humanitarianism in Crisis* (Simon & Schuster 2003).
Robinson AH, *Early Thematic Mapping in the History of Cartography* (University of Chicago Press 1982).
Rodogno D, *Against Massacre: Humanitarian Interventions in the Ottoman Empire, 1815–1914* (Princeton University Press 2012).
Samana N, *Global Positioning: Technologies and Performance* (Wiley 2008).

Scholz T and Schneider N, *Ours to Hack and to Own: The Rise of Platform Cooperativism, a New Vision for the Future of Work and a Fairer Internet* (OR Books 2016).
Seaman V, *An Account of the Epidemic Yellow Fever, as It Appeared in the City of New-York in the Year 1795* (Hopkins, Webb & Co. 1796).
Serres M, *The Parasite* (Lawrence R Schehr tr., Johns Hopkins University Press 1982).
Shapin S and Schaffer S, *Leviathan and the Air-Pump: Hobbes, Boyle, and the Experimental Life* (Princeton University Press 1985).
Sharma S, *Famine, Philanthropy and the Colonial State: North India in the Early Nineteenth Century* (Oxford University Press 2001).
Shaw C, *Britannia's Embrace: Modern Humanitarianism and the Imperial Origins of Refugee Relief* (Oxford University Press 2015).
Shaw D, *The World's Largest Humanitarian Agency—The Transformation of the UN World Food Programme and of Food Aid* (Palgrave Macmillan Limited 2011).
Shaw D, *World Food Security: A History Since 1945* (Palgrave Macmillan UK 2007).
Smirl L, *Spaces of Aid: How Cars, Compounds and Hotels Shape Humanitarianism* (Zed Books 2015).
Stamatov P, *The Origins of Global Humanitarianism: Religion, Empires, and Advocacy* (Cambridge University Press 2013).
Suchman LA, *Plans and Situated Actions: The Problem of Human-Machine Communication* (Cambridge University Press 1987).
Tesner S, *The United Nations and Business: A Partnership Recovered* (Macmillan 2000).
Tsing AL, *The Mushroom at the End of the World: On the Possibility of Life in Capitalist Ruins* (Princeton University Press 2015).
Tzouvala N, *Capitalism as Civilisation: A History of International Law* (Cambridge University Press 2020).
van Dijck J, *The Culture of Connectivity: A Critical History of Social Media* (Oxford University Press 2013).
Vaughan L, *Mapping Society: The Spatial Dimensions of Social Cartography* (UCL Press 2018).
Venzke I and Heller KJ (eds.), *Contingency in International Law: On the Possibility of Different Legal Histories* (Oxford University Press 2021).
Weber M, *Economy and Society* (Keith Tribe tr., Harvard University Press 2019).
Weizman E, *Forensic Architecture: Violence at the Threshold of Detectability* (MIT Press 2017).
Whyte J, *The Morals of the Market: Human Rights and the Rise of Neoliberalism* (Verso Books 2019).
Wilden A, *System and Structure: Essays in Communication and Exchange* (2nd ed., Tavistock 1980).
Wilson RA and Brown RD (eds.), *Humanitarianism and Suffering: The Mobilization of Empathy* (Cambridge University Press 2008).
Winichakul T, *Siam Mapped: A History of the Geo-Body of a Nation* (University of Hawai'i Press 1994).
Worboys M, *Spreading Germs: Disease Theories and Medical Practice in Britain, 1865–1900* (Cambridge University Press 2000).
Zammit A, *Development at Risk: Rethinking UN-Business Partnerships* (The South Centre and UNRISD 2003).
Zuboff S, *The Age of Surveillance Capitalism: The Fight for a Human Future at the New Frontier of Power* (Profile Books 2019).

## Book Chapters

Abou-bakr AJ (ed.), "The Emergence of Disaster-Oriented PPPs," in *Managing Disasters through Public-Private Partnerships* (Georgetown University Press 2013), 15–42.

Anderson M and Gerber M, "Introduction to Humanitarian Emergencies," in David Townes (ed.), *Health in Humanitarian Emergencies: Principles and Practice for Public Health and Healthcare Practitioners* (Cambridge University Press 2018), 1–8.

Barthes R, "The Structuralist Activity," in Richard Howard (tr.), *Critical Essays* (Northwestern University Press 1972), 213–220.

Barthes R, "The Reality Effect," in Richard Howard (tr.), *The Rustle of Language* (University of California Press 1969), 141–148.

Benjamin W, "The Task of the Translator," in Marcus Bullock and Michael W Jennings (eds.), *Walter Benjamin: Selected Writings Volume 1, 1913–1926* (Harvard University Press 1996), 253–263.

Bourdieu P, "The Forms of Capital," in JG Richardson (ed.), *Handbook of Theory and Research for the Sociology of Education* (Greenwood 1986), 241–258.

Brett A, "What Is Intellectual History Now?," in David Cannadine (ed.), *What Is History Now?* (Palgrave Macmillan 2002), 113–131.

Cabanes B (ed.), "Human Disasters: Humanitarianism and the Transnational Turn in the Wake of World War I," in *The Great War and the Origins of Humanitarianism, 1918–1924* (Cambridge University Press 2014), 1–17.

Cannon T, "Vulnerability Analysis and the Explanation of 'Natural' Disasters," in Ann Varley (ed.), *Disasters, Development and Environment* (John Wiley & Sons, Ltd. 1994), 14–30.

Christie R, "Critical Readings of Humanitarianism," in Roger Mac Ginty and Jenny H. Peterson (eds.), *The Routledge Companion to Humanitarian Action* (Routledge 2015), 38–48.

Coen DR, "The Advent of Climate Science," in Hans von Storch (ed.), *Oxford Research Encyclopedia of Climate Science* (Oxford University Press 2020), <https://oxfordre.com/climatescience/view/10.1093/acrefore/9780190228620.001.0001/acrefore-9780190228620-e-716> (accessed October 10, 2022).

Crary J, "Eclipse of the Spectacle," in Brian Wallis (ed.), *Art After Modernism: Rethinking Representation* (New Museum of Contemporary Art with David Godine 1984), 283–294.

Deleuze G, "How Do We Recognize Structuralism?," in David Lapoujade (ed.); Michael Taormina (tr.), *Desert Islands and Other Texts, 1953–1974* (Semiotexte 2004), 170–192.

Derrida J, "Des Tours de Babel," in Joseph F Graham (tr.), *Difference in Translation* (Cornell University Press 1985), 165–207.

Eller KH, "Transnational Contract Law," in Peer Zumbansen (ed.), *The Oxford Handbook of Transnational Law* (Oxford University Press 2021), 513–530.

Foucault M, "On the Genealogy of Ethics: An Overview of Work in Progress," in Paul Rabinow (ed.), *The Foucault Reader* (Pantheon 1984), 340–372.

Gangadharan SP, "Digital Exclusion: A Politics of Refusal," in Lucy Bernholz, Hélène Landemore, and Rob Reich (eds.), *Digital Technology and Democratic Theory* (University of Chicago Press 2021), 113–140.

Gillespie T, "Algorithm," in Benjamin Peters (ed.), *Digital Keywords: A Vocabulary of Information Society and Culture* (Princeton University Press 2016), 18–30.

Glasze G and Perkins C, "Social and Political Dimensions of the OpenStreetMap Project: Towards a Critical Geographical Research Agenda," in Jamal Jokar Arsanjani et al. (eds.), *OpenStreetMap in GIScience: Experiences, Research, and Applications* (Springer International Publishing 2015), 143–166.

Greenhalgh S, "Globalization and Population Governance in China," in Aihwa Ong and Stephen J Collier (eds.), *Global Assemblages: Technology, Politics, and Ethics as Anthropological Problems* (John Wiley & Sons, Ltd., 2008), 354–372.

Grove K, "Disaster Biopolitics and the Crisis Economy," in Jennifer L Lawrence and Sarah Marie Wiebe (eds.), *Biopolitical Disaster* (Routledge 2018), 30–46.

Hermanstrand H, "Identification of the South Saami in the Norwegian 1801 Census: Why Is the 1801 Census a Problematic Source?," in Håkon Hermanstrand et al. (eds.), *The Indigenous Identity of the South Saami: Historical and Political Perspectives on a Minority within a Minority* (Springer 2019), 49–63.

Johns F, "Data Territories: Changing Architectures of Association in International Law," in Martin Kuijer and Wouter Werner (eds.), *Netherlands Yearbook of International Law 2016: The Changing Nature of Territoriality in International Law* (TMC Asser Press 2017), 107–129.

Koskenniemi M, "A History of International Law Histories," in Bardo Fassbender and Anne Peters (eds.), *The Oxford Handbook of the History of International Law* (Oxford University Press 2012), 943–971.

Mannan M and Pek S, "Solidarity in the Sharing Economy: The Role of Platform Cooperatives at the Base of the Pyramid," in Israr Qureshi, Babita Bhatt, and Dhirendra Mani Shukla (eds.), *Sharing Economy at the Base of the Pyramid* (Springer 2021), 249–279.

Montasari R and Jahankhani H, "The Application of Technology in Combating Human Trafficking," in Hamid Jahankhani, Arshad Jamal, and Shaun Lawson (eds.), *Cybersecurity, Privacy and Freedom Protection in the Connected World* (Springer 2021), 149–156.

Mukherjee B and Koren O, "Food Riots, Urbanization, and Mass Killing Campaigns: Indonesia and Malaysia," in Bumba Mukherjee and Ore Koren (eds.), *The Politics of Mass Killing in Autocratic Regimes* (Springer International Publishing 2019), 197–252.

Peters B, "Digital," in *Digital Keywords: A Vocabulary of Information Society and Culture* (Princeton University Press 2016), 93–108.

Rahman R and Salehin M, "Flood Risks and Reduction Approaches in Bangladesh," in Rajib Shaw, Fuad Mallick, and Aminul Islam (eds.), *Disaster Risk Reduction Approaches in Bangladesh* (Springer Japan 2013), 65–90.

Rhind D, "National Mapping as a Business-Like Enterprise," in Fraser Taylor (ed.), *Policy Issues in Modern Cartography*, vol. 3 (Elsevier 1998), 1–18.

Riles A, "Is the Law Hopeful?," in Hirokazu Miyazaki and Richard Swedberg (eds.), *The Economy of Hope* (University of Pennsylvania Press 2017), 126–146.

Riles A, "Legal Amateurism," in Christopher Tomlins and Justin Desautels-Stein (eds.), *Searching for Contemporary Legal Thought* (Cambridge University Press 2017), 499–516.

Rose N, "Governing 'Advanced' Liberal Democracies," in Nikolas Rose, Thomas Osborne, and Andrew Barry (eds.), *Foucault and Political Reason* (Taylor & Francis Group 1996), 37–64.

Rouvroy A, "The End(s) of Critique: Data Behaviourism versus Due Process," in Mireille Hildebrandt and Katja De Vries (eds.), *Privacy, Due Process and the Computational Turn: The Philosophy of Law Meets the Philosophy of Technology* (Taylor & Francis Group 2013), 143–167.
Samuelson P, "The Strange Odyssey of Software Interfaces and Intellectual Property Law," in Mario Biagioli, Peter Jaszi, and Martha Woodmansee (eds.), *Making and Unmaking Intellectual Property: Creative Production in Legal and Cultural Perspective* (University of Chicago Press 2009), 321–335.
Sandvik KB, Messelken D, and Winkler D, "Humanitarian Wearables: Digital Bodies, Experimentation and Ethics," in Daniel Messelken and David Winkler (eds.), *Ethics of Medical Innovation, Experimentation, and Enhancement in Military and Humanitarian Contexts* (Springer International Publishing 2020), 87–104.
Schaar J, "The Birth of the Good Humanitarian Donorship Initiative," in *The Humanitarian Response Index 2007* (Palgrave Macmillan 2008), 37–44.
Star SL and Bowker GC, "How to Infrastructure," in Leah A Lievrouw and Sonia Livingstone (eds.), *Handbook of New Media: Updated Student Edition* (SAGE Publications 2006), 230–245.
Sterne J, "Analog," in Benjamin Peters (ed.), *Digital Keywords: A Vocabulary of Information Society and Culture* (Princeton University Press 2016), 31–44.
Thürer D, "Soft Law," in Rüdiger Wolfrum (ed.), *Max Planck Encyclopedia of Public International Law (Online)* (Oxford University Press 2011), <https://opil.ouplaw.com/home/mpil> (accessed October 10, 2022).
Weber M, "Politics as a Vocation," in David Owen and Tracy B Strong (eds.), Rodney Livingstone (tr.), *The Vocation Lectures: Science as a Vocation; Politics as a Vocation* (Hackett Publishing 2004), 32–94.
Williams E, "Plagues—Account of the Spasmodick Cholera," in *The Treasury of Knowledge, and Library of Reference*, vol. 3 (7th ed., Collins, Keese & Co. 1839), 89–95.

## Articles in Journals

Aalberts TE, "Interdisciplinarity on the Move: Reading Kratochwil as Counter-Disciplinarity Proper" (2016) 44 Millennium 242.
Albuquerque JP de, Herfort B, and Eckle M, "The Tasks of the Crowd: A Typology of Tasks in Geographic Information Crowdsourcing and a Case Study in Humanitarian Mapping" (2016) 8 Remote Sensing 859.
Ali SF, "Crowd-Sourced Governance in a Post-Disaster Context" (2015) 64 International & Comparative Law Quarterly 211.
Allensworth RH, "Antitrust's High-Tech Exceptionalism Antitrust and Digital Platforms" (2020) 130 Yale Law Journal Forum 588.
Amoore L, "Data Derivatives: On the Emergence of a Security Risk Calculus for Our Times" (2011) 28 Theory, Culture & Society 24.
Amoore L, "Lines of Sight: On the Visualization of Unknown Futures" (2009) 13 Citizenship Studies 17.
Anderson J, Sarkar D, and Palen L, "Corporate Editors in the Evolving Landscape of OpenStreetMap" (2019) 8 ISPRS International Journal of Geo-Information 232.
Aradau C, Blanke T, and Greenway G, "Acts of Digital Parasitism: Hacking, Humanitarian Apps and Platformisation" (2019) 21 New Media & Society 2548.

Asad T, "Reflections on Violence, Law, and Humanitarianism" (2015) 41 Critical Inquiry 390.
Auerbach S, "'The Law Has No Feeling for Poor Folks Like Us!': Everyday Responses to Legal Compulsion in England's Working-Class Communities, 1871–1904" (2012) 45 Journal of Social History 686.
Awad O and Abu Harb S, "Palestinian Census 2017—Harnessing the Modernization Initiative" (2020) 36 Statistical Journal of the IAOS 77.
Back A and Marjavaara R, "Mapping an Invisible Population: The Uneven Geography of Second-Home Tourism" (2017) 19 Tourism Geographies 595.
Balibar E, "Structuralism: A Destitution of the Subject?" (2003) 14 Differences 1.
Barnett M, "Evolution without Progress? Humanitarianism in a World of Hurt" (2009) 63 International Organization 621.
Barnett MN, "Humanitarian Governance" (2013) 16 Annual Review of Political Science 379.
Beach H, "Self-Determining the Self: Aspects of Saami Identity Management in Sweden" (2007) 24 Acta Borealia 1.
Beer S, "What Is Cybernetics?" (2002) 31 Kybernetes 209.
Beer S, "Cybernetics—A Systems Approach to Management" (1972) 1 Personnel Review 28.
Benjamin R, "Informed Refusal: Toward a Justice-Based Bioethics" (2016) 41 Science, Technology & Human Values 967.
Berger J and Milkman KL, "What Makes Online Content Viral?" (2012) 49 Journal of Marketing Research 192.
Blumenstock JE, "Inferring Patterns of Internal Migration from Mobile Phone Call Records: Evidence from Rwanda" (2012) 18 Information Technology for Development 107.
Booth C, "Condition and Occupations of the People of East London and Hackney, 1887" (1888) 51 Journal of the Royal Statistical Society 276.
Boyce JK, "Birth of a Megaproject: Political Economy of Flood Control in Bangladesh" (1990) 14 Environmental Management 419.
Bradley M, "The International Organization for Migration (IOM): Gaining Power in the Forced Migration Regime" (2017) 33 Refuge: Canada's Journal on Refugees 97.
Brammer H, "After the Bangladesh Flood Action Plan: Looking to the Future" (2010) 9 Environmental Hazards 118.
Brammer H, "Floods in Bangladesh: II. Flood Mitigation and Environmental Aspects" (1990) 156 The Geographical Journal 158.
Breiman L, "Statistical Modeling: The Two Cultures (with Comments and a Rejoinder by the Author)" (2001) 16 Statistical Science 199.
Brun C, "There Is No Future in Humanitarianism: Emergency, Temporality and Protracted Displacement" (2016) 27 History and Anthropology 393.
Bühlmann P and van de Geer S, "Statistics for Big Data: A Perspective" (2018) 136 Statistics & Probability Letters 37.
Burns R, "New Frontiers of Philanthro-Capitalism: Digital Technologies and Humanitarianism" (2019) 51 Antipode 1101.
Burns R, "Moments of Closure in the Knowledge Politics of Digital Humanitarianism" (2014) 53 Geoforum 51.
Casas-Cortés M et al., "Clashing Cartographies, Migrating Maps: The Politics of Mobility at the External Borders of E.U.Rope" (2017) 16 ACME: An International Journal for Critical Geographies 1.

Casemajor N et al., "Non-Participation in Digital Media: Toward a Framework of Mediated Political Action" (2015) 37 Media, Culture & Society 850.

Cesarz M, "The Diversity of Citizenship of Palestinians and Its Impact on Their Mobility: Passport and Visa Issues" (2018) 47 Polish Political Science Yearbook 284.

Chander A, "How Law Made Silicon Valley" (2013) 63 Emory Law Journal 639.

Charles-Edwards E et al., "A Framework for Official Temporary Population Statistics" (2020) 36 Journal of Official Statistics 1.

Chen GM, "Tweet This: A Uses and Gratifications Perspective on How Active Twitter Use Gratifies a Need to Connect with Others" (2011) 27 Computers in Human Behavior 755.

Chimni BS, "Globalization, Humanitarianism and the Erosion of Refugee Protection" (2000) 13 Journal of Refugee Studies 243.

Chouliaraki L, "Post-Humanitarianism: Humanitarian Communication beyond a Politics of Pity" (2010) 13 International Journal of Cultural Studies 107.

Chowdhury R, "An Assessment of Flood Forecasting in Bangladesh: The Experience of the 1998 Flood" (2000) 22 Natural Hazards 139.

Chun WHK, "On Software, or the Persistence of Visual Knowledge" (2005) 18 Grey Room 26.

Cohen JE, "Law for the Platform Economy" (2017) 51 UC Davis Law Review 133.

Compton C, "The Temporality of Disaster: Data, the Emergency, and Climate Change" (2020) 1 Anthropocenes—Human, Inhuman, Posthuman 14.

Compton C, "The Unheeded Present and the Impossible Future: Temporalities of Relocation after Typhoon Haiyan" (2018) 50 Critical Asian Studies 136.

Cook B, "Flood Knowledge and Management in Bangladesh: Increasing Diversity, Complexity and Uncertainty" (2010) 4 Geography Compass 750.

Crabtree K and Geara P, "Safety Planning for Technology: Displaced Women and Girls' Interactions with Information and Communication Technology in Lebanon and Harm Reduction Considerations for Humanitarian Settings" (2018) 3 Journal of International Humanitarian Action 3.

Crary J, "Spectacle, Attention, Counter-Memory" (1989) 50 October 97.

Crawford K and Finn M, "The Limits of Crisis Data: Analytical and Ethical Challenges of Using Social and Mobile Data to Understand Disasters" (2015) 80 GeoJournal 491.

Curtis B, "Foucault on Governmentality and Population: The Impossible Discovery" (2002) 27 The Canadian Journal of Sociology 505.

Daas PJH et al., "Big Data as a Source for Official Statistics" (2015) 31 Journal of Official Statistics 249.

Dalton CM and Stallmann T, "Counter-Mapping Data Science: Counter-Mapping" (2018) 62 The Canadian Geographer/Le Géographe Canadien 93.

Dean J, "Enclosing the Subject" (2016) 44 Political Theory 363.

Deleuze G, "Postscript on the Societies of Control" (1992) 59 October 3.

Desai D, "Reflexive Institutional Reform and the Politics of the Regulatory State of the South" (2022) 16 Regulation & Governance <https://doi.org/10.1111/rego.12336> (accessed October 10, 2022).

Desautels-Stein J, "International Legal Structuralism: A Primer" (2016) 8 International Theory 201

Deville P et al., "Dynamic Population Mapping Using Mobile Phone Data" (2014) 111 Proceedings of the National Academy of Sciences 15888.

Doarn CR and Merrell RC, "Spacebridge to Armenia: A Look Back at Its Impact on Telemedicine in Disaster Response" (2011) 17 Telemedicine and e-Health 546.

Donders K, Van den Bulck H, and Raats T, "The Politics of Pleasing: A Critical Analysis of Multistakeholderism in Public Service Media Policies in Flanders" (2019) 41 Media, Culture & Society 347.

Duffield M, "The Resilience of the Ruins: Towards a Critique of Digital Humanitarianism" (2016) 4 Resilience 147.

Edkins J, "Humanitarianism, Humanity, Human" (2003) 2 Journal of Human Rights 253.

Edmonds P and Johnston A, "Empire, Humanitarianism and Violence in the Colonies" (2016) 17 Journal of Colonialism & Colonial History <doi:10.1353/cch.2016.0013> (accessed October 10, 2022).

Eisenberg MA, "The Role of Fault in Contract Law: Unconscionability, Unexpected Circumstances, Interpretation, Mistake, and Nonperformance" (2009) 107 Michigan Law Review 1413.

Elrick J and Schwartzman LF, "From Statistical Category to Social Category: Organized Politics and Official Categorizations of 'Persons with a Migration Background' in Germany" (2015) 38 Ethnic and Racial Studies 1539.

Farnham JW, "Disaster and Emergency Communications Prior to Computers/Internet: A Review" (2005) 10 Critical Care 207.

Fassin D, "Ethics of Survival: A Democratic Approach to the Politics of Life" (2010) 1 Humanity: An International Journal of Human Rights, Humanitarianism, and Development 81.

Fechter A-M and Schwittay A, "Citizen Aid: Grassroots Interventions in Development and Humanitarianism" (2019) 40 Third World Quarterly 1769.

Feinmann J, "How MSF Is Mapping the World's Medical Emergency Zones" (2014) 349 BMJ g7540.

Fink S, "The Science of Doing Good" (2007) 297 Scientific American 98.

Foody GM et al., "Accurate Attribute Mapping from Volunteered Geographic Information: Issues of Volunteer Quantity and Quality" (2015) 52 The Cartographic Journal 336.

Foucault M, Bennington G, and Lévy B-H, "The History of Sexuality: Interview" (1980) 4 Oxford Literary Review 3.

Fourcade M and Gordon J, "Learning Like a State: Statecraft in the Digital Age" (2020) 1 Journal of Law and Political Economy 78.

Fourcade M and Healy K, "Seeing like a Market" (2017) 15 Socio-Economic Review 9.

Fourcade M and Johns F, "Loops, Ladders and Links: The Recursivity of Social and Machine Learning" (2020) 49 Theory and Society 803.

Fourcade M and Kluttz D, "A Maussian Bargain: Accumulation by Gift in the Digital Economy" (2020) 7 Big Data & Society <https://doi.org/10.1177/2053951719897092> (accessed October 10, 2022).

Fredriksen A, "Crisis in 'a Normal Bad Year': Spaces of Humanitarian Emergency, the Integrated Food Security Phase Classification Scale and the Somali Famine of 2011" (2016) 48 Environment and Planning A: Economy and Space 40.

Fukuda-Parr S and McNeill D, "Knowledge and Politics in Setting and Measuring the SDGs: Introduction to Special Issue" (2019) 10 Global Policy 5.

Galeano P and Peña D, "Data Science, Big Data and Statistics" (2019) 28 TEST 289

Galloway AR, "Mathification" (2019) 47 Diacritics 96.

Gardiner C, "Principles of Internet Contracting: Illuminating the Shadows" (2019) 48 Common Law World Review 208.
Geertz C, "What Is a State If It Is Not a Sovereign?" (2004) 45 Current Anthropology 577.
Givoni M, "Between Micro Mappers and Missing Maps: Digital Humanitarianism and the Politics of Material Participation in Disaster Response" (2016) 34 Environment and Planning D: Society and Space 1025.
Guttal S and Shoemaker B, "Manipulating Consent: The World Bank and Public Consultation in the Nam Theun 2 Hydroelectric Project" (2004) 10 Watershed 18.
Haklay M (Muki), "Neogeography and the Delusion of Democratisation" (2013) 45 Environment and Planning A: Economy and Space 55.
Hamka F et al., "Mobile Customer Segmentation Based on Smartphone Measurement" (2014) 31 Telematics and Informatics 220.
Harig S et al., "The Tsunami Scenario Database of the Indonesia Tsunami Early Warning System (InaTEWS): Evolution of the Coverage and the Involved Modeling Approaches" (2020) 177 Pure and Applied Geophysics 1379.
Harley JB, "Deconstructing the Map" (1989) 26 Cartographica 1.
Harman G, "Technology, Objects and Things in Heidegger" (2010) 34 Cambridge Journal of Economics 17.
Harris LM and Hazen HD, "Power of Maps: (Counter) Mapping for Conservation" (2005) 4 ACME: An International Journal for Critical Geographies 99.
Haselkorn M and Walton R, "The Role of Information and Communication in the Context of Humanitarian Service" (2009) 52 IEEE Transactions on Professional Communication 325.
Haskell TL, "Capitalism and the Origins of the Humanitarian Sensibility, Part 2" (1985) 90 The American Historical Review 547.
Haskell TL, "Capitalism and the Origins of the Humanitarian Sensibility, Part 1" (1985) 90 The American Historical Review 339.
Hassani H et al., "Big Data and Energy Poverty Alleviation" (2019) 3 Big Data and Cognitive Computing 50.
Hayles NK, "Virtual Bodies and Flickering Signifiers" (1993) 66 October 69.
Helmreich S, "Recombination, Rationality, Reductionism and Romantic Reactions: Culture, Computers, and the Genetic Algorithm" (1998) 28 Social Studies of Science 39.
Higgitt RF and Dolan G, "Greenwich, Time and the Line" (2010) 34 Endeavour 35
Hilhorst D, "Being Good at Doing Good? Quality and Accountability of Humanitarian NGOs" (2002) 26 Disasters 193.
Hill H, "What's Happened to Poverty and Inequality in Indonesia over Half a Century?" (2021) 38 Asian Development Review 68.
Hilton M et al., "History and Humanitarianism: A Conversation" (2018) 241 Past & Present e1.
Hinwood AL and Rodriguez CM, "Potential Health Impacts Associated with Peat Smoke" (2005) 88 Journal of the Royal Society of Western Australia 133.
Hossain MdS, "Flood Forecasting and Warning in Bangladesh" (2018) 67 WMO Bulletin 1.
Houtchens BA et al., "Telemedicine and International Disaster Response: Medical Consultation to Armenia and Russia via a Telemedicine Spacebridge" (1993) 8 Prehospital and Disaster Medicine 57.

Humphreys L and Liao T, "Mobile Geotagging: Reexamining Our Interactions with Urban Space" (2011) 16 Journal of Computer-Mediated Communication 407.
Hunt A and Specht D, "Crowdsourced Mapping in Crisis Zones: Collaboration, Organisation and Impact" (2019) 4 Journal of International Humanitarian Action 1.
Ilcan S and Rygiel K, "'Resiliency Humanitarianism': Responsibilizing Refugees through Humanitarian Emergency Governance in the Camp" (2015) 9 International Political Sociology 333.
Isin E and Ruppert E, "The Birth of Sensory Power: How a Pandemic Made It Visible?" (2020) 7 Big Data & Society 1.
Jablonsky R, Karppi T, and Seaver N, "Introduction: Shifting Attention" (2021) 47 Science, Technology, & Human Values 235.
Jacobsen KL, "Making Design Safe for Citizens: A Hidden History of Humanitarian Experimentation" (2010) 14 Citizenship Studies 89.
Jeffrey C, "Waiting" (2008) 26 Environment and Planning D: Society and Space 954.
Johns F, "State Changes: Prototypical Governance Figured and Prefigured" (2022) 33 Law & Critique <https://doi.org/10.1007/s10978-022-09329-y> (accessed October 10, 2022).
Johns F, "Centers and Peripheries in a World of Blockchain: An Introduction to the Symposium" (2021) 115 AJIL Unbound 404.
Johns F, "Governance by Data" (2021) 17 Annual Review of Law and Social Science 53.
Johns F, "From Planning to Prototypes: New Ways of Seeing Like a State" (2019) 82 Modern Law Review 833.
Johns F, "Data, Detection, and the Redistribution of the Sensible in International Law" (2017) 111 American Journal of International Law 57.
Johns F, "The Temporal Rivalries of Human Rights" (2016) 23 Indiana Journal of Global Legal Studies 39.
Johns F, The Deluge" (2013) 1 London Review of International Law 9.
Johns F, "Financing as Governance" (2011) 31 Oxford Journal of Legal Studies 391.
Johns F, "Performing Party Autonomy" (2008) 71 Law and Contemporary Problems 243.
Johns F, "Guantánamo Bay and the Annihilation of the Exception" (2005) 16 European Journal of International Law 613.
Johns F and Compton C, "Data Jurisdictions and Rival Regimes of Algorithmic Regulation" (2020) 16 Regulation & Governance 63.
Joyce R, "Anarchist International Law(Yers)? Mapping Power and Responsibility in International Law" (2017) 5 London Review of International Law 397.
Junka-Aikio L, "Can the Sámi Speak Now?" (2016) 30 Cultural Studies 205.
Kaika M, "'Don't Call Me Resilient Again!': The New Urban Agenda as Immunology ... or ... What Happens When Communities Refuse to Be Vaccinated with 'Smart Cities' and Indicators" (2017) 29 Environment and Urbanization 89.
Kandel S et al., "Research Directions in Data Wrangling: Visualizations and Transformations for Usable and Credible Data" (2011) 10 Information Visualization 271.
Kapczynski A, "The Law of Informational Capitalism" (2020) 129 Yale Law Journal 1460.
Kennedy D, "The Political Stakes in 'Merely Technical' Issues of Contract Law" (2001) 1 European Review of Private Law 7.
Kibanov M et al., "Mining Social Media to Inform Peatland Fire and Haze Disaster Management" (2017) 7 Social Network Analysis and Mining 30.

## BIBLIOGRAPHY

Kim J, Cha M, and Lee JG, "Nowcasting Commodity Prices Using Social Media" (2017) 3 PeerJ Computer Science e126.

Kimball MA, "London through Rose-Colored Graphics: Visual Rhetoric and Information Graphic Design in Charles Booth's Maps of London Poverty" (2006) 36 Journal of Technical Writing and Communication 353.

Kingsbury B, "Infrastructure and InfraReg: On Rousing the International Law 'Wizards of Is'" (2019) 8 Cambridge International Law Journal 171.

Kingsbury B and Maisley N, "Infrastructures and Laws: Publics and Publicness" (2021) 17 Annual Review of Law and Social Science 353.

Klabbers J, "Counter-Disciplinarity" (2010) 4 International Political Sociology 308.

Klinenberg E, "Denaturalizing Disaster: A Social Autopsy of the 1995 Chicago Heat Wave" (1999) 28 Theory and Society 239.

Koch T, "The Art of Medicine: Knowing Its Place: Mapping as Medical Investigation" (2012) 379 The Lancet; London 887.

Koch T, "Mapping the Miasma: Air, Health, and Place in Early Medical Mapping" (2005) 52 Cartographic Perspectives 4.

Koskenniemi M, "What Is Critical Research in International Law? Celebrating Structuralism" (2016) 29 Leiden Journal of International Law 727.

Koskenniemi M, "Law, Teleology and International Relations: An Essay in Counterdisciplinarity" (2012) 26 International Relations 3.

Koslov L, "How Maps Make Time" (2019) 23 City 658.

Krieger N, "Who and What Is a 'Population'? Historical Debates, Current Controversies, and Implications for Understanding 'Population Health' and Rectifying Health Inequities" (2012) 90 The Milbank Quarterly 634.

LaCapra D, "Rethinking Intellectual History and Reading Texts" (1980) 19 History and Theory 245.

Legg S, "Foucault's Population Geographies: Classifications, Biopolitics and Governmental Spaces" (2005) 11 Population, Space and Place 137.

Li Y, "Red Cross Society in Imperial China, 1904–1912: A Historical Analysis" (2016) 27 Voluntas: International Journal of Voluntary and Nonprofit Organizations 2274.

Litt E and Hargittai E, "The Imagined Audience on Social Network Sites" (2016) 2 Social Media + Society <https://doi.org/10.1177/2056305116633482> (accessed October 10, 2022).

Madianou M, Longboan L, and Ong JC, "Finding a Voice Through Humanitarian Technologies? Communication Technologies and Participation in Disaster Recovery" (2015) 9 International Journal of Communication 19.

Manovich L, "Media After Software" (2013) 12 Journal of Visual Culture 30.

Marks S, "Law and the Production of Superfluity" (2011) 2 Transnational Legal Theory 1.

Marwick AE and boyd d, "I Tweet Honestly, I Tweet Passionately: Twitter Users, Context Collapse, and the Imagined Audience" (2011) 13 New Media & Society 114.

Matin N and Taher M, "The Changing Emphasis of Disasters in Bangladesh NGOs" (2001) 25 Disasters 227.

Mbembe A, "Aesthetics of Superfluity" (2004) 16 Public Culture 373.

Mbembe A, "Necropolitics" (2003) 15 Public Culture 11.

McFarland DA and McFarland HR, "Big Data and the Danger of Being Precisely Inaccurate" (2015) 2 Big Data & Society <https://doi.org/10.1177/2053951715602495> (accessed October 10, 2022).

McGurk TJ and Caquard S, "To What Extent Can Online Mapping Be Decolonial? A Journey throughout Indigenous Cartography in Canada" (2020) 64 The Canadian Geographer/Le Géographe Canadien 49.

Meier P, "New Information Technologies and Their Impact on the Humanitarian Sector" (2011) 93 International Review of the Red Cross 1239.

Meier P and Munro R, "The Unprecedented Role of SMS in Disaster Response: Learning from Haiti" (2010) 30 The SAIS Review of International Affairs 91.

Miller M, "Geospatial Data and Software Reviews: Mapbox.Js" (2020) 165 Association of Canadian Map Libraries and Archives Bulletin 32.

Miraftab F, "Public-Private Partnerships: The Trojan Horse of Neoliberal Development?" (2004) 24 Journal of Planning Education and Research 89.

Mirowski P, "The Philosophical Basis of Institutional Economics" (1987) 21 Journal of Economic Issues 1001.

Moats D and Seaver N, "'You Social Scientists Love Mind Games': Experimenting in the 'Divide' between Data Science and Critical Algorithm Studies" (2019) 6 Big Data & Society <https://doi.org/10.1177/2053951719833404> (accessed October 10, 2022).

Mock N, Morrow N, and Papendieck A, "From Complexity to Food Security Decision-Support: Novel Methods of Assessment and Their Role in Enhancing the Timeliness and Relevance of Food and Nutrition Security Information" (2013) 2 Global Food Security 41.

Mutascu M, "Influence of Climate Conditions on Tax Revenues" (2014) 8 Contemporary Economics 315.

North DC, "Institutions" (1991) 5 The Journal of Economic Perspectives 97.

O'Sullivan K, Hilton M, and Fiori J, "Humanitarianisms in Context" (2016) 23 European Review of History: Revue Européenne d'Histoire 1.

Ogie RI et al., "Crowdsourced Social Media Data for Disaster Management: Lessons from the PetaJakarta.Org Project" (2019) 73 Computers, Environment and Urban Systems 108.

Oppenheimer M et al., "Resilient Humanitarianism? Using Assemblage to Re-Evaluate the History of the League of Red Cross Societies" (2021) 43 The International History Review 579.

Orgad S and Seu BI, "'Intimacy at a Distance' in Humanitarian Communication" (2014) 36 Media, Culture & Society 916.

Osborne T and Rose N, "Spatial Phenomenotechnics: Making Space with Charles Booth and Patrick Geddes" (2004) 22 Environment and Planning D: Society and Space 209.

Pánek J, "From Mental Maps to GeoParticipation" (2016) 53 The Cartographic Journal 300.

Paul BK, "Relief Assistance to 1998 Flood Victims: A Comparison of the Performance of the Government and NGOs" (2003) 169 The Geographical Journal 75.

Paul BK, "Flood Research in Bangladesh in Retrospect and Prospect: A Review" (1997) 28 Geoforum 121.

Peluso NL, "Whose Woods Are These? Counter-Mapping Forest Territories in Kalimantan, Indonesia" (1995) 27 Antipode 383.

Perrin WG, "The Prime Meridian" (1927) 13 The Mariner's Mirror 109.

Pirotti F et al., "An Open Source Virtual Globe Rendering Engine for 3D Applications: NASA World Wind" (2017) 2 Open Geospatial Data, Software and Standards 4.

Pitts J, "The Critical History of International Law" (2015) 43 Political Theory 541.

Plantin J-C et al., "Infrastructure Studies Meet Platform Studies in the Age of Google and Facebook" (2018) 20 New Media & Society 293.

Pottage A, "The Materiality of What?" (2012) 39 Journal of Law and Society 167.

Preci A, "Fixing the Territory, a Turning Point: The Paradoxes of the Wichí Maps of the Argentine Chaco" (2020) 64 The Canadian Geographer/Le Géographe Canadien 20.

Purnomo H et al., "Fire Economy and Actor Network of Forest and Land Fires in Indonesia" (2017) 78 Forest Policy and Economics 21.

Quinn SD and Tucker DA, "How Geopolitical Conflict Shapes the Mass-Produced Online Map" (2017) 22 First Monday <https://doi.org/10.5210/fm.v22i11.7922> (accessed October 10, 2022).

Rab Á, "Social Media and Emergency—New Models and Policies Enhancing Disaster Management" (2015) X ME.DOK Média-Történet-Kommunikáció 45.

Rahman A, "Peoples' Perception and Response to Floodings: The Bangladesh Experience" (1996) 4 Journal of Contingencies and Crisis Management 198.

Rahman S, "Bangladesh in 1988: Precarious Institution Building Amid Crisis Management" (1989) 29 Asian Survey 216.

Rajkovic NM, "The Visual Conquest of International Law: Brute Boundaries, the Map, and the Legacy of Cartogenesis" (2018) 31 Leiden Journal of International Law 267.

Rasid H and Pramanik MAH, "Areal Extent of the 1988 Flood in Bangladesh: How Much Did the Satellite Imagery Show?" (1993) 8 Natural Hazards 189.

Rasid H and Pramanik MAH, "Visual Interpretation of Satellite Imagery for Monitoring Floods in Bangladesh" (1990) 14 Environmental Management 815.

Raustiala K, "Governing the Internet" (2016) 110 American Journal of International Law 491.

Raustiala K, "The Architecture of International Cooperation: Transgovernmental Networks and the Future of International Law" (2002) 43 Virginia Journal of International Law 1.

Rawat P and Mahajan AN, "ReactJS: A Modern Web Development Framework" (2020) 5 International Journal of Innovative Science and Research Technology 698.

Raymond M and DeNardis L, "Multistakeholderism: Anatomy of an Inchoate Global Institution" (2015) 7 International Theory 572.

Redfield P, "Fluid Technologies: The Bush Pump, the LifeStraw® and Microworlds of Humanitarian Design" (2016) 46 Social Studies of Science 159.

Riley D, "The New Durkheim: Bourdieu and the State" (2015) 2 Critical Historical Studies 261.

Rohde RA and Muller RA, "Air Pollution in China: Mapping of Concentrations and Sources" (2015) 10 PLOS ONE e0135749.

Rossum M van, "Labouring Transformations of Amphibious Monsters: Exploring Early Modern Globalization, Diversity, and Shifting Clusters of Labour Relations in the Context of the Dutch East India Company (1600–1800)" (2019) 64 International Review of Social History 19.

Rouvroy A and Stiegler B, "The Digital Regime of Truth: From the Algorithmic Governmentality to a New Rule of Law" (2016) 3 La Deleuziana 6.

Rubenstein JC, "Emergency Claims and Democratic Action" (2015) 32 Social Philosophy and Policy 101.

Ruppert E, "The Governmental Topologies of Database Devices" (2012) 29 Theory, Culture & Society 116.

Ruppert E, "Population Objects: Interpassive Subjects" (2011) 45 Sociology 218.

Sachs JD, "Goal-Based Development and the SDGs: Implications for Development Finance" (2015) 31 Oxford Review of Economic Policy 268.
Sadowski J, "'Anyway, the Dashboard Is Dead': On Trying to Build Urban Informatics" [2021] New Media & Society 1.
Saluveer E et al., "Methodological Framework for Producing National Tourism Statistics from Mobile Positioning Data" (2020) 81 Annals of Tourism Research 102895.
Sandvik KB, "Making Wearables in Aid: Digital Bodies, Data and Gifts" (2019) 1 Journal of Humanitarian Affairs 33.
Scholz S et al., "Volunteered Geographic Information for Disaster Risk Reduction—The Missing Maps Approach and Its Potential within the Red Cross and Red Crescent Movement" (2018) 10 Remote Sensing 1239.
Scott-Smith T, "Sticky Technologies: Plumpy'nut®, Emergency Feeding and the Viscosity of Humanitarian Design" (2018) 48 Social Studies of Science 3.
Seaman V, "An Inquiry into the Cause of the Prevalence of the Yellow Fever in New-York" (1798) I The Medical Repository 315.
Seu IB, "'The Deserving': Moral Reasoning and Ideological Dilemmas in Public Responses to Humanitarian Communications" (2016) 55 British Journal of Social Psychology 739.
Sheller M, "The Islanding Effect: Post-Disaster Mobility Systems and Humanitarian Logistics in Haiti" (2013) 20 Cultural Geographies 185.
Shringarpure B, "Africa and the Digital Savior Complex" (2020) 32 Journal of African Cultural Studies 178.
Siegert B, "Coding as Cultural Technique: On the Emergence of the Digital from Writing AC" (2018) 70 Grey Room 8.
Silbey SS, After Legal Consciousness" (2005) 1 Annual Review of Law and Social Science 323.
Skinner R and Lester A, "Humanitarianism and Empire: New Research Agendas" (2012) 40 The Journal of Imperial and Commonwealth History 729.
Slim H, "Dissolving the Difference between Humanitarianism and Development: The Mixing of a Rights-Based Solution" (2000) 10 Development in Practice 491.
Snape J, "Tax Law: Complexity, Politics and Policymaking" (2015) 24 Social & Legal Studies 155.
Sobocinska A, "New Histories of Foreign Aid" (2020) 17 History Australia 595.
Stanley L, "A Philosopher Manqué?: Simone de Beauvoir, Moral Value and 'The Useless Mouths'" (2001) 8 European Journal of Women's Studies 201.
Stevenson LG, "Putting Disease on the Map: The Early Use of Spot Maps in the Study of Yellow Fever" (1965) 20 Journal of the History of Medicine and Allied Sciences 226.
Taylor L and Broeders D, "In the Name of Development: Power, Profit and the Datafication of the Global South" (2015) 64 Geoforum 229.
Ticktin M, "From the Human to the Planetary" (2019) 6 Medicine Anthropology Theory 133.
Tomlins C, "How Autonomous Is Law?" (2007) 3 Annual Review of Law and Social Science 45.
Topalov C, "The City as Terra Incognita: Charles Booth's Poverty Survey and the People of London, 1886–1891" (1993) 8 Planning Perspectives 395.
Turing AM, "Computing Machinery and Intelligence" (1950) 59 Mind 433.
Turk C, "Cartographica Incognita: 'Dijital Jedis', Satellite Salvation and the Mysteries of the 'Missing Maps'" (2017) 54 The Cartographic Journal 14.

Twomey C, "Framing Atrocity: Photography and Humanitarianism" (2012) 36 History of Photography 255.

Tzouvala N, "TWAIL and the 'Unwilling or Unable' Doctrine: Continuities and Ruptures" (2015) 109 AJIL Unbound 266.

Vavilina ND and Skalaban IA, "Social Mapping as a Tool for Public Participation" (2015) 5 Regional Research of Russia 66.

Viljoen S, "The Promise and Limits of Lawfulness: Inequality, Law, and the Techlash" (2021) 2 Journal of Social Computing 284.

Vismann C, "Cultural Techniques and Sovereignty" (2013) 30 Theory, Culture & Society 83.

von Czechowski AS, "Humanitarianism: Histories, Erasures, Repetitions" (2017) 37 Comparative Studies of South Asia, Africa, & the Middle East 614.

Wagner-Pacifici R, "Theorizing the Restlessness of Events" (2010) 115 American Journal of Sociology 1351.

Walden VM, Scott I, and Lakeman J, "Snapshots in Time: Using Real-time Evaluations in Humanitarian Emergencies" (2010) 19 Disaster Prevention and Management: An International Journal 283.

Wang D and Liu S, "Performing Artivism: Feminists, Lawyers, and Online Legal Mobilization in China" (2020) 45 Law & Social Inquiry 678.

Watenpaugh KD, "The League of Nations' Rescue of Armenian Genocide Survivors and the Making of Modern Humanitarianism, 1920–1927" (2010) 115 The American Historical Review 1315.

Wayland HL, "A Scientific Basis of Charity" (1894) 3 The Charities Review 263.

Wezel FC and Ruef M, "Agents with Principles: The Control of Labor in the Dutch East India Company, 1700 to 1796" (2017) 82 American Sociological Review 1009.

White P, "The Role of UN Specialised Agencies in Complex Emergencies: A Case Study of FAO" (1999) 20 Third World Quarterly 223.

Wiener N, "Cybernetics" (1948) 179 Scientific American 14.

Wilden A, "Analog and Digital Communication: On the Relationship between Negation, Signification, and the Emergence of the Discrete Element" (1972) 6 Semiotica 50.

Wobcke W, Compton C, Johns C, Lamchek J, and Mariyah S, "Nowcasting for Hunger Relief: A Study of Promise and Perils" (2022) Information Technology for Development, <https://doi.org/10.1080/02681102.2022.2092438> (accessed October 10, 2022).

Wood D and Fels J, "Designs on Signs/Myth and Meaning in Maps" (1986) 23 Cartographica 54.

Yam P, Minkel J, and Schultz K, "Updates" (2008) 298 Scientific American 18.

Yeung K, "Algorithmic Regulation: A Critical Interrogation" (2018) 12 Regulation & Governance 505.

Yu FLT, "Private Enterprise Development in a One-Party Autocratic State: The Case of Alibaba Group in China's E-Commerce" (2018) 54 Issues & Studies 1850001.

Zagatti GA et al., "A Trip to Work: Estimation of Origin and Destination of Commuting Patterns in the Main Metropolitan Regions of Haiti Using CDR" (2018) 3 Development Engineering 133.

## Newspapers, Magazines, Blogs, and Website Posts

Amazon Web Services, "Helping to End Future Famines with Machine Learning" (*AWS*, November 29, 2018), <https://aws.amazon.com/blogs/publicsector/helping-to-end-future-famines-with-machine-learning/> (accessed October 10, 2022).

# BIBLIOGRAPHY 253

antiAtlas of borders, "Hackitectura—Critical Cartography of Gibraltar" (*antiatlas*, August 14, 2013), <https://www.antiatlas.net/hackitectura-critical-cartography-of-gibraltar-en/> (accessed October 10, 2022).

Australian Government Department of Foreign Affairs and Trade, "Stability in Indonesia" (*DFAT Development Partnership in Indonesia*, 2021), <https://www.dfat.gov.au/geo/indonesia/development-assistance/stability-in-indonesia> (accessed October 10, 2022).

Bauer J-M, "Mobile Phone Surveys Can Help World Food Programme Reach Hungry People," *The Guardian* (London, March 10, 2016).

Blakemore E, "Help First Responders in Ecuador Without Leaving Your Desk" *Smithsonian Magazine* (Washington, D.C., April 19, 2016).

Bock Clark D, "Why the Tsunami in Indonesia Struck Without Warning," *The New Yorker* (New York, October 4, 2018).

Brown M, "Nicaraguan Invasion? Blame Google Maps," *Wired* (San Francisco, November 8, 2010).

Butler D, "AI Summit Aims to Help World's Poorest," *Nature* (Berlin, June 6, 2017).

Cahill J, "MapSwipe—The Story Continues" (*Missing Maps*, June 25, 2018), <https://www.missingmaps.org/blog/2018/06/25/mapswipe-story/> (accessed October 10, 2022).

Cornish L, "Under New Management, DFAT Dumps Innovation Role" (*Devex*, February 14, 2020), <https://www.devex.com/news/sponsored/exclusive-under-new-management-dfat-dumps-innovation-role-96559> (accessed October 10, 2022).

Currion P, "'If All You Have Is a Hammer . . .'—How Useful Is Humanitarian Crowdsourcing?" (*Medium*, November 10, 2015), <https://paulcurrion.medium.com/if-all-you-have-is-a-hammer-how-useful-is-humanitarian-crowdsourcing-fed4ef33f8c8> (accessed October 10, 2022).

Delattre F and Colchester S, "Team Up in the New Tasking Manager" (*Humanitarian OpenStreetMap Team*, May 6, 2020), <https://www.hotosm.org/updates/tm4launch/> (accessed October 10, 2022).

Digital Democracy, "Waorani Territory Mapping Project" (*Digital Democracy*, 2021), <https://www.digital-democracy.org/ourwork/waorani/> (accessed October 10, 2022).

The Economist, "Monitoring Nuclear Weapons: The Nuke Detectives," *The Economist* (London, September 3, 2015).

Emergency Relief Coordination Centre, OCHA-Geneva, "GDACS—Global Disaster Alerting and Coordination System" (*GDACS*, N.D.), <https://www.gdacs.org/About/overview.aspx> (accessed October 10, 2022).

FAO, "Complex Emergencies: FAO in Emergencies" (*FAO*, N.D.), <https://www.fao.org/emergencies/emergency-types/complex-emergencies/en/> (accessed October 10, 2022).

FAO, "Drought and Financial Crisis Leave Indonesia Facing Record Food Deficit" (*FAO*, April 24, 1998), <https://www.fao.org/NEWS/GLOBAL/GW9810-e.htm> (accessed October 10, 2022).

Field Papers, "About Field Papers" (*Field Papers*, N.D.), <http://fieldpapers.org/about> (accessed October 10, 2022).

Fisher A, "Indicators 2.0: From Ranks and Reports to Dashboards and Databanks" (*Völkerrechtsblog*, November 23, 2021), <https://voelkerrechtsblog.org/indicators-2-0-from-ranks-and-reports-to-dashboards-and-databanks/> (accessed October 10, 2022).

Grower's Information Services Coop, "Grower's Information Services Coop" (*GISC*, N.D.), <https://www.gisc.coop/> (accessed October 10, 2022).

Hackitectura, "Acerca de—hackitectura.net" (*Hackitectura*, N.D.), <https://hackitectura.net/es/acerca-de/> (accessed October 10, 2022).

Heaven WD, "Hundreds of AI Tools Have Been Built to Catch Covid. None of Them Helped." (*MIT Technology Review*, July 30, 2021).

Hewlett-Packard, "CeNSE, HP Official Site" (*HP*, 2014), <https://www.hp.com/us-en/hp-information/environment/cense.html#.YOwEmBMzYUr> (accessed October 10, 2022).

Humanitarian OpenStreetMap Team, "Consolidated Mapping Projects—Base Roads Check vs Open Data References" (*Open Street Map Wiki*, N.D.), <https://wiki.openstreetmap.org/wiki/Consolidated_mapping_projects_-_base_roads_check_vs_open_data_references> (accessed October 10, 2022).

Humanitarian OpenStreetMap Team, "HOT Code of Conduct" (*HOTOSM*, N.D.), <https://www.hotosm.org/code-of-conduct> (accessed October 10, 2022

Humanitarian OpenStreetMap Team, "HOT Tasking Manager" (*HOTOSM*, N.D.), <https://tasks.hotosm.org> (accessed October 10, 2022).

Humanitarian OpenStreetMap Team, "Missing Maps" (*Missing Maps*, N.D.), <https://www.missingmaps.org/> (accessed October 10, 2022).

IBM Research, "The Possibilities of Project Lucy" (*IBM Research Blog*, October 13, 2014), <https://www.ibm.com/blogs/research/2014/10/the-possibilities-of-project-lucy/> (accessed October 10, 2022).

Ioanes E, "Hong Kong Protesters Destroyed 'Smart' Lampposts Because They Fear China Is Spying on Them," *Business Insider* (New York, August 26, 2019).

Jindia S, "Tech Startups to the Rescue? How Technology Can Deepen Inequality in Detroit—and How 'Civic Tech' Could Help End It" (*Medium*, November 23, 2016), <https://medium.com/latterly/tech-startups-to-the-rescue-978ec1f0f68f> (accessed October 10, 2022).

JMMB Group, "Investor Update: Digicel Group Limited" (*JMMB*, April 2019), <https://www.jmmb.com/sites/default/files/Jamaica/Attachments/Research/2019/JMMB_Digicel_InvestorUpdate_APRIL_2019.pdf> (accessed October 10, 2022).

Knight P, "Missing Maps Project Awarded at the Red Cross Humanitarian Technology Awards—A Year of Blogs—Oct 2020" (*Missing Maps*, October 26, 2020), <https://www.missingmaps.org/blog/2020/10/26/a-year-of-blogs/> (accessed October 10, 2022).

Lassa J, "Reviewing Indonesia's Tsunami Early Warning Strategy: Reflections from Sulawesi Island" (*The Conversation*, October 3, 2018), <http://theconversation.com/reviewing-indonesias-tsunami-early-warning-strategy-reflections-from-sulawesi-island-104257> (accessed October 10, 2022).

Leake F, "Suspect in Custody Following Arson Attack on 5G Mast" (*5Gradar*, March 10, 2019), <https://www.5gradar.com/news/suspect-in-custody-following-arson-attack-on-5g-mast> (accessed October 10, 2022).

Lin Y, "#DeleteFacebook Is Still Feeding the Beast—But There Are Ways to Overcome Surveillance Capitalism? (*The Conversation*, March 26, 2018), <http://theconversation.com/deletefacebook-is-still-feeding-the-beast-but-there-are-ways-to-overcome-surveillance-capitalism-93874> (accessed October 10, 2022).

London School of Economics, "Charles Booth's London: Poverty Maps and Police Notebooks" (*LSE*, 2016), <https://booth.lse.ac.uk/> (accessed October 10, 2022).

Makis P and Vari M, "Loloho Digicel Tower Equipment Torched," *Post Courier* (Papua New Guinea, February 14, 2019).

Maron M, "HOT's Tasking Manager 4: How We Built It" (*Mapbox.com*, May 15, 2020), <https://blog.mapbox.com/hots-tasking-manager-4-how-we-built-it-53ebaa3cafd0> (accessed October 10, 2022).

Meier P, "A Brief History of Crisis Mapping (Updated)" (*iRevolutions*, March 12, 2009), <https://irevolutions.org/2009/03/12/a-brief-history-of-crisis-mapping/> (accessed October 10, 2022).

Microsoft, "Microsoft Appoints Senior Government Affairs Leaders in Brussels and New York, Establishes New York Office to Work with the United Nations" (*EU Policy Blog*, January 17, 2020), <https://blogs.microsoft.com/eupolicy/2020/01/17/senior-gov-affairs-leaders-appointed-brussels-new-york/> (accessed October 10, 2022).

MVAMBLOG, "Introducing HungerMap LIVE" (*MVAM: THE BLOG*, October 22, 2019), <https://mvam.org/2019/10/22/introducing-hunger-map-live/> (accessed October 10, 2022).

MVAMBLOG, "Mapping Our Way towards Zero Hunger" (*MVAM: THE BLOG*, July 20, 2018), <https://mvam.org/2018/07/20/mapping-our-way-towards-zero-hunger-2/> (accessed October 10, 2022).

NDTV, "Indonesians Loot Markets After Tsunami Creates Shortage of Food, Water" (*NDTV.com*, September 30, 2018), <https://www.ndtv.com/world-news/indonesians-loot-supermarkets-after-tsunami-earthquake-create-shortage-of-food-water-1924504> (accessed October 10, 2022).

Oleson T, "Beyond the Bomb: The World's Nuclear Watchdog Expands Its Science" *Earth Magazine* (Alexandria, Virginia, April 7, 2015).

Ong AG, "WFP Launches HungerMap Live" (*WFP Stories*, January 20, 2020), <https://www.wfp.org/stories/wfp-launches-hungermap-live> (accessed October 10, 2022).

OpenMapKit, "OpenMapKit Website" (*OpenMapKit*, N.D.), <http://openmapkit.org/> (accessed October 10, 2022).

OpenStreetMap Foundation, "Contributor Terms (Rest of the World)" (*OpenStreetMap*, N.D.), <https://www.openstreetmap.org/user/terms> (accessed October 10, 2022).

OpenStreetMap Wiki, "Walking Papers" (*OpenStreetMap Wiki*, N.D.), <https://wiki.openstreetmap.org/wiki/Walking_Papers> (accessed October 10, 2022).

Perez de Lama J, de Soto P, and Moreno S, "Fadaîlat. Through Spaces at Fortress EU's Southwest Border," *Fadaiat: Freedom of Movement, Freedom of Knowledge* (Indymedia, 2006), <https://www.in-no.org/pdfs/furthur2/fadaiat_f2.pdf>.

Permanent Mission of France to the UN and International Organisations in Vienna, "CTBTO: Around the World in 16 Stations" (*delegfrance.org*, March 9, 2018), <https://onu-vienne.delegfrance.org/CTBTO-Around-the-world-in-16-stations> (accessed October 10, 2022).

Pramestri Z et al., "Estimating the Indicators on Education and Household Characteristics and Expenditure from Mobile Phone Data in Vanuatu," *Poster Session 2* (NetMob, 2017), <https://www.netmob.org/www17/assets/img/bookofabstract_poster_2017.pdf#page=82>.

Pulse Lab Jakarta, "VAMPIRE" (*Pulse Lab Jakarta*, N.D.), <http://vampire.pulselabjakarta.org/#m-home> (accessed October 10, 2022).

Pulse Lab Jakarta, "Understanding Population Movement after the 2018 Central Sulawesi Natural Disasters" (*Medium*, December 17, 2019), <https://medium.com/pulse-lab-jakarta/understanding-population-movement-after-the-2018-central-sulawesi-natural-disasters-70ab95b7741b> (accessed October 10, 2022).

Pulse Lab Jakarta, "Managing Relevant Information in the Aftermath of Natural Disasters: Launching PLJ's Latest Data Analytics Platform" (*Medium*, June 1, 2019), <https://medium.com/pulse-lab-jakarta/managing-relevant-information-in-the-aftermath-of-natural-disasters-launching-pljs-latest-data-de3b4cbae07b> (accessed October 10, 2022).

Pulse Lab Jakarta, "After Dark: Encouraging Safe Transit for Women Travelling at Night" (*Pulse Lab Jakarta*, 2019), <https://pulselabjakarta.org/ourwork> (accessed October 10, 2022).

Pulse Lab Jakarta, "Fusing Datasets to Track the Impact of Disasters in Indonesia and Beyond . . . VAMPIRE Is on It!" (*Medium*, January 30, 2018), <https://medium.com/pulse-lab-jakarta/fusing-datasets-to-track-the-impact-of-disasters-in-indonesia-and-beyond-vampire-is-on-it-ed13fe8e6ff6> (accessed October 10, 2022).

Pulse Lab Jakarta, "Stories of Change: Haze Gazer & VAMPIRE" (*Pulse Lab Jakarta*, 2018), <https://pulselabjakarta.org/ourwork> (accessed October 10, 2022).

Pulse Lab Jakarta, "Using Big Data Analytics for Improved Public Transport" (*Pulse Lab Jakarta*, 2017), <https://pulselabjakarta.org/assets/uploadworks/2018-08-02-13-21-05.pdf> (accessed October 10, 2022).

Pulse Lab Kampala, "Using Machine Learning to Analyse Radio Content in Uganda: Opportunities for Sustainable Development and Humanitarian Action" (*UN Global Pulse*, September 2017), <https://www.unglobalpulse.org/wp-content/uploads/2017/09/Radio-Analysis-Report_Preview.pdf> (accessed October 10, 2022).

Pulse Lab New York, "Using Call Detail Records to Understand Refugee Integration in Turkey" (*United Nations Global Pulse*, 2018), <https://www.unglobalpulse.org/projects/using-call-detail-records-understand-refugee-integration-turkey> (accessed October 10, 2022).

Quaggiotto G, "Tech4Labs Issue 6: Inverting the Logic of Government through User Insights" (*nesta*, June 2015), <https://www.nesta.org.uk/blog/tech4labs-issue-6-inverting-the-logic-of-government-through-user-insights/> (accessed October 10, 2022).

Reuters, "Gunmen Destroy Mobile Phone Tower in Afghan South" (*Reuters*, March 2, 2008), <https://www.reuters.com/article/us-afghan-violence-idUSISL20878120080302> (accessed October 10, 2022).

SDG2 Advocacy Hub, "HungerMap LIVE: A Tool for Timely Action on Food Insecurity" (*sdg2advocacyhub*, January 22, 2021), <https://sdg2advocacyhub.org/news/hungermap-live-tool-timely-action-food-insecurity> (accessed October 10, 2022).

Singhvi A, Saget B, and Lee JC, "What Went Wrong with Indonesia's Tsunami Early Warning System," *The New York Times* (New York, October 2, 2018).

Smith B, "Microsoft Deepens Longstanding Commitment to Philanthropy with Expanded Vision, New Organization" (*The Official Microsoft Blog*, December 15, 2015), <https://blogs.microsoft.com/blog/2015/12/15/microsoft-deepens-longstanding-commitment-to-philanthropy-with-expanded-vision-new-organization/> (accessed October 10, 2022).

Tani S and Maulia E, "Indonesia's Tsunami Warning Blamed as Death Toll Reaches 1,200" (*Nikkei Asia*, October 2, 2018), <https://asia.nikkei.com/Economy/Indonesia-s-tsunami-warning-blamed-as-death-toll-reaches-1-200> (accessed October 10, 2022).

Tivany Wargadiredja A, "Indonesia's Tsunami Warning System Is Broken" (*VICE*, October 3, 2018), <https://www.vice.com/en/article/yw954g/broken-stripped-and-stolen-indonesias-tsunami-warning-system-is-a-mess> (accessed October 10, 2022).

Twitter, "Twitter for Good" (*Twitter*, N.D.), <https://about.twitter.com/en_us/company/twitter-for-good.html> (accessed October 10, 2022).

UN Department of Economic and Social Affairs, "Sustainable Development Goals—Goal 17" (*Global Goals*, N.D.), <https://www.globalgoals.org/17-partnerships-for-the-goals> (accessed October 10, 2022).

UN Department of Economic and Social Affairs, "Sustainable Development Goals—Goal 9" (*SDGs*, N.D.), <https://sdgs.un.org/goals/goal9> (accessed October 10, 2022).

UN Environment Programme, "UN Environment and Google Announce Ground-Breaking Partnership to Protect Our Planet" (*UNEP News and Stories*, July 16, 2018), <https://www.unenvironment.org/news-and-stories/press-release/un-environment-and-google-announce-ground-breaking-partnership> (accessed October 10, 2022).

UN Global Pulse, "PulseSatellite: Human-AI Interaction for Satellite Analysis" (*UN Global Pulse*, 2020), <https://www.unglobalpulse.org/microsite/pulsesatellite/> (accessed October 10, 2022).

UN Global Pulse, "Haze Gazer Demo" (*UN Global Pulse*, 2018), <https://www.youtube.com/watch?v=YVZV9fpoxTQ> (accessed October 10, 2022).

UN Global Pulse, "Where We Work" (*UN Global Pulse*, February 27, 2018), <https://www.unglobalpulse.org/labs/> (accessed October 10, 2022).

UN Global Pulse, "Haze Gazer: A Crisis Analysis Tool" (*UN Global Pulse*, March 16, 2016), <https://www.unglobalpulse.org/2016/03/haze-gazer-a-crisis-analysis-tool/> (accessed October 10, 2022).

UN Global Pulse, "MIND: Managing Information in Natural Disasters" (*UN Global Pulse*, N.D.), <https://www.unglobalpulse.org/microsite/mind/> (accessed October 10, 2022).

UN Global Pulse, "Project Brief: Mapping the Risk-Utility Landscape of Mobile Data for Sustainable Development and Humanitarian Action" (*UN Global Pulse*, July 2015), <https://www.unglobalpulse.org/document/mapping-the-risk-utility-landscape-of-mobile-data-for-sustainable-development-and-humanitarian-action/> (accessed October 10, 2022).

UN Global Pulse, "Project Brief: Nowcasting Food Prices in Indonesia Using Social Media Signals" (*UN Global Pulse*, January 2014), <https://www.unglobalpulse.org/document/nowcasting-food-prices-in-indonesia-using-social-media-signals/> (accessed October 10, 2022).

UN Global Pulse, "Taking the Global Pulse: Using New Data to Understand Emerging Vulnerability in Real-Time" (*UN Global Pulse*, 2012), <https://www.unglobalpulse.org/document/taking-the-global-pulse-using-new-data-to-understand-emerging-vulnerability-in-real-time/> (accessed October 10, 2022).

UNHCR, "UNHCR and IOM Announce Technology Partnership to Set up System to Register Kosovo Refugees in Albania" (May 11, 1999), <https://www.unhcr.org/en-au/news/press/1999/5/3ae6b81723/unhcr-iom-announce-technology-partnership-set-system-register-kosovo-refugees.html (accessed October 10, 2022).

Webb A and Usher D, "A New Tool for Assisting Vulnerable Populations During Droughts" (*Medium*, February 28, 2017), <https://medium.com/pulse-lab-jakarta/a-new-tool-for-assisting-vulnerable-populations-during-droughts-a54e5022cb9e> (accessed October 10, 2022).

West H, "Missing Maps Mapathon 2021. UWE Bristol—Department of Geography and Environmental Management" (*Missing Maps Mapathon 2021*, November 17, 2021), <https://storymaps.arcgis.com/stories/14918b56fedf4e5ab548b9f2431a9ea3> (accessed October 10, 2022).

Wibawa T and Ibrahim FM, "Tsunami Early Detection Buoys Haven't Worked for Six Years: Disaster Agency" (*ABC News*, October 1, 2018), <https://www.abc.net.au/news/2018-10-01/indonesia-tsunami-early-detection-buoys-broken-for-six-years/10324200> (accessed October 10, 2022).

Winfrey C, "Noxious Bogs & Amorous Elephants," *Smithsonian Magazine* (November 2005), <http://archive.is/gdNP1> (accessed October 10, 2022).

Woodrow Wilson International Center for Scholars, "Improving Disaster Response and Humanitarian Aid in Times of Crisis" (*PR Newswire Association*, December 15, 2010), < https://www.prnewswire.com/news-releases/improving-disaster-response-and-humanitarian-aid-in-times-of-crisis-111911154.html> (accessed October 10, 2022).

World Food Programme, "WFP and the Iraqi Ministry of Trade Launch a Food Ration Smartphone App for 1.6 Million People in Iraq" (*WFP News*, June 28, 2021), <https://www.wfp.org/news/wfp-and-iraqi-ministry-trade-launch-food-ration-smartphone-app-16-million-people-iraq> (accessed October 10, 2022).

World Food Programme, "WFP Indonesia Country Brief" (*WFP Countries: Indonesia*, 2021), <https://www.wfp.org/countries/indonesia> (accessed October 10, 2022).

World Food Programme, "Palantir and WFP Partner to Help Transform Global Humanitarian Delivery" (*WFP News*, February 5, 2019), <https://www.wfp.org/news/palantir-and-wfp-partner-help-transform-global-humanitarian-delivery> (accessed October 10, 2022).

World Food Programme, "WFP Supports Iraq in Modernising Its Public Distribution System" (*WFP News*, January 9, 2019), <https://www.wfp.org/news/wfp-supports-iraq-modernising-its-public-distribution-system> (accessed October 10, 2022).

World Food Programme, "News Release: WFP and Alibaba Enter Strategic Partnership to Support UN Sustainable Development Goal of a World with Zero Hunger" (*WFP News*, November 5, 2018), <https://www.wfp.org/news/wfp-and-alibaba-enter-strategic-partnership-support-un-sustainable-development-goa> (accessed October 10, 2022).

World Food Programme, "WFP Introduces Iris Scan Technology to Provide Food Assistance to Syrian Refugees in Zaatari" (*WFP News*, October 6, 2016), <https://www.wfp.org/news/wfp-introduces-innovative-iris-scan-technology-provide-food-assistance-syrian-refu> (accessed October 10, 2022).

World Meteorological Organization (WMO), "Weather-Related Disasters Increase over Past 50 Years, Causing More Damage but Fewer Deaths" (*WMO*, August 31, 2021), <https://public.wmo.int/en/media/press-release/weather-related-disasters-increase-over-past-50-years-causing-more-damage-fewer> (accessed October 10, 2022).

Wright S, "'None of the 22 Buoys Are Functioning': Tsunami Warning System Might Have Saved Lives in Indonesia" *National Post* (Ontario, Canada, October 1, 2018).

Zahara A, Kusumawati UD, and Carruthers D, "Adapting to Data-Driven Diplomacy with Machine Learning" (*UN Global Pulse*, February 25, 2021), <https://www.unglobalpulse.org/2021/02/adapting-to-data-driven-diplomacy-with-machine-learning/> (accessed October 10, 2022).

# Reports and Materials of the United Nations, Regional Organizations, and Specialized Agencies

Almuna I et al., "Pulse Stories. After Dark: Encouraging Safe Transit for Women Travelling at Night" (UN Women, Pulse Lab Jakarta, 2019).

## BIBLIOGRAPHY

Annan K, "Secretary-General Proposes Global Compact on Human Rights, Labour, Environment, in Address to World Economic Forum in Davos Press Release SG/SM/6881" (United Nations, February 1, 1999).

Asian Development Bank, "Poverty: Indonesia" (Asian Development Bank, May 14, 2021).

Asian Development Bank, "Mapping the Spatial Distribution of Poverty Using Satellite Imagery in Thailand" (Asian Development Bank, April 2021).

Asian Development Bank, "Mapping the Spatial Distribution of Poverty Using Satellite Imagery in the Philippines" (Asian Development Bank, March 2021).

Bindraban PS et al., "Focus on Food Insecurity and Vulnerability—A Review of the UN System Common Country Assessments and World Bank Poverty Reduction Strategy Papers" (FAO, 2003).

Boutrif E, "Establishing a Food Insecurity and Vulnerability Information and Mapping System" (FAO, 1998), Appendix to the 17th Session of the Asia Pacific Commission on Agricultural Statistics APCAS/98/7.

Capgemini Consulting, "Technological Innovation for Humanitarian Aid and Assistance" (European Parliament, Scientific Foresight Unit (STOA), Panel for the Future of Science and Technology, May 2019).

FAO, "Food Insecurity and Vulnerability Information and Mapping Systems (FIVIMS)" (FAO, 2000).

FAO Committee on World Food Security, "Guidelines for National Food Insecurity and Vulnerability Information and Mapping Systems (FIVIMS): Background and Principles" (FAO 24th Session, June 2, 1998).

FAO Office of Evaluation, "Evaluation of FAO's Role and Work in Nutrition" (FAO, 2011), PC 108/6.

Inter-Agency Standing Committee, "IASC Operational Guidance on Data Responsibility in Humanitarian Action" (February 3, 2021).

International Labour Organization, "EIIP Technical Brief: Using Digital Technologies in Employment-Intensive Works" (International Labour Organization, July 2020).

International Organization for Migration, "Methodological Framework Used in Displacement Tracking Matrix Operations for Quantifying Displacement and Mobility" (International Organization for Migration, 2017).

IPCC, "Global Warming of 1.5°C" (World Meteorological Organization 2018).

ITU, "Turning Digital Technology Innovation into Climate Action" (International Telecommunication Union, 2019).

OCHA Centre for Humanitarian Data, "Guidance Note: Data Responsibility in Public-Private Partnerships" (OCHA, February 2020).

OCHA Centre for Humanitarian Data, "Data Responsibility Guidelines (Working Draft)" (March 2019).

OCHA Policy Development and Studies Branch, "OCHA and Slow-Onset Emergencies" (UN Office for the Coordination of Humanitarian Affairs, 2011), OCHA Occasional Policy Briefing Series No. 6.

OECD, "OECD Digital Government Index (DGI): Results and Key Messages" (OECD, 2020), Highlights Brochure: OECD Working Papers on Public Governance.

Sphere, "Humanitarian Charter" (1997).

UN Department of Economic and Social Affairs, "World Economic Situation and Prospects" (UN Department of Economic and Social Affairs, 2021), Monthly Briefing No. 151.

UN Department of Economic and Social Affairs, "United Nations E-Government Survey 2020: Digital Government in the Decade of Action for Sustainable Development" (UN Department of Economic and Social Affairs, 2020).
UN Development Group, "Data Privacy, Ethics and Protection: Guidance Note on Big Data for Achievement of the 2030 Agenda" (2017).
UNGA Res 69/283 (June 23, 2015) UN Doc A/RES/69/283.
UNGA Res 60/214 (August 10, 2005) UN Doc A/RES/60/214.
UNGA Res 45/95 (December 14, 1990) UN Doc A/RES/45/95.
UNGA Res 2093(XX) "United Nations Development Programme" (December 20, 1965) UN Doc A/RES/2093(XX).
UN Global Pulse, "UN Global Pulse Annual Report 2020" (UN Global Pulse, 2021).
UN Global Pulse, "UN Global Pulse Annual Report 2018" (UN Global Pulse, 2019).
UN Global Pulse, "Risks, Harms and Benefits Assessment Tool" (United Nations, 2016, updated 2019).
UN Global Pulse and International Association of Privacy Professionals (IAPP), "Building Ethics into Privacy Frameworks for Big Data and AI" (United Nations, 2018).
UN Global Working Group on Big Data for Official Statistics, "Handbook on the Use of Mobile Phone Data for Official Statistics" (United Nations, 2019).
UN Inter-agency Task Force on Financing for Development, "Financing for Sustainable Development Report 2021" (United Nations, 2021).
UN Statistics Division, "Global Assessment of Institutional Readiness for the Use of Big Data in Official Statistics" (UN Statistics Division, 2020), Background document E/CN.3/2020/24.
United Nations, "Principles on Personal Data Protection and Privacy" (United Nations, 2018).
United Nations Development Group, "Data Privacy, Ethics and Protection: Guidance Note on Big Data for Achievement of the 2030 Agenda" (United Nations, 2017).
United Nations Office for Disaster Risk Reduction, "Sendai Framework for Disaster Risk Reduction 2015–2030" (United Nations, 2015).
United Nations Statistics Division, "Draft Handbook on Civil Registration, Vital Statistics and Identity Management Systems: Communication for Development" (UN Statistics Division, April 2019).
WFP Office of Evaluation and Avenir Analytics, "Strategic Evaluation of Funding WFP's Work" (World Food Programme, 2020), Evaluation Report OEV/2019/018.
World Bank Asia Region Technical Department, "Flood Control in Bangladesh—A Plan for Action" (1990), World Bank Technical Paper 119.
World Food Programme, "Vulnerability Analysis and Mapping: Food Security Analysis at the World Food Programme" (World Food Programme, November 2018).
World Food Programme, "WFP's Safety Net Policy: The Role of Food Assistance in Social Protection" (World Food Programme, June 23, 2021).
World Food Programme, "HungerMap LIVE," <https://hungermap.wfp.org/> (accessed October 10, 2022).
Ziesche S, "Innovative Big Data Approaches for Capturing and Analyzing Data to Monitor and Achieve the SDGs" (UN ESCAP, 2017).

## Treaties and Government Agreements

Constitution and Convention of the International Telecommunication Union (opened for signature December 22, 1992, entered into force July 1, 1994), 1825 UNTS 330.

Convention on Rights and Duties of States (adopted by the Seventh International Conference of American States on December 26, 1933, entered into force December 26, 1934), 165 LNTS 19.
"Memorandum of Understanding between the Government of the Republic of Indonesia and the United Nations" (August 15, 2012) (on file with the author).
Statute of the International Court of Justice (opened for signature October 24, 1945, entered into force April 18, 1946), 33 UNTS 993.
"UNDP Mutual Non-Disclosure Agreement" (2018) (on file with the author).

## Cases

*Certain Activities Carried Out by Nicaragua in the Border Area (Costa Rica v. Nicaragua) and Construction of a Road in Costa Rica Along the San Juan River (Nicaragua v. Costa Rica), Judgmen*t [2015] ICJ Rep 665.
*The Corfu Channel Case (UK v. Albania)* [1949] ICJ Rep 4.

## Conference Proceedings and Other

Aal K, Weibert A, and Talhouk R, "Refugees & Technology: Determining the Role of HCI Research" (Group '18: 2018 ACM Conference on Supporting Groupwork, Florida, January 7–10, 2018).
Ananny M and Gillespie T, "Public Platforms: Beyond the Cycle of Shocks and Exceptions" (IPP2016 The Platform Society, Oxford, September 22–23, 2016).
Bangladesh Water Development Board, "Annual Flood Report" (Bangladesh Water Development Board 2016), Annual Report, <https://www.ffwc.gov.bd/images/annual16.pdf> (accessed October 10, 2022).
Bangladesh Water Development Board, "Flood Forecasting & Warning in Bangladesh" (Bangladesh Water Development Board, N.D.), Project Brief, <https://www.bwdb.gov.bd/archive/pdf/190.pdf> (accessed October 10, 2022).
Berditchevaskaia A et al., "Collective Crisis Intelligence for Frontline Humanitarian Response" (NESTA, 2021).
Campo SR et al., "The Signal Code: Ethical Obligations for Humanitarian Information Activities" (Harvard Humanitarian Initiative, 2018), 5/2018.
Center for International Earth Science Information Network—CIESIN—Columbia University and Information Technology Outreach Services—ITOS—University of Georgia, "Global Roads Open Access Data Set, Version 1 (GROADSv1)," <https://sedac.ciesin.columbia.edu/data/set/groads-global-roads-open-access-v1> (accessed October 10, 2022).
Cohen JL and Kharas H, "Using Big Data and Artificial Intelligence to Accelerate Global Development" (The Brookings Institution, Washington, D.C., November 15, 2018).
Development Initiatives, "Global Humanitarian Assistance Report 2021" (Development Initiatives, June 22, 2021).
Dodgson K et al., "A Framework for the Ethical Use of Advanced Data Science Methods in the Humanitarian Sector" (Humanitarian Data Science & Ethics Group, 2020).
Eick S, "A History of Indonesian Telecommunication Reform 1999–2006" (40th Annual Hawaii International Conference on System Sciences, Hawaii, January 3–6, 2007).
Florescu D et al., "Will 'Big Data' Transform Official Statistics?" (Q2014: European Conference on Quality in Official Statistics, Vienna, June 2–5, 2014).

Fulton M et al., "Digital Technologies and the Big Data Revolution in the Canadian Agricultural Sector: Opportunities, Challenges, and Alternatives" (Canadian Center for the Study of Cooperatives, August 2021).

Good Humanitarian Donorship (GHD) Initiative, "Principles and Good Practice of Humanitarian Donorship" (2018).

Hammond AL et al., "The Next 4 Billion: Market Size and Business Strategy at the Base of the Pyramid" (The World Bank, 2007).

ICRC, "Code of Conduct for Employees of the International Committee of the Red Cross" (ICRC, 2018).

IFRC, "Guidelines for the Domestic Facilitation and Regulation of International Disaster Relief and Initial Recovery Assistance (IDRL Guidelines)" (2007).

JICA, "The Study for Rural Development Focusing on Flood Proofing in the People's Republic of Bangladesh Final Report" (Japan International Cooperation Agency, 2002).

Lassa J, "When Heaven (Hardly) Meets the Earth: Towards Convergency in Tsunami Early Warning Systems" (Indonesian Students' Scientific Meeting Conference Proceedings, Delft, May 1, 2008).

Logar T et al., "PulseSatellite: A Tool Using Human-AI Feedback Loops for Satellite Image Analysis in Humanitarian Contexts" (Indonesian Students' Scientific Meeting Conference Proceedings, Delft, May 1, 2008).

Malcolm J, "Arresting the Decline of Multi-Stakeholderism in Internet Governance" (2011 GigaNet Conference, Nairobi, September 26, 2011).

Pfaff A et al., "Policy Impacts on Deforestation: Lessons Learned from Past Experiences to Inform New Initiatives," Nicholas Institute Report (Duke University, 2010).

Ralston L and Tiwari S, "No One Left Behind: Rural Poverty in Indonesia" (World Bank, 2020), Report.

Recalde P, "An Overview of Vulnerability Analysis and Mapping (VAM)" (United Nations Meeting on Cartography and Geographic Information Science, New York, March 28–30, 2000).

Reynders P (tr.), "A Translation of the Charter of the Dutch East India Company" (Australasian Hydrographic Society, 2009), <https://www.australiaonthemap.org.au/voc-charter/> (accessed October 10, 2022).

Saracco R, "Augmented Machines and Augmented Humans Converging on Transhumanism" (IEEE-FDC Symbiotic Autonomous Systems Initiative, 2019), White Paper.

Scazza M and Nenquimo O, "From Spears to Maps: The Case of Waorani Resistance in Ecuador for the Defence of Their Right to Prior Consultation" (International Institute for Environment and Development (IIED), February 2021), Report.

Stanley JD, "Planetary Skin Institute ALERTS: Automated Land Change Evaluation, Reporting and Tracking System" (COM.Geo 11: Proceedings of the 2nd International Conference on Computing for Geospatial Research & Applications, Washington, D.C., May 23–25, 2011).

Sumadiwiria C, "Putting Vulnerable Communities on the Map: A Research Report on What Influences Digital Map-Making with Young Volunteers in Bangladesh" (Y Care International, 2015).

Tkacz N, "Connection Perfected: What the Dashboard Reveals" (Digital Methods Initiative Winter School, Amsterdam, January 16, 2015).

Zhilou Y and Hua J, "Research of Tax Revenue Intelligent Forecast System" (International Forum on Information Technology and Applications, Kunming, July 16–18, 2010).

## Interviews

Interview with A, August 18, 2015.
Interview with I, August 18, 2015.
Interview with J, August 18, 2015.
Interview with K, August 18, 2015.
Interview with H, August 19, 2015.
Interview with L, August 20, 2015.
Interview with M1 & M2, August 20, 2015.
Interview with N, April 11, 2018.
Interview with F, June 13, 2018.
Interview with G, June 13, 2018.
Interview with A, July 23, 2018.
Interview with B, July 23, 2018.
Interview with C1 & C2, July 23, 2018.
Interview with A, July 26, 2018.
Interview with D, July 27, 2018.
Interview with E, July 31, 2018.
Interview with B, August 28, 2018.
Interview with O, September 11, 2018.
Interview with P, September 11, 2018.
Interview with Q1, Q2, & Q3, September 11, 2018.
Interview with Y, November 1, 2018.
Interview with K, November 21, 2018.
Interview with R, December 4, 2018
Interview with T, January 13, 2019.
Interview with V, May 5, 2019.
Interview with D, September 5, 2019.
Interview with X, October 17, 2019.
Interview with Z, November 28, 2019.
Interview with AA, December 17, 2019.
Interview with AB, January 28, 2020.
Interview with AC & D, February 18, 2020.
Interview with AE, April 20, 2020.
Interview with AG, April 22, 2020.
Interview with AF, April 28, 2020.
Interview with AD, April 30, 2020.
Interview with AH, October 26, 2020.
Interview with AI & AJ, November 12, 2020.
Interview with AC, June 9, 2021.
Interview with AC, June 11, 2021.
Interview with AC, June 16, 2021.
Interview with AI, June 24, 2021.
Interview with AJ, July 8, 2021.
Interview with AK, July 16, 2021.

# Index

*For the benefit of digital users, indexed terms that span two pages (e.g., 52–53) may, on occasion, appear on only one of those pages.*
Figures are indicated by *f* following the page number

#DeleteFacebook campaigns, 211–12

1988 Bangladesh floods, 48–54

abuse value, 217–18
adaptability, 32
advanced very high-resolution radiometer (AVHRR) data, 49–50
Agency for International Development, 139
Ahmed, Sara, 206–8, 211–12
AI (artificial intelligence), 141–42
AI for Good Global Summit, 141–42, 180, 182
AI for Humanitarian Action, 30–31
Air Quality Index China, 111
alert for price spikes (ALPS) indicator, 123–24
algorithmic culture, 16
algorithms, 16–18, 185
Alianza Ceibo, 68–69
Alibaba, 15, 122–23
Amazon Web Services (AWS), 144
American Red Cross, 30
Amoore, Louise, 62–63, 220–21
analog logics
  humanitarian mapping, 33–35
  states, 136–44
Annan, Kofi, 143–44
anti-formalism, 62–63
application programming interfaces (APIs), 9
Aradau, Claudia, 220
Arendt, Hannah, 73
artificial intelligence (AI), 141–42
Asian Development Bank, 120–21, 153, 158
atmospheric infrasound, 152
attention-directing guidance, 80–81
automatic identification system, 79–80
automatic sensing technologies, 150–51
AVHRR (advanced very high-resolution radiometer) data, 49–50
AWS (Amazon Web Services), 144

Bangladesh, 48–54
Bangladesh Water Development Board (BWDB), 49, 50

BAPPENAS (National Development Planning Agency of Indonesia), 140
Barthes, Roland, 33, 174–75
baseline data layer, 118–19
Bashford, Alison, 87
Beauvoir, Simone de, 215–16
Becker Lorca, Arnulf, 146–47
Benton, Lauren, 94–95, 138
bias, 77, 79
big data, 95–96, 99
Bigelow, Julian, 34
biopolitics, 73, 74–75
Blakemore, Erin, 7–8
blockchain technologies, 19, 35
Booth, Charles, 44–48
Bourdieu, Pierre, 130–31
bourgeois alarm, 47
Bourguet, Marie-Noëlle, 43–44
Brahmaputra River, 48
British imperialism, 138, 142
British Red Cross, 30
Brun, Catherine, 114
Bucher, Taina, 212–13
budgets, 190–91
BWDB (Bangladesh Water Development Board), 49, 50

calibrated machine learning, 154*f*
Canetti, Elias, 61
Casemajor, Nathalie, 213
CATI (computer-assisted telephone interviewing), 123–24, 125–26
Central Bureau of Statistics, 118–19
Central Nervous System for the Earth (CeNSE) project, 152–53
choropleth map, 51
Chouliaraki, Lilie, 88
chronic waiting, 114
click-wrap contracting, 192
closures, humanitarian mapping, 64–70
cloud hosting, 186–87
coaxial correlation diagrams, 49

CODATA Global Roads Data Development
    Task Group, 148–50
Code of Conduct (HOT), 37
Cohen, Julie E., 14
Cold War period, 139, 155
collaborative networking, 55
Colonial Development Corporation, 139
colonialism, 138, 146–47
commercial firms, 142
complex emergency, 104–5
Comprehensive Nuclear-Test-Ban Treaty
    Organization (CTBTO), 152
computer-assisted telephone interviewing
    (CATI), 123–24, 125–26
Comte, August, 43–44
consciousness, 172–73
contracts, 85, 192–96
copperplate maps, 39, 41–43
*Corfu Channel Case*, 155
Costa Rica, 61–62, 153–55
counterdisciplinary approaches, 22–23
counter-mapping, 32, 67–70
COVID-19 pandemic, 8–9
Crary, Jonathan, 209–10
Crawford, Kate, 134
crowds, 60–61
crowdsourcing, 61–62, 78
CTBTO (Comprehensive Nuclear-Test-Ban
    Treaty Organization), 152
Curtis, Bruce, 85
customer relations management software, 80–81

Danish Hydraulic Institute, 49
dashboard illustration, 127
Daston, Lorraine, 43–44
data
    access, 96, 185–88
    becoming crazy with, 222–24
    emergencies viewed as deficiencies of, 130
    harvesters, 156
    misuse of, 219
    storage capacity, 80–81
    UN Principles on Personal Data Protection
        and Privacy, 189
data responsibility, 198–99
data streams, 83, 150–51
Dean, Jodi, 61
dehumanization, 100
#DeleteFacebook campaigns, 211–12
Department of Foreign Affairs and Trade
    (DFAT), 159
Desrosières, Alain, 43–44
Digicel, 96

digital data flows, 16–17
Digital Democracy, 68–69
digital aggregates, 71, 73–74, 75–76, 82, 83, 92–
    93, 95–96, 98–99, 100–1
digital humanitarianism, 1–2
    disuse of, 211–18
    misuse of, 218–21
    overview, 4–8
    populations in, 77–93
    stakes of, 8–9
    stakes of digital aggregation in humanitarian
        field, 93–101
    usage, kinds of, 207–11
    what could become of, 222–24
digital interfaces, 10–11
    with emergencies, 110–14
    emergencies and rhythms of, 114–16
digital logics
    humanitarian mapping, 33–35
    states, 145–47
digital poorhouse, 99
digitization, of humanitarian mapping, 57–64
Diouf, Jacques, 54–55
disaster relief
    biosocial goals of, 83
    Flood Action Plan, 51–52
    IDRL Guidelines, 188
    MIND, 77–80
    tracking human displacement, 71–72
disease mapping, 39–43
Displacement Tracking Matrix (DTM), 71–73
disuse, 211–18
doctrines, 12–13
Douglas, Mary, 222
drainage infrastructure, 49
Droid Destruction Kit, 220
drought data, 118–19
DTM (Displacement Tracking Matrix), 71–73
Dunant, Henry, 4–5
Durkheim, Émile, 43–44
Dutch East India Company (VOC), 142

Eagleton, Terry, 172
Early Warning System (EWS), 111–13, 121
Economic Cooperation Agency, 139
economic inequality, 8–9
Ecuador, 68–69
Edelman, Lee, 114–15
Edkins, Jenny, 138–39
egalitarianism, 61
e-governance champions, 159
eighteenth-century disease mapping, 39–43
El Niño cycle, 118

INDEX  267

Elementary Education Act, 44
emergencies, 102–33
　emergence of and rhythms of digital
　　interface, 114–16
　HungerMap LIVE, 122–29
　interfacing digitally, 110–14
　international humanitarian emergencies, 103–6
　overview, 102–3
　VAMPIRE, 117–22
　for whom, 106–10
end-of-the-millennium vulnerability
　　mapping, 54–57
Ershad, H.M, 52–53
Esmeir, Samera, 100
ethical codes, 93–94, 197–202
Eubanks, Virginia, 99
European Recovery Program, 139
European Space Agency, 49–50
EWS (Early Warning System), 111–13, 121
Extreme Gradient Boosting (XGBoost)
　　algorithm, 123–24

Facebook, Inc. (Meta, Inc.), 30–31, 81–82, 212–13
faith-based organizations, 142–43
FAO (Food and Agriculture Organization), 54–
　　57, 104–5, 116–17, 141
Fassin, Didier, 136, 217–18
FCS (food consumption score), 122–24
FFWC (Flood Forecasting and Warning
　　Center), 49
Field Papers, 57–58, 58f, 62–63
financial models, 23–24
Fink, Sheri, 1
Fiori, Juliano, 139
FIVIMS (Food Insecurity and Vulnerability
　　Information and Mapping Systems), 54–
　　57, 116–17
Flood Action Plan, 51–52
Flood Forecasting and Warning Center
　　(FFWC), 49
flood mapping, 48–54
Flood Monitoring Cell, 50
Floridi, Luciano, 85
Food and Agriculture Organization (FAO), 54–
　　57, 104–5, 116–17, 141
food consumption score (FCS), 122–24
food insecurity, 116–17
　HungerMap LIVE, 122–29
　Palantir, 159–61
　VAMPIRE, 117–22
Food Insecurity and Vulnerability Information
　　and Mapping Systems (FIVIMS), 54–
　　57, 116–17

Ford, Lisa, 94–95, 138
foreign relations. *See* states
Forensic Architecture, 95–96
Foucault, Michel, 73, 74–75. *See also* biopolitics
*Framework for The Ethical Use of Advanced
　Data Science Methods in the Humanitarian
　Sector*, 165–66, 197, 200
futurity, 114–15, 116, 216

G7 Summit, 52–53
Galloway, Alexander, 10, 64
Ganges River, 48
GDACS (Global Disaster Alert and
　　Coordination System), 78, 84, 115–16
Geertz, Clifford, 136
geographic information systems (GIS), 29–30,
　　55, 121
geotagging, 85, 98–99
GISC (Grower's Information Service
　　Cooperative), 219–20
GitHub, 220
Global Disaster Alert and Coordination System
　　(GDACS), 78, 84, 115–16
Global Humanitarian Assistance Report 2021, 8–9
Global Positioning System (GPS), 56, 150–51
Global Roads Open Access Data Set
　　(gROADS), 148–50
Global South, 161–62
global warming, 8–9
Global Working Group on Big Data for Official
　　Statistics, 90, 98, 157–58, 191
Google, 78, 144
Google Maps, 65–66, 150–51, 153–55
Google PageRank algorithm, 17
Google Trends, 88–89
government, governing digitally, 157–61
GPS (Global Positioning System), 56, 150–51
grammar, 171–73
graphical user interfaces (GUIs), 9, 10–11
Greenhalgh, Susan, 74
gROADS (Global Roads Open Access Data
　　Set), 148–50
Grower's Information Service Cooperative
　　(GISC), 219–20
Guidelines for the Regulation of Computerized
　　Personnel Data Files, 197

Hacking, Ian, 43–44
Hackitectura, 67–68, 218–19
Halpern, Orit, 205
Handbook on Data Protection in Humanitarian
　　Action (ICRC), 190
harbor statistics, 79–80

hardware, 10
Harley, Brian, 36
Harvard Humanitarian Initiative, 197
Haskell, Thomas, 139–40
Haze Gazer, 110–14, 129
HDX (Humanitarian Data Exchange), 208
Heartfield, James, 106–7
Hewlett-Packard, 152–53
Hilton, Matthew, 139
Hirschman, Albert, 211–12
history, 38–57
　eighteenth-century disease mapping, 39–43
　end-of-the-millennium vulnerability mapping, 54–57
　of humanitarianism, 4–5
　nineteenth-century poverty mapping, 43–48
　twentieth-century flood mapping, 48–54
Hookway, Branden, 11
hope, 223–24
HOT. *See* Humanitarian OpenStreetMap Team (HOT)
HOT Tasking Manager, 11, 15, 30–31, 31*f*, 32*f*, 148–50
human suffering, 4–5, 6–7, 37
humanism, 100
Humanitarian Charter, 200
Humanitarian Data Exchange (HDX), 208
Humanitarian Data Science and Ethics Group, 197
humanitarian imperialism, 106–7
humanitarian mapping, 29–70
　analog and digital logics, 33–35
　closures and openings, 64–70
　digitization of, 57–64
　historical snapshots of, 38–57
　HungerMap LIVE, 122–29
　mismatches and overruns, 64–70
　overview, 29–32, 35–38
　poverty mapping using satellite imagery, 158
Humanitarian OpenStreetMap Team (HOT), 57–58. *See also* HOT Tasking Manager
　boundaries and, 153
　Code of Conduct, 37
　overview, 30–32
humanitarianism. *See also* digital humanitarianism
　history of, 4–5
　process of transformation, 2–4
　stakes of digital aggregation in, 93–101
Hunger Monitoring Unit, 125
HungerMap LIVE, 11, 115–16, 122–29, 209
hydroacoustic centers, 152

IBM, 162
ICJ (International Court of Justice), 153–55
ICRC (International Committee of the Red Cross), 4–5, 140, 190, 200

ICT. *See* information and communication technologies (ICT)
ideas, interfaces vs., 18–19
IDRL Guidelines (International Disaster Relief and Initial Recovery Assistance), 188
IFRC (International Federation of Red Cross and Red Crescent Societies), 188
imperialism, 138
InaTEWS
　disuse of, 213–18
　misuse of, 218
incrementality, 116
indicators, laws and policies, 202–4
Indonesian National Socio-Economic Household Survey, 118–19
Indonesian Telecommunication Regulatory Authority, 96
inference, 77
information and communication technologies (ICT), 1–2, 94–95, 182
　interfaces, 9, 10
　misuse of, 96–98
information capitalism, 75–76
informational infrastructure, 49
infra-legality, 21, 175–76
infrastructures, 175–78
　international legal infrastructures of interfaces, 178–79
　laws and policies as, 169–78
InnovationXChange, 159
*Inquiry into Life and Labour in London* (Booth), 44–46
institutions, 13–14
interested simulacrum, 33
interfaces, 1–28, 175–77
　algorithms vs., 16–18
　designed for revenue-generation, 219
　digital humanitarianism, 4–9
　doctrines vs., 12–13
　ideas vs., 18–19
　infra-investigations, 19–25
　institutions vs., 13–14
　laws and policies on, 169–78
　overview, 9–11
　platforms vs., 14–16
international
　law, 24–25
　legal infrastructures of interfaces, 178–79
　organizations' guidelines, 188–91
　treaties, 180–82
International Committee of the Red Cross (ICRC), 4–5, 140, 190, 200
International Court of Justice (ICJ), 153–55
International Disaster Relief and Initial Recovery Assistance (IDRL Guidelines), 188

International Electrotechnical
    Commission, 203–4
International Federation of Red Cross and Red
    Crescent Societies (IFRC), 188
international humanitarian emergencies, 103–6
International Labour Organization, 141
International Organization for Migration
    (IOM), 71–72, 165
International Organization for Standardization
    (ISO), 203–4
International Relief Organization, 141
International Science Council, 148–50
International Telecommunication Union (ITU),
    141–42, 180
Internet, 5–6, 109, 212–13
IOM (International Organization for
    Migration), 71–72, 165
Iraqi Ministry of Trade, 11
IrisGuard, 160–61
Isin, Engin, 92–93
ISO (International Organization for
    Standardization), 203–4
ITU (International Telecommunication Union),
    141–42, 180

James, William, 210
Japan International Cooperation Agency
    (JICA), 139
Japanese Aerospace Exploration Agency
    (JAXA), 49–50
JavaScript programming library, 30–31
JAXA (Japanese Aerospace Exploration
    Agency), 49–50
Jeffrey, Craig, 130–31
JICA (Japan International Cooperation
    Agency), 139

Kennedy, David, 170
Kennedy, Duncan, 172–73
Koskenniemi, Martti, 23, 170
Kosovo War, 1, 209–10

Landsat, 148–50
LAPOR! 111
laws and policies, 168–204
    contracts, 192–96
    ethical codes, 197–202
    goals, targets, and indicators, 202–4
    as interfaces, structures, and
        infrastructures, 169–78
    international legal infrastructures of
        interfaces, 178–79
    international organizations' guidelines, 188–91
    international treaties, 180–82
    misuse of, 221

multistakeholder arrangements, 182–88
    overview, 168–69
    real-time forecasting, 131–32
League of Nations, 140
League of Red Crescent Societies, 140
legal consciousness, 172–73
Libyan crisis mapping, 61–62
*Life and Labour of the People* (Booth), 44
local emergency, 104
London, England, 43–44
London School Board Visitors, 44
Loveland Technology, 62, 211

machine learning, 82, 141–42, 154f
    of diplomatic engagement, 162
    HungerMap LIVE, 122–24, 128–29
    use of algorithms, 220–21
Macy Conferences, 34
Managing Information in Natural Disasters. *See*
    MIND (Managing Information in Natural
    Disasters)
Manovich, Lev, 10–11
Mapbox GL-JS, 30–31
Mapeo, 68–69
mapping. *See also* humanitarian mapping
    becoming humanitarian, 36–38
    overview, 35–36
MapSwipe, 57–58
market capitalism, 143–44
Marx, Karl, 209–10
Mbembe, Achille, 217–18
McLuhan, Marshall, 210
Médecins Sans Frontières (MSF), 15, 30–31,
    59, 143
Meghna River, 48
Meier, Patrick, 5–6, 109, 223
Memorandum of Understanding, 181
*Mestizo International Law* (Becker Lorca), 146–47
Meta, Inc. (Facebook, Inc.), 30–31, 81–82, 212–13
micro-censusing, 80
Microsoft, 1, 144
Microsoft Philanthropies, 30–31
MIKE11, 49
Millennium Development Goals, 7
MIND (Managing Information in Natural
    Disasters), 11, 15–16, 77–80, 84
    continual updating of data, 209
    interface waiting on user, 115–16
    misuse of, 220
    navigating interface, 86–90
mismatches, humanitarian mapping, 64–70
Missing Maps Project (MMP), 13–14, 30, 80
    overview, 57–63
    terms of conditions, 193–94, 196
misuse, 218–21

Mitterand, Danielle, 52–53
Mitterand, François, 52–53
Miyazaki, Hirokazu, 223–24
mobile phone surveys, 126, 128–29, 183
mobile phone towers, 80–81
modern governance, 74–77
Montevideo Convention, 135, 145–47, 157, 161–62, 163–65
moral intervention, 46
Morgan, Mary, 43–44
Moyn, Samuel, 134
MSF (Médecins Sans Frontières), 15, 30–31, 59, 143
multistakeholder arrangements, 182–88
Muskingum-Cunge methods, 49
mutual dependence, 73
Mutual Security Agency, 139
mVAM, 125
My Food Ration (Tamwini) smartphone application, 11, 159–60

nanoscale sensors, 152–53
NASA (National Aeronautics Space Administration), 49–50, 118–19
NASA WorldWind initiative, 152–53
National Development Planning Agency of Indonesia (BAPPENAS), 140
National Food Security and Vulnerability Atlas, 121–22
National Map Accuracy Standards, 62
National Statistical Office of Thailand, 158
New York City, 37–43
NGOs (nongovernmental organizations), 52, 53–54, 106–7
Nicaragua, 61–62, 153–55
night lights, 158–59
nineteenth-century poverty mapping, 43–48
noise level, 151–52
nongovernmental organizations (NGOs), 52, 53–54, 106–7
nuclear testing, 152

OECD (Organization for Economic Co-operation and Development), 159
OECD Digital Government Index, 159, 162–63
Open Data Commons Open Database License (ODbL), 31*f*, 32*f*
openings, humanitarian mapping, 64–70
OpenMapKit, 57–58
open-source code repository, 30–31
open-source software, 93–94
OpenStreetMap (OSM), 15, 57–58, 66–67, 193–94
Organization for Economic Co-operation and Development (OECD), 159

Osborne, Thomas, 46
O'Sullivan, Kevin, 139
OTCA (Overseas Technical Cooperation Agency), 139
overruns, humanitarian mapping, 64–70
Overseas Economic Cooperation Fund, 139
Overseas Resources Development Act, 139
Overseas Technical Cooperation Agency (OTCA), 139

Palantir, 159–60
Palestine, 164–65
Palestinian Central Bureau of Statistics, 164–65
pay-for-data practice, 119–20
permanent population, 147–48
philanthro-capitalism, 174–75
Philippine Statistics Authority, 158
Planetary Skin Institute, 152–53
platforms, 14–16
PLJ. *See* Pulse Lab Jakarta (PLJ)
populations, 71–101
　assembling permanent population, 147–48
　in digital humanitarianism, 77–93
　in modern governance, 74–77
　overview, 71–74
　stakes of digital aggregation in humanitarian field, 93–101
Porter, Theodore, 43–44
post-humanitarianism, 88
post-structuralism, 170–75
poverty mapping, 11, 43–48
PPPs. *See* public-private partnerships (PPPs)
precise inaccuracy, 41
private data
　Seaman's maps, 41–43
　VAMPIRE development, 119
private international law, 179
Project Lucy, 162–63
public data, 185
　Seaman's maps, 41–43
　VAMPIRE development, 119
public health emergency, 104
public law emergency, 104
public-private partnerships (PPPs), 106–7, 143–44
　governmental operations, 159–60
　International Telecommunication Union (ITU), 180
　promoting, 191
　VAMPIRE development, 119
Pulse Lab Jakarta (PLJ), 19–21, 71–73
　abiding by UNDP regulations, 181
　applying data, 211
　Haze Gazer interface, 111–13

Memorandum of Understanding, 181
MIND, 78
VAMPIRE development, 117–18
PulseSatellite, 150–51

Quaker anti-slavery movement, 142
quantum information theory, 35

radionuclide detecting stations, 152
Rajkovic, Nikolas, 36
rapid-onset humanitarian emergencies, 104–5
React, 30–31
reality effects, 169, 175
Red Cross societies, 140
reduced coping strategy index (rCSI), 122–24
Refugee.info website, 220
registered users, 210
religious organizations, 142–43
reproductive futurity, 114–15
resource extraction, 37–38
revenue generating interfaces, 219
Riles, Annelise, 22
*Risk, Harm and Benefit Assessments Tool*, 165–66
Robinson, Arthur H., 36
Rose, Nikolas, 46
Royal Statistical Society, 47
Ruppert, Evelyn, 92–93

Saami Nordic Convention, 164–65
sampling, 77
satellite imagery, 49–51, 60–61, 150. *See also* Missing Maps Project (MMP)
  data, 11
  obscure data with, 156
  poverty mapping using, 158
satellite luminosity data, 158–59
scientific charity, 44–46
scientific philanthropy, 141
SDG (Sustainable Development Goal) 2, 122–23, 126
SDGs (Sustainable Development Goals), 7, 92, 144, 180, 202–3
Seaman, Valentine, 37–43
security, 74–75
SeisComP3 software, 213–14
seismic stations, 152
self-help, 216–17
Sendai Framework for Disaster Risk Reduction, 188–89
senso-political digital interfaces, 99–100. *See also* MIND (Managing Information in Natural Disaster)
sensor networks, 150–51, 214–15
sentiment index, 81–82

Serres, Michel, 217–18
Sheller, Mimi, 150
Signal Code Obligations, 197, 200
signaling, 82
Silicon Valley, 107–8
slave trading, 94–95, 142
slow-onset humanitarian emergencies, 104–5
small occurrences, 41
smart meters, 152–53
social listening, 90
social mapping, 37
social media, 78, 85, 91, 186, 219.
  *See also* MIND (Managing Information in Natural Disaster)
social survey, 44–46
Social Systems Team, 183
sociology, 43–44
software, 10
Space Research and Remote Sensing Organization (SPARRSO), 49–50
speculative projection, 92–93
Spencer, Herbert, 43–44
Sphere, 200
squatters, 218–19
states, 134–66
  analog logic, 136–44
  assembling permanent population, 147–48
  defined, 135–36
  defining and controlling territory, 148–57
  digital futures of statehood, 163–66
  digital logic, 145–47
  governing digitally, 157–61
  overview, 134–35
  relating to other states digitally, 161–63
statistical bias, 82
Statistics and Data Innovation Unit, 158
Stigler, Stephen, 43–44
Strait of Gibraltar, 67–68
structuralism, 170–75
structuralist analysis, 33
structures, laws and policies as, 169–78
Sullivan, Gavin, 21
Sumadiwiria, Carmen, 63
Sustainable Development Goal (SDG) 2, 122–23, 126
Sustainable Development Goals (SDGs), 7, 92, 144, 180, 202–3
syntaxes, 171–72

Tamwini (My Food Ration) smartphone application, 11, 159–60
targets, 202–4
tech-abolitionism, 217
temporariness, 32

terms of service, 192
territories, 148–57
text messaging, 119–20, 214
thematic mapping, 36
Ticktin, Miriam, 76–77
TOAST (Tsunami Observation and Simulation Terminal), 213–14
Trading Economics, 123–24
transparency, 201–2
treaties, 85, 180–82
trust, 210
*Tsunami Early Warning Service Guidebook for InaTEWS*, 216, 218
tsunami early warning system, 213–14
Tsunami Observation and Simulation Terminal (TOAST), 213–14
twentieth-century flood mapping, 48–54
Twitter, 15, 78, 81–82, 87–89
   Haze Gazer interface, 111
   misuse of data from, 219–20
   Pulse Lab Jakarta (PLJ) and, 119–20
   UN Global Pulse collaboration, 144, 181

UN Charter, 181
UN Global Pulse project, 19–21, 90, 144
UN OCHA (United Nations Office for the Coordination of Humanitarian Affairs), 104–5
UNDG Guidance Note, 199–200
UNDP (United Nations Development Programme), 181, 193
UNDRO (United Nations Disaster Relief Organization), 105
UNEP (United Nations Environment Programme), 144
UNHCR (United Nations High Commissioner for Refugees), 141
UNICEF (United Nations Emergency Children's Fund), 141
United Nations, 1, 15
   Annan, Kofi, 143–44
   population data systems, 76–77
   Principles on Personal Data Protection and Privacy, 189
   Relief and Rehabilitation Administration, 141
United States Agency for International Development (USAID), 50
UNIX operating system, 56
UNOSAT (United Nations Satellite Center), 150–51
US Geological Survey, 118–19
usage, 205–24
   disuse, 211–18
   kinds of, 207–11
   misuse, 218–21
   what digital humanitarianism could become, 222–24
USAID (United States Agency for International Development), 50
use value, 209–10, 217–18
use-for-survival, 217
utility, 207–8

VAM (Vulnerability Analysis and Mapping), 54–57, 125–26
VAMPIRE (Vulnerability Analysis Monitoring Platform for Impact of Regional Events), 117–22, 129
vandalism, 213–18, 223–24
Vismann, Cornelia, 171
VOC (Dutch East India Company), 142
volunteered geographic data, 64
vulnerability, 54–57, 116–17, 220
Vulnerability Analysis and Mapping (VAM), 54–57, 125–26
Vulnerability Analysis Monitoring Platform for Impact of Regional Events (VAMPIRE), 117–22, 129

Waorani people, 68–69
Watenpaugh, Keith, 140–41
wearables, 6–7
Weber, Max, 135–36, 198–99
WHO (World Health Organization), 141
Wikipedia, 87
World Bank Flood Action Plan, 51–52
World Data Lab, 158
World Economic Forum, 143–44
World Food Programme (WFP), 11, 56–57, 117–18, 141
   Alibaba partnership, 122–23
   HungerMap LIVE, 122–29
   Palantir, 159–60
World Food Summit, 54–55
World Health Organization (WHO), 141
World Meteorological Organization, 51
World War One, 140–41
World War Two, 141

XGBoost (Extreme Gradient Boosting) algorithm, 123–24

yellow fever epidemic, 37–43
YouTube, 14–15, 111